Third International Conference on Credit Analysis and Risk Management

Third International Conference on Credit Analysis and Risk Management

Edited by

Joseph Callaghan, Austin Murphy
and Hong Qian

Cambridge
Scholars
Publishing

Third International Conference on Credit Analysis
and Risk Management

Edited by Joseph Callaghan, Austin Murphy and Hong Qian

This book first published 2015

Cambridge Scholars Publishing

Lady Stephenson Library, Newcastle upon Tyne, NE6 2PA, UK

British Library Cataloguing in Publication Data
A catalogue record for this book is available from the British Library

ISBN (10): 1-4438-7648-8
ISBN (13): 978-1-4438-7648-3

TABLE OF CONTENTS

INTRODUCTION

A SUMMARY OF THE THIRD INTERNATIONAL CONFERENCE ON CREDIT ANALYSIS AND RISK MANAGEMENT

AUSTIN MURPHY[1]

The Third International Conference on Credit Analysis and Risk Management was held on August 21-22, 2014, in Rochester, MI, at Oakland University, whose Enterprise Risk Analysis Institute in the Department of Accounting and Finance founded the conference series in 2011. The conference was as informative, useful, and enjoyable as the prior two. The chapters in this book summarize some of the presentations and discussions that occurred in the 2014 conference.

Terry Benzschawel, Global Bond Portfolio Analysis Director at Citibank, led off the conference with a fabulous review of past trends in credit analysis that provided substance for forecasting future directions for this vital financial science. The first chapter is devoted to his writing on this presentation.

Subsequent chapters by various authors summarize presentations on numerous topics. These include an investigation into the actual risks associated with money market funds, a credit card loss analysis, an overview of macroeconomic credit risks in emerging markets, a sovereign bond trading strategy, models of collateralized debt obligations, loan screening with credit transfer, credit risk with off-balance-sheet obligations, counterparty risk, a model of bank credit risk with contagion, internal liquidity management issues, general models of estimating default risk, hedging debt portfolios, a new measure of debt systematic risk, losses upon default, Basel III analysis, and the effect of sovereign risk on domestic corporate credit spreads.

[1] The author is from Oakland University. Email: jamurphy@oakland.edu.

There were also many other informative seminars, including ones given by three other keynote speakers. Kevin Cooper of Ford Motor Credit provided a fascinating talk on credit risk management for automobile loans. Professor Tyler Shumway of the University of Michigan at Ann Arbor supplied a unique analysis of the credit risk involved in the private firm loan market. Kevin Bodie of Comerica Bank supplied great insights into the management of commercial loan risk. A listing of all the conference sessions is provided in Exhibit 1.

The next conference in this series is scheduled for August 27-28, 2015, in Basel, Switzerland. See http://www.oakland.edu/business/creditconf

Exhibit 1 Schedules for the Third International Conference on Credit Analysis and Risk Management*

Thursday, August 21, 2014

1p.m. - 2:00 p.m.	**Credit Risk Models: Past, Present, and Future (Introductory Keynote Speaker Terry Benzschawel, Citibank)**
2 p.m. – 2:30 p.m.	Industry Characteristics and Debt Contracting (Alon Kalay and Gil Sadka, Columhia Business School)
	Introducing the Exchange Traded Pieced Loan (Richard Bussman, Central China Normal University)
2:45 p.m. – 3:15 p.m.	Proper Computation of Credit Exposures under the Real World and Risk Neutral Measures (Harvey Stein, Bloomberg)
	Systematic Risk and Yield Premiums in Bonds (Austin Murphy, Oakland University)
3:45 p.m. – 4:15 p.m.	The Stochastic Recovery Rate in CDS (Chanatip Kitwiwattanachai, University of Connecticut)
	Sovereign Risk Spreads in Europe (Yan Sun, IMF, and Frigyes Ferdinand Heinz, IMF)
4:30 p.m. – 5:00 p.m.	*The Relation between Counterparty Default and Interest Rate Volatility, and its Impact on the Credit Risk of Interest-Rate Derivatives (Tao Wu, Illinois Institute of Technology)*
	Assessing Credit Risk in Money Market Portfolios (Emily Gallagher, Paris School of Economics)

6 p.m. - 8:45 p.m.	**Dinner with Keynote Speaker Kevin Cooper (Ford Motor Credit) at Oakland University Meadow Brook Hall**

Friday, August 22, 2014

8 a.m. – 9 a.m.	**Day's Opening Keynote Speaker Kevin Bodie (Comerica)**
9:15 a.m. – 9:45 a.m.	Banks' Loan Screening Incentives with Credit Risk Transfer (Marc Arnold, University of St. Gallen) The Credit Risk Premium: Measurement, Hedging, and Prediction (Terry Benzschawel, Citibank)
10 a.m. – 10:30 a.m.	Applying Technology to Enhance Decisioning throughout the Credit Lifecycle (Tara kinner, SAS) Does the Macro-economy Impact Industry Credit Risk: A Study in an Emerging Market (Rimpa Saha, Arunkumar Gopalaswamy, Indian Institute of Technology)
10:45 a.m.–11:15 a.m.	Forecasting Loan Loss Rates using Multivariate Time-Series Models (Hongbing Chen, Stonegate Mortgage) Model for Sovereign Default Risk and Relative Value (Terry Benzschawel, Citibank)
11:30 a.m. – 12:45 p.m.	**Lunch with Keynote Speaker Tyler Shumway (University of Michigan), "Forecasting Defaults of Private Firms"**
1 p.m. – 1:30 p.m.	*Can Balance Sheet Diversification Substitute for the Bank Capital? (Matjaz Steinbacher. Kiel Institute for the World Economy)* Liquidity and Corporate Governance: Evidence from Family Firms (Liang Fu, Oakland University)
1:45 p.m. – 2:15 p.m.	*How Does Government Borrowing Affect Corporate Financing and Investment? (Mark Leary, Washington University)* Credit Risk Measurement, Leverage, and Basel III (Marianne Ojo, North West University, South Africa)

2:30 p.m. – 3:00 p.m.	*Consumer Credit on American Indian Reservations (Peter Grajzl, Washington & Lee University* Credit Risk and Off-balance-sheet Contractual Obligations (Shao Zhao, Oakland University)
3:15 p.m. – 3:45 p.m.	Sovereign Risk and the Pricing of Credit Default Swaps (Matthias Haerri, University of Applied Sciences Northwestern Switzerland) Joining Risk and Rewards (Harvey Stein, Bloomberg)
3:50 p.m. – 4:20 p.m.	*"Forecasting Credit Cards' Portfolio Losses in the Great Recession: a Study in Model Risk" (Sougata Kerr, Federal Reserve Bank of Philadelphia)*
4:30 p.m. – 5:00 p.m.	Merton's Model with Stochastic Recovery (Albert Cohan, Michigan State University) *Two Risk Models for CMOs with Credit Tranching (Dror Parnes, University of South Florida,* and Michael Jacobs Jr. (Price Waterhouse Coopers)

* *Sessions in italics indicate live video teleconferencing*.
For more information, see http://www.oakland.edu/internationalcreditconference.

CHAPTER ONE

DEFAULT MODELS: PAST, PRESENT, AND FUTURE

TERRY BENZSCHAWEL[1]

Abstract

The roots of default models can be found in the origins of credit markets, beginning with fundamental analysis, the development of financial ratios, and the emergence of credit rating agencies and agency ratings in the early 1900s. Altman's (1968) z-score model marks the beginning of the modern era, consisting also of applications of the risk neutral pricing framework to credit and the development of Merton-type structural default models and hybrid statistical-structural models. The recently-developed market-implied PD model (Benzschawel and Assing, 2012) bridges the current and post-modern modeling eras. The post-modern period is characterized by development of expert systems and big data methods, whose potential is just beginning to be exploited. Models are presented from a practitioner's viewpoint, focusing on each's accuracy, ease of implementation, advantages and limitations as well as how each has increased our predictive ability with regard to obligor risk and asset relative value. Each level of model improvement requires greater amounts of input data, computational power, and theoretical complexity. Also, despite ongoing improvements in model accuracy and comprehensiveness, all model types continue to find uses among various investor types and for different applications.

---

[1]The author is from Citi Institutional Clients Group.
Email: terry.l.benzschawel@citi.com.

Introduction

As expressed in the motto of the original Dun & Bradstreet credit rating agency, credit is "Man's Confidence in Man" (Downes and Goodman, 1991): the exchange of a liquid asset (i.e., cash) for a documented promise of payments in the future. In general, credit instruments consist of loans, bonds, charge-account balances with commercial firms, and, more recently, credit default swaps and other financial obligations. A common feature of these instruments is that their returns are subject to the risk of default.[2] This report describes the history of methods for analyzing the default risk of credit issuers from its origins in the fundamental analysis of government bond risk to the latest applications of "big data" techniques to predict corporate bankruptcy. Although most previously successful forms of credit analysis continue to play various roles in financial markets, the modern demand for quantitative estimates of default probabilities has resulted in the dominance of risk-neutral and structural credit models for use by broker dealers and investment firms for trading and risk management.

Over the past several decades, models of default risk have evolved from fundamental analysis, agency ratings, and regression-based models to become dominated by structural models and reduced form approaches in their various forms. In addition, evaluations of default model accuracies have transitioned from anecdotal descriptions of predictive success to quantification using methods derived from statistical decision theory. It is important to note that default prediction is a statistical problem; one rarely knows with certainty if a borrower will default prior to the actual non-payment of an obligation. Given the inherent uncertainty in the default process, it appears that after several decades of refinements within modern modelling approaches, we are reaching a limit in our ability to accurately predict default over time horizons of a year or more.[3] That fact, along with limitations of existing frameworks to provide reliable estimates of default risk for sovereign nations, municipalities, financial firms, and private companies, is fueling demand for new classes of credit models. In fact, applications of "expert consensus" and "big data" methods have been proposed to fill that demand, examples of which are described below.

---

[2] These now include structured credit products such, as collateralized loan obligations (CLOs), single-tranche CDOs, credit options, and even counterparty credit risk.

[3] For example, the "best" available credit models all capture roughly 60%-70% of firms who will default within the next year within the top 10% of firms that are ranked as riskiest.

Most of the discussion herein concerns the application of quantitative techniques for estimating credit risk and relative value. However, at present, no credit model can serve as an adequate substitute for fundamental analysis in making investment decisions. In fact, a fundamental evaluation of a credit investment should be the final step in the credit vetting process; a process that should also involve analysis using quantitative techniques. Although no current model is adequate to capture the complexity of reality, being ahead of the competition can be profitable. That perspective is useful when considering the development and applications of credit models to problems in credit risk and valuation.

Origins of the Bond Market and Early Credit Analysis

The development of credit analysis is closely linked to the evolution of financial markets, and that relationship is considered briefly in this section.[4] The creation of modern financial assets is generally attributed to the Dutch who, in 1609, invented common stock to finance the Dutch East India Company. The Dutch also established the first version of a central bank at that time (Neal, 1990). By the 1600s, the Dutch already had a government bond market for decades and soon thereafter had all major components of a modern financial system. In 1688, the British invited William of Orange, the Dutch leader, to be their king, and he brought experienced Dutch financiers to England. The Bank of England was subsequently established in 1694 and England went on to have the first industrial revolution and to lead the world economy in the eighteenth and nineteenth centuries (Dickson, 1967).

A century later, Alexander Hamilton, the first U.S Secretary of the Treasury from 1789-1795, worked to establish a modern financial system modeled on Dutch, English, and French precedents. Thus, by 1795, the United States, essentially a bankrupt country before 1789, had strong public finances, a stable dollar, a banking system, a central bank, and bond and stock markets in several cities. And just as the English had succeeded the Dutch in economic and financial leadership, the Americans went on to displace the English as the world's pre-eminent national economy within a century.

For much of the four-century history of modern capital markets, there were few questions regarding credit quality because most bond investing was in the public or sovereign debt of nations and governments, and

---

[4] An extensive and informative treatment of the historical development of the bond market and credit analysis can be found in Sylla (2002).

investors trusted the willingness and ability of countries and municipalities to honor their commitments. In fact, up until the nineteenth century, only the Dutch, the English, and the Americans, people with representative governments, issued significant amounts of sovereign debt. The development of the railroads in the 1800s fueled the demand for capital in the United States. Early on, this demand for capital could be met with bank credit and stock issues. However, after 1850, railroad corporations grew larger and expanded into territories where few local banks and investors were willing to provide financing. The solution to that problem was the development of a huge market, both domestic and international, for the bonded debt of U.S. railroad corporations. Along with it came the demand for information on the investment quality of those firms

Still, it was not until 1909 that John Moody devised a scale for rating the credit quality of risky obligors, in this case the railroads. By that time, the railroad bond market was a half-century old and the sovereign bond market had been operating for centuries. Thus, both sovereign and corporate bond markets were able to operate without the benefit of agency ratings. How was this possible? Sylla (2002) argues that three important American developments combined to lead to the emergence of bond-rating agencies. These are the credit-reporting (but not rating) agency, the specialized financial press, and the investment banker. The development of each of these institutions is summarized in Figure 1. The agency started by Moody in 1909 represents a fusion of the function of the three institutions that preceded it.

Credit Reporting Agencies	Financial Press	Investment Bankers
• Letters of recommendation from a known source sufficed until the 1830s • Lewis Tappan founded the Mercantile Agency in 1841 that sold information to subscribers (became Dun & Bradstreet in 1859) – by 1900, over one million subscribers • John Bradstreet founded a similar firm in Cincinnati and published the first commercial rating book in 1851 • Merged with Dunn in 1933 to become Dunn & Bradstreet and acquired by Moody's in 1962	• Railroads were America's first big business • *The American Railroad Journal* began in 1832 and Henry Poor became its editor in 1849 • After the Civil War, Poor and his son published *Poor's Manual of the Railroads of the U.S.*, the recognized authority on railroads • The Poor company entered the rating business in 1915 and merged with Standard Statistics in 1941 to form Standard & Poor's (S&P), later acquired by McGraw Hill publishers	• Bankers who underwrote the deals put their reputations (and capital) on the line in all deals • The banker was an insider, insisting that companies disclose relevant information, even insisting on being on their boards of directors • International contacts for capital depended on the bankers reputation (e.g., J.P. Morgan, Kuhn Loeb & Co, Goldman Sachs) • Resentment rose over bankers access to inside information, rather than banker dominance of corporations

Figure 1. Precursors to the bond rating agency that represent a fusion of functions performed by these institutions prior to the 1900s.

Credit, Credit Risk, and Credit Models

Model-based approaches for estimating credit risk and relative value make some common assumptions and have some common objectives. First, they assume that accurate estimates of the likelihood of default can be derived from information in financial statements, analysts' reports, news services, and market prices. That is, one can build useful models of default. Also, changes in agency credit ratings tend to lag market perceptions of changing credit quality (see below), thereby fueling demand for alternative approaches to estimating default risk. In addition, agency rating scales provide only a ranking of risk and serve to estimate default risk "through the credit cycle," whereas modern investors demand more quantitative and timely estimates of obligors' credit quality. Finally, as shown below, changes in credit quality from equity based models and expert systems can often predict moves in bond yields.

Credit is the provision of access to liquid assets today in return for a promise of repayment in the future. Typically, credit is thought of as the debt that one party owes another. In a credit transaction, there is usually a lender, the provider of credit, and a borrower, also called the obligor or debtor. Most common instruments of credit, particularly with maturities greater than one year, are coupon-bearing instruments called bonds and loans. The simplest debt instrument is one without coupons, called a zero-coupon or discount bond. A diagram of cash flows from the lender to the borrower of a zero-coupon bond appears in Figure 2. The fundamental question in credit analysis is "How much should an investor charge the obligor for lending money to be repaid at a future date?"

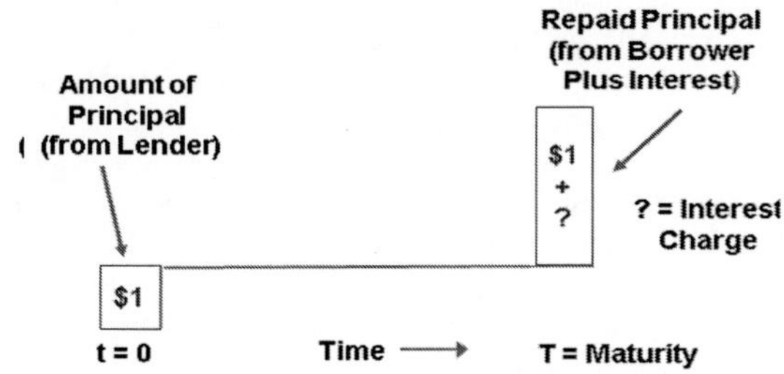

Figure 2. A single risky cash flow of $1 to be received at time T.

Credit risk involves several types of risk, but what separates credit risk from interest rate risk is the potential that an obligor may not make the coupon payments and may fail to pay back the principal. The main risk thought to be associated with credit is default risk.[5] When such a credit event occurs, the due date for repayment of principal is usually accelerated to the date of non-payment and all future coupons are forfeited.[6] The lender has a claim on the borrower's assets for the principal and accrued interest up to that time. Although there is room for legal disagreement about what constitutes default on a financial asset, there is general agreement that it involves several types of credit events (Moody's, 2010). These are:

1. A missed, delayed payment of interest and/or principal;
2. Bankruptcy, administration, legal receivership, or other legal block to the timely payment of interest and/or principal; or
3. A distressed exchange whereby the issuer offers debt holders a security that amounts to a diminished financial obligation, and the exchange has the apparent purpose of helping the borrower avoid default.

In default, lenders rarely receive the full value of principal and interest, and their claims have levels of priority depending on whether the debt is secured, senior, or subordinated.[7] In addition, the recovery value, or, more specifically, the loss given default (LGD), also depends on the firm's industry sector, economic conditions, geography, and other factors.[8] Finally, there is market risk associated with credit investments because the

---

[5] In fact, although default risk plays a major role in what drives credit spreads, market risk is likely a greater factor in most changes in the value of credit instruments—see the discussion of credit risk premium below.

[6] Also, there are typically provisions of cross-default, whereby failure to make a specified payment on one obligation triggers defaults on the firm's other debt instruments, even if no payment from those are due at that time.

[7] The position of a given type of debt in the firm's capital structure has legal implications in recovery via the Absolute Priority Rule (Eberhart, Moore, and Rosenfelt, 1990). However, despite legal priority, in practice the strict priority rule is violated routinely. Despite routine violations of the Absolute Priority Rule, the effect of priority on amount recovered in default has been confirmed (Altman and Eberhart, 1994; Fridson, and Garman, 1997). An excellent discussion of the role of seniority in recovery value during default can be found in Schuermann (2005).

[8] In fact, the likelihood of default has been much more well-documented and received greater attention from modelers than has loss given default, but its importance in risk and relative value is coming to be widely recognized, particularly with recent changes in the regulatory environment (i.e., Basel regulations). Although recovery models are not the subject of this report, extensive treatments can be found in Benzschawel (2012) and Benzschawel and Su (2013).

value of a credit instrument may change prior to maturity. Market risk results from changes in interest rates, changes in market liquidity, and the credit risk premium. The credit risk premium, described in detail below, reflects interplay between the willingness of lenders to lend and borrowers' demands for credit.

Historical Default Rates and Recovery Values

Credit rating agencies have been tracking corporate defaults for nearly a century and have been documenting cumulative default rates over time for each initial letter-rating category. To provide a historical perspective on the cyclicality of corporate defaults, Figure 3 displays average annual default rates since 1920 for firms with speculative grade ratings, (i.e., rated below Baa3; see Figure 8 for the credit rating scale) as reported by Moody's (Emery, Tennant, Kim, and Cantor, 2008, and Moody's 2013). The figure reveals that default rates are far from uniform, displaying large spikes and clusters in times of economic stress and periods of little or no default. Also, rarely is a very high default year followed by a very low one; default rates tend to change gradually. Finally, the figure shows that we have just emerged from another cycle of high default rates. Benzschawel and Su (2013) estimate that the annual default rate for 2014 will be just over 2%.

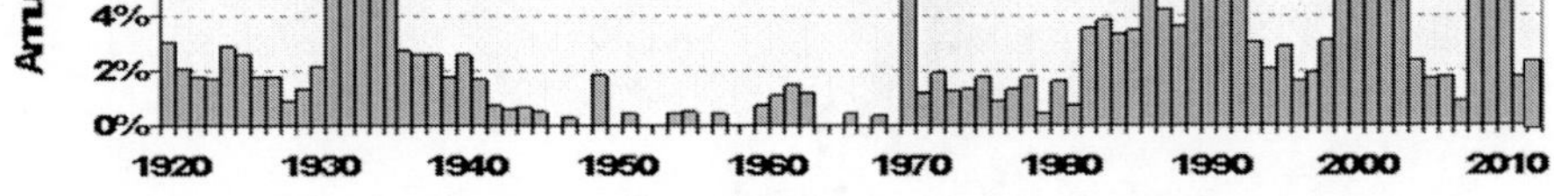

Figure 3. Annual speculative grade (Moody's ratings below Baa3) default rates from 1920-2012.

Other aspects of annual default rates are worth noting, as illustrated by the frequency distribution of annual default rates presented in Figure 4. First, default rates are not normally distributed (i.e., not Gaussian); they are highly skewed toward higher values. Although the average annual default rate is 2.8%, that rate only occurs in about 10% of the years. In fact, during most years, the annual high yield default rate is between 0% and 1%. Historical annual default rates for individual rating categories (not shown) are also skewed. Thus, although one often hears reference to average historical default rates, historical averages are clearly not appropriate measures of their central tendency.

Although measuring and modeling the default rates on risky debt has a long history, the amount recovered in default has received much less attention. This is surprising in that the recovery value in default plays an equal part with default probability in losses from default on risky assets. The expected loss given default, EL, depends on both default and recovery. That is,

$$EL = PD * (1 - RV), \quad (1)$$

where PD is the probability of default and RV is the recovery value in default. Despite the fact that expected loss depends on both recovery value and default probability, when estimating portfolio losses, managers commonly assign PDs based on a model, but assume a constant RV. In recent years, major credit rating agencies have reported statistics on recovery values in default because subsequent research has greatly increased our understanding of recovery value and our ability to construct predictive models.[9]

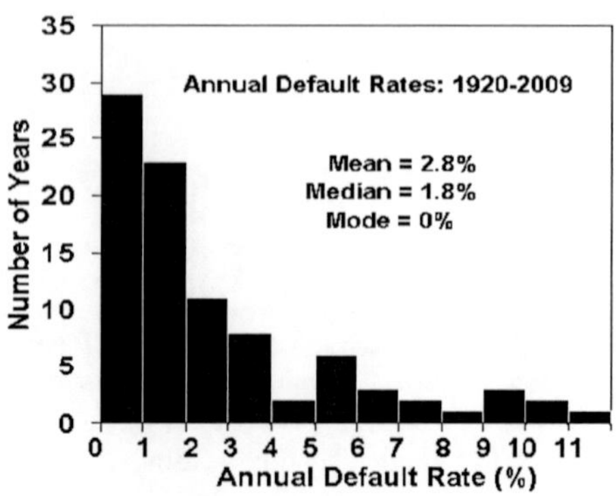

Figure 4. Annual value-weighted default rates, 1920-2008.

[9] For examples, see Verde (2003); Varma and Cantor (2004); Vazza, Aurora, and Miller (2007); and Emery, Ou, and Tennant (2010).

The earliest calculations of historical bond prices just after default averaged roughly 40% of face value (Hickman, 1958; Altman and Nammacher, 1984; Altman and Kishore, 1996). In fact, those early studies provide the basis for the oft-used constant value of 40% recovery of face value by market practitioners. However, the left panel of Figure 5 reveals the wide range of recovery values observed for defaulted firms. Moreover, the shape of the distribution of recovery rates is highly skewed and even bimodal. Also, it appears that neither the mean recovery rate of 40% nor the median of 34.5% are very good predictors of the recovery rate for any single case and that the most common amount recovered in default is about 20%.

The business cycle has also been shown to have a significant influence on recovery in default. That is, results reported by Frey (2000a, b) indicate that recoveries are lower in recessions than during expansions, which was later corroborated by Altman, Brady, Resti, and Sironi (2003). For example, the middle and right panels of Figure 5 display average annual default rates and recovery values, respectively, for senior unsecured debt. In the middle panel, the bars indicate default rates and the connected circles show recovery rates on an inverted scale on the right side. Clearly high and low extremes in recovery rates occur during low and high default periods, respectively. The dependence of recovery on default is demonstrated more clearly in the right panel of Figure 5, which plots average annual recoveries against average annual default rates.

Figure 6 shows that the amount recovered in default depends on other factors as well. These include the seniority of the debt in the capital structure (left panel), industry sector (middle), and agency rating prior to default (right). The interdependencies of all these factors and the relative lack of historical data on recoveries have made it difficult to generate accurate estimates of recovery value in default. Thus, despite the crucial role of recovery value on expected losses in default, very few well-tested models of recovery value have been proposed.[10] Issues regarding recovery value are presented herein to illustrate an existing problem for which newer types of model, such as crowd sourcing and big data, offer potential for greatly improving our ability to accurately estimate expected losses on credit portfolios.

---

[10] These include Moody's LossCalc (Dwyer and Korablev, 2008), S&P's Ratings Direct (Standard and Poor's, 2008), and Citi's E-3 Ensemble Model (Benzschawel and Su, 2013).

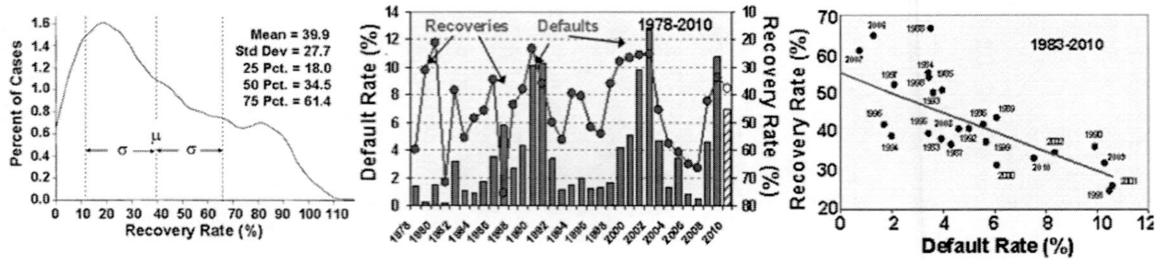

Figure 5. Left: Frequency Distribution of Recovery Rates for Bonds and Loans, Moody's 1970-2003; Middle: Annual Default Rates (Bars) and Recovery Rates (Circles; Inverted Axis); and Right: Scatterplot of Annual Recoveries versus Defaults.

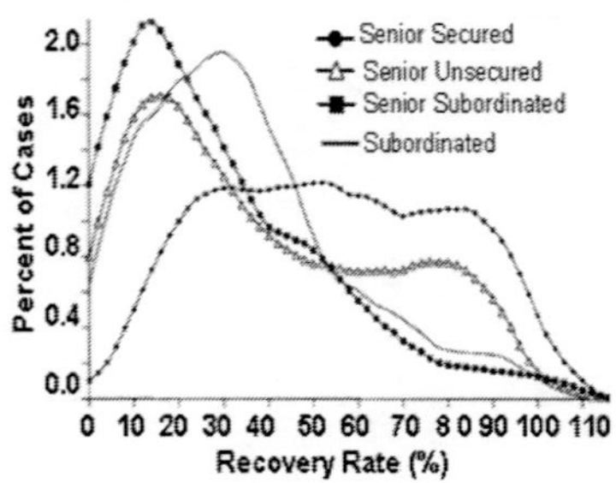

Sector Name	SIC code (4 digit)	SIC code (2 digit)	Average (%)	Std. Dev. (%)	Count
Agriculture / Mining	0199-1499	01-14	53	26	187
Construction	1500-1799	15-17	47	27	110
Food / Tobacco / Clothing	2000-2299	20-22	53	31	106
Clothes / Wood / Furniture	2300-2599	23-25	43	27	65
Paper / Printing	2600-2799	26-27	38	27	150
Chemicals / Rubber	2800-3099	28-30	44	30	136
Leather / Stone / Metal	3100-3499	31-34	44	30	156
Machinery / Electronics	3500-3699	35-36	45	30	134
Transportation Equipment	3700-3799	37	40	31	127
Manufacturing (Misc.)	3800-3999	38-39	40	29	55
Land Transportation	4000-4499	40-44	44	22	54
Transport / Pipelines (Other)	4500-4799	45-47	33	19	284
Communications	4800-4899	48	37	30	371
Utilities	4900-4999	49	58	33	229
Wholesale Trade	5000-5199	50-51	42	33	89
Retail Trade	5200-5999	52-59	49	29	266
Depository Financial	6000-6099	60	33	30	144
Nondepository Financial	6100-6199	61	63	27	150
Securities / Broker Dealer	6200-6299	62	9	2	294
Insurance / Real Estate	6300-6799	63-67	39	29	149
Travel / Entertainment Services	7000-7999	70-79	53	29	244
Services (Misc.)	8000-8799	80-87	62	22	431

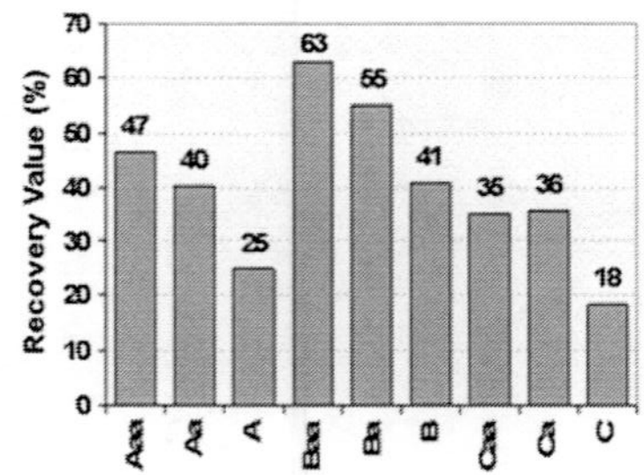

Figure 6. Diagram of median log default probabilities from Citi's HPD model as a function of agency rating category (lower axis) and five-year CDS spread (top axis) illustrating the mapping between HPD score and inferred credit rating or CDS spread.

Early Credit Models: Fundamental Analysis, Agency Ratings, and Financial Ratios

To begin the discussion of credit models, consider first the origins of quantitative credit analysis as embodied in fundamental analysis, including agency ratings and the initial applications of financial ratios to default risk.

Fundamental Analysis. Fundamental credit analysts examine in detail a firm's balance sheet, income statement, management, position within its industry, and future prospects. On that basis, they form opinions regarding whether a firm's credit is improving, deteriorating, or stable, and possibly if its debt is trading rich, cheap or is priced fairly. For example, financial analysts typically consider a firm's past records of:

- Assets,
- Earnings,
- Sales,
- Products,
- Management, and
- Market positioning.

From that analysis, they predict future trends in those indicators and their implications for firms' success or failure. They may even make qualitative judgments about firms' default risk relative to other firms and whether or not firms' assets are fairly priced.

Fundamental analysis is a well-established and critical aspect of investment strategy and will continue to be so. Despite its usefulness, fundamental analysis has many limitations. Figure 7 lists some advantages and disadvantages of fundamental analysis. An advantage of fundamental analysis is that it can provide a close and in-depth monitoring of a firm's activities and provide a detailed assessment of its management. Analysts are also forward looking in that they attempt to project the prospects of the firm in the context of its industry and the economic environment. Fundamental analysis is particularly useful for avoiding credit spread "blow-ups" and for early identification of financial problems. Furthermore, analysts can identify potential event risk, such as leveraged buyouts, equity buybacks, mergers, etc., events that are often challenging for model-based approaches.

Advantages

- Close and in depth monitoring of firm's activities
- Useful for avoiding "blowups" and defaults
- Can identify potential "event risk" (LBO, equity buybacks, etc.)
- Forward looking

Disadvantages

- Only single analyst's opinion
- Difficult to quantify
- Intermittent, incomplete, and inconsistent coverage of universe of firms
- Don't always respond to market movements and events
- Analysts are expensive

Figure 7. Advantages and limitations of fundamental analysis.

Nevertheless, analysts' views of a firm's prospects often differ and, even at the same advisory company, a new analyst's opinion of a given firm may differ from that of his or her predecessor. In particular, analysts' views can be difficult to quantify; they rarely assign firms' probabilities of default or a spread value of richness or cheapness, tending to prefer qualitative assessments. Fundamental analysts typically do not provide daily opinions, so it is not always clear that one has his latest opinion and an analyst may not respond in a timely way to market moves or events. Also, coverage of a firm may be intermittent; an analyst may leave, and coverage of a firm or industry may be suspended. In fact, there is necessarily incomplete coverage of a large number of firms issuing debt, so tracking analysts' performances can be difficult. Finally, analysts are "expensive," particularly relative to model-based approaches.

Credit Rating Agencies. Credit agencies began analyzing firm default risk in the 19th century. As listed in Figure 1, Lewis Tappan founded the Mercantile Agency in 1941 and the forerunner of Dunn and Bradstreet, Inc. was organized in Cincinnati, Ohio, in 1849 to provide investors with independent credit investigations based on fundamental analysis. At that time, information of firms' credit quality was particularly scarce, and firms found that they could issue debt more cheaply if it had been reviewed by a respected credit agency. Still, it was not until 1909 when John Moody developed the credit rating scale, which he first applied to characterize the relative riskiness of railroad bonds.

Moody's credit rating scale appears along with those of its major competitors, Fitch and Standard and Poor's (S&P), in Figure 8.[11] The

---

[11] It is difficult to overemphasize the contribution of the agency rating scale to the development of credit markets and to credit modeling efforts. Not only did it allow quantification of judgments about firms' credit qualities, thereby aiding issuers and

major features of rating scales are well known; credits rated AAA/Aaa by S&P/Moody's are of the highest quality, and bonds in all categories down through BBB-/Baa3 are called investment-grade because they have very little near-term risk of default. Typically, investors in investment-grade bonds are concerned with either managing liability or collecting steady income from coupons while monitoring their exposure to mark-to-market risk from changes in credit spreads. Bonds rated below BBB-/Baa3 are called speculative grade or high yield bonds. High yield bonds are typically held in different investment funds than investment-grade bonds and traded by different individuals within the same investment firms. Also, high yield bond investors typically seek higher yields, speculating on price appreciation and on decreases in firms' default risk over time.

Number Code	S&P / Fitch	Moody's	Yield Book	PD Range From	To	Avg	Interpretation	Class
0			a4	0	0	0	Risk-Free	Investment Grade
1	AAA	Aaa	a3	0	0.03	0.03	Highest Quality	
2	AA+	Aa1	a2+	0.03	0.05	0.04	High Quality	
3	AA	Aa2	a2	0.05	0.06	0.06		
4	AA-	Aa3	a2-	0.06	0.08	0.07		
5	A+	A1	a1+	0.08	0.10	0.09	Strong Payment Capacity	
6	A	A2	a1	0.10	0.16	0.13		
7	A-	A3	a1-	0.16	0.23	0.19		
8	BBB+	Baa1	b3+	0.23	0.37	0.28	Adequate Payment Capacity	
9	BBB	Baa2	b3	0.37	0.61	0.50		
10	BBB-	Baa3	b3-	0.61	0.84	0.73		
11	BB+	Ba1	b2+	0.84	1.1	0.96	Likely to Fulfill Oligations; Ongoing Uncertainty	High Yield
12	BB	Ba2	b2	1.1	1.3	1.2		
13	BB-	Ba3	b2-	1.3	1.6	1.4		
14	B+	B1	b1+	1.6	2.1	1.8	High Risk Obligations	
15	B	B2	b1	2.1	2.8	2.4		
16	B-	B3	b1-	2.8	3.4	3.2		
17	CCC+		c3+	3.4	4.0	3.7	Current Vulnerability to Default	
18	CCC	Caa	c3	4.0	6.3	4.2		
19	CCC-		c3-	6.3	14	9.4		
20	CC	Ca	c2	14	31	21	In Backruptcy or Default, or Exhibits Other Shortcomings	Distresse
21	C	C	c1	31	67	45		
22	D	D	d	67	100	100		

Figure 8. Credit rating scales from S&P, Fitch, and Moody's along with Citigroup's Yield Book risk categories and average one-year default probabilities by rating category from Citi's HPD model.

---

investors, but also it enabled historical tracking of defaults and credit spreads by generating ratings for use by subsequent generations of credit modelers.

Bonds' initial agency credit ratings appear to order well their long-term default risk. For example, Figure 9 shows cumulative default rates by year as a function of initial agency rating on linear (left plot) and logarithmic (right panel) default axes. The graphs indicate clearly that bonds in each lower rating category (see Figure 8 for the ordering) have subsequently higher cumulative default rates across the entire 30-year time period. Also, the logarithmic plot shows a very regular vertical spacing of cumulative default curves by rating category. Notice in the right panel of Figure 9 that after about 7-10 years, curves for all rating categories are parallel. That is, marginal default rates settle in, but at rates that are higher for each successively lower-rated category.

The pattern of yield spreads by maturity for each agency rating category also indicates, at least on average, general agreement between agency ratings and investors' perceptions of credit risk. To demonstrate this, consider first the top left panel of Figure 10, which displays a typical bond with promised annual coupons, *c*, paid at semi-annual intervals and a bullet payment at maturity. The equation at the lower left in Figure 10 specifies how the yield on a bond is determined as the single annual discount rate, *y*, which serves to equate the sum of discounted cash flows to the current market price. That equation can be used to derive the curves in the plot at the right in Figure 10. That graph displays, for each letter-rating category, average yield curves as a function of maturity fit to US Treasury bonds and corporate bonds in Citigroup's Broad Investment Grade (BIG) and High Yield Indexes.[12] The lowest yields are for US Treasury bonds (UST), which serve as a benchmark for comparison with the riskier corporate bonds, whose average yield curves are higher for all rating categories and at all maturities. In particular, as bonds go down the credit quality scale (i.e., as agency ratings get lower), magnitudes of yields at each maturity increase monotonically; the lower the agency rating, the higher the yield. Finally, notice that for almost all risk categories, the yield curves are upward sloping; they increase with maturity. However, for the riskiest bonds (i.e., the ones rated triple-C), the curve is inverted, with yields for bonds having short maturities higher than longer maturity ones. In fact, this pattern, while not always present, is typical and is generally assumed to indicate that the marginal risk of high-default obligors decreases over time.[13]

---

[12] Citigroup Index Group (2013) describes the criteria for inclusion of bonds in the corporate indexes.

[13] That is, if a risky obligor with default probability $p_{0,1}$ survives one year , the one-year probability between years 1 and 2, $p_{1,2} < p_{0,1}$. But see Berd, Mashal, and Wang (2004) for an alternative interpretation.

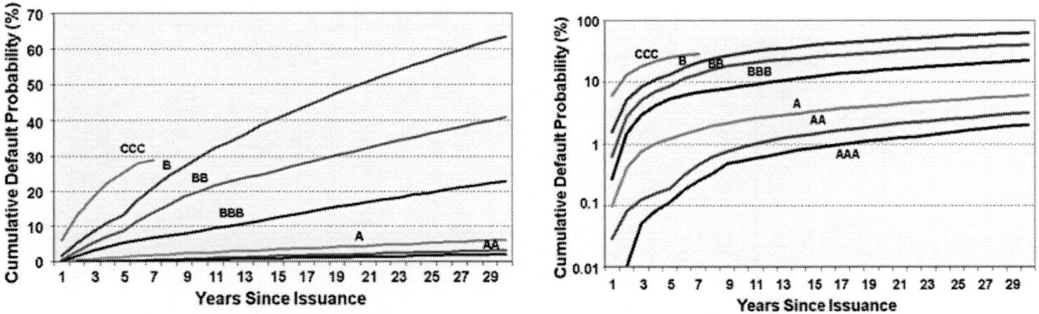

Figure 9. Cumulative default rates by time since issuance and initial rating category on linear (left) and logarithmic (right) axes.

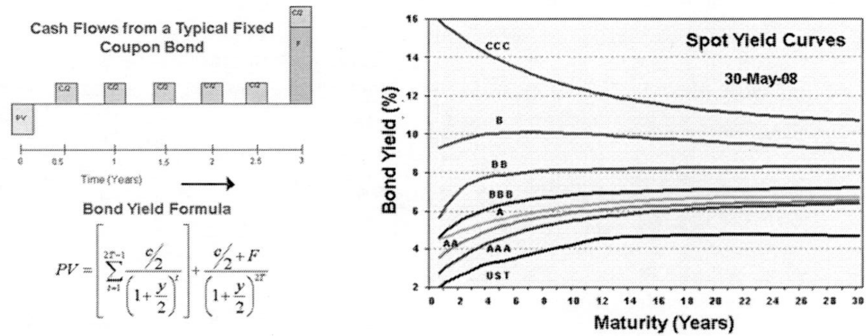

Figure 10. Left: Cash flows from a semi-annual fixed coupon bond and a formula for its yield; Right: par yield curves by agency credit rating.

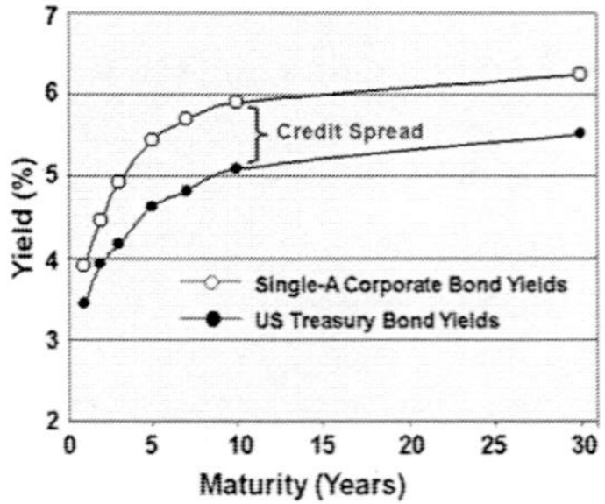

The present value, *PV*, of a bond with maturity, *T* for:

US Treasuries $PV = \left[\sum_{t=1}^{2T-1} \frac{c/2}{\left(1+\frac{r_{t/2}}{2}\right)^t}\right] + \frac{c/2+100}{\left(1+\frac{r_T}{2}\right)^{2T}}$

Corporates $PV = \left[\sum_{t=1}^{2T-1} \frac{c/2}{\left(1+\frac{r_{t/2}+s}{2}\right)^t}\right] + \frac{c/2+100}{\left(1+\frac{r_T+s}{2}\right)^{2T}}$

Credit Spread

Where *PV* is the price of bond with coupons (*c*), r_t is the term structure of US Treasury spot yields at 0.5 year intervals, and *s* is the yield spread of the bond to US Treasuries.

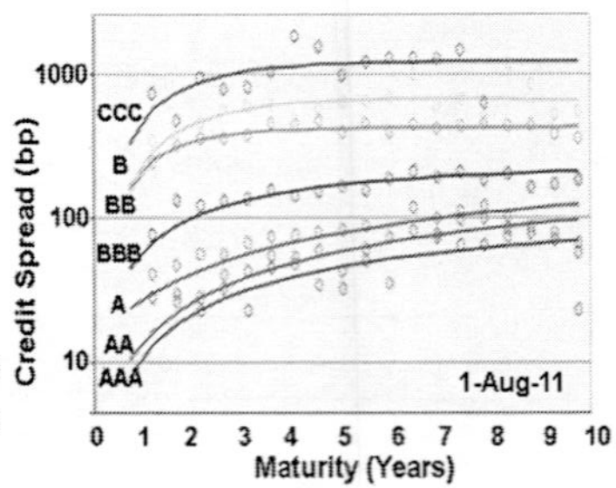

Figure 11. Left: Yield curves for US Treasuries and for single-A corporate bonds; Middle: Formula for calculating yield spreads to Treasuries; and Right: Yield spreads-to-Treasuries by rating.

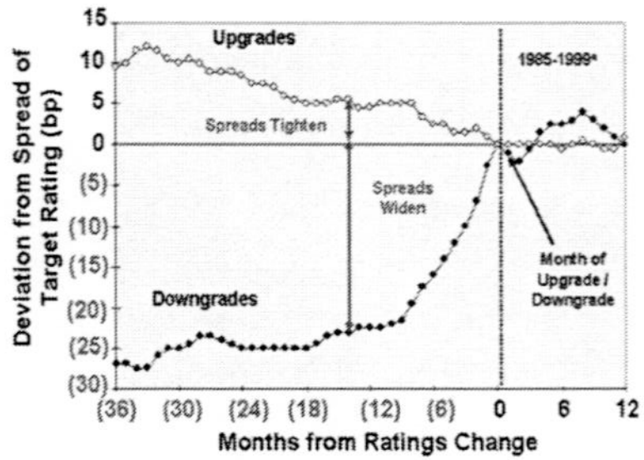

Portfolio Construction Rules:

1. 100 Credits
2. Uniform Ratings from Single-A to Single-B+
3. Average Rating: Triple-B-
4. Maturities from 4 to 12 years
5. Sector / Issuer Maximum: 20%/2%

RANDOM: **Pick Bonds at Random**

GREEDY: **Select Highest Yielding Bonds First**

CONSERVATIVE: **Select Bonds with Lowest Expected PDs from the KMV Model first**

Defaults per Portfolio

	Random	Greedy	Conservative
1994	0.00	0.00	0.00
1995	0.00	0.00	0.00
1996	0.00	0.00	0.00
1997	0.25	1.47	0.00
1998	0.11	0.40	0.00
1999	0.95	3.26	0.00
2000	0.70	0.22	0.00
2001	0.46	1.67	0.00
2002	2.68	4.82	0.00
Mean	0.57	1.32	0.00

Figure 12. Left: Average credit spreads are at agency rating averages in the month of change; Middle and Right: 500 Annual identically-rated portfolios constructed using different rules have different average default rates per portfolio.

The price of a bond is typically quoted in terms of yield spread: the increment in yield over the yield of a Treasury bond of similar maturity (or the term structure of credit spreads) required to match the market price of a bond with a coupon. The bond's spread serves to isolate the price of its credit risk and is typically quoted in basis points (where 1bp is 1/100 of 1%) of yield increment relative to Treasuries (or some other reference such as the London Interbank Borrowing Rate – LIBOR). The left panel of Figure 11 illustrates the credit spreads of hypothetical triple-A corporate bonds of various maturities as the differences in yields between those bonds and US Treasuries of similar maturities. The concept of a credit spread has become an important measure for describing the relative riskiness of bonds.

In addition to the positive features of agency ratings, there are also some well-documented limitations. Consider first the left panel of Figure 12 from Benzschawel and Adler (2002). They tracked differences between spreads of over 2,500 downgraded bonds and over 2,000 upgraded bonds to the average spreads of their future rating categories before and after ratings' changes. The chart shows average differences for upgrades and downgrades separately. For upgrades, spreads start to tighten two- to three-years prior to the upgrade, arriving at the average spread during the month of upgrade. For downgrades, spreads start to widen only nine-months prior to downgrade, but are also at the spread of the target-rating category at the month of downgrade. The middle and right hand panels of Figure 12 show results of a study by McDermott, Skarabot, and Kroujiline (2003, 2004), who constructed portfolios each year from 1994 to 2002 using identical rules for agency ratings' distributions, maturities, and industry sectors, but different selection rules:

1. RANDOM: Select bonds at random as long as they satisfy the rules (i.e., the benchmark).
2. GREEDY: Select the highest yielding bonds first.
3. CONSERVATIVE: Select the bonds with the lowest expected PDs from Moody's KMV model first.

Multiple portfolios of 100 corporate bonds were selected each year from the bonds in Citi's BIG and High Yield Indexes. The right panel of Figure 12 shows the average number of defaults per portfolio by year and the overall average. Note that according to agency criteria, all of those portfolios should be equally risky. Clearly, that is not the case. Selecting the highest yielding bonds as in the "Greedy" method produced over twice the number of defaults per portfolio as the "Random" method. Conversely, the "Conservative" method, picking safe credit according to the KMV model (described below), avoided all defaults, thereby also demonstrating its ability to outperform agency ratings at predicting default risk (or safety in this case).

The development of agency credit rating scales have proven critical to the expansion function of modern credit markets over the last century. Some positive features of agency ratings appear in the left column of Figure 13, with limitations presented in the right column. For example, the agencies have developed consistent rating methodologies, they cover a wide range of corporate, municipal and sovereign issuers, and they have collected and shared publically their detailed data on bond defaults since the 1920s. Furthermore, agency ratings have proven useful, at least on average, as indicators of credit risk and relative value. Nevertheless, as listed in the right portion of Figure 13, agencies are slow to react to credit events. On average, the market recognizes changes in credit quality months, and even years, prior to ratings changes—that is typically, changes in agency ratings trail changes in credit spreads. Also, although the rating agencies have long histories and present average default rates by year and credit quality; Figure 3 and Figure 4 illustrate that default rates are highly dependent on the credit cycle and rarely are they at their mean values. Finally, subscriptions to agency ratings are expensive and, as will be shown below, are inferior to other types of models in ordering bonds by default risk.

Advantages

- Ratings by Moody's, S&P, and Fitch are reliable and generally correct when made
- The agencies cover a wide spectrum of debt issuers
- Provide accurate long-term rankings of default probabilities
- Agreement, on average, between market spreads and rating

Disadvantages

- Agencies are slow to react to credit events
- Reluctant to change a rating, often erring on the conservative side
- Subscriptions are expensive
- Rating changes tend to trail changes in credit spreads
- Use of average historical defaults ignores effects of the credit cycle on default rates
- Other models perform better at predicting defaults

Figure 13. Advantages and limitations of agency ratings.

Despite the limitations of agency ratings, it is difficult to overstate their importance in the development of financial markets, not only in the United States, but globally. One is hard pressed to identify a major corporate or sovereign bond issuer who has found it unnecessary to have an agency credit rating. Furthermore, agency credit ratings have been written into legislation, loan agreements, pension targets, and fund indentures. Although the rating agencies have been criticized as being slow to react to credit changes and to have overstepped their expertise for the rating of structured credit products, no other credit scoring system has had comparable acceptance over such an extended period. In fact, the agency rating is arguably the most successful credit model in existence.

Financial Ratio Analysis

The first reference to ratio analysis can be traced to Euclid, who described its benefits and properties in 300 B.C. (Heath, 1956). However, the application of ratio analysis in finance originated much later, its origins being traced to the late nineteenth century.[14] A financial ratio (or accounting ratio) is a quotient of two numbers where both numbers are taken from an enterprise's financial statements. The earliest reference to a financial ratio is the "quick ratio," attributed to Rosendale (1908), but Horrigan (1968) claims that James Cannon, a pioneer of financial statement analysis, was using ten different ratios as early as 1905, and Foulke (1961) suggests that the current ratio may have emerged as early as 1891.[15] In any case, the use of financial ratios for credit analysis developed rapidly with the introduction of the first ratio criterion for risk, the 2-to-1 current ratio, and inter-firm comparisons and relative ratio criteria. Despite this, few analysts used financial ratios prior to World War I, and those who did were inclined to use only the current ratio. The passage of the Federal income tax code in 1913 and establishment of the Federal Reserve System in 1914 increased demand for financial statements and improvement in their analysis. Wall (1919) responded to this need with his now classic study of seven different financial ratios for 981 firms, stratified by industry and location.

---

[14] See Horrigan (1968) for a detailed history of the development of ratio analysis. Additionally, Brown (1955) provides a more detailed description of the early history of financial ratio analysis.

[15] The quick ratio is a measure of a firm's liquid assets relative to its current liabilities.

A rapid development of different ratios took place during the 1920s and that proliferation continued until the 1960s.[16] There are now many financial ratios linked to financial risk, and several of the most widely used ratios are listed in Figure 14. Although quantitative, financial ratios are typically viewed as part of fundamental analysis because, until relatively recently, their relationship to default was not explicitly specified. Fisher (1959) and Beaver (1966) were the first to attempt to systematically evaluate the relationship between financial ratios and corporate failure, and Beaver identified many of the ratios that we view as important today. In fact, that effort by Beaver can be said to have provided the bridge between classical and modern periods in credit risk analysis.

- Quick Ratio (Liquid Ratio):
  - The ability of a company to use its cash or quick assets to extinguish or retire its current liabilities immediately

$$\text{Quick Ratio} = \frac{\text{Cash} + \text{Marketable Securities} + \text{Accounts Receivable}}{\text{Current Liabilities}}$$

- Return on Equity (ROE):
  - The rate of return on the ownership interest of the common stock

$$\text{Return on Equity} = \frac{\text{Net Income}}{\text{Average Shareholders Equity}}$$

- Debt Ratio (Leverage):
  - The percentage of a company's assets that are provided via debt

$$\text{Debt Ratio} = \frac{\text{Total Debt}}{\text{Total Assets}}$$

- Operating Margin (Profitability):
  - The ratio of operating divided by net sales

$$\text{Operating Margin} = \frac{\text{Operating Income}}{\text{Net Sales}}$$

Figure 14. Advantages and limitations of agency ratings.

---

[16] In fact, Lincoln (1925) already discusses and illustrates 40 different financial ratios.

The Modern Era: Quantitative Default Models

The modern era in credit modeling can arguably be traced to the development of statistical models based on financial ratios. Those models generate probabilistic estimates of future default risk based on historical relationships observed between measurable characteristics of firms and their past payment performance. Along with those models, a characteristic feature of the modern period is the application of techniques from statistical decision theory for assessing the accuracy of models at predicting defaults.

Statistical Credit Models: Altman's Z-Score

The first, and most notable of the early statistical models is Altman's (1968) Z-Score, whose formulation is presented in Figure 15. Altman derived his Z-Score model by performing a discriminant analysis between defaulting and non-defaulting firms using five financial ratios calculated from data in their financial statements. The ratios chosen for analysis were those that had been highlighted by Fischer (1959) and Beaver (1966) and that were available from the financial statements of publicly-traded firms. In fact, Beaver had already demonstrated that ratio analysis could be useful for discriminating defaulters from non-defaulters, but had not combined them into a predictive model. To build the Z-Score model, Altman assembled financial information from 66 manufacturing firms, half of which had defaulted within a year of reporting those financials, whereas the other 33 did not. The resulting discriminant function appears at the top of the lower portion of the figure, which shows the five financial ratios and the $Z=2.6$ cut-off between bankrupt and non-bankrupt firms reported by Altman. These values of Z were mapped to historical one-year default rates to produce the first quantitative estimates of firms' default probabilities.

Not only was the Z-Score model an immediate success, it has continued to be useful, even though its particular applications have evolved. Although the Z-Score was widely used in the next couple decades for estimating default probabilities for individual firms, its relative usefulness for that purpose has declined due to several factors. First, the model is backward looking. That is, the financial ratios in Figure 15 are already at least a month or two old when reported and firms' financial prospects may have changed since their publication. Furthermore, firms' financial reports are updated quarterly at best, with some information updated only annually. This is too infrequent for modern credit investors, who now typically rely more on structural and risk-neutral models (described below) for assessing individual firm risk. Those latter models, incorporating market information, are inherently forward looking and can produce updated estimates of default daily.

The success of the Z-Score spawned an entire class of statistical approaches to predicting default risk. These include ordinary least-squares models and Probit and Logit models as well as non-linear models and others based on neural networks (Odom and Sharda, 1990), decision trees (Bozsik, 2012), genetic algorithms (Marose, 1990; Marose, Rothenberg, and Sankaran, 1992), and Bayesian inference (Kazemi and Mosleh, 2012), to name a few. Although some of these models have proven useful for understanding certain aspects of default, none of these models has displaced Altman's Z-score. Often, investors have found these models too difficult to interpret in terms of their relationship to actual properties of firms, and they tend to view the more complicated statistical models as "black boxes," often lacking economic intuition, prone to over-fitting the data, and too computationally intensive and complex. Thus, none has achieved the acceptance or longevity accorded to the Z-score model and its offshoots.

$Z = .012X_1 + .014X_2 + .033X_3 + .006X_4 + .999X_5$

X_1 = Working Capital / Total Assets
X_2 = Retained Earnings / Total Assets
X_3 = Earning Before Interest & Taxes / Total Assets
X_4 = Market Value of Equity / Book Value of Debt
X_5 = Sales / Total Assets
Z = Overall Index

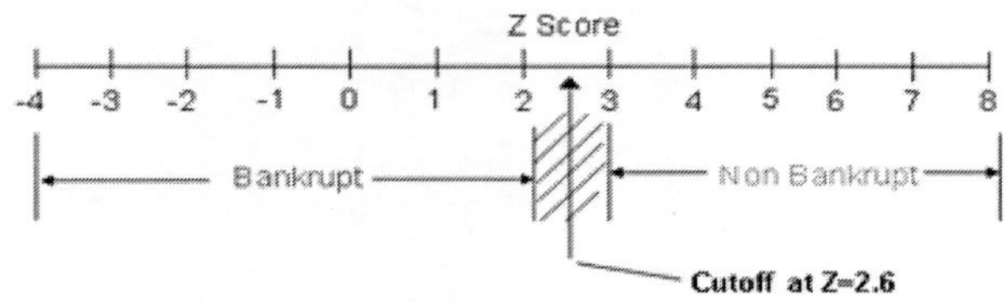

Figure 15. Altman's (1968) Z-Score model for estimating corporate default risk.

Statistical Credit Models: Adaptive Non-Linear Regression

Statistical approaches to modeling default have become more sophisticated since the development of the Z-score model. As described in detail in this section, more recent statistical models use adaptive non-linear modeling techniques to predict defaults and to evaluate model performance using a methodology derived from statistical decision theory. An example of such an application can be found in Campbell, Hilscher, and Szilagyi (2008). The logistic regression function (see the middle panel of Figure 16) is commonly used for transforming model input variables when the values of the inputs are non-linearly related to the desired output. The adaptive method is so called because it deploys a walk forward construction method to compute a new model by selecting input variables each year from a set of candidates, while adding the data from the previous year to the development sample. We illustrate the non-linear adaptive modeling approach using a model developed by Benzschawel, Li, and Lee (2013) because it embodies the non-linear adaptive approach, along with step-wise variable selection, and evaluates performance using cumulative accuracy profile (CAP) curves.

Major features of the bank default model are presented in Figure 16. The equation in the upper left panel of the figure specifies the model, whose variable inputs are shown just below it. The variables shown were chosen via step-wise variable selection from a set of 20 candidate financial ratios, with all input variables transformed into standard normal distributions testing as inputs to each annual model. Model construction begins with only the logistic function:

$$PD = \frac{1}{1+e^{-(\alpha_i+\beta_i x_i)}} \quad . (2)$$

For each candidate input variable, values of αi and βi are selected that best predict default on the development sample. The variable with the greatest predictive power with respect to default is chosen as the first input variable.[17] After selection of the first variable, the process repeats to select a second variable, and so on, until model performance ceases to improve.

[17] We chose the Bayesian Information Criterion (BIC) developed by Schwartz (1978) as our measure of predictive power. The BIC measures how well the model fits the data, but also imposes a penalty for having too many variables, thereby guarding against over-fitting the data. A detailed description of model construction can be found in Benzschawel et al. (2013).

Once all the variables for the model are selected, the value of the constant β0 and coefficients βi (i=1, … , n) for each variable are refit to minimize errors in logistic regression. The variables and their values of β for the 2013 one-year model appear on the left in Figure 16.

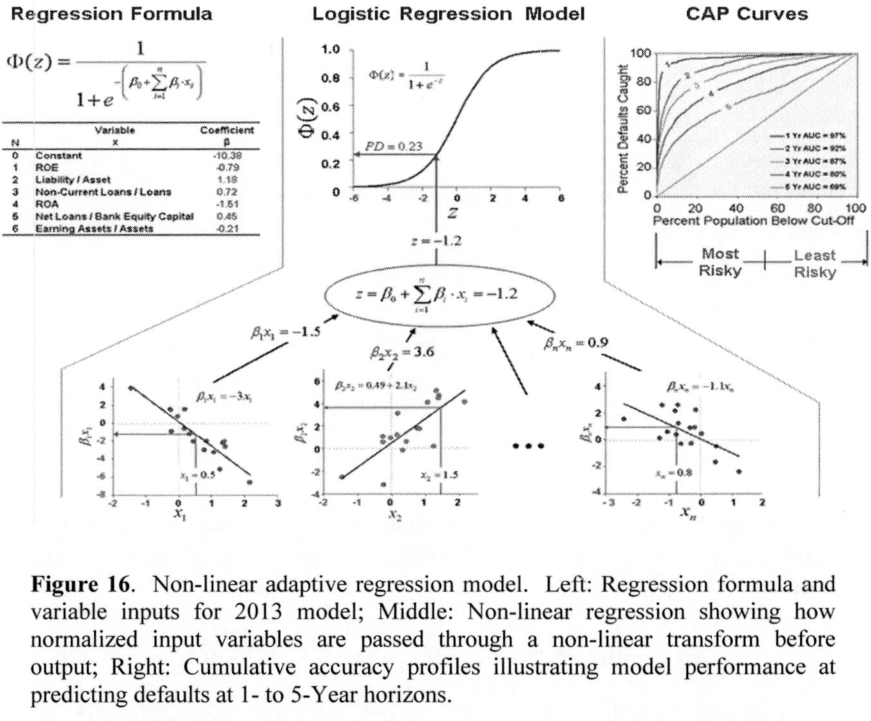

Figure 16. Non-linear adaptive regression model. Left: Regression formula and variable inputs for 2013 model; Middle: Non-linear regression showing how normalized input variables are passed through a non-linear transform before output; Right: Cumulative accuracy profiles illustrating model performance at predicting defaults at 1- to 5-Year horizons.

Benzschawel et al. constructed annual series bank models using all available US bank data from 1992 to 2012. To ensure no look-forward bias in model construction and to determine out-of-sample performance, they used a walk-forward procedure as illustrated in Figure 17. Data from the years 1992 through 1999 were used to construct the first annual model. The one-year model for 1999 was then used to score all non-defaulting banks existing at the beginning of 2000, and its ability to predict defaults in 2000 was determined. That procedure was repeated annually until 2012.

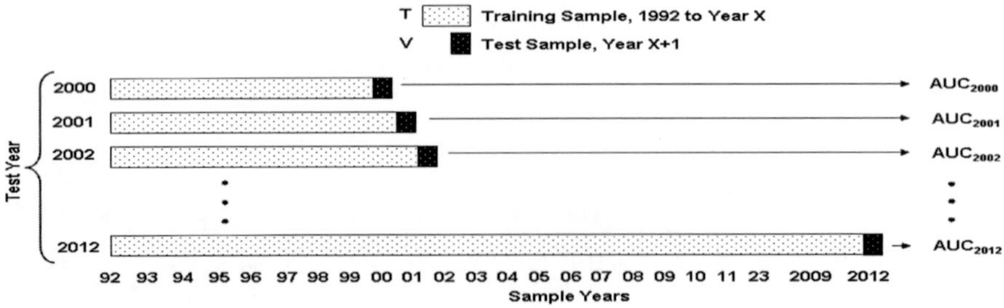

Figure 17. Walk-forward development and testing procedure for one-year models. A new model is developed each year from 1999 to 2011 using data from all previous years and tested on the defaulted and non-defaulted banks in each subsequent year from 2000 to 2012.

Out-of-sample performance of the bank model at default prediction was evaluated at horizons of one- to five-years for each year from 2002 through 2012.[18] The model has proven superior to agency ratings at predicting defaults at all horizons (see below). In addition, Benzschawel and Lommaert (2014) present a detailed analysis of factors contributing to default risk over the credit cycle and how those factors change in importance when predicting default over different time horizons. Before describing those results further, it is useful to describe methods for evaluating the relative accuracy of default models. These methods will be used throughout the remainder of this report for comparing default model performance.

Analyzing Model Performance: CAP Curves

Although several studies have related financial ratios to corporate distress (Fischer, 1966; Beaver, 1966), powerful quantitative methods for evaluating model performance at predicting default have only been applied in the past 20 years. Quantifying default model performance can be challenging because only a small fraction of existing firms default in any year, and many firms with very high risk may not default. Furthermore, default is typically not known with certainty before the actual event. Thus, evaluating model performance must necessarily rely upon probabilistic comparisons. Along with the development of more sophisticated default

[18] The test set is sufficiently large, with a total of 499 defaulters out of 11,114 distinct banks. For models at horizons longer than one year, testing was only able to be done to year 2012 minus the horizon year.

models in the 1990s came the application of more rigorous methods for evaluating model performance at predicting defaults. Most notable of these improvements is the application of cumulative accuracy profile (CAP) curves from statistical decision theory.[19] The earliest reports of using CAP curves to evaluate the predictive power of default models are those of Sobehart, Keenan, and Stein (2000) and Kealhofer and Kurbat (2001). A detailed treatment of the history and application of statistical decision theory to financial model validation appears in Stein (2007). The construction of CAP curves is presented briefly in this section because CAP curves will be used frequently in the following sections.

Figure 18 illustrates how CAP curves are constructed from both agency ratings and model-derived default probabilities (PDs) for a hypothetical example of 100 firms. The first step in the process, shown at left, involves ordering firm risk (either by agency ratings or PDs) from highest to lowest, typically at the beginning of each year. At the end of the year, each firm's risk score is associated with a "D" or "N" depending on whether it defaulted or did not default, respectively. The middle panel shows how the ranked scores and associated outcomes (D or N) are used to construct the CAP curve. Consider the dashes between ranks 10 and 11 in the left portion of Figure 18 that divide the upper 10% and remaining 90% of the riskiest firms by agency rating and the PD model. Assume that of the 100 firms, there are 15 total defaults. Then, in the top 10%, the agency ratings capture 5 of the 15 or 33% of the defaulters. This is the value of the red bar at 10% on the x-axis of the CAP curve in the middle panel of Figure 18. Similarly, the PD model captures 8 of the 15 defaults or 53% of the defaulters in the top10%, the green bar at 10% population cut-off. The other bars of the curve are constructed similarly as the criterion is expanded at 10-percentile intervals on the ranked risk dimension. The CAP curve reveals that, for all percentiles, the PD model outperforms the agency ratings. Finally, note that a model assigning risk scores at chance would catch 10% of the defaulters in the top 10%, 20% in the top 20%, and so on. This "chance line" is the diagonal line in the figure, indicative of no ability to sort defaulters from non-defaulters. Hence, the area above the chance line is a measure of the relative classification ability of the model.

[19] Receiver Operating Characteristic (ROC) curve, the precursor to the CAP curve, and its analysis were originally described by Green and Swets (1966) and Egan (1975) to quantify the detection of signals in noise. The relationship between ROC and CAP curves is described in Sobehart, Keenan, and Stein (2000).

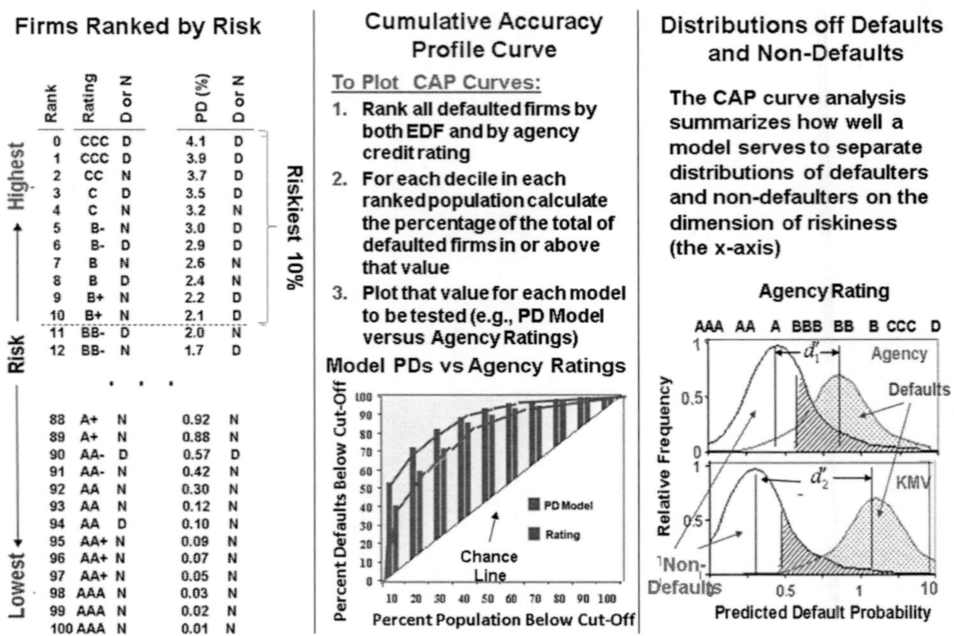

Figure 18. Demonstration of how distributions of defaulted and non-defaulting firms ranked by risk from agency ratings and a PD model is used to calculate cumulative accuracy profile (CAP) curves. The larger the area under the CAP curve, the better the model predictions.

The right portion of Figure 18 shows how the CAP curve summarizes the discriminatory power of a given model. Frequency distributions can be constructed from the ranked scores and their associated outcomes (D or N). These plots separately show how scores for defaulters and non-defaulters are distributed by risk score (i.e., the x-axis). Greater separation between the distributions of defaulters and non-defaulters is indicative of a model with better accuracy. CAP curve analysis has become standard procedure in evaluating credit models, and we will see several examples of its use below.

Bank Model Performance

Having described construction of CAP curves, we are now in a position to analyze the performance of Benzschawel, Li, and Lee's (2013) bank default model. The right panel of Figure 16 shows CAP curves that summarize the accuracy of bank models to predict defaults at one- to five-year horizons over the period from 1999 to 2012. The curves show how discriminatory power decreases with time horizon, being nearly perfect at one year, but still demonstrating a good deal of ability to rank default risk five years out. A useful measure of predictive power from CAP analysis is the Area under the Curve (AUC), the percentage of the area under each CAP curve, which is inset in the figure.

For comparison with agency ratings, Figure 19 presents CAP curves from agency ratings and the bank model for one- to four-year horizons. The top row shows results for Bank Holding Companies and the bottom row is for Savings and Loans. Clearly, both the bank default model and Kroll agency ratings order banks' risk at better than chance levels, even out to four years. It is also evident that predictive accuracy for both models decreases as the year of prediction gets farther out in time.[20] Visual comparison of CAP curves in Figure 19 indicates that for all horizons, the adaptive non-linear bank model outperforms Kroll agency ratings. Although performance decreases for both models as the time horizon increases from two to four years, decreases are greater for Kroll ratings than for Citi's bank model.

---

[20] Recall that for each model the prediction for each year is dependent on the firm surviving up to the year of prediction. Thus, when predicting defaults for year two, all firms that defaulted in the first year after date of prediction are excluded from the sample.

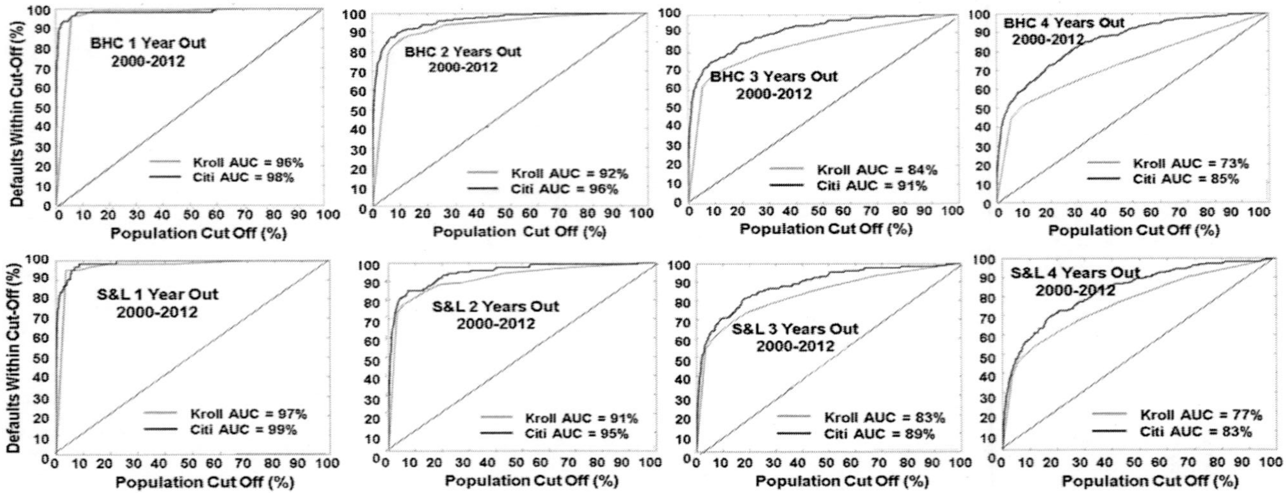

Figure 19. Comparison of CAP curves for Bank Holding Companies (top) and Savings and Loans between Kroll agency ratings and Citi's bank model from 2000-2012.

To demonstrate the richness of the adaptive non-linear modeling approach, Figure 20 presents a quantitative analysis of variable contributions by time horizon of prediction. The left table in the figure shows the likelihood of each variable being selected for the one- to five-year default models in each year over the period from 2000 to 2012. The table at the right displays the average order of selection if the variable was included in the model at the listed horizons. Consider first the probabilities of variable selection. Although return on equity (ROE) and the ratio of liabilities to assets are included in all one-year models, their contributions drop off rapidly at two to five years. Also, performance on earning assets (earning assets to assets) is important at one- and two-year horizons, but it is not included in three- and four-year models, with only moderate contributions to five-year models.

Variables	Probability of Selection					Average Order if Selected				
	1y	2y	3y	4y	5y	1y	2y	3y	4y	5y
ROE	100%	92%	15%	0%	0%	1.0	2.7	4.5	-	-
Liabilities / Assets	100%	23%	31%	31%	23%	2.1	5.7	3.0	4.0	4.3
Non-Current Loans / Loans	92%	100%	100%	69%	15%	3.9	1.1	2.1	2.4	8.0
Net Operation Income / Assets	92%	0%	69%	69%	8%	4.9	-	3.9	2.7	2.0
Earning Assets / Assets	85%	85%	0%	0%	31%	3.5	4.3	-	-	1.0
Yield on Earning Asset	46%	85%	92%	77%	54%	5.8	4.2	4.3	2.3	2.6
ROA	23%	0%	0%	8%	8%	4.0	-	-	6.0	2.0
Assets	23%	23%	23%	15%	46%	5.7	5.7	5.7	4.0	4.0
Non-Current Loans / Loan Loss Allowance	15%	0%	8%	0%	0%	5.0	-	11.0	-	-
Net Loans / Bank Equity Capital	0%	100%	100%	31%	23%	-	3.6	1.8	3.0	2.7
Annual Default Rate	0%	23%	23%	31%	31%	-	5.3	2.0	2.0	2.5
Assets 90 days Past Due / 30 - 89 Days Past Due	0%	31%	23%	23%	23%	-	5.8	6.0	1.3	3.0
Net Interest Income / Earning Assets	0%	15%	15%	8%	23%	-	8.0	9.0	8.0	6.7
Net Interest Margin	0%	0%	8%	8%	38%	-	-	10.0	7.0	3.6

Figure 20. Probabilities of variable selection by model horizon (left) and average order of inclusion if selected at a given horizon (right) for annual models over the period from 2000-2012 from Benzschawel and Lommaert (2014).

The most consistently important variable is the percentage of non-current loans, included in nearly all annual models from one to three years and dropping off to 69% at four years and 15% at five years. Return on equity is important in the short term (i.e., one- and two-year models), but drops off rapidly for longer dated ones. For two- to four-year horizons, the yield on earning assets and net loans to bank equity capital becomes important, while having less influence in one- and five-year models. In fact, five-year models appear to have the most diversity of variable contributions, with no model in more than 54% of annual models. Finally, net interest margin appears relatively unimportant, except at the five-year horizon, with the ratio of non-current loans to loan loss allowance only included in a small fraction of models at one- and three-year horizons.

The bank model is presented to illustrate the high predictive power of the adaptive non-linear modeling approach, a modern extension of the statistical approach that originated with Altman's Z-Score. In addition, the analysis demonstrates the richness of information yielded by the model regarding determinants of default over time horizon and credit cycle provided by the dynamic variable selection method. Despite these advantages, the adaptive linear model can be difficult to implement because it requires highly standardized financial information, which may not be available for all other types of firms.[21] Also, the predictive power and analytical richness of the adaptive non-linear approach comes at the cost of much greater mathematical and computational complexity. It also requires annual assembly of updated data and new model construction for one- to five-year models. Thus, the approach is not suitable for all applications.

Reduced Form Models: Risk-Neutral Default Probabilities

Many default models were proposed between Altman's Z-Score in the late 1960s and the mid-1990s. However, for various reasons, none proved satisfactory for use by broker dealers for hedging their credit exposure. First, there had been little out-of-sample testing of the models' abilities to predict defaults. This lack of testing was partially the result of researchers' lack of access to data on individual defaults and the fact that methods from statistical decision theory had not yet been applied to default models. There were also difficulties and limitations associated with access to data necessary for input to models in a trading setting. Finally, early evidence suggested problems with default predictions from the Merton structural model (discussed in the section on structural models below).

To meet the need for an easy-to-apply, simple to understand, and general framework for measuring credit risk, the risk neutral pricing framework was applied to credit risk as embodied in the reduced form model. Reduced form credit models generate default probabilities directly from market credit spreads without any assumptions regarding the source or causes of obligors' credit risk premiums. In that sense, reduced form models represent another type of statistical approach to measuring default risk. It is unlikely that a liquid credit derivatives market would have

[21] In the case of the bank model, all data are posted on the Federal Deposit Insurance Corporation's website, so they are in standardized form and easily sourced for model calibration.

emerged without the availability of reduced form credit models. Applications of risk-neutral pricing theory to credit can be traced to several sources that include Hull and White (1995), Jarrow and Turnbull (1995), Perry (1995), and Duffie and Singleton (1999), and this approach has given rise to a large body of research since then.

Risk-neutral pricing theory specifies that the present value of a set of cash flows is equivalent to their expected likelihoods of receipt discounted from the time of their receipt by the corresponding risk-free rates of return. Recall Figure 2 that depicts a single default-risky cash flow to be received one year from now. Note that one can view a one-period bond as a portfolio of two securities:

1. One that pays $1 at time T if the issuer does not default; and
2. One that pays an amount R if default occurs before maturity T.

Also, one can express the present value PV of that single cash flow of $1 at time T as:

$$PV = e^{-rt} \text{. (3)}$$

Let the probability of non-payment (i.e., default) of the $1 cash flow be pT and its recovery value in default be R. Then, within risk-neutral pricing theory, the expected value of the $1 to be received at time T is the probability-weighted sum of receiving the $1 or the recovery value. That is

$$E[T] = \{[(1 - p_T) * 1] + p_T R\} \text{. (4)}$$

Furthermore, given the price-yield formula in Equation 3 and the expected cash flows in Equation 4, one can express the discount yield y on the $1 resulting from the fraction pT of times one expects to only receive the recovery value R as the sum of the risk-free yield r plus a yield spread s such that

$$e^{-T(r+s)} = e^{-rT}\{[(1 - p_T) * 1] + p_T R\} \text{. (5)}$$

By noting the loss given default LGD = (1-R) and taking the natural logarithms of both sides and rearranging, we can write:

$$s = -\frac{1}{T}\ln[1 - (p_T * LGD)] \text{. (6)}$$

An example of how risk neutral pricing can be applied to solve for a default rate, the risk neutral default rate, for a one-period risky bond is depicted in Figure 21. Assume that the bond has an 8% coupon, a one year maturity, and is priced at par (i.e., its price is 100) as well as that its recovery rate in default is 50% of face value and the one-year risk free rate is 6%.

One can calculate the risk neutral default probability pTQ using the following:[22]

$$100 = \frac{1}{1.06}\left\{\left[\left(1 - p_1^Q\right)*108\right] + \left(p_T^Q * 50\right)\right\} \quad . (7)$$

Solving for p_1^Q in Equation 7 gives a risk-neutral default rate of 3.5%. Note that while Equations 3-7 are useful for illustrating the concepts behind the risk-neutral model, they do not illustrate the formal richness of the approach, one that appeals to many academics and practitioners.[23]

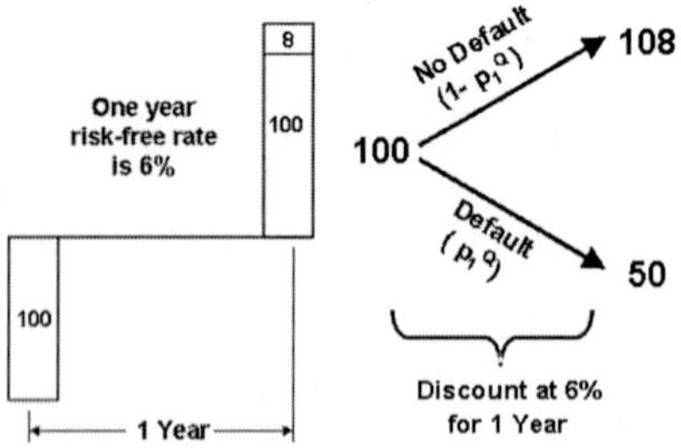

Figure 21. Representation of a one-period par bond within the risk-neutral framework.

More generally, one can calculate the compounded rate of return on a risk-free asset over a time interval t as e^{rt} and the rate of return on a risky asset as $e^{(r+s)t}$. Assuming that the recovery value is zero, the risk-neutral default probability can be calculated as $(1 - p_t^Q)e^{(r+s)t}$ and can be written as:

[22] The superscript Q is used to denote the fact that default probabilities are determined under a risk-neutral measure.
[23] See Jarrow and Turnbull (1995) for an application of risk-neutral pricing theory in continuous time.

$$(1-p_t^Q)e^{(r+s)t}=e^{rt}\text{, (8)}$$

and solving for p_t^Q gives

$$p_t^Q=1-e^{st}\text{. (9)}$$

Equation 9 can be used to calculate default probabilities from credit spreads on bonds. However, in most cases, Equation 8 must be modified to include another term that accounts for the usual non-zero recovery value of bonds in default as:

$$(1-p_t^Q)e^{(r+s)t}+Rp_t^Q e^{(r+s)t}=e^{rt}\text{, and (10)}$$

$$p_t^Q=1-e^{st}\text{. (11)}$$

Equation 11 can be used to determine risk neutral default probabilities for an entire corporate yield curve. Despite the wide use of the reduced-form approach, comprehensive studies of the probabilities of default inferred from these models have been sparse or very limited in scope.[24] To demonstrate how the formulas in Equations 10 and 11 are employed in practice, the left portion of Figure 22 shows how risk-neutral default curves by ratings are generated from par bond yield curves 8-Jun-09 and assuming an average recovery rate of 40%.

One reason for the success of reduced form credit models is that they require only information about securities' nominal cash flows, their yields, and risk-free interest rates. That is, one only needs bond market prices and assumed recovery rates to calculate risk neutral PDs for all credits. Unfortunately, one-year default rates implied by the risk neutral models are much higher than even the highest default rates observed historically. Consider, for example, the right portion of Figure 22, which presents risk neutral default rates (top) with average historical default rates (bottom). Clearly, the risk neutral default rates are much larger than their physical counterparts. The vertical line spanning the figures connects 10-year historical and risk neutral default rates for triple-B credits and serves to highlight the contrast between the 8% cumulative historical rate and its

[24] See for example, Chava and Jarrow (2002) and Janossi, Jarrow, and Yildrim (2003).

corresponding 52% risk neutral value. In fact, ten-year cumulative default rates are over 70% for the entire set of high yield credits, much higher than those ever observed historically. The overestimation of actual default probabilities poses problems for using the reduced form model for estimating default probabilities. Reasons for the consistent overestimation of physical default probabilities by risk-neutral measures will be made evident in the context of the discussion in the chapter on the credit risk premium (see below).

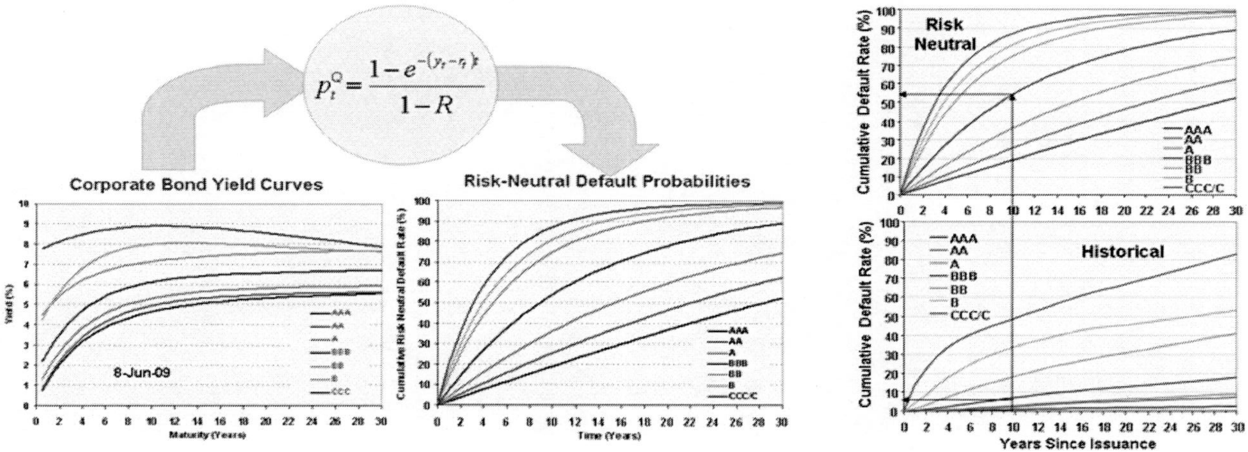

Figure 22. Left: Deriving risk-neutral default probabilities from corporate bond yield curves; Right: Risk-neutral default probabilities (top) and physical default probabilities (bottom), 8-Jun-09

It is difficult to overstate the importance of the risk-neutral framework in our understanding of credit, the development of the credit markets, and for quantitative financial modeling in general. Still, there are limitations of this approach for understanding and quantifying credit risk. The overestimation of default probabilities has already been discussed. In addition, although reduced form models appear to make few assumptions about physical default, they require the assumption of a recovery value to infer PDs or hazard rates. The reduced form approach has also been criticized as providing investors with few insights regarding factors that influence credit risk or any guidance about the relative values of various bonds. Also, the notion of a hazard rate, which is a jump to default that underlies most applications, is suspect, particularly for high quality credits.[25] That is, default is not a surprise for the firm and often not for investors either. Finally, hazard rates are typically calculated from bond or credit default swap spreads.

Several authors have attempted to account for the overestimation of physical default rates by risk-neutral methods (Bonn, 2000; Gray and Malone, 2008).[26] The calculation of "physical" or actual probability of default is outside the contingent claims analysis (CCA) or "Merton" model (discussed in the next section), but it can be combined with an equilibrium model of underlying expected returns to produce estimates of expected returns. However, those frameworks require viewing the entire credit risk premium as an actual default as depicted in Figure 23. This has resulted in problems in valuation and hedging of credit default swaps (Benzschawel and Corlu, 2010). Recently, Duan, Sun, and Wang (2012) proposed a model that incorporates financial and economic variables in an intensity-based framework, whose outputs are calibrated to physical probabilities of default. Although it may prove useful for predicting defaults and for analyzing factors underlying corporate failure, it will be less useful for hedging purposes, which provided the initial motivation for the intensity-based framework.

---

[25] In fact, examination of calculations of risk neutral default probabilities reveal them to be simply logarithmic transformations of spreads modified by expected recovery values in default.

[26] Bielecki and Rutkowski (2002) describe various extensions of reduced form models.

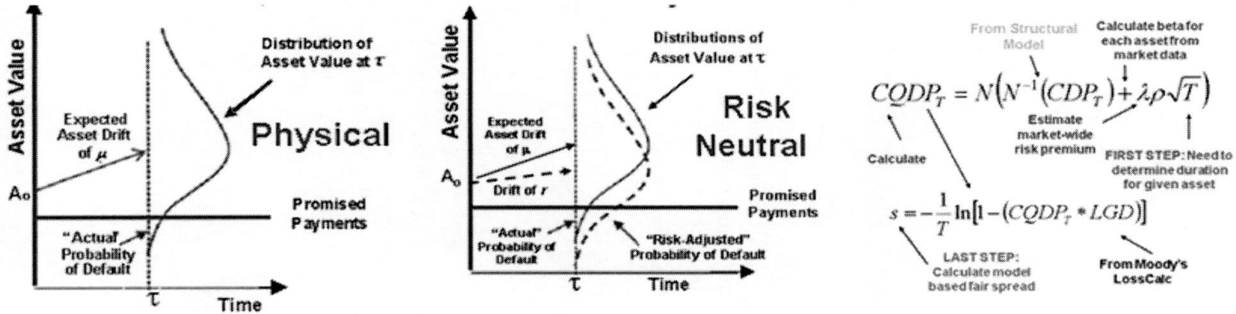

Figure 23. Bohn's (2000) model linking physical and risk-neutral default probabilities.

Finally, accurate valuation of assets that depend on non-default credit state transitions is particularly problematic within the risk neutral framework. This is so because, when adjusting historical ratings transitions to risk neutral ones, overstatement of default risk requires one to transfer probabilities from non-default credit states to the default state to account for the larger than physical risk-neutral default rates. This leaves other non-default transitions at a deficit, which can be important when valuing embedded options in bonds or loans. Thus, the risk-neutral framework is not useful for valuing corporate loans with credit-state-dependent optionality, for calculations of value-at-risk (VaR) for credit portfolios, or for evaluating firm risk for regulatory purposes.

The Merton Model: Equity-Debt Relationship

Decades before development of the risk-neutral framework, Robert Merton (1973, 1974) formalized Black and Scholes (1973) suggestion that a firm's equity and debt resembled contingent claims on the firm's assets and liabilities. The relationship between a firm's equity and debt within the Merton theory is depicted in Figure 24. The left portion of the figure shows that the firm's assets consist of its equity and its debt. The equity holders of the firm are viewed as having a call option on its assets, whereby those investors share in the profitability of the firm. Conversely, the debt holders of a firm are long a risk-free asset, having loaned the firm money at a risk free rate, and are short a put that they sold to the equity holders in exchange for the premium over the risk free rate. The strike price of the call and put is the face value of the firm's outstanding debt, which can be determined from the firm's balance sheet. The market value of the firm's assets can be inferred from the stock price and shares outstanding and asset volatility from equity price volatility. The importance of the Merton formulation is that, if correct, a firm's equity and debt can be valued using the Black-Scholes option pricing formula.

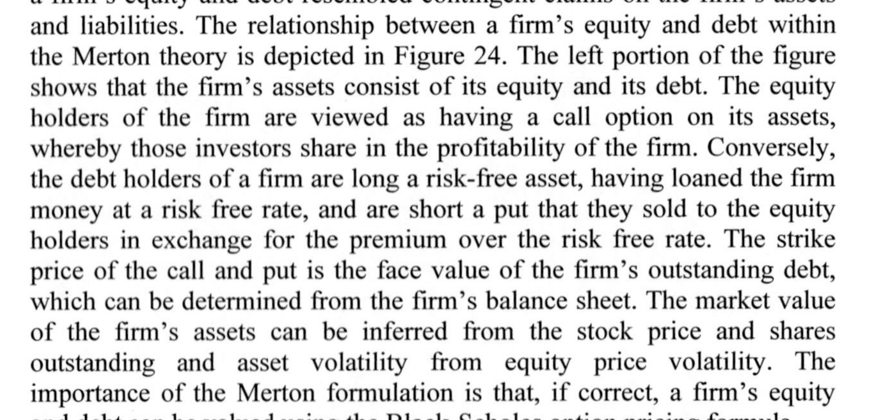

Figure 23. Relationship between a firm's equity and debt in the Merton structural model.

Inputs to the Merton model come from equity markets and firms' financial statements. The three main drivers of firm value are the market value of assets, V_A, asset volatility, σ_A, and the level of the debt K. These values are used to calculate the distance-to-default, DD over a given time horizon T. That is, the distance-to-default is calculated as:

$$DD = \frac{V_A - K}{(V_A * \sigma_A)\sqrt{T}}, \quad (13)$$

where the numerator measures the magnitude that the business value exceeds the level of the debt and the denominator measures investors' uncertainty regarding the future value of the firm.

Problems with the Merton Model

Although successful implementations of the Merton structural model framework are described below, consider first some issues concerning the validity of the assumptions underlying the model. The original Merton model formulation comes directly from the Black-Scholes' option pricing model, placing it on a firm foundation within financial theory. Accordingly, if assumptions underlying the Merton formulation are correct, one ought to be able to use the Black-Scholes option pricing formula to determine a firm's probability of default and the "fair" yield spread to Treasuries (or price) of its bonds from the firm's equity price and balance sheet information. For several reasons, including lack of data and difficulty in its acquisition, it was not until the 1980s that Jones, Mason, and Rosenfeld (1984) found that the Black-Sholes Merton model formulation consistently underestimates by large amounts the credit spreads observed in the market.

This failure to predict credit spreads resulted in minimal use of the Merton model for assessing or hedging credit exposure, particularly by traders, much of which continues to this day. Nevertheless, the work of Jones et al. spurred many attempts in academia to adapt the Merton model to account for credit spreads. Examples include the addition of uncertainty to the default boundary and estimates of firms' assets (Geske, 1979; Finger, Finkelstein, Pan, Lardy, and Ta, 2002) and adding correlations among Treasury yields and credit risk (Longstaff and Schwarz, 1995).[27] Other adaptations include jumps in the value of assets, bond indenture

[27] Many of these modifications are discussed in Anderson and Sundaresan (2000).

provisions, taxes, bankruptcy costs, stochastic volatility, and interest rates.[28]

In addition to the empirical problems, there are issues regarding the application of contingent claims analysis to value corporate liabilities. These relate to the unobservable character of the market value of firms' assets, the relatively illiquid nature of firms' liabilities, and the unrealistic dynamics of borrowing and lending implied by the model.[29] With respect to the market value of unobservable assets implied from equity prices, even fully informed equity prices are marginal prices, and therefore, primarily reflect marginal supply and demand conditions rather than the value of the aggregate capital stock of the firm. Also, with respect to the Merton model's characterization of firms' debt, the liabilities of most institutions do not possess the same characteristics as the securities for which many of the contingent claims models were first developed. That is, the issuance of debt is not associated with any bona fide hedging activity that would tend to result in a high volume of incremental rebalancing trades. This is important because the ideal hedge portfolio concept, which underlies the options-pricing equation, requires an infinitesimal hedging/trading environment as a precondition.

Another problem is that the Merton framework specifies a tight linkage between risk premiums in the equity and debt markets. However, Fridson (1999) suggests that those risk premiums frequently diverge. For example, as shown in the stylized leverage clock in the left panel of Figure 24 adapted from King (2012), the equity and debt risk premiums are positively correlated in only two parts of the credit cycle. That is, both markets rally when profits are growing faster than debt, and they sell off together when the level of debt to profits cannot sustain existing debt and equity prices. In the other parts of the cycle equity and debt prices move inversely. When firms are deleveraging after a debt and equity downturn, their debt rallies, but earnings are insufficient to raise equity prices. Also, amid an equity rally, debt tends to grow faster than profits, leading to an increase in the credit risk premium.

---

[28] See, for example, Black and Cox (1976), Kim, Ramaswamy, and Sunderasan (1993), Longstaff and Schwartz (1995), Levin and van Deventer (1997), Briys and Varenne (1997), Leland (1999), Schwartz, and Moon (2000), Kao (2000) and references therein.

[29] A detailed description of these issues appears in Benzschawel (2013), so they are described only briefly herein.

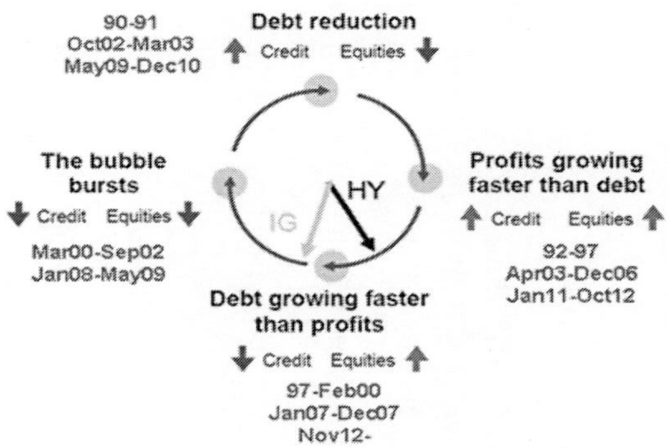

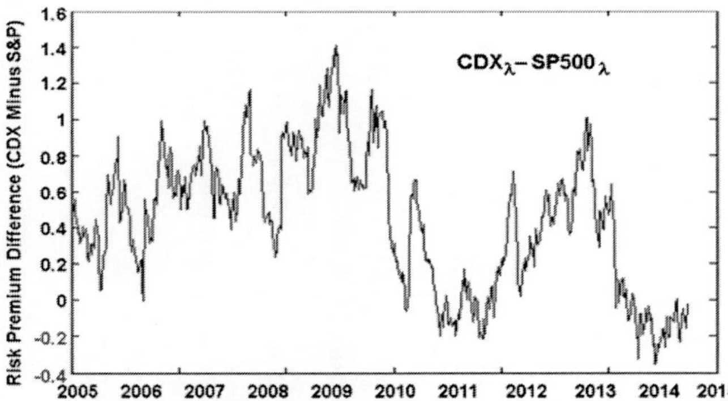

Figure 24. Left: The leverage clock; Right: Debt risk premium from the CDS Index minus the equity risk premium from the S&P 500 Index.

The hypothesized divergence between equity and debt risk premiums was recently documented by Benzschawel, Su, Lee, and Lommaert (2104), who measured daily equity and debt risk premiums from 2005 through mid-2014. The differences they reported between the daily debt premium for the CDX.NA.IG debt index and that of the S&P 500 equity index appear in the right panel of Figure 24. Clearly, although there are patterns of short-term deviations among equity and debt risk premiums, those deviations are superimposed on a lower frequency cyclical pattern of differences in their risk premiums. Furthermore, as will be shown below, these relations have implications for default probabilities generated using the Merton model formulation.

The KMV Model

Despite difficulties with the Merton framework, Kealhofer, McQuown, and Vasicek formed the KMV Company in 1988 and developed a modified version of Merton's structural model, called the KMV model, to measure default risk (Vasicek, 1995). KMV abandoned the use of the Merton framework for estimating credit spreads and focused on its ability to predict defaults. Also, instead of using the total liabilities of the firm, TL, as the default boundary, K, KMV set the boundary equal to the firm's current liabilities, CL, (debt due in less than one year) plus one-half its long-term debt, LTD, where $LTD = TL - CL$ (Kealhofer, 1999), That is,

$$K = CL + LTD/2 \quad . (14)$$

Of particular importance is that KMV abandoned the tight linkage between options theory and default, choosing to leave that relationship unspecified. Instead, they opted for an empirical approach, whereby they mapped the historical relationship between firms' distances-to-default in Equation 13 and their subsequent likelihoods of default over time intervals of one to five years.[30] A demonstration of that mapping for one-year default probabilities appears in Figure 25. The figure shows how a given

[30] KMV made several other modifications of the Merton framework including bounding default probabilities between 0.02% (best) and 20% (worst) and adjusting asset volatilities for certain types of industrial firms. A detailed description of the KMV Model can be found in Crosbie and Bohn (2001). The KMV corporation was sold to Moody's Investors Service in 2002 for $210 million and the company was renamed Moody's/KMV. The model is currently marketed by that corporation.

distance-to-default expressed in standard deviation units, in this case 3.7σ, corresponds to a given one-year default probability, 1.0% in the example. Thus, for a given distance-to-default from Equation 12, the KMV model can assign a historically-derived probability of default, called the Expected Default Frequency (EDF), at annual horizons of one to five years.

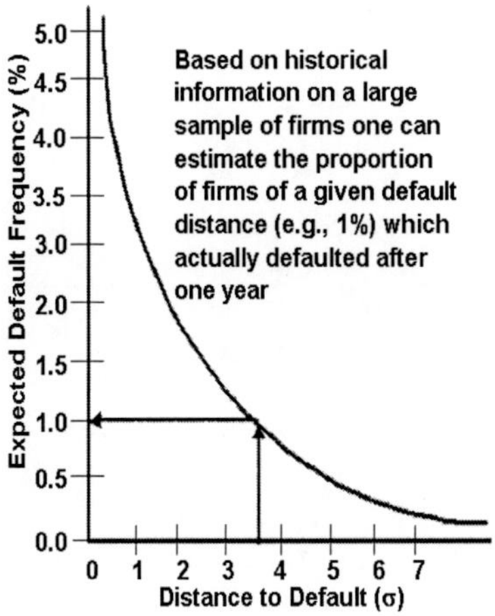

Figure 25. Mapping from distance-to-default to historical default probabilities.

Importantly, Kealhofer and Kurbat (2001) used CAP curve analysis to demonstrate the superiority of the KMV model to agency ratings at predicting corporate defaults. In fact, the performance of the KMV model relative to agency ratings is presented in the illustration of CAP curve analysis in Figure 18. The KMV model has had a great deal of commercial success and continues to be widely used for investment and risk management purposes. However, that success has come at the cost of abandoning the strict linkage to the Merton and Black-Sholes formulation. (In fact, no known successful implementation of the Merton framework follows that original formulation explicitly.) Despite the success of the KMV model, it has failed to displace the risk-neutral model as the method preferred by broker/dealers for managing risk of credit derivative positions.

Hybrid Structural/Statistical Models

The above-described issues with the Merton model have become central to the debate over quantitative risk assessment models, particularly regarding the completeness of the Merton formulation for estimating firms' default probabilities and valuing their liabilities. For example, Stein (2000) found that adding firms' return-on-assets to the Merton model could add discriminatory power between defaults and non-defaults. Thus, acknowledging that firms' equity and debt premiums diverge over the credit cycle and allowing for the possible relevance of additional variables related to the firm's debt capacity is the essence of the hybrid approach. That is, the hybrid approach blends a variant of the Merton model to capture firms' asset valuations, while adding a set of variables selected to assess firms' borrowing capacities. Deviations of the hybrid approach from the standard Merton model concern three main issues. These are:

1. The impact of divergence of equity and debt markets on estimates of firms' default probabilities;
2. The role of firms' debt capacities; and
3. The concept of the default point.

A detailed theoretical treatment of each of these issues and implications for their inclusion in a hybrid Merton-statistical model appears in Sobehart and Keenan (2003). Thus, we address those issues only briefly below. That discussion is followed by a definition and evaluation of a hybrid-statistical model.

Note that in the Merton model and KMV's implementation, there is no specification regarding firms' abilities to restructure their liabilities when under financial stress. In practice, however, if the firm has borrowing capacity, it can reduce the amount currently due by rolling over its debt, thereby reducing its probability of default in the short term. In fact, several extensions of the Merton model have relaxed this limitation, introducing variable liabilities (Colin-Dufresne and Goldstein, 2001), multiple liabilities with different time horizons (Geske, 1979; Longstaff and Schwartz, 1995), continuous rollover of debt (Leland, 1999), stochastic assets (Huang and Kong, 2003), stochastic liabilities and default boundary (Finger, Finkelstein, Pan, Lardy, and Ta, 2002; Hsu, Saa-Reqeujo, and Santa Clara, 2010), and stochastic macroeconomic variables (Li, 2013), to name a few.[31]

The relationship between an obligor and its lending institutions is another factor to consider in estimating likelihood of default. Obligors having large exposures to their lenders create incentives for lenders to roll over debt under times of stress. Also, lenders can extend additional credit based on their estimation of borrowers' capacity to service that debt. These

[31] See Huang (2010) for a description of various extensions of credit risk structural models.

factors are related to key accounting information, such as the borrower's profitability, liquidity, and capital structure as well as information on the business environment and the borrower's competitiveness. Additional variables in hybrid models are intended to capture these factors. In fact, Duffie, Eckner, Horel, and Saita (2009) introduced the idea of frailty to capture the effects of these risk factors on expected defaults under times of stress.

Thus, despite the success of the KMV model, the considerations above suggest that adding relevant variables to structural models of default risk might improve the model's performance at predicting defaults. Working on this assumption, Sobehart, Stein, Mikityanskaya, and Li (2000) proposed a hybrid approach called the HPD model that incorporates the Merton model framework along with financial variables related to firms' size, profitability, and cash flow.[32] The model, described in detail by Sobehart and Keenan (2002, 2003), appears in Figure 26.

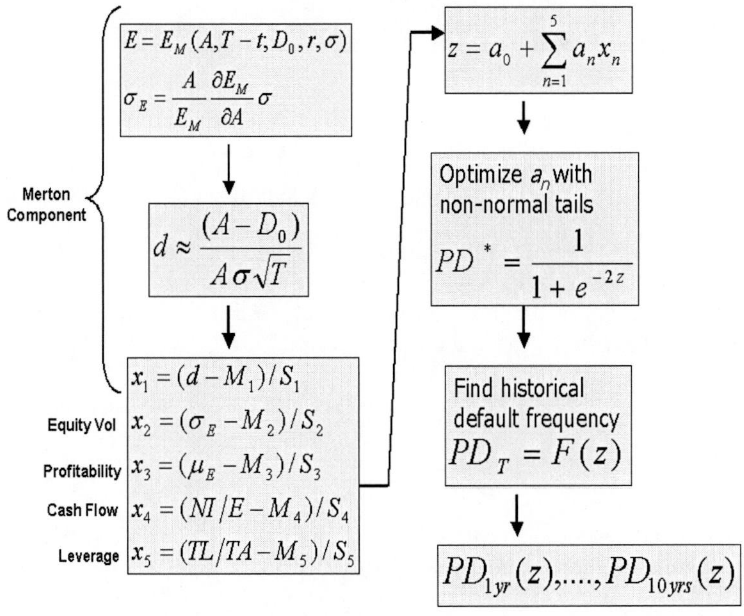

Figure 26. The Sobehart-Keenan HPD Model.

[32] HPD stands for *hybrid probability of default.*

To begin, Sobehart and Keenan selected a set of market and accounting variables to describe the value of the firm's assets and its borrowing capacity. They retained much of the Merton model formulation and variables required for the asset valuation portion of the model. Variables that account for firms' borrowing capacity were selected from those available in the market or firms' financial statements by a trial and error process, placing emphasis on those variables that were available for the widest number of firms. The selected variables are:

1. The firm's market value of equity, E,
2. 12-month volatility of the firm's equity price, σ_E,
3. The firm's 12-month return on equity, μ_E,
4. Book value of total assets, TA,
5. The book value of current liabilities, CL,
6. The book value of total liabilities TL, and
7. Net income NI.

The default boundary of the firm, D_0 in Figure 26, is calculated according to the method introduced by Kealhofer (1999) in Equation 13, where D_0 equals short-term liabilities plus one-half long-term debt.[33] To capture the asset valuation of the firm, Sobehart and Keenan also used KMV's variation of the Merton model formulation in Equation 12, whereby the distance-to-default, d, is defined as:

$$d = \frac{(A - D_0)}{A\sigma\sqrt{T}} \text{, (15)}$$

where A corresponds to Merton's V_A, and D_0 is K, respectively, and T is the time horizon, typically one or five years.

To capture a firm's borrowing capacity, Sobehart and Keenan chose a linear combination of the following variables:

---

[33] Sobehart and Keenan explored other combinations of current liabilities and long-term-debt and found only small changes in the performance of the model given their available data set.

1. 12-month equity volatility, σ_E ,
2. 12-month equity return relative to the S&P 500 index:

   $\mu_E - \mu_{S\&P500}$,

3. Profitability ratio: net income to equity, NI / E , and
4. Book value of leverage TL/TA .

The purpose of these variables is to penalize volatile, highly leveraged, and/or unprofitable companies, thereby reducing their borrowing capacity.

Figure 26 shows the two general stages of the he HPD model. The first stage involves assembling and transforming the input variables as preparation for the second stage, which computes firms' estimated PDs. Having defined the quantities for input, the inputs to the model are used to generate five variables, $x_1, \ldots, x_5$, where the first variable is the distance-to-default, and the others characterize the firm's equity volatility, profitability, cash flow, and size. In particular, Figure 24 shows that each of the variables, including distance-to-default, is normalized with respect to its means and standard deviations calculated from non-defaulting firms in the development sample.

The second state of the model first combines the variables $x_1, \ldots, x_5$ linearly to generate a single quantity z that characterizes the risk of the firm as:

$$z = a_0 + \sum_{n=1}^{5} a_n x_n \quad , (15)$$

which is identical in form to Altman's z-score. Because the x_i variables are normalized with respect to non-defaulted firms in the sample, and the variable z measures the deviation of firms' credit quality from the historical average of healthy firms. Finally, Sobehart, and Keenan use the following functional form to approximate firms' probabilities of default, PD:

$$PD \approx \frac{1}{1+e^{-2z}} \quad . (16)$$

Sobehart and his colleagues have tracked the relative predictive power of the HPD and KMV models over the past decade and a recent summary of those analyses from Sobehart (2013) appears in Figure 27. The CAP curve at the left in Figure 27 is a composite of results from annual analysis from 2000-2011, based on over 800 firm defaults and 50,000 non-default observations. At the beginning of each year, both models were presented with the same sample of firms that defaulted during the subsequent 12 months and along with non-defaulting firms in that year.[34] The CAP curve demonstrates that, for all population percentile criteria, the HPD model isolates more defaulters in the sample than KMV. For example, the vertical line in the CAP curve illustrates model accuracy for the 10% of the population ranked riskiest (i.e., largest PDs) by both models. In that 10%, KMV captures about 57% of defaulters in that sample, performing well above chance (i.e., 10%).[35] Nevertheless, HPD is performing even better, capturing roughly 65% of the defaulting firms in their riskiest top 10%.

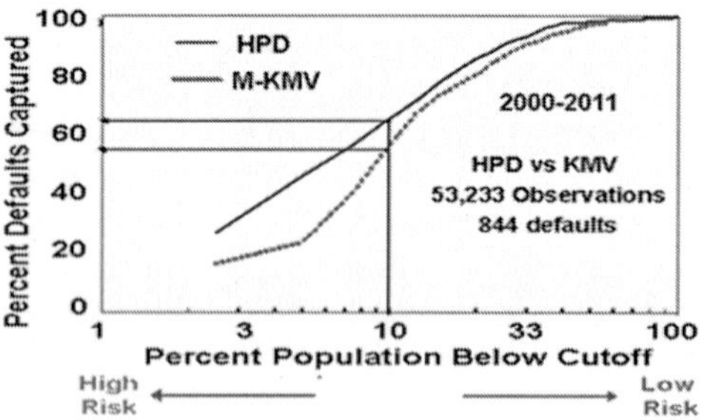

	Sample		Accuracy Ratio	
Year	N(Obs)	Defaults	HPD	KMV
2000	3,104	75	79%	73%
2001	3,271	107	80%	71%
2002	3,382	89	83%	76%
2003	3,501	81	80%	72%
2004	3,524	37	82%	72%
2005	3,649	39	80%	71%
2006	3,989	31	87%	80%
2007	4,161	44	87%	84%
2008	4,156	97	80%	76%
2009	4,075	118	81%	79%
2010	4,229	39	73%	74%
2011	4,287	32	77%	78%
Avg			81%	75%
StdDev			4%	4%

Figure 27. Cumulative Accuracy Profile (CAP) curves (left) and sample statistics by year and corresponding accuracy ratios (right) for HPD and KMV models.

The right panel of Figure 27 lists accuracy ratios (ARs) by year for the HPD and KMV models along with numbers of defaulting and non-defaulting firms.[36] The HPD model has higher ARs than KMV for 10 of the 12 years tested. Also, when HPD underperforms KMV, as in 2010 and 2011, its ARs lag by only by 1% and those years were among those with

[34] Note that the HPD model was last recalibrated in 2000, so all results for the HPD model are out-of-sample. Most results are also out-of-sample for the KMV model, but after being acquired by Moody's in 2004, the model was recalibrated in 2008, and its performance appears to have improved slightly relative to HPD since then, but default rates have also been low since 2008.

[35] Note that the value of 57% at the 10% criterion is very similar to that presented by Kealhofer and Kurbat (2001), which appears in Figure 18.

[36] Recall from above that the accuracy ratio from a CAP curve is the ratio of the area between the CAP curve and the negative diagonal to the total potential area of the CAP curve for a "perfect" model.

the lowest defaults over the period. Finally, the average annual AR for the HPD model is 81% as opposed to the 75% average annual AR for the KMV model.

Implications of Equity-Debt Risk Premium Divergence for Credit Models

Practitioners familiar with the KMV model will likely have noticed how swings in equity market values move predicted default probabilities, which are not necessarily followed by changes in overall default probabilities. For example, the top left and right panels of Figure 28 presents analysis from Sobehart (2005) on expected one-year default frequencies (EDFs) from Moody's/KMV model on December 31, 2002, for 4,997 North American firms.[37,38] Based on the EDFs assigned by the KMV model to those firms, one would have expected an overall default rate of 8.7% in 2003, but only 84 of those firms defaulted, a 1.7% rate. Furthermore, a rough estimate of the default rate for high yield firms in the sample is 20%, but Moody's Investors Service (Ou, Chiu, and Metz, 2012) reports a 5.3% default rate for high yield firms in 2003. These types of results underlie often-voiced criticism that Merton models, as embodied in the KMV formulation, generate too many "false positive" default signals.

---

[37] A more detailed explanation of this study appears in Benzschawel (2012).

[38] Some may recall the situation in debt and equity markets near the end of 2002. The telecom bubble in equity markets had burst, capped by large and high profile defaults by WorldCom and Enron. The massive sell-off in the equity markets led to high estimates of one-year PDs for 2003 from the KMV model as illustrated in Figure 33. Yet, by that time, firms' balance sheets had begun to improve and the high yield default rate dropped to 5.3% in 2003.

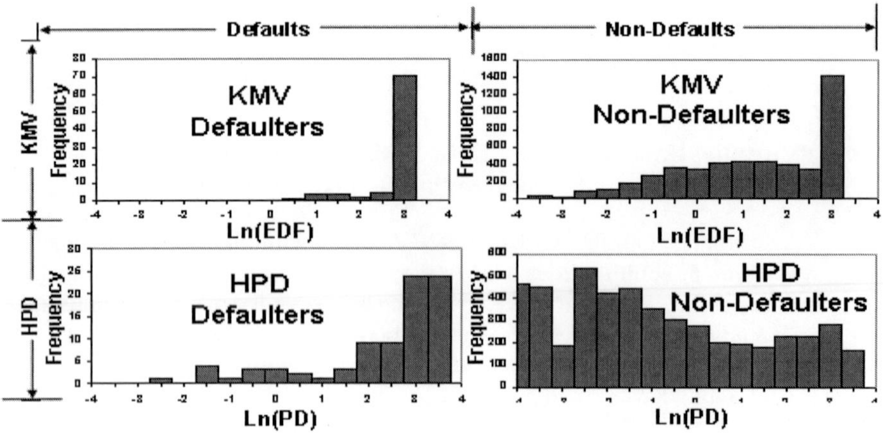

Figure 28. Frequency of estimated default probabilities for defaulted and non-defaulting firms in 2003 from the KMV (top) and the HPD (bottom) models on 31-Dec-02.

The results in Figure 28 are also useful for illustrating the importance of variable normalization in the HPD model.[39] Consider scores assigned by the HPD model to those same defaulting (lower left) and non-defaulting firms (lower right) at the end of 2002. A comparison of the distributions of defaulters between KMV and HPD (i.e. the left panels) would seem to indicate better performance of the KMV model—the defaulters appear to have higher default probabilities.[40] However, when one considers the distributions of the non-defaulters in the right-hand panels, one observes a huge number of non-defaulters to which KMV assigns high default probabilities. In contrast, the HPD model maintains very low estimates of default probabilities for the non-defaulting firms amid the huge equity sell-off in late 2002, but with the resulting average realized defaults in 2003. In fact, regardless of population criterion, KMV excludes more non-defaulters for each defaulter excluded than the HPD model. For example, if one sets its investment criterion for scores >= 3 (i.e. default greater than 20%), the ratio of non-defaulters excluded to defaulters detected is:

[39] Recall that the input variables to the HPD model are all z-scores calculated relative to their means and standard deviations in the development sample.

[40] The x-axes in the figures are scaled in natural logarithms of PDs because the logarithms of PDs are linearly related to agency rating categories. Also, note that the natural logarithm of 20 is 3.

- KMV: 1400 non-defaulters: 70 defaulters, or 20:1
- HPD: 450 non-defaulters: 50 defaulters, or 9:1

Structural and Hybrid Models: Advantages and Limitations

Although structural and hybrid credit models have proven superior to agency ratings at predicting defaults, they also have limitations. Before discussing more recent innovations in credit modeling, we consider briefly the advantages and disadvantages of the structural and hybrid structural/statistical approach, particularly regarding gaps in our ability to predict defaults for a range of risky asset classes. A summary of such features appears in Figure 29. Each is described briefly in turn below.

Figure 29. Advantages and limitations of structural and statistical models.

Consider first some positive features of the structural and hybrid models as embodied in the KMV and HPD models, respectively. The basic concept of equity and debt as options on the firms' assets is deeply rooted in financial theory. Also, inputs to the models are available from public information and are directly verifiable. Importantly, these models are forward looking, incorporating information from the equity market. In particular, structural and hybrid models have been demonstrated to be useful for predicting ratings changes and superior to agency ratings at predicting defaults. In addition, although not the subject of this report, the KMV and HPD models have proven useful for predicting changes in credit spreads (Benzschawel, Lee, Lommaert, and Su, 2014).[41]

Consider now some limitations of structural and hybrid models. First, to be successful, both types of model had to abandon their strict linkage to the theoretical foundations of the Merton/Black-Scholes' framework. Although that break has proven advantageous in practice, it provides no insight into the relationship between defaults and credit spreads. In addition, Merton-based models can be "fooled" by equity friendly/bond unfriendly events such as leveraged buyouts and equity buybacks. Both types of events cause equities to rally and bonds to sell off, leaving bonds looking erroneously cheap. These models do not do well at estimating default probabilities for banks or firms with both a manufacturing and a financial arm, such as the major automakers. These firms appear highly leveraged relative to most non-financial firms, leading to overly high probabilities of default. Also, unlike non-financial companies, banks tend to fail rapidly, often due to a lack of confidence, making it impossible to fund their liabilities.

The most general problem with equity-based structural and hybrid models is that they cannot estimate PDs for obligors without public financials and tradable equity. Thus, the structural framework cannot be applied to the risk of sovereign debt, municipalities, or private firms. Although Gray, Merton, and Bodie (2007) have recently attempted to expand the Merton contingent-claims' framework to estimate sovereign risk, that model requires extensive and critical user-defined estimates of macroscopic conditions and linkages between private and public sector debt. Thus, the model, while of particular interest for macroeconomic analysis, has not yet found widespread use for estimating likelihoods of default for trading and risk management purposes.

---

[41] In fact, KMV and HPD models have proven extremely useful for predicting spread market moves and have given rise to many well-documented successful trading strategies.

The Credit Risk Premium and the Market-Implied Default Model

This lack of a framework for predicting defaults for countries, municipalities, and private firms has led to development of other classes of models as described below. In this section, we describe the development of a market-implied default model (MKI) that is an amalgamation of the structural model, the risk-neutral model, and the Capital Asset Pricing Theory (CAPM). The foundation of the model relies on the ability to separate the yield spread over Treasuries into two components: the compensation for not receiving the cash flows due to default and the credit risk premium resulting from exposure to the volatility of credit spreads. Since an understanding of the credit risk premium is a critical feature of the MKI model, we describe it in detail in the next section, followed by a subsequent description of how that risk premium is used in the MKI model.

The Credit Risk Premium

Although the early work of Jones, Mason and Rosenfeld (1984) established firmly that Merton's structural model underestimates the spread values of risky debt, only relatively recently have market participants begun to unravel the components that underlie the spread compensation for investing in default-risky assets. Elton, Gruber, Agrawal, and Mann (2001) first documented the role of the credit risk premium in corporate bond spreads.[42] Using the logic embedded in Equations 5 and 6, Elton et al. used historical default rates for double-A rated corporate bonds, their duration, and an assumed recovery value of 40%, as input into Equation 5. Their calculations revealed that only a small fraction of the yield spread over Treasuries could be attributed to not receiving the cash flows because of default. Some other factor, since termed the credit spread puzzle (Amato. and Remolona, 2003; Driessen, 2003) and later the credit risk premium, is the major determinant of credit spreads, and Turnbull (2005) argues that the relationship between default and credit spreads is a major unsolved issue in credit modeling.

[42] Yield spreads to Treasuries also contain a premium for liquidity/illiquidity. For now, we use the term credit risk premium to refer to the entire spread compensation over and above that necessary for the present value of expected cash flows to equal that of an equal-duration US Treasury security.

Benzschawel (2012) confirmed the results of Elton et al. in a more systematic analysis of the credit risk premium for corporate bonds, providing estimates by agency rating category. Those results are summarized in Figure 30. The table lists average cumulative 4.5-year default probabilities by rating category from Sobehart and Keenan's (2002, 2003) Hybrid Probability of Default (HPD) model for corporate bonds in Citi's Broad Investment Grade (BIG) and High Yield Indexes over the period from 1994-2010.[43] 4.5-year cumulative default rates were used as they correspond roughly to the average duration of the bonds in those indexes. The figure also shows average monthly spreads S by rating category over the 17-year period along with the spread compensation for default S_d calculated using Equation 5 from the average PDs by rating, 4.5-year duration, and a 40% recovery value in default. The last column of the table presents differences by rating category between average spreads and spread due to default, the non-default spread or risk premium, designated as S_λ. For all rating categories magnitudes of S_λ are multiples of S_d with ratios of S_λ to S_d increasing for less risky credits, whereby the risk premium accounts for nearly the entire credit spread to US Treasuries.

The dark area in the middle panel of Figure 30 presents by rating category average values of the default spread S_d, and the light area represents average values of the credit risk premium S_λ. Values of S_d can be viewed as the spreads necessary to compensate investors for the expected loss of cash flows due to default. That is, an investor who receives a yield spread to US Treasuries equal to S_d receives only an amount equal to the expected return from an equivalent-duration US Treasury security. For this reason, S_d could be called a rock bottom spread.

[43] See Citigroup Index (2013) for descriptions of Citigroup's BIG Index and High Yield Index.

S&P Credit Rating	4.5 Year Implied PD	Average Spread (bp)	Spread Due to Default (bp)	Non-Default Spread (bp)
AAA	0.3%	70	1	69
AA+	0.3%	87	4	82
AA	0.4%	88	5	83
AA-	0.5%	104	6	98
A+	0.6%	113	8	105
A	0.7%	122	9	112
A-	0.9%	137	11	126
BBB+	1.0%	160	14	146
BBB	1.3%	178	17	161
BBB-	1.6%	223	21	201
BB+	1.9%	326	25	301
BB	2.3%	366	30	336
BB-	2.7%	383	36	347
B+	3.8%	438	51	386
B	5.7%	511	77	433
B-	8.2%	588	113	476
CCC+	11.8%	891	164	727

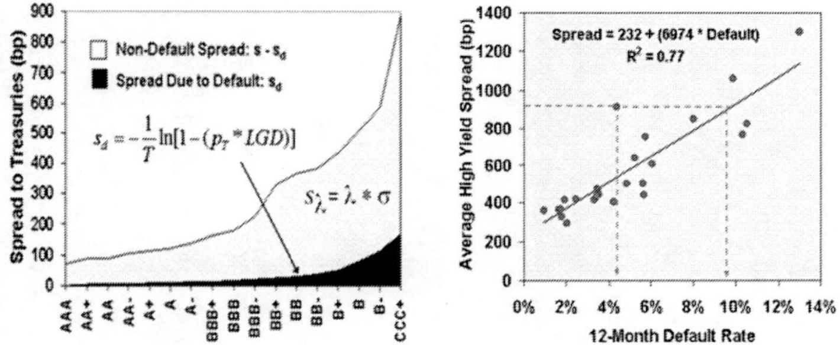

Figure 30. Left and Center: Average credit spreads due to default and non-default spreads by agency rating category, 1994-2010; Right: Annual average high yield credit spreads and annual default rates, 1986-2009.

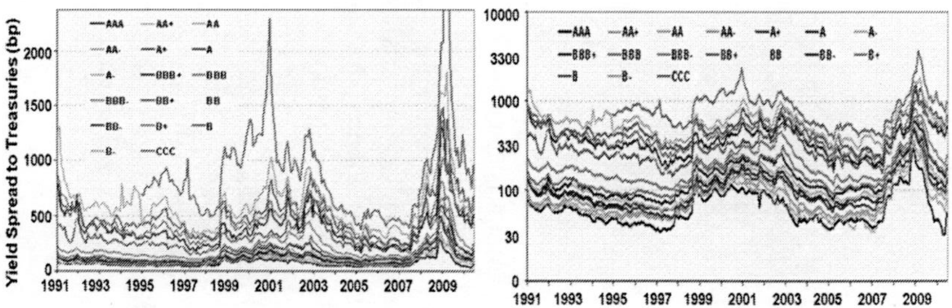

Figure 31. Monthly average yield spreads to US Treasuries by rating category on linear (left) and logarithmic (right) axes, 1991-2010.

Although the left and middle portions of Figure 30 show average values of the risk premium, default rates vary over the credit cycle as do credit spreads. Perhaps by determining the relationship between credit spreads and default rates, one could make inferences as to PDs from current values of credit spreads or vice versa. Then, applying this knowledge to individual credits, one could determine what a given difference in credit spread implies regarding probability of default or how a change in default probability would impact a bond's credit spread. Unfortunately, this has not proven satisfactory as illustrated in the right panel of Figure 30, which displays annual average high yield credit spreads against comparable default rates over the period from 1986 to 2009. That is, even though overall spread levels and defaults are correlated (R2=0.77), that relationship is not sufficiently useful for accurate prediction of overall spread levels, much less credit spreads by rating category or for individual firms. The dashed lines in the Figure 30 show that errors can be large. For example, in 2008, the average spread was 912bp, but the default rate was only 4.37% as opposed to the predicted value of 9.7%. The divergence between factors controlling default and credit spreads was also noted by Colin-Dufresne, Goldstein, and Martin (2001), who found that changes in spreads are highly correlated among issuers, but are unrelated to macroeconomic or financial variables that influence default.

A key to understanding the credit risk premium comes from observations of historical credit spreads by rating categories over time. The left panel of Figure 31 shows monthly average yield spreads to US Treasuries by rating category. Clearly, spread values vary widely over the credit cycle. However, when plotted on logarithmic axes, as in the right panel of Figure 31, one sees that credit spreads by rating seem to move in tandem at a constant ratio across rating categories. This suggests that while default rates and the credit risk premium may not be perfectly correlated, spread moves for default-risky credits, regardless of rating, are related by changes in a single common factor.

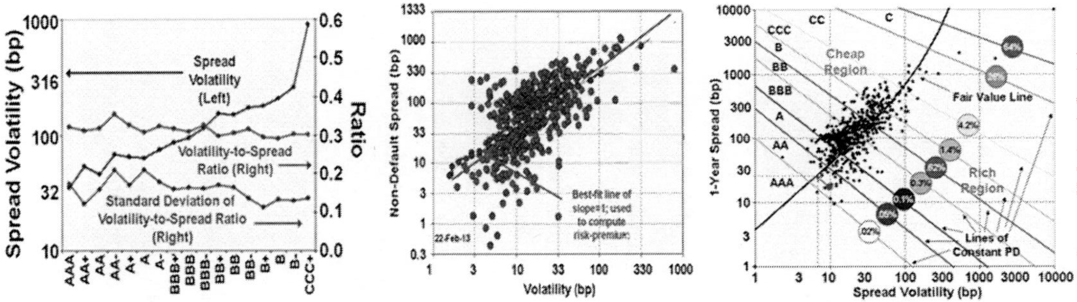

Figure 32. Left: Spread volatility by rating (left axis) and ratio of volatility to spread (right axis) and the volatility of rolling five-year volatility-to-spread ratio; Middle: Non-default spreads by volatility for the calibration universe using HPD PDs; Right: One-year spreads by 60-day trailing spread volatilities for commercial and industrial firms with HPD PDs in Citigroup's Investment-Grade and High Yield Indexes. Lines of constant PDs and implied rating categories are also shown.

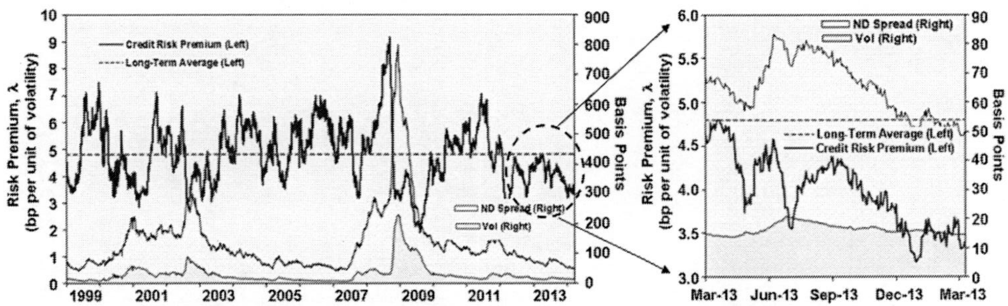

Figure 33. Historical values of the credit risk premium, λ , from 1999 to 2014 (left) and from Mar-13 to Mar-14 (right).

Benzschawel and Assing (2012) provided insight into the factor controlling the non-default spread s_d from examination of the volatility of average credit spreads over time. For example, the connected blue dots in the left panel of Figure 32 show that average monthly spread volatility as a function of rating category is a straight line when plotted on a logarithmic spread axis. Furthermore, the volatility-to-spread ratio (red points referenced to right axis) is a constant of roughly 0.3 for all rating categories. Importantly, this implies that the market charges the same average spread per unit of volatility. Finally, we find the volatility of the rolling spread-to-volatility ratio (the green dots) is also constant across rating categories.

The results in the left panel of Figure 32 suggest that the credit risk premium might be related to spread volatility. To test this, Benzschawel and Assing first computed values of default spreads s_d for bonds in Citi's Investment-Grade and High Yield Indexes using the HPD model. As shown in the middle panel of Figure 32, one can think of p_T in the structural framework of Merton (1974) as the likelihood that a given firm is insolvent at time T. Then, given a firm's p_T (from HPD), its duration, and an assumed value for LGD, in this case 60%, one can use Equation 6 to determine the spread values of default for its bonds. By subtracting the value of s_d from the bond's overall spread s, one can determine the value of the non-default spread s_λ. That is, we model the bond's spread as $s = s_d + s_\lambda$. The resulting values of s_λ for the bonds in our sample appear on a logarithmic scale as a function of log spread volatility in the middle panel of Figure 32. If the market charges the same amount on average per unit of volatility regardless of its source, then the relationship between non-default spread and spread volatility should have a slope of 1.0 in log-log coordinates. In fact, the red line in Figure 32, with a slope equal to 1.0, fits the points well. Note that all points on the red line have the same ratio of spread to volatility and we call this ratio λ and designate $\lambda\sigma = s_\lambda$ as the value of the daily risk premium for a given bond.[44]

---

[44] The text presented a simplified description of how the points in the middle panel of Figure 32 were determined. In fact, as described in Benzschawel and Lee (2011), a Nelson-Siegel (1987) procedure is used to determine one-year equivalent spreads (i.e., $T=1$) for all firms in the sample, and these are the values that appear

Historical analyses of plots of non-default spreads versus volatility as in Figure 32 indicate that, at least to a first approximation, lines of slope equal to1.0 fit the data well. Accordingly, one can compute historical values of the daily ratio of spread-to-volatility (i.e., λ). The resulting values of λ appear in Figure 33. Average spreads and spread volatilities are also shown. The left panel of Figure 33 displays daily values of λ since 1999, whereas the right panel shows λ over the past year. The dashed line in each plot is the average value of λ, which is 4.8bp per unit of spread volatility. The right panel of Figure 33 indicates that, as of the past year or so, the spread value of volatility has been consistently below average. Thus, despite historically low volatility, investors have been willing to accept much less spread per unit of volatility than average. Presumably, this reflects a demand for yield amid the low yields resulting from the U.S. Federal Reserve's qualitative easing program.

To summarize the credit risk premium and its relation to default probabilities, bonds' credit spreads are decomposed into compensation for default s_d and into compensation for spread volatility s_λ, where

$$s_d = -\frac{1}{T}\ln[1-(p_T * LGD)] \quad \text{, and} \quad s_\lambda = \lambda_T \sigma \quad , \qquad (17)$$

where T is the duration of the bond, p_T is the cumulative default probability to time T, LGD is the expected loss in default, σ is the spread volatility, λ_T is the price of spread volatility on day t (i.e., the "Sharpe ratio"), and λ_T is the same for all credits. Putting these two expressions together, we can express the overall yield spread to US Treasuries on day t as:

$$s = \lambda_t \sigma - \frac{1}{T}\ln[1-(p_T * LGD)] \quad . \qquad (18)$$

Thus, the model of spreads represented in Equation 18 requires physical probabilities of default (PDs) from the structural model, risk neutral theory to convert PDs to spreads, and the Sharpe ratio from the

---

in Figure 32. Also, we compute spread volatility on the trailing 60 daily spread values, but impose an exponential decay with a half-life of 66 days on trailing spread values.

Capital Asset Pricing Theory (CAPM) to estimate the daily spread value of volatility λ_T.

Estimating Obligor PDs

The previous section presented a framework for interpreting the relationship between credit spreads, default, recovery, and spread volatility, but estimating firms' p_T remains a challenge. That is, even if one has bond spreads and volatilities and a reasonable assumption for LGD (e.g., 1-RV = 60%), one still requires an estimate of the current market price of risk at time t, λ_t. One-year PDs from the HPD model are used to provide daily estimates of λ_t for the commercial and industrial firms in Citi's investment-grade and high yield bond indexes to construct a plot like that in the middle panel of Figure 32. Once λ_t is determined, firms' one-year spreads and spread volatilities are plotted, as in the right panel of Figure 32, and those points are fit with a quadratic function as shown in the figure.[45] Having inferred that day's value of λ_t, one can estimate a firm's p_1 using a recent history of its credit spreads. The bond's current spread and spread volatility are used to infer fair spreads and volatilities at the intersection of the line perpendicular to the bond's spread and volatility and the best-fit line in the left panel of Figure 32. For example, assume that the value of $\lambda_t =$ 4.7bp/vol and that a bond has a volatility of 10bp and spread of 20bp (the red dot in the right panel of Figure 32). That point would be referred to the point 7bp volatility and 29bp spread as shown by the arrow. If one assumes an LGD of 60%, the obligor would have a one-year market-implied default probability from Equation 5 of 1.6bp or 0.016%.

---

[45] A quadratic function has a term with and exponent of 2 such as $s = a_0 + a_1\sigma + a_2\sigma^2$.

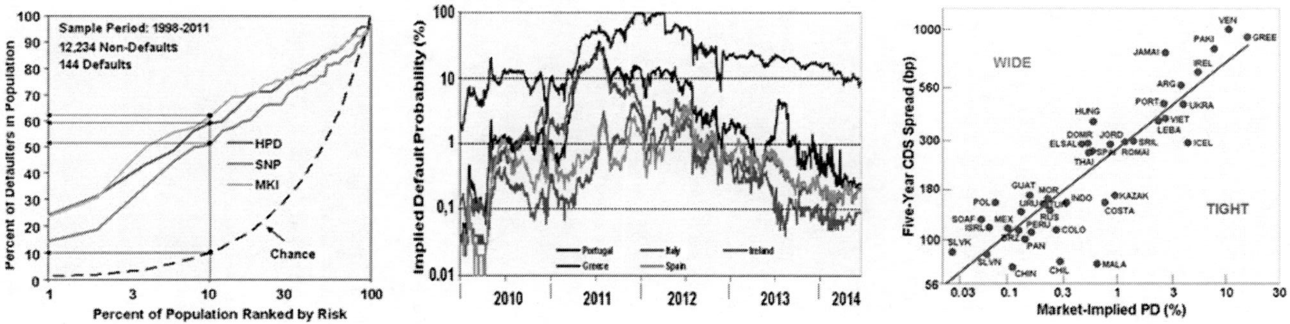

Figure 34. Left: Cap curves for the MKI and HPD models and S&P credit ratings; Middle: Market implied default probabilities for European peripheral sovereigns; Right: Five-year CDS spreads versus market-implied default probabilities, 26-Jan-11.

The left panel of Figure 34 displays CAP curves for HPD and MKI models along with S&P agency ratings on the same set of 144 defaults and over 12,000 non-defaults over the period from 1998 through 2011.[46] Although the sample size of defaulters is relatively small, the CAP curves indicate that the MKI model performs similarly to HPD at predicting defaults, and both outperform agency ratings. The accuracy similarity of HPD and MKI is not surprising since PDs from the HPD model are used to determine the risk premium and the spread versus volatility curve.

More generally, once λ_t is determined, then for any obligor having a series of bond spreads, one can calculate a market-implied PD. For example, the middle panel of Figure 34 illustrates how the MKI model can be used to generate PD estimates for sovereigns, not scored by structural models. The graph displays time series of PDs for peripheral European sovereigns that span the most critical part of the European credit crisis. It also shows how, after PDs spiked in early 2012, they have been decreasing steady since then. The right panel of Figure 34 from Benzschawel, Assing, Haroon, and Lee (2012) show how PDs generated from sovereign bond data by the MKI model can be used to identify rich and cheap five-year credit default swaps (CDS). That is, sovereigns' five-year CDS premiums versus logarithms of PDs are fit well by a straight line. CDS plotting above the line might be viewed as cheap, with those below the line as rich.

The market-implied approach is relatively new, but interesting and unique applications already have been demonstrated. For example, the CDX index (CDX.NA.IG) can be an effective hedge for the credit risk premium (Benzschawel and Su, 2014a), predicted default rates can be used to forecast the credit risk premium (Benzschawel and Su, 2014b), and the MKI framework can be used to estimate bail-in probabilities for banks' contingent conversion (Co-co) bonds (Benzschawel, Lee, Su, and Lommaert, 2014). As described above, the MKI model has already proven useful for tracking sovereign risk, and we are currently applying that model to measure the risk premium in the municipal bond market and to estimate MKI PDs for municipal bonds.

---

[46] The sample size was limited to firms for which scores were available from both HPD and KMV models at the beginning of each year as well as credit ratings from Standard and Poor's.

The Future: Consensus Models and Big Data

Although statistical, structural, and hybrid models have had a good deal of success at predicting defaults at one-year horizons for commercial and industrial firms and perhaps banks, predictive models of default with similar accuracy remain to be developed for private firms, sovereign issuers, and municipalities. Most of the frameworks described above, with the possible exception of the market-implied approach, are not well-suited to those problems or remain untested in those domains.[47] Furthermore, as has already been noted above, predicting default is inherently a probabilistic endeavor. Given the convergence of accuracies of existing models at predicting default, it seems likely that we are reaching an asymptote in our ability to predict defaults at the one-year horizon from publically available financial and market information. This fact and our lack of models for sovereign and municipal defaults has prompted the search for models that embed other sources of information, such as news stories, analyst reports, and expert opinions, as input to predictive models of default. We consider several such approaches in this section.

This section presents examples of model classes that are expected to play an important role in future credit modeling. Currently, these models are in their infancy, but are sufficiently detailed to allow testing of their predictive power, albeit over relatively restricted time frames. One of the classes considered is referred to as an expert system or consensus model. This approach involves soliciting views from "experts" on various aspects of obligor creditworthiness on a regular basis. Examples include Euromoney's Country Risk Scorecard-based model (Mortimer, 2013) or current determinants of bonds' yield spreads to Treasuries from Capital Market Exchange (Biller and Gerlanc, 2012). The other class includes big data models, as embodied in Thompson-Reuters StarMine model (Roser, Bonne and Smith-Hill, 2013), which incorporates information from news services, published research, conference call transcripts, and company filings to generate daily estimates of obligor default risk. To illustrate these approaches and their potential for addressing unsolved issues in credit modeling, the Euromoney and Thompson Reuters models are described briefly below along with some preliminary tests of their abilities to predict credit changes.

---

[47] In fact, several statistical models for sovereign defaults have recently been proposed (Altman and Rijken, 2011), but these remain largely untested, require user-determined inputs, and/or are difficult to implement (Gray, Merton, and Bodie, 2007).

Euromoney's Country Risk Score

Although models for estimating physical default probabilities (PDs) for corporate borrowers abound, estimating physical PDs for sovereign issuers within existing frameworks has proven problematic. Although agency ratings for sovereign debt issues are useful for some applications, their use has several shortcomings. Also, macroeconomic models, while also useful for some applications, rarely generate default probabilities, are backward-looking, or otherwise require user-estimated inputs of future economic performance. A novel approach to sovereign default risk was introduced by Euromoney in 2011. Its Euromoney Country Risk (ECR) score embeds experts' estimates of political, economic, and structural risk into a standard framework to generate a Country Risk Score (ECR score) that varies from 100 (no default risk) to 0 (default). The ECR score does not generate an estimate of physical default, per se, but Benzschawel, Lee, and Li (2013) have demonstrated how ECR scores can be converted to default probabilities using average defaults by rating category from the Sobehart-Keenan HPD model or from defaults by rating from the market-implied PD model.

The ECR scorecard is presented in the left panel of Figure 35.[48] The ECR scores are opinions of over 400 experts worldwide on two main dimensions: country risks and qualitative factors, with each contributing 70% and 30%, respectively, to the total score. The top three sections of the scorecard show country score categories, each consisting of expert scores on 15 variables relating to economic, political, and structural factors. The country scores consist of 30% contributions from economic factors and political factors, and a 10% contribution from structural factors. The items in each factor are as follows:

- Economic Assessments: Participants rate each country from 0-10 across 5 sub factors, each weighed 6%, for a maximum score of 30%. Categories of economic risk are bank stability/risk, GNP outlook, unemployment rate, government finances, and monetary policy/currency stability;
- Political Risk: Participants rate countries from 0-10 across 6 sub factors, each weighted 5%, for a maximum score 30%. The political risk categories are corruption, government non-payments/non-repatriation, government stability, information access/transparency, institutional risk, and regulatory and policy environment;

[48] A more detailed description of the ECR methodology can be found in Benzschawel, Lee, and Li (2013).

- Structural Risk: Participants rate countries from 0-10 across 4 sub factors, each weighted 2.5%, for a maximum score of 10%. The categories are demographics, hard infrastructure, labor market/ industrial relations, and soft infrastructure.

The remaining 30% contribution is from three qualitative factors (labeled "Other Inputs" in Figure 35): overall credit ratings,[49] debt indicators, and access to capital, with each contributing 10% to the ECR score. The scores on all of the factors are averaged across experts, and average scores are summed to produce a composite ECR score. The ECR score can have a value from 100 to 0, with 100 being nearly devoid of any risk, and 0 being completely exposed to every risk (at or near default).

A diagram of the ECR rating system appears in the right portion of Figure 35. The first stage, the assembling of "experts," is depicted in the top left panel. The experts are domiciled globally, not just in major financial centers, and their occupations span the financial industry, government, and academia. This diversification of expert backgrounds is intentional, as Euromoney wishes to capture a broad survey of sentiment, rather than only one sector of interest. In addition, the backgrounds of the experts and the countries to which they contribute their views are also available.

The experts input their views on each sub-factor into the ECR system using a system shown at the top right in the right panel of Figure 35. Items in each major category are scored using sliders (see figure) to set ratings on scales of 10 (best) to 0 (worst). Then, for a given country, scores from the experts assigned to that country are aggregated to produce a country report. An example of that report for Russia in December of 2013 appears in the lower right portion of Figure 35. That report contains the overall county rating, in this example an ECR score of 51.96, along with changes in ECR score, country rank, and information on the number of expert opinions. In addition, the summary provides information on ratings for each of the factors (economic, political, and structural) and their momentum as well as their rating, access to capital, and debt indicators.

---

[49] The credit rating is a composite of the average of ratings from Fitch, Moody's, and Standard and Poor's converted to numerical scales and normalized to the range between 10 (highest) and 0 (default).

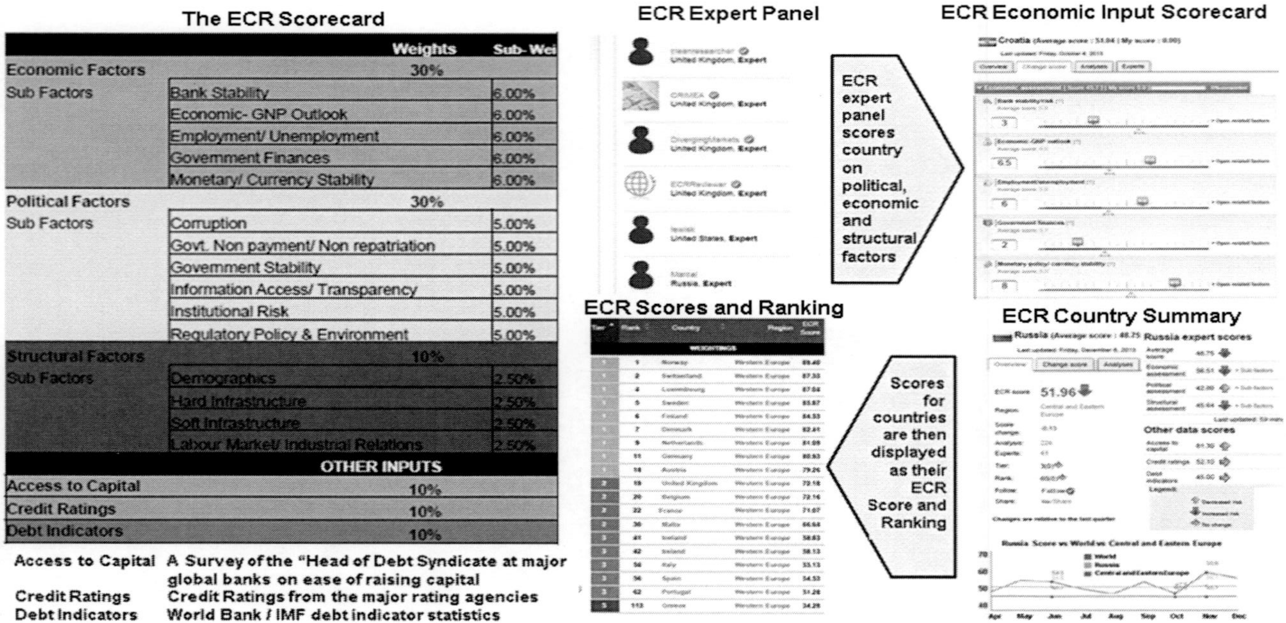

Figure 35. Left: The ECR scorecard for sovereign issuers; Right: How the ECR system works: A panel of experts (top left) inputs views via scorecards (top right) that are aggregated into country scores and summaries (bottom right) to create a set of country scores and risk rankings (bottom left).

Full synchronised results provided on quarterly basis in EXCEL format

Dec-11 Rank	Country	ECR Score	Euromoney Country Risk , December 2011					
			Economic Risk	Political Risk	Structural Risk	Debt Indicators	Credit ratings	Access to Capital
Weightings			30 '(100)	30 '(100)	10 '(100)	10 '(10)	10 '(10)	10 '(10)
1	Norway	91.17	88.17	92.36	82.15	8.85	10.00	10.00
2	Singapore	88.51	79.25	87.94	84.69	10.00	10.00	9.88
3	Switzerland	88.40	82.92	88.42	86.03	8.39	10.00	10.00
4	Luxembourg	87.84	79.88	91.85	85.75	8.76	10.00	9.00
5	Denmark	85.36	73.11	90.71	81.72	8.10	10.00	9.75
6	Finland	85.10	75.36	89.09	78.48	7.92	10.00	10.00
7	Sweden	85.08	78.83	90.15	82.35	8.24	10.00	7.88
8	Netherlands	84.71	75.93	86.79	78.29	8.02	10.00	10.00
9	Canada	84.70	77.40	88.37	77.95	7.24	10.00	9.88
10	Hong Kong	83.68	79.33	82.18	80.11	8.23	9.58	9.00
11	New Zealand	82.33	68.50	89.73	72.94	7.52	9.58	9.75
12	Australia	82.14	73.50	85.59	75.53	7.52	9.79	9.75
13	Germany	82.12	72.55	85.04	78.48	7.59	10.00	9.50
14	Austria	81.59	72.50	82.40	76.21	7.34	10.00	10.00
15	USA	76.28	56.89	83.99	78.63	6.51	9.79	9.92
16	Taiwan	76.19	71.87	73.54	72.32	7.60	7.92	9.67
17	France	76.10	61.20	78.34	73.38	6.58	10.00	10.00
18	Chile	75.24	77.05	78.52	70.14	4.53	7.71	9.00
19	UK	75.20	58.11	82.53	73.83	6.51	10.00	9.08
20	Qatar	73.20	78.43	62.66	57.88	7.34	8.75	9.00

Figure 36. Sample of highest ECR composite scores, along with category scores and qualitative scores, Dec-2011.

The output of the ECR system is a table of country scores and rankings as shown in the lower part of Figure 35. A sample of a more detailed report by country appears in Figure 36, which presents ECR scores and ratings on each of the six factors for the top ranked portion of the 186-country sovereign universe. As mentioned, the ECR score ranges from 100 to 0, with Norway having the highest ECR score of 91.17 (on December 1, 2011). The sum of the sub-factor ratings contributing to each of the three country factor scores are normalized to provide a score on each factor in the range from 100 to 0. The three qualitative factors are expressed on a scale of 10 to 1.

Although useful for a relative ranking of country risk, the ECR does not provide an estimate of likelihood of default (i.e., PDs), per se, and is therefore of limited use for quantifying expected losses on sovereign credit portfolios. For this reason, Benzschawel, Lee, and Li (2013) devised a method for linking ECR scores with PDs from the Sobehart-Keenan HPD model using agency credit ratings as a bridge. As mentioned above, the HPD model cannot generate PDs for sovereigns because countries do not have tradable equity. However, one can construct a map between HPD model ECR scores as illustrated in Figure 37.

The first step in mapping ECR scores to default probabilities is to determine a correspondence between the ECR scores on a given day and rating categories. For example, the left panel of Figure 37 shows the mapping between credit ratings and ECR scores for August 1, 2013. That map is constructed by determining the number of triple-A-rated sovereigns in the sample and that same number of sovereigns with the highest ECR scores. Assume that number is 10. Given that the upper bound on the ECR scores is 100, we need only establish the lower bound, which is given by the average ECR score of the 10th and 11th ranked countries. In this example, that score is 81. We proceed similarly down the rating categories scale until we get to single-C rated credits. We set the boundary between single-C and default at the average of the ECR score of the lowest single-C sovereign and 0.

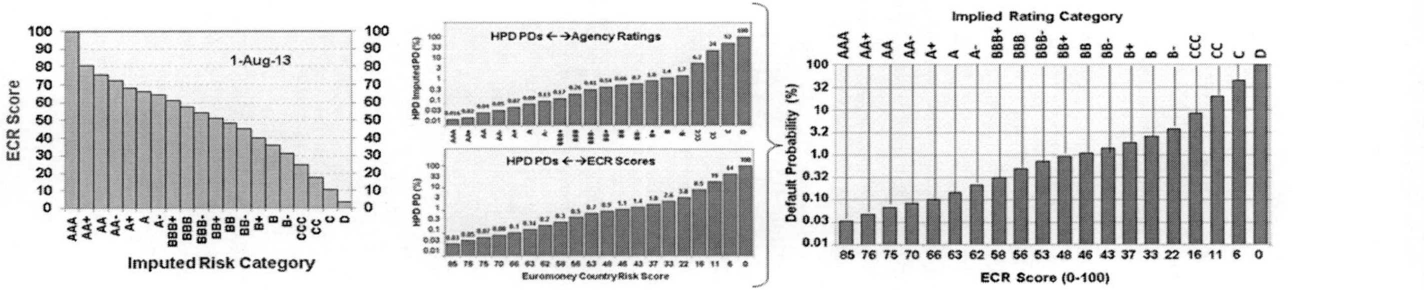

Figure 37. Monthly average yield spreads to US Treasuries by rating category on linear (left) and logarithmic (right) axes, 1991-2010.

Next as illustrated in the middle panels of Figure 37, similar correspondences between HPD model PDs and agency ratings and HPD PDs and ECR scores are determined using agency ratings as the bridge. The right panel of Figure 37 combines results of the middle panel into a three-way map between agency ratings, default probabilities from the HPD model, and ECR scores.[50]

Benzschawel et al (2013) examined if changes in ECR scores would anticipate sovereigns' upgrades and downgrades by credit rating agencies. To that end, acquired monthly agency credit ratings were acquired for the 143 sovereigns in the ECR scoring system over the sample period from December 2011 through August 2013.[51] The sample contained 44 upgrades and 69 downgrades. For each month preceding the sovereign upgrade/downgrade, differences were computed between that sovereign's ECR score and the average ECR score of that country's target rating category. The left panel of Figure 38 displays the differences in ECR scores for the upgrades (green circles) and downgrades (red circles) in months relative to that of the upgrade and downgrade (0 on the x-axis).[52] The ECR model scores lead agency ratings changes: average ECR scores for upgrades increase prior to the upgrade and scores for downgrades decrease. Furthermore, in the month of the ratings change, the average sovereign ECR scores for both upgrades and downgrades are at the averages of their target rating categories.[53]

Benzschawel et al. (2013) also simulated long/short sovereign CDS trades based on ECR scores similar to that devised for long/short investment-grade corporate CDS trades based on the HPD model (Benzschawel and Lee, 2012). The middle panel of Figure 38 plots five-year CDS spreads versus ECR scores for sovereigns in Citi's World Government Bond Index (Citigroup Index, 2012). Corresponding ECR-

---

[50] We have since determined that the mapping of PDs using the sovereign PDs from the Market-Implied model (Benzschawel and Assing, 2012) provides more intuitive estimates of physical PDs than the corporate scale from the HPD model. In either case, the procedure is described herein.

[51] A rating change could be triggered by any of the major rating agencies: S&P, Moody's, or Fitch. To avoid double counting, for sovereigns having similar ratings changes in subsequent months, we kept only the scores related to the first rating change.

[52] Note that because the various upgrades and downgrades took place over different periods in the 19-month ECR score sample, their histories do not overlap completely on the graph in Figure 38.

[53] For a detailed description of the results of the ECR-HPD model, see Benzschawel, Lee, and Li (2013).

based inferred PDs from the HPD model, denoted PDS, are plotted on the top axis. A regression line is fit to five-year CDS spreads versus ECR scores (and/or) PDS, which is defined as the "fair value" line. Although points deviate from the line, a linear function provides a good functional form for the relationship between ECR scores or PDS and CDS premiums. As regards value, CDS spreads that plot above regression line (i.e., fair value) in Figure 38 are inferred to be cheap, offering investors above average compensation for their credit risk. Conversely, sovereign CDS spreads below the line are rich. Lines of +/-0.5σ are chosen to define sell/buy boundaries for short/long CDS trades. In each month, a long/short CDS trade was simulated by:

1. Eliminating from the trade the 10% of the credits with the largest PDs;
2. Selling protection on all the CDS above given; and
3. Buying credit protection on sovereign CDS below the given criterion (e.g., between -0.5σ or, for other studies, a fixed number of CDS).

The right panel of Figure 38 presents cumulative P/L from the monthly series of simulated three-month long/short sovereign CDS trades (solid lines) and the benchmark (i.e., just sell protection) long-only strategy (dashed lines). P/L is broken out by total P/L (blue lines), carry (green) and convergence (red), where convergence for the long-only strategy is from spread tightening only. Consider first the total P/L. The long-only benchmark portfolio is profitable, generating roughly 6.5% from December 2011 to August 2013. However, total P/L from the long/short CDS trades is almost double the long only, topping 10% over the period. Both long/short and long-only CDS trades produce consistent positive carry as indicated by the green line and green dashes, respectively. For the long only strategy, the 2.2% return from carry comes from premiums on the 30% of CDS nearest to fair value. In comparison, positive carry from the three-month long/short CDS trades is 4.0% over the period, reflecting the difference between premiums received from selling protection on cheap CDS over those paid for protection on rich CDS. P/L from

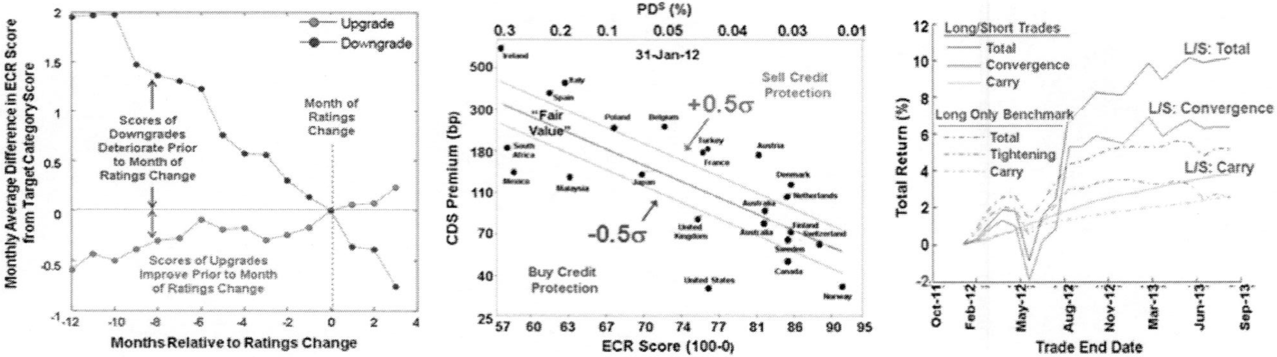

Figure 38. Left: Time series of average ECR scores for upgraded (N=44) /downgraded (N=69) sovereigns relative to average scores of their target rating categories in months relative to the ratings change; Middle: Five-Year WGBI sovereign CDS premiums versus ECR scores and ECR-HPD PDs, illustrating "cheap" and "rich" CDS defined by +/-0.5σ from the "fair value" regression; Right: Cumulative P/L for long/short trades and long-only benchmark with three-month holding periods.

convergence is just over 6% for the long/short strategy (the red line), topping the 2% spread tightening for the long-only strategy (the red dashes).[54]

Clearly the ECR model with inferred PDs from the HPD model holds promise for providing investors with a forward looking model for sovereign credit risk and relative value. A major limitation of the model is the relatively short history of ECR scores available for back testing the model; the model history does not include a negative part of the credit cycle. Still, no other model is known to have demonstrated similar success at predicting ratings' downgrades and CDS spread convergence. Also, preliminary testing indicates that ECR scores may prove useful as predictors of foreign currency moves for non-G10 sovereigns. The ECR framework has also been criticized for having arbitrary scorecard weights. However, Benzschawel, Lee, and Li (2013) have shown that those weights can be optimized adaptively to predict market data and ratings' changes. Thus, a fixed-weight standardized scorecard is an advantage in terms of consistency of rater's judgments and, by subsequent optimization, allowing analysis of changing determinants of global sovereign default risk.

Finally, although useful for modeling sovereign risk, the crowd sourcing model approach as embodied in the ECR score is more difficult to apply to corporate or municipal default risk. That is, unlike the manageable 194 countries scored by the Euromoney model, there are over 30,000 corporations globally and over 100,000 municipal issuers in the U.S. from which scores would need to be solicited. However, models for a subset of those firms, banks for example, may be a more manageable application for the consensus approach. Another new approach that holds promise for estimating default risk for corporations and municipalities is the "big data" approach described in the next section.

Big Data – The Thomson Reuters TMCR Model

This section presents a model that employs a "big data" methodology to predict likelihoods of default for corporate firms. Thomson Reuters' StarMine Text Mining Credit Risk Model (TMCR) described by Roser, Bonne and Smith-Hill (2013) is the first commercially available credit risk model to measure corporate default risk by quantitatively analyzing text.

---

[54] For a long-only portfolio, over the long run, one would expect little P/L from spread tightening because CDS premiums should fluctuate around their average value. The fact cumulative P/L from spread tightening on the long only trades is 2% (roughly equal to the carry), which is indicative of the rally in sovereign CDS spreads over the relatively small sample period available for testing.

More importantly, as shown below, Roser et al. present evidence of the predictive power of the TMCR model.

The StarMine TMCR, depicted in Figure 39, assesses the default risk of publically traded companies by systematically evaluating the language in Reuters News, StreetEvents conference call transcripts, corporate filings (10-K, 10-Q, and 8-K), and research documents from over 600 participating brokers. The TMCR model scores over 25,000 companies daily. StarMine TMCR creates a ranked component score for each of the four document sources and combines the component scores to provide an overall rating of company credit risk. The overall score is available as a letter grade, probability of default, and a rank form 1-100.

The core of the TMCR model is a "bag of words" (Salton and McGill, 1983) text-mining algorithm. A bag of words text-mining algorithm breaks a document into its constituent words and phrases and establishes relationships between the frequencies of these words and phrases and a known training variable, such as empirical default probability. Development of the StarMine TMCR consisted of extensive research to determine unique dictionaries of language for each document source within the context of financial analysis that are useful for robustly assessing the credit risk of a company. In developing the dictionaries, StarMine analyzed the text in millions of individual documents across more than ten years of history to identify which words and phrases have the strongest and most robust relationship to company credit risk. StarMine TMCR calculates the frequency of the dictionary words and phrases for each document and then uses a learning algorithm to calculate an overall score for the document from these frequencies. From that analysis, StarMine creates a ranked component score from each of the four document sources on the four dimensions of interest at shown in the left panel of Figure 40. These are:

1. Income – income statement related;
2. Structural – balance sheet and debt structure related;
3. Legal – legal obligations and terms; and
4. External – terms related to external and market factors.

The category outputs are not used in the calculation of the overall TMCR score, but are designed to provide insight into the language that drives the TMCR score. Figure 40 indicates that each TMCR component contains a different combination of language relating to the four relevant dimensions.

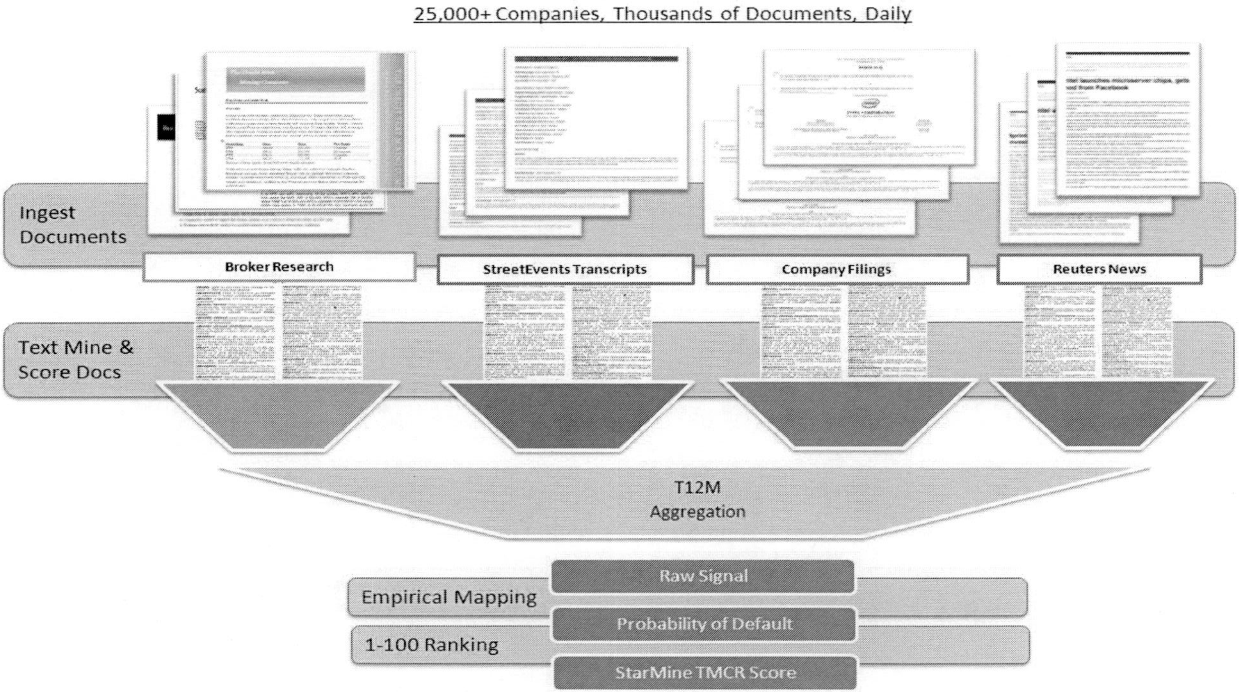

Figure 39. Thomson Reuters' StarMine TMCR model.

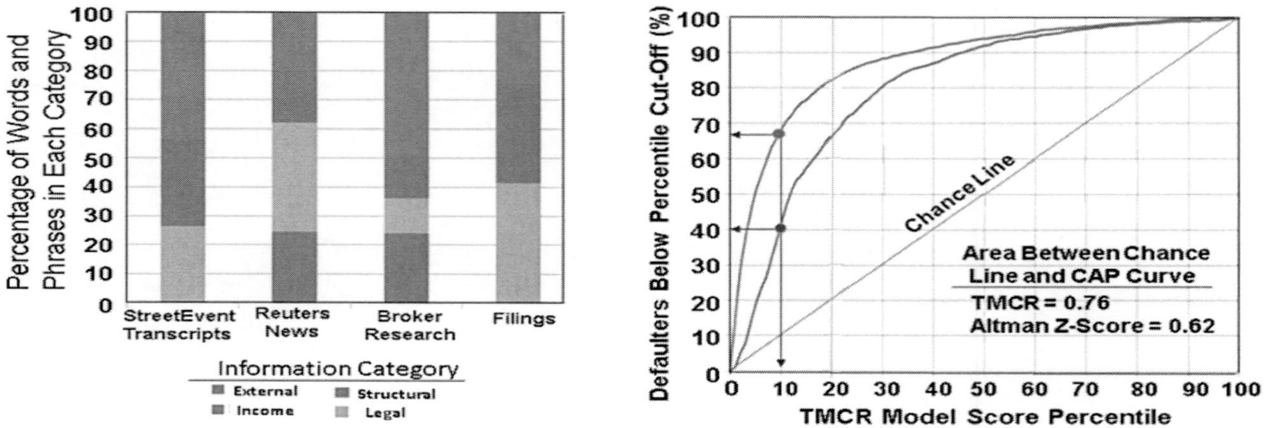

Figure 40. Monthly average yield spreads to US Treasuries by rating category on linear (left) and logarithmic (right) axes, 1991-2010.

Roser, Bonne, and Smith-Hill (2013) present CAP curves and Accuracy Ratios for the TMCR score and Altman's Z-Score model for all years from 2002-2010, and these are reproduced in the right panel of Figure 40. The figure indicates that StarMine TMCR performs significantly better than the Z-Score, capturing 68% of default events in the bottom 10% (most risky) of model scores versus 40% for the Z-Score. Although the samples differ somewhat, the TMCR model's CAP curve is roughly equivalent to that of the HPD model in Figure 27 and superior to that of the KMV model. Given the additional complexity of the data mining approach for predicting default, it is somewhat disappointing that, at least for the one-year horizon, default predictions from TMCR are roughly equivalent to the previously best models. The similarity of model performances is consistent with the idea that, at least for one year out and the inherent uncertainty of default, default prediction models based on publicly available information are approaching an asymptote in accuracy. However, the TMCR model may still prove superior as an indicator of relative value, but that remains untested.

The performance of the TMCR model at predicting corporate defaults suggests that its application to municipal and sovereign defaults may prove useful. In fact, the municipal default problem is particularly well-suited for data mining approaches due to the large number (i.e. over 100,000) of municipalities and the lack of competing models. An interesting possibility is to use big data techniques to generate forward-looking estimates of parameters for existing credit models. Other potential problems are estimating recovery value in default, which remains a difficult problem and is important for expected losses and relative value. In addition, the data mining approach holds particular promise for shorter-term predictions of index and asset relative value, but remains relatively untested for those purposes. For example, the ability to predict the next day's closing CDS index prices or market opening prices after a night of new information would be particularly useful. Also, applying data mining to firm specific information for over- and underweighting various bonds over short intervals is another potential application.

Figure 41 presents some of the potential uses and challenges of data mining approaches to credit. Consider first some potential uses of sentiment data. Big data can provide an information advantage as it goes beyond traditional fundamental analysis. It also offers potential for the creation of indices based on traditional structured data (e.g. macro and market data). The application of sentiment modeling can provide first movers with a competitive advantage over slower-to-adopt competitors. It also holds promise for determining proxy measures for data that is not available (e.g., financial information from private firms). There may be data that can be leveraged quickly to add immediate value.

Potential Uses

- Timeliness of the data can provide an information advantage
- Potential to provide first movers with a key differentiator from the slower-to-adopt competitors
- Sentiment data can be leveraged as proxy measures for data that is currently not available to improve our analysis (e.g. private firms)
- There may be a subset of data ("low hanging fruit") that can be leveraged quickly and add immediate value
- Forecasting the short- to medium-term returns remain elusive and pioneering this area will be a significant competitive advantage

Challenges

- Not yet clear how to best use the data
- Developing an appropriate front-end to extract and analyze the data is critical
- Text analysis in the financial sector has only recently transitioned from high-frequency and event-based trading
- Not just about trading on sentiment (positive or negative)
- News volume, timing and market absorption of news needs to be understood and varies across securities and asset classes
- Determinants of returns and relationship to sentiment data need to be determined

Figure 41. Big Data: Potential uses and challenges.

Despite the potential of big data and sentiment models, challenges remain regarding their application to credit modeling. Effective use of sentiment data requires new ways of thinking, hypothesis creation, and relevant data. There are technical challenges as well; the dataset is massive, involving storage and retrieval, handling, and display. These involve knowledge of how the data is to be used and how to integrate it within existing applications. Also, technologists need to be engaged in dialogue with data analysts and quants to develop effective models. There are also problems to be solved with respect to prediction of default, recovery, and market movements.

Summary

This report presents a history of quantitative approaches to credit risk modeling from a practical point of view, concentrating on default prediction and relative value. It begins by describing the origin of credit modeling along with debt markets and carries through various innovations, such as statistical, structural and reduced form models to modern consensus and big data sentiment models. The discussion highlights the advantages and disadvantages of each approach. A major theme that emerges from an historical analysis of credit modeling is that older successful models typically do not become extinct even though they give way to more cutting-edge models. That is, for each type of innovation from financial ratios to agency ratings and even Altman's Z-Score, there remains a range of applications for which the level of accuracy of those models is sufficient. The survival of less powerful approaches results from the fact that nearly every innovation in credit modeling has come at the expense of increasing requirements for input data, enhancements in computational power, and greater theoretical complexity. Furthermore, although those innovations have enabled greater accuracy at predicting defaults and credit relative value, that information is not required for all investor applications. This leads one to suspect that the models we see today will continue to be used in the future, albeit likely in more restricted domains. One can also foresee the trend for consensus models and big data sentiment models to play a greater role in the very near future and to even help solve some of the tougher credit modeling problems as described above. Finally, none of these models can currently substitute for human judgment, which remains as the last step in the analytical credit analysis process, particularly as it involves investment decisions. Although the emergence of high powered computational machines, such as embodied in IBM's Watson, may someday be as accurate and reliable as the best human fundamental analysts, that day has not arrived yet.

References

Altman, E.I. Financial Ratios, Discriminant Analysis and the Prediction of Corporate Bankruptcy, *Journal of Finance, 28*(4), September 1968

Altman, E. I. and Eberhart, A. Do Seniority Provisions Protect Bondholders' Investments? *Journal of Portfolio Management 20*, pp.67-75, 1994.

Altman, E. and Kishore, V. Almost Everything You Wanted to Know about Recovery on Defaulted Bonds, *Financial Analysts Journal* 52(6), pp. 57-64, 1966.

Altman, E. and Nammacher, S. The Default Rate Experience of High Yield Corporate Debt, *Financial Analysts Journal 40*(4), pp. 25-41, 1984

Altman, E. A., Resti, A. and Sironi, A. *Recovery Risk*, Risk Books, London, 2005.

Altman, E. A., Brady, B. Resti, A. and Sironi, A. The Link between Default and Recovery Rates, NYU Working Paper No. S-CDM-04-07, September 2003.

Altman, E. and Rijken, H. Toward a Bottom-Up Approach to Assessing Sovereign Default Risk, *Journal of Applied Corporate Finance* 23(1), pp. 20-31, 2011.

Amato, J. and Remolona, E. The Credit Spread Puzzle, *BIS Quarterly Review*, pp 51-63, December 2003.

Anderson, R. and Sundaresan, S. A Comparative Study of Structural Models of Corporate Bond Yields: An Exploratory Investigation, *Journal of Banking and Finance 24*, pp. 255-269, 2000.

Beaver, W. H. Financial Ratios as Predictors of Failure, *Journal of Accounting Research 4*, pp. 71-111, 1966.

Benzschawel T., Adler D. Empirical Analysis of Corporate Bond Spreads, *Quantitative Credit Analyst 1*, Citigroup, pp. 5-33, 2002.

Benzschawel, T. and Assing, A. Inferring Default Probabilities from Credit Spreads, *Journal of Fixed Income 13*, pp. 16-24, Spring 2012.

Benzschawel, T., Assing, A., Haroon, A. and Lee, M. Market-Implied Default Probabilities for Sovereign Credits, Citi, January, April 8, 2011.

Benzschawel, T. and Corlu, A. Cash Flow Analysis of Credit Default Swaps, *Journal of Fixed Income 20*(3), pp. 40-54, 2010.

Benzschawel, T. *Credit Modeling: Facts, Theory and Applications*, Incisive Media, London, 2012.

Benzschawel, T. and Lee, M. A Rule-Based Long/Short CDS Strategy, Citi, April 30, 2012.

Benzschawel, T., Li, J. and Lee, M. Predicting Bank Failure: An Adaptive Statistical Model for Estimating Banks' Default Risk, Citi, August 6, 2013.

Benzschawel, T., Lee, M. and Li, J. Sovereign Default Risk and Relative Value, Citi, December 23, 2013.

Benzschawel, T. Citi's Hybrid Probability of Default Model: The Sobehart-Keenan HPD Model – Ten Years After, Citi, July 10, 2013.

Benzschawel, T. and Su, Y. Recovery Value in Default: An Ensemble Model (E-3), Citi, December 3, 2013.

Benzschawel, T. and Su, Y. Hedging the Credit Risk Premium, Citi, January 22, 2014a.

Benzschawel, T. and Su, Y. Predicting the Credit Risk Premium, Citi, May 21, 2014b.

Benzschawel, T., Lee, M., Lommaert, C. and Su, Y. Beating Global Credit Indexes, Citi, February 21, 2014.

Benzschawel, T., Su, Y., Lee, M. and Lommaert, C. Equity and Debt Risk Premiums and Applications, Citi, June 19, 2014.

Benzschawel, T., Lommaert, C. and Li, J. Predicting Bank Failure II: Further Model Validation, Analysis, and Enhancements, Citi, January 10, 2014.

Berd, A., Mashal, R. and Wang, P. Defining, Estimating and Using Credit Term Structures: Part I: Consistent Valuation Measures, Lehman Brothers, Nov 2004.

Bielecki, T. and Rutkowski, M. *Credit Risk: Modeling, Valuation and Hedging*, Springer-Verlag, 2002.

Biller, S. and Gerlance, D. Capital Market Exchange (available at www.capital-market-exchange.com), 2013.

Black F. and Scholes M. The Pricing of Options and Corporate Liabilities, *Journal of Political Economy 81*, pp. 637-659, 1973.

Black F., and Cox J.C., Valuing Corporate Securities: Some Effects of Bond Indenture Provisions, *Journal of Finance 31*, pp. 351-367, 1976.

Bohn, J. A Survey of Contingent-Claims Approaches to Risky Debt Valuation, *Journal of Risk Finance 1*(3), pp. 53-70, 2000.

Bozsik, J. Decision Tree Combined with Neural Networks for Financial Forecast, Periodica Polytechnica, *Electrical Engineering 55*(1-2), pp. 95-101, 2011.

Briys, E. and Varenne, F., Valuing Risky Fixed Rate Debt: An Extension, Journal of Financial and *Quantitative Analysis 32*(2), 239-248, 1997.

Brown, I. *The Historical Development of the Use of Ratios in Financial Statement Analysis to 1993*, Doctoral Dissertation, School of Social Science, Catholic University of America, 1955.

Campbell, J., Hilscher, J. and Szilagyi, J. In Search of Distress Risk, *The Journal of Finance 63*(6), pp. 2899-2939, 2008.

Chava S. and Jarrow R.A., Bankruptcy Prediction with Industry Effects, Working paper, *Johnson Graduate School of Management*, Cornell University, 2002.

Citigroup Index Group, Citigroup Global Fixed-Income Index Catalog – 2012 Edition, Citi, January 17, 2012.

Citigroup Index Group, Index Guide – 2013 Edition, Citigroup, January 2013.

Collin-Dufresne, P. and Goldstein, R. Do Credit Spreads Reflect Stationary Leverage Ratios, *The Journal of Finance 56*, pp. 1929-1958, 2001.

Colin-Dufresne, P., Goldstein, R. and Martin, J. The Determinants of Credit Spread Changes, *Journal of Finance 56*(6), pp. 2177-2207, 2001

Crosbie, P. and Bohn, J. Modeling Default Risk (KMV LLC), 2001.

Dickson, P. *The Financial Revolution in England: A Study in the Development of Public Credit. 1688-1756*, London: Macmillan, 1967.

Driessen, J. Is default event risk priced in corporate bonds? Mimeo, University of Amsterdam, 2003.

Downs, J. and Goodman, J., *Dictionary of Finance and Investment Terms*, Barron's Educational Series, Hauppauge, New York, 1991.

Duan, J.-C., Sun, J. and Wang, T. Multiperiod Corporate Default Prediction — A Forward Intensity Approach, *Journal of Econometrics 170*, pp. 191–209, 2012.

Duffie, D. and Singleton, K. Modeling Term Structures of Defaultable Bonds, *Review of Financial Studies 12(4)* pp. 687-720, 1999

Duffie, D., Eckner, A., Horel, G. and Saita, L. Frailty Correlated Default, *The Journal of Finance 64*(5), pp. 2089-2123, 2009.

Dwyer, D. and Korablev, I. LossCalc 3.0 Methodology Document, Moody's/KMV, December 12, 2008.

Eberhart, A., Moore, C. and Rosenfelt, E. Security Pricing and Deviations from the Absolute Priority Rule in Bankruptcy Proceedings, *Journal of Finance 45*(5), pp. 1457-1479, 1990.

Eberhart, A., and Weiss, L. The Importance of Deviations from the Absolute Priority Rule in Chapter 11 Bankruptcy Proceedings, *Financial Management 27*(4), pp. 106-110, 1998.

Emory, K. Ou, S., Tennant, J., Kim, F. and Cantor, R. Corporate Default and Recovery Rates, 1920-2007, Moody's Investors Service, February 2008.

Egan, J. *Signal Detection Theory and ROC Analysis*, Academic Press, 1975.

Elton, J., Gruber, M., Agrawal, D. and Mann, D. Explaining the Rate Spread on Corporate Bonds, *Journal of Finance 56*, pp. 449-470, 2001

Fisher, L. Determinants of Risk Premiums on Corporate Bonds, *Journal of Political Economy 67*(3), pp.217-237, 1959.

Finger, C., Finklestein, V., Pan, G., Lardy, J.P. and Ta, T. CreditGrades Technical Document, RiskMetrics Group, pp. 23-30, 2002.

Frey, J. Collateral Damage, *RISK*, April, pp. 91-94, 2000a.

Frey, J. Depressing Recoveries, *RISK*, November, pp. 108-111, 2000b.

Fridson, M. Anomaly in Intercapital Pricing? Merrill Lynch High Yield, October 1999.

Fridson, M. and Garman, M. Valuing Like-Rated Senior and Subordinated Debt, *Journal of Fixed Income*, pp. 83-93, December 1997.

Foulke, R. *Practical Financial Statement Analysis*, Fifth Edition, McGraw-Hill Book Company, pp. 13-19, 1961.

Geske, R. The Valuation of Compound Options, *Journal of Financial Economics 12*, pp. 211-235, 1979.

Gray, D. and Malone, S. *Microfinancial Risk Analysis*, John Wiley & Sons, Ltd., West Sussex, England, 2008.

Gray, D., Merton, R. and Bodie, Z. Contingent Claims Approach to Measuring and Managing Sovereign Credit Risk, *Journal of Investment Management* 5(4), pp. 5-28, 2007.

Green, D. and Swets, J. *Signal Detection Theory and Psychophysics*, John Wiley and Sons, New York, 1966.

Hickman, W. B. Corporate Bond Quality and Investor Experience, *Princeton University Press*, Princeton, N.J., 1958.

Horrigan, J. A Short History of Financial Ratio Analysis, *The Accounting Review 43* (2), pp. 284-294, 1968.

Hsu, J. Saa-Requejo, J. and Santa-Clara, P. A Structural Model of Default Risk, *Journal of Fixed Income*, pp. 77-94, Winter 2010.

Huang, J-Z. and Kong, W. Explaining Credit Spread Changes: New Evidence from Option-Bond Indexes, *Journal of Derivatives 11*, pp. 30-44, 2003.

Huang, J-Z. The Structural Approach to Modeling Credit Risk, In *Handbook of Quantitative Finance and Risk Management*, C.F. Lee (ed.), pp. 665-673, 2010.

Hull, J. and White, A. The Impact of Default Risk on the Prices of Options and Other Derivative Securities, *Journal of Banking and Finance 19*, pp. 299-322, 1995.

Janossi T., Jarrow R.A., and Yildirim Y., Estimating Default Probabilities Implicit in Equity Prices, *Journal of Investment Management*, First Quarter, pp. 1-30, 2003.

Jarrow, R. and Turnbull, S. Pricing Options on Derivatives Subject to Credit Risk, *Journal of Finance 1*, pp. 53-85, 1995.

Jones, E., S. Mason and Rosenfeld, E. Contingent Claims Analysis of Corporate Capital Structures: An Empirical Investigation, *Journal of Finance 39*, pp. 611-625, 1984.

Kao D.L., Estimating and Pricing Credit Risk: An Overview, *Financial Analysts Journal, 56*(4), pp. 50–66, 2000.

Kazemi, R. and Mosleh, A. Improving Default Risk Prediction using Bayesian Model Uncertainty Techniques, *Risk Analytics 32*(11), pp.1888-1900, 2012.

Kealhofer S. Credit Risk and Risk Management, AIMR Conference Proceedings, pp. 80–94, 1999.

Kealhofer, S. and Kurbat, M. The Default Prediction Power of the Merton Approach, Relative to Debt Ratings and Accounting Variables (KMV LLC), 2001.

Kim J., Ramaswamy, K. and Sunderasan, S., Does Default Risk in Coupons Affect the Valuation of Corporate Bonds? A Contingent Claims Model, *Financial Management*, pp. 117-131, 1993.

King, M. Why Good Gardeners Should Take Credit, Citi, November 2012

Lee, M., Su, Y. and Benzschawel, T. *Corporate Markets Quantitative Review*, Citi, June 17, 2014.

Leland, H.E. The Structural Approach to Credit Risk, *Frontiers in Credit-Risk Analysis*, AIMR Conference Proceedings, pp, 36–46, 1999.

Levin, J.W. and van Deventer D. R., The Simultaneous Analysis of Interest Rate and Credit Risk in *Controlling and Managing Interest Rate Risk* (A.G. Cornyn, R.A. Klein, and J. Lederman eds., New York Institute of Finance, New York, 1st Edition, pp. 494-506, 1997.

Li, W. A Default Risk Model under Macroeconomic Conditions, *Journal of Fixed Income 23*(2), pp. 98-113, 2013.

Lincoln, E. *Applied Business Finance*, 3rd revised edition, A. W. Shaw and Company, pp. 339-358, 1925.

Longstaff, F.A. and Schwartz, E.S., A Simple Approach to Valuing Risky Fixed and Floating Rate Debt, *Journal of Finance 50*, pp. 789–819, 1995.

Marose, R. A Financial Neural-Network Application, *AI Expert 5*, May 1990.

Marose, R., Rothenberg, D. and Sankaran, S. Knowledge Based Decision Support System for Accounting Auditors, In *Decision Support Systems: Experiences and Expectations*, T. Jelassi, M. Klein, and W. Mayon-White (Eds.), North-Holland, Amsterdam, 1992.

McDermott, G., Skarabot, J. and Kroujiline, A. Optimizing Selection of Credit Portfolios, *Quantitative Credit Analyst 1*, Citigroup, pp. 50-69, 2003.

McDermott, G., Skarabot, J. and Kroujiline, A. Optimizing Selection of Credit Portfolios, *The Journal of Portfolio Management 30*(3), pp. 112-123, 2004.

Merton, R. The Theory of Rational Options Pricing, *Bell Journal of Economics and Management Science 4*, pp. 141–183, 1973.

Merton, R. On the Pricing of Corporate Debt: The Risk Structures of Interest Rates. *Journal of Finance 29*, pp. 449-470, 1974.

Moody's Investors Service, Corporate Default and Recovery Rates, 1920-2009, February 2010.

Moody's Investors Service, Corporate Default and Recovery Rates, 1920-2009, February 2012.

Mortimer, A. Euromoney Country Risk, Euromoney Institutional Investor, PLC, http://www.euromoneycountryrisk.com, (Also available on request), 2013.

Neal, L. *The Rise of Financial Capitalism: International Capital Markets in the Age of Reason*, Cambridge: Cambridge University Press, 1990.

Nelson, C. R. and Siegel, A. F., Parsimonious Modeling of Yield Curves, *Journal of Business 60*(4), pp. 473-489, 1987.

Odom, M. D. and Sharda, R. A Neural Network Model for Bankruptcy Prediction, *Proceedings of the International Joint Conference on Neural Networks, Vol. II.* IEEE Neural Networks Council, pp. 163–171, 1990.

Ou, S., Chiu, D. and Metz, A. Annual Default Study: Corporate Default and Recovery Rates, 1920-2011, Moody's Investors Service, February 29, 2012.

Perry, C. Implied Default Probabilities: A New Approach to Risky Debt, *CS First Boston*, April 26, 1995.

Rosendale, W. H., Credit Department Methods, *Bankers' Magazine*, 1908

Roser, R., Bonne, G. and Smith-Hill, C. StarMine Text Mining Credit Risk Model: Overview and Performance, Thomson Reuters, 2013.

Schuermann, T. What Do We Know About Loss Given Default, In, *Recovery Risk*, Altman, Resti and Sironi (Eds.), Risk Books, London, pp. 3-24, 2005.

Schwarz, G. E. Estimating the Dimension of a Model, *Annals of Statistics 6*(2), pp. 461–464, 1978.

Schwartz E. S. and Moon, M. Rational Pricing of Internet Companies. *Financial Analysts Journal 5*, pp. 62-75, 2000.

Sobehart, J., Keenan, S. and Stein, R. Benchmarking Quantitative Default Risk Models: A Validation Methodology, Moody's Risk Management Services, 1999.

Sobehart, J. and Keenan, S. Hybrid Contingent Claims Models: A Practical Approach to Modeling Default Risk, *Credit Ratings: Methodology, Rationale and Default Risk*, M. Ong (ed.), Risk Books, 2002.

Sobehart, J. and Keenan, S. Hybrid Probability of Default Models: A Practical Approach to Modeling Default Risk, *Quantitative Credit Analyst 3*, pp. 5-29, 2003.

Sobehart, J., Keenan, S. and Stein, R. Benchmarking Quantitative Default Risk Models: A Validation Methodology, Moody's Special Comment, Moody's Investors Service, 2000.

Sobehart, J., Stein, R., Mikityanskaya, V. and Li, L. Moody's Public Firm Risk Model: A Hybrid Approach to Modeling Short-Term Default Risk, Moody's Investors Service, 2000.

Sobehart, J. Modeling Default Risk beyond Statistical, Structural and Reduced Form Approaches, Citigroup Risk Architecture, Presentation at Conference Advanced Credit Risk Measurement and Modeling Techniques, New York, March 14-15, 2005.

Sobehart, J. Citi Risk Architecture, Personal Communication, 2013.

Standard and Poor's, Standard and Poor's Extends Recovery Ratings to Unsecured Speculative-Grade Corporate Issuers, Ratings Direct, March 21, 2008.

Stein, R. Evidence on the Incompleteness of Merton-type Structural Models for Default Prediction, Moody's Risk Management Services, January 2, 2000.

Stein, R. Benchmarking Default Prediction Models: Pitfalls and Remedies in Model Validation, *Journal of Risk Model Validation 1*(1), pp. 77-113, 2007.

Salton, G. and McGill, M.J., *Introduction to Modern Information Retrieval*, McGraw Hill, New York, 1983.

Sylla, R. A Historical Primer on the Business of Credit Rating, Chapter 1 *in Ratings, Rating Agencies and the Global Financial System*, R.M Levich, G. Majnoni, and C. Reinhart (Eds.) Kluwer Academic Publishers, Boston, 2002.

Turnbull, S. Unresolved Issues in Modeling Credit-Risky Assets, *Journal of Fixed Income 15*(1), pp. 68-87, 2005.

Vasicek, O. EDF and Corporate Bond Pricing, KMV, 1995.

Varma, P. and Cantor, R. Determinants of Recovery Rates on Defaulted Bonds and Loans for North American Corporate Issuers: 1983-2003. Moody's Investors Service, December 2004.

Vazza, D., Aurora, D. and Miller, C. U.S. Recovery Study: Liquidity Avalanche Propels Recovery Rates into the Stratosphere, Standard & Poor's, February 2007.

Verde, M. Recovery Rates Return to Historic Norms, Fitch Ratings, September 2003.

Wall, A. Study of Credit Biometrics, *Federal Reserve Bulletin*, 229-243, March 1919.

CHAPTER TWO

A SUMMARY OF "ASSESSING THE CREDIT RISK OF MONEY MARKET FUNDS DURING THE EUROZONE CRISIS"

SEAN COLLINS AND EMILY GALLAGHER[1]

Based on our working paper entitled "Assessing the Credit Risk of Money Market Funds During the Eurozone Crisis," this chapter summarizes a new measure for assessing credit risk in prime money market funds (MMFs) and studies how such credit risk evolved during the Eurozone crisis of 2011-2012.[2]

An analysis of this type is important because, in the five business days following the default of Lehman Brothers in September 2008, MMFs experienced redemptions totaling over $300 billion. Unlike banks, MMFs neither hold capital against credit losses nor are insured by the federal government. Instead, credit risks in MMFs are mitigated by liquidity, maturity, credit rating, and diversification limits on funds' portfolios as mandated by the Securities and Exchange Commission (SEC). In the aftermath of the Lehman Brothers default, the SEC significantly tightened money market fund regulations. Regulators, press reports, and some academic studies (e.g., Chernenko and Sunderam, 2014; Rosengren, 2012) have questioned whether the new, tighter regulations were sufficient to constrain credit risks in MMF portfolios during periods of market stress. These studies cite the rapidly deteriorating credit quality during 2011-2012 of certain European banks in which MMFs held substantial investments.

---

[1] The authors are from the Paris School of Economics. Email: emgallag@gmail.com.

[2] We focus only on the credit risk in prime MMF portfolios. Prime MMFs are money market funds that invest in a range of money market securities, including commercial paper, bank CDs, medium-term and floating-rate notes, repurchase agreements (repos), and Treasury and agency securities. Government money market funds typically invest only in Treasury or agency securities or repos backed by Treasuries and agencies and therefore should be default-risk-free.

Based on the scale of their investments in European banks, these studies suggest that credit risk in prime MMFs rose markedly during the second half of 2011. If true, this could indicate that the SEC's 2010 reforms to MMFs were insufficient to prevent a replay of September 2008.

Our working paper offers a detailed analysis of the scale and sources of credit risk in MMF portfolios during the Eurozone crisis. We begin by developing a method for assessing credit risks in MMF portfolios. At first glance, the most obvious way to estimate the credit risk on an MMF is by the difference between the yield on a prime MMF and the yield on a comparable government-only MMF. If a fund holds a security and that security's credit quality declines, the security's market price should also decline, boosting the security's market yield. But because funds use amortized cost accounting, a rise in the security's yield would not be immediately reflected in the fund's yield. Generally speaking, only if that security matures and the fund rolls over its holding of that security, would the fund's yield then rise to reflect the increased credit risk. Thus, to study credit risk in MMFs, we must first develop a market-based risk measure. Next, we use this measure to study the evolution of MMF portfolio credit risks during the Eurozone crisis of 2011-2012. The goal is to understand (a) how much credit risk resided in MMF portfolios over this period and (b) whether increases in MMF credit risks were attributable to their investments in European banks or other factors.

In theory, CDS premiums could be used to measure the credit risk in MMF portfolios. Numerous recent studies have sought either to assess the credit risk or capital adequacy of banks using CDS premiums. For example, Segoviano and Goodhart (2009) treat the entire banking system as a portfolio, the riskiness of which is based on the CDS premiums of individual banks. Other studies have used 5-year CDS premiums to assess systemic risk in bank portfolios at a fixed horizon, such as over the next quarter or the coming year (Avesani, Pascual, and Li, 2006; Huang, Zhou, and Zhu, 2009). Money market funds pose a unique problem in that the bulk of their assets are very short-term, typically maturing in 3 months or less, while CDS premiums are not generally quoted at maturities of less than 6 months.

To deal with this, we use a novel dataset of "synthetic" CDS premiums for short-dated securities based on default probabilities obtained from the Risk Management Institute (RMI) at the University of Singapore. We match these estimated CDS premiums with the characteristics of the securities money market funds hold (such as a security's issuer, amortized cost value, maturity, and security type) collected from SEC form N-MFP. For example, if a fund holds a Ford Motor medium-term note that has a remaining maturity of 3 months, that note is matched with Ford Motor's annualized 3-month cumulative default probability. This default probability is multiplied by the presumed default loss rate on Ford Motor to generate a synthetic 3-month CDS premium for the security. Aggregating (on an asset-weighted basis) across all of a fund's holdings provides an estimate of the "expected loss-to-maturity" (ELM) of the fund's portfolio under the assumption that the fund holds each security until it matures (or defaults). Because the term structure of CDS premiums is normally upward sloping for high quality issuers (Agrawal and Bohn, 2006; Han and Zhou, 2011), we expect ELM to be lowest for those MMFs with the shortest portfolio maturities.

Specifically, we define expected loss-to-maturity (ELM) for a given fund at a given moment in time to be:

$$ELM = \sum_i^I \sum_j^J w_{ij} CDS_i(T_j) \qquad (1)$$

where w_{ij} is the proportion of a fund's assets invested in security j issued by issuer I, and $CDS_i(T_j)$ is the expected loss (annual rate) on security j issued by i with remaining life T_j.

As noted, CDS premiums are not generally quoted for maturities of fewer than 6 months. To make Equation (1) operational, we use default probabilities provided by RMI. As the next section discusses, RMI creates forward-looking default probabilities for about 50,000 issuers worldwide for maturities of 1, 3, 6, 9, 12, 18, and 24 months. We interpolate these to obtain $p_i(T_j)$ for any intervening maturity. These maturity-matched cumulative default probabilities are then annualized such that $\widetilde{p}_i(T_j)$ is the annualized counterpart of $p_i(T_j)$. Given the RMI default probabilities (or interpolated values), we approximate the annualized CDS premium for insuring against credit losses on issuer i as:

$$C\widehat{D}S_i(T_j) = (1 - R_i)\widetilde{p}_i(T_j) = (1 - R_i)\{1 - [1 - p_i(T_j)]^{360/T_j}\} \qquad (2)$$

where R_i is the recovery rate on an issuer i's securities in the event of a default. Substituting Equation (2) into Equation (1) gives:

$$ELM = \sum_i^I \sum_j^J w_{ij} (1 - R_i)\widetilde{p}_i(T_j) \qquad (3)$$

ELM approximates the expected loss on a fund's portfolio and is useful for measuring a fund's overall credit risk.

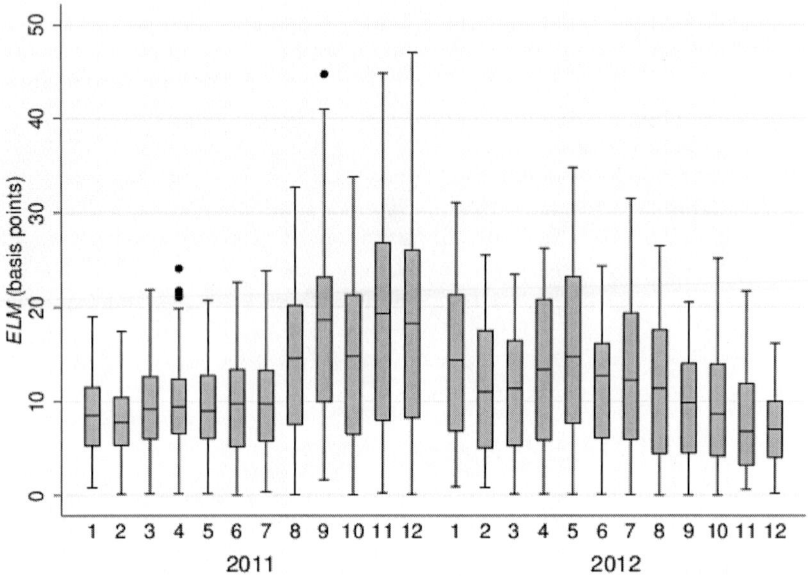

Figure 1. Distribution of ELM by Fund, Jan 2011-Dec 2012. This figure shows box-and-whisker plots of ELM, respectively, across funds by month. Rectangles represent the interquartile range (IQR), which extends from the 25th to 75th percentile, and the median is the horizontal line in the middle of the rectangle. The ends in the lines extending from below and above the rectangle represent the minimum and maximum values in the ranges from Q1 − 1.5*IQR to Q1 and from Q3to Q3 + 1.5*IQR, respectively. If observations exist outside of this range (i.e., in the top or bottom 0.35 percentiles of a normal distribution), they are considered to be outliers and are denoted with a dot.

Our results indicate that credit risk in prime MMFs, as measured by ELM, is small, averaging just 15 basis points from January 2011 to December 2012 on an asset-weighted basis. By comparison the 6-month and 5-year CDS premium on JPMorgan Chase, a relatively higher credit-quality large U.S. bank, averaged 36 and 112 basis points, respectively, and the 6-month CDS premium on BNP Paribas averaged 106 basis points over this same period. Nonetheless, the credit risk exposure of prime funds doubled during the peak of the Eurozone crisis. ELM rose from 12 basis points in January 2011 to 23 basis points in December 2011 before receding to 10 basis points in December 2012. That rise is consistent with the market's intensifying concerns about Eurozone banks, a deteriorating outlook for the U.S. economy, and the looming U.S. federal government debt ceiling crisis. Still, the rise was small compared to increases in CDS premiums on global banks over the same period. Asset-weighted averages of ELM across time, however, mask cross-sectional variation in funds' credit risks (Figure 1). The standard deviation of ELM was 4 basis points in January 2011. This rose to 11 basis points in December 2011. The maximum expected loss in any individual prime MMF was 47 basis points in December 2011, while the minimum was just slightly above zero. This reflects heterogeneity in the funds' portfolio holdings, some concentrating a larger portion of their assets in U.S. Treasury and agency securities and others more invested in bank-issued debt.

The common perception is that the credit risk of prime MMFs increased in mid-to-late 2011 because these funds held, or even increased, their holdings of securities issued by Eurozone banks in order to boost fund yields (e.g., Chernenko and Sunderam, 2014; Rosengren, 2012). Our results present a rather different picture. Our key finding is that MMF holdings of Eurozone or other European banks did not contribute importantly to the increase in the average credit risk of prime MMFs in the second half of 2011.

In the second half of 2011, prime fund managers acted to reduce their exposure to the Eurozone crisis. Most notably, prime MMFs reduced the portion of their bank holdings issued by French-domiciled banks from 20 percent in May 2011 to just 3 percent by December 2011. As prime funds pulled back from the Eurozone, they reallocated their investments to regions presumably more insulated from the Eurozone crisis, including the U.S., Canada, certain Northern European countries, and, most notably, the Asia/Pacific region. Prime funds' assets attributable to Asian/Pacific-domiciled banks rose by $55 billion and went from 15 to 26 percent of prime MMF bank-issued investments. This increase went primarily to banks headquartered in Japan. From May to December 2011, the portion of prime funds' bank assets issued by Japanese banks doubled. By December 2011, prime funds had more assets invested in Asian/Pacific banks than they did in France, Germany, and the UK combined, representing a sharp reversal from earlier in the year.

In addition, prime funds mitigated credit risks from European issuers by lowering the WAL (final legal maturity) of their remaining holdings in European-domiciled banks. The WAL for prime funds' French, German, and UK bank holdings fell from around 70 days in May 2011 to below 30 days in December 2011. At the same time, the maturities of funds' U.S. and Canadian bank holdings remained roughly constant.

The actions prime funds took to insulate themselves from the Eurozone crisis would have been more effective had financial conditions not deteriorated outside the Eurozone. Figure 2 plots the index of 5-year CDS premiums for large European financial institutions (i.e., the Markit iTraxx senior financial index).[3] The figure also plots the averages of 5-year CDS premiums for selected large Japanese, Australian, and U.S. banks. The CDS premiums on Japanese and Australian banks are almost always lower than the European CDS index. Thus, all else equal, by shifting their portfolios toward banks in Japan and Australia, prime MMFs expected to reduce risk. But, as shown here, the three series are correlated. Notably, the 5-year CDS premiums for the Japanese and Australian banks rose from low levels (100 basis points or less) in January 2011 to over 250 basis points on October 4, the same day the 5-year CDS index for European financials hit its highest level (296 basis points) up to that point in 2011. CDS premiums on Japanese banks, and to a lesser extent on Australian banks, spiked again in late November when the CDS index on European financials hit its highest point ever (355 basis points).

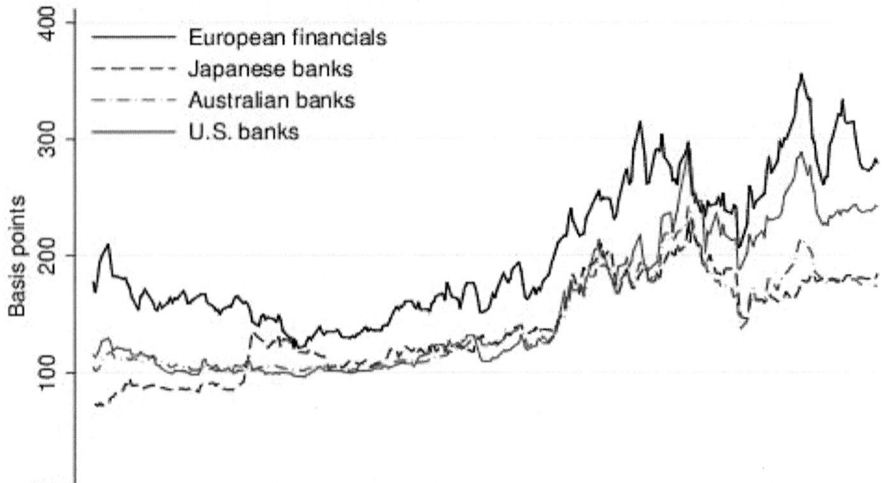

Note: The CDS premium for European financials is the iTraxx senior financial index for Europe. The CDS premiums for large Japanese, Australian, and U.S. banks is the average of 5-year CDS premiums for (Sumitomo Bank and Mizuho Bank), (National Australia Bank, Westpac, and ANZ), and (Bank of America, JPMorgan Chase, Citi, Wells Fargo, and Goldman Sachs), respectively.

Figure 2. 5-Year CDS Premiums for Banks, by Region, 2011.

[3] Canadian banks are excluded because their CDS is thinly traded.

Results from our ELM measure are consistent with the circumstantial evidence presented above, which indicates that prime funds were, at least to some extent, passive recipients of contagion from Eurozone banks to the global banking system. A fund's ELM is just the weighted sum of the estimated CDS on the fund's portfolio securities. Therefore, to determine the contributions to the credit risk of a group of funds by region, we simply calculate a weighted sum of the estimated CDS premiums on these funds' portfolio securities by the region of the issuer. We restrict our sample to only funds with top quartile credit risk (as measured by ELM) as of May 2011, just before the worsening of the Eurozone crisis. These funds tended to have higher European bank exposure and were arguably least prepared for the coming shock. Figure 3 shows results of a counterfactual comparing ELM to the ELM that would have occurred had prime funds continued throughout the remainder of 2011 to hold the portfolios they held in May 2011 (in other words, had they not taken steps to insulate their portfolios from the Eurozone crisis). It confirms that funds made significant efforts to lower their credit exposure to European banks. Among this group of funds, the actual contribution from Europe to ELM increased by 4 basis points from May to December. This is small compared to a counterfactual increase of 14 basis points had these funds not acted to reduce their European credit exposure. It also confirms that, even among the riskiest funds, the Asian/Pacific region contributed more than Europe to funds' credit risk during the Eurozone crisis. This is true both in absolute terms and in relative changes.

Funds' European investments do not appear to be the primary reasons the credit risks of prime MMFs rose in the second half of 2011. Instead, the rise was primarily due to an increased contribution from prime fund investments in banks domiciled in the Asian/Pacific region. As credit conditions deteriorated for Eurozone banks in the fall of 2011, MMFs drastically reduced their holdings of Eurozone bank debt and shortened the maturities of their remaining Eurozone holdings. This offset, to a great extent, an increase in the credit risk attributable to Eurozone banks. At the same time, prime funds increased their holdings of bank debt in Canada, Norway, Australia/New Zealand, and Japan. In the fall of 2011, however, as the economic outlook deteriorated in the Eurozone, CDS premiums rose on banks across the world, including through the Asian/Pacific region. Some of this likely reflected concerns that the failure of a large Eurozone bank would reverberate across the world financial system. More generally, slowing global economic growth might also have lowered the credit quality of banks in the Asian/Pacific region and other export-driven economies. Standard and Poor's August 5th, 2011, downgrade of the U.S.

sovereign debt credit rating also may have contributed to the rise in CDS premiums among large global banks. Finally, the credit quality of Japanese banks might have suffered from the lingering impact of the March 2011 tsunami (including Japan's nuclear power plant issues).

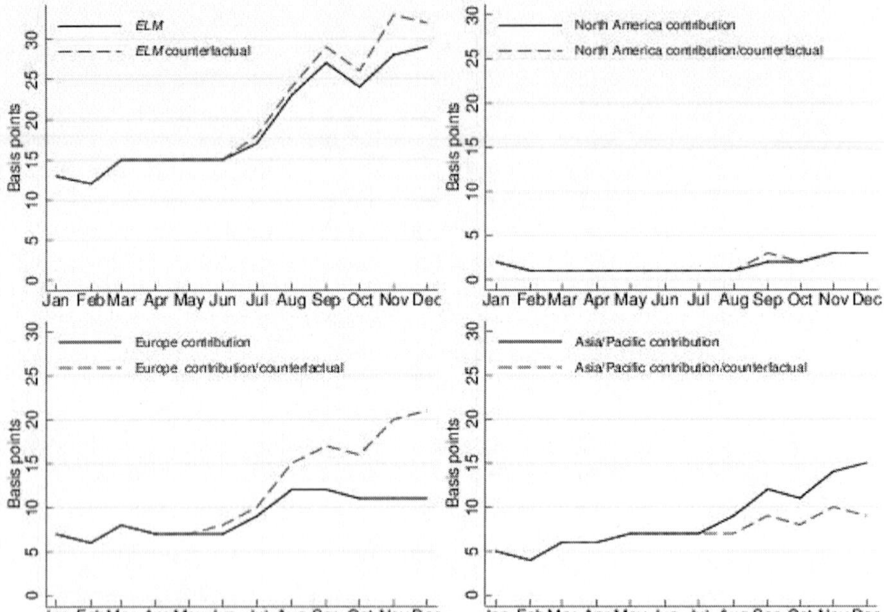

Figure 3. Actual and Counterfactual ELM, 2011, Top Quartile Funds by Credit Exposure, Contributions by Region. Note: Using a restricted sample of funds with top quartile credit risk (as measured by ELM) as of May 2011, this figure shows actual and counterfactual values for ELM (upper left panel). ELM is the value-weighted sum of the estimated CDS premiums on portfolio securities. Counterfactual values are constructed on the assumption that prime funds continued to hold throughout 2011 the portfolios they held in May 2011. The other panels in the chart show the contributions of the three regions (North America, Europe, and Asia/Pacific) to ELM or to counterfactual ELM, respectively. The contributions of the three regions total to the actual and counterfactual ELM measures in the upper-left panel.

This growth in global credit risk, combined with the increased holdings of MMFs in regions outside the Eurozone, largely explains why prime MMFs experienced a rise in measured credit risk in the second half of 2011. Given that Eurozone developments only indirectly affected banks in the Asian/Pacific region, we conclude that the increase in the credit risk of prime MMFs in the second half of 2011 reflected contagion in the worldwide banking system, not actions taken by MMFs.

References

Agrawal, D., J. Bohn: *Humpbacks in Credit Spreads*. 2006.

Han, B., Y. Zhou: *Understanding the Term Structure of Credit Default Swap Spreads*. 2011.

Avesani, R., A. Pascual, J. Li: *A New Risk Indicator and Stress Testing Tool: A Multifactor Nth-to-Default CDS Basket*. 2006.

Rosengren, E.: *Money Market Mutual Funds and Financial Stability*. 2012.

Segoviano, M., C. Goodhart: *Banking Stability Measures*. 2009.

Chernenko, Sergey, Adi Sunderam: "Frictions in Shadow Banking: Evidence from the Lending Behavior of Money Market Funds," *Review of Financial Studies*, pp. 1717-1750, 2014.

Huang, Xin, Hao Zhou, Haibin Zhu: "A Framework for Assessing the Systemic Risk of Major Financial Institutions," *Journal of Banking and Finance*, pp. 2036-2049, 2009.

CHAPTER THREE

CREDIT RISK MODELING IN SEGMENTED PORTFOLIOS: AN APPLICATION TO CREDIT CARDS

JOSÉ J. CANALS-CERDÁ AND SOUGATA KERR[1]

Abstract

The Great Recession offers a unique opportunity to analyze the performance of credit risk models under conditions of economic stress. We focus on the performance of models of credit risk applied to risk-segmented credit cards portfolios. Specifically, we focus on models of default and loss and analyze three important sources of model risk: model selection, model specification, and sample selection. Forecast errors can be significant along any of these three model-risk dimensions. Simple linear regression models are not generally outperformed by more complex or stylized models. The impact of macroeconomic variables is heterogeneous across risk segments. Model specifications that do not take into account this heterogeneity display large projection errors across risk segments. Prime segments are proportionally more severely impacted by downturn economic conditions relative to subprime or near-prime segments. The

---

[1] The views expressed in the paper are those of the authors and do not necessarily reflect the views of the Federal Reserve Bank of Philadelphia or the Federal Reserve System. Any errors or omissions are the responsibility of the authors. We thank Sharon Tang for outstanding research assistance and Jessica Weber for outstanding editorial assistance. Contact information: José J. Canals-Cerdá, Federal Reserve Bank of Philadelphia, 10 Independence Mall, Philadelphia, PA 19106. Phone: (215) 574-4127, Fax: (215) 574-4146, e-mail: Jose.Canals-Cerda@phil.frb.org. Corresponding author: Sougata Kerr, Federal Reserve Bank of Philadelphia, 10 Independence Mall, Philadelphia, PA 19106. Phone: (215) 574-4127, Fax: (215) 574-4146, e-mail: sougata.kerr@phil.frb.org.

sensitivity of modeled losses to macroeconomic factors is conditional on the model development sample. Models estimated over a period that does not incorporate a significant period of the Great Recession may fail to project default rates, or loss rates, consistent with those experienced during the Great Recession.

Introduction

In this paper we analyze the relative loss-forecasting performance of credit risk models applied at an aggregated risk-segment level to a representative credit card portfolio. Our main emphasis is on the analysis of model development elements that may impact default/loss forecasting under stressed economic conditions, while the lessons learned may also apply more broadly to the modeling of credit risk in segmented portfolios.

Although the use of loan level models is widespread, risk segmentation continues to be widely used across banks and other financial companies with different levels of complexity. The use of segmentation is also an important component in the analysis of credit risk within the advanced Basel II framework. Reasons for the use of data at an aggregate segment level vary from data availability, to time constraints, to simplicity of approach, among others. In this paper we analyze the performance of a variety of models and model specifications taking advantage of a panel dataset of a representative credit card portfolio aggregated at a risk-segment level. Specifically, our primary focus is on the analysis of the one-year default rate and loss rate at the segment level. We focus our attention on three dimensions of model risk: model selection, model specification assumptions, and sample selection.

Our analysis employs a panel data set of credit card accounts from the Equifax Credit Bureau over the period 2001-2011. The data cover the Great Recession and afford us the opportunity to analyze the performance of credit risk models under conditions of significant economic stress. We consider a variety of approaches for the estimation of models of default and loss rate. Linear regression represents the most simple and straightforward approach. We also consider potential improvements on simple regression that have been suggested in recent empirical literature, relying on transformations of the dependent variable (Ferrari and Cribari–Neto, 2004; Ospina and Ferrari 2010, 2012). Finally, we also consider flexible parametric and semi-parametric model specifications (for a survey, see Li, Qi, Zhang and Zhao, 2014). Interestingly, the linear regression projections compare favorably to other, more sophisticated models. The regression model seems to have a slight edge in the projection of the initial increase in default rates at the start of the recession. In contrast, flexible parametric models seem to have a slight edge in the projection of the decrease in default rates as the recession subsides. It is not possible to isolate what aspect of model design contributes to the better performance of a specific model in certain circumstances, but it seems that the simplicity and flexibility of the regression approach allows it to overcome some well-known limitations of the model.

Our analysis also indicates that loss projections can be significantly impacted by model specification assumptions. Models that overlook potential interactions between macroeconomic conditions and segment characteristics can result in the significant under-projection of prime portfolio losses under stressed economic conditions. Surprisingly, relative to the subprime borrowers, near-prime and prime borrowers in the portfolio are proportionally more severely impacted by economic downturns and model specification assumptions. Also, models estimated over a time frame that does not include a representative economic downturn period may not project levels of credit loss consistent with losses experienced during the Great Recession of 2007-09. Once again, the projection error seems to be much larger for the prime segment relative to the subprime segment.

Reliance on models as tools for effective supervision and risk surveillance has increased significantly within regulatory agencies over the years, with the advent of the Internal Ratings Based (IRB) approach to regulatory capital postulated in the Basel II accord. More recently, in the Comprehensive Capital Analysis and Review (CCAR) exercise now mandated by the Dodd-Frank Wall Street Reform and Consumer Protection Act, the Federal Reserve conducts its own independent assessment of capital adequacy through periodic stress testing across participant banks as a benchmark of the banks' own stress-test analysis. Because complex credit risk models are the foundation for these exercises, it is paramount to evaluate and mitigate risks associated with the development and implementation of these models. Recent regulatory guides on model risk (OCC Bulletin 2011-12 and FED SR Letter 11-7, "Supervisory Guidance on Model Risk Management"), along with their antecedents (primarily OCC Bulletin 2000-16), stress and highlight the important aspects of model risk management, including model development, implementation, use, validation, governance, policies, and controls' structure.

Credit card portfolios constitute the largest unsecured loan portfolios at most large banks. The net charge□off rate for credit card portfolios increased more than twofold for a number of large banks during the peak of the financial crisis, and it is estimated that more than $160 billion of credit card debt has been charged off since 2008.[2] Further, recent stress tests conducted by banks and regulators showed the importance of credit card portfolios as a potential source of losses for banks in the event of a severe economic downturn. In particular, projected losses from card portfolios of the largest banks participating in the 2012-13 DFAST stress-test exercise totaled $87 billion, or 19% of overall projected losses, over the projected stress period. Only trading and counterparty losses represented a larger share of projected losses, at $97 billion, while losses from first-mortgage portfolios were projected at $61 billion, and losses for other types of mortgage exposure (junior liens, HELOC, etc.) were projected at $56 billion.[3]

Early studies on credit card portfolios over the business cycle did not find conclusive evidence of macroeconomic factors having an impact on portfolio losses. Gross and Souleles (2002) analyze credit card delinquency and personal bankruptcy in the 1990s using panel data on credit card accounts. The authors conclude that the relationship between default and economic fundamentals appears to have changed substantially over the period of study in ways not explained by their control variables; however, they did not find unemployment to have a significant impact on credit card default. Agarwal and Liu (2003) also examine credit card delinquency and bankruptcy behavior. They note that previous empirical studies did not consistently find a significant effect of macroeconomic factors on bankruptcy either because of inadequate data or a lack of sufficient variation in the unemployment variable during the period of analysis. Their analysis indicates that the level of unemployment appears to be a significant determinant of default, while the change in unemployment is usually insignificant. In contrast, Banerjee and Canals-Cerdá (2012), taking advantage of significant variation in macroeconomic variables, risk exposure, and performance outcomes experienced during the Great Recession, report that both the level and the change in unemployment are statistically and materially significant determinants of credit card defaults. Banerjee and Canals-Cerdá (2012) also report that unemployment was not a relevant factor in the account balance exposure at default (EAD) during the Great Recession.

---

[2] Data are from bank call reports and other regulatory filings (Figure 1); see also Hunt (2013). The net charge-off rate peaked at the time of the financial crisis, propelled by an increase in the net dollar charge-off rate and a decline in dollars outstanding.

[3] Board of Governors of the Federal Reserve System (2013): "Dodd-Frank Act Stress Test 2013: Supervisory Stress Test Methodology and Results, March 2013."

A recent paper by Canals-Cerdá and Kerr (2014) explores potential sources of model risks in loan level credit risk models. In their paper, loan level credit losses are decomposed into probability of default (PD) and exposure at default (EAD) and modeled separately using survival analysis and linear regression. Their analysis shows that macroeconomic variables have a strong and heterogeneous impact on an account's likelihood and timing of default but play a much smaller role in an account's projected exposure at default. The proportionally larger impact of unemployment on the near-prime and prime segments in the Great Recession lead them to conclude that model specifications matter more for prime segments than for subprime. Finally, they extend their analysis to alternative scenarios and show the dramatic importance of scenarios in loss projection. The analysis conducted in this paper complements research by Canals-Cerdá and Kerr (2014) by looking at the impact of model choice and model specification assumptions, as well as sample selection, with a focus on aggregated segment-level panel data models.

In the next section, we present the data and provide descriptive statistics for some key variables in our sample. Section 3 contains the empirical methodology. Section 4 presents empirical results and analysis, while Section 5 concludes the paper. Tables and figures are presented in Section 7.

Data and Descriptive Analysis

We have access to a panel data set containing historical trade-line credit card information from a 5% random sample of individuals with a credit file in Equifax's consumer database, one of the major credit bureaus in the United States. The data is updated biannually and includes information on credit card account characteristics, such as account age, line, and utilization; account balances; and current and past delinquencies as well as an individual's Equifax credit score. Given the enormous size of the original data set, we employ a 1% random sub-sample from the sample described above in our analysis.

For simplicity of exposition, we focus our analysis on the one-year default experience of accounts current at the time of observation, and we expand our research to an analysis of losses. The one-year default experience of accounts delinquent at the time of observation can also be modeled using the framework developed in this paper, but it is recommended to model delinquent accounts separately from current accounts due to their significantly higher default rate. Delinquent accounts represent a small percentage of accounts in a representative cards portfolio due to a low incidence of delinquency and a high rate of transition to default. Thus, delinquent accounts are likely to contribute significantly to portfolio losses in the short run, whereas current accounts are likely to contribute to portfolio losses over a longer time horizon.

Table 1 lists the primary risk drivers employed in our statistical analysis of credit risk. Relevant variables include a proprietary account-specific Equifax risk score, account balance, account line, and account utilization (defined as the percentage of the credit line that is being utilized). We consider level and change in unemployment as primary measures of economic activity driving credit card default. We also include a second quarter dummy in our models to account for potential patterns of seasonality in credit card defaults.

In our investigation, we employ segmented data; the unit of analysis is a segment of accounts where at each observation point segments are defined according to the score, line, and utilization ranges described in table 1, as well as state as the unit of regional variation in macroeconomic risk drivers. We employ a panel with information on credit card account performance from 2001 to 2011. We observe account information in the months of June and December, including historical information on monthly account performance. The payment status of each loan in a cohort is followed for four consecutive quarters, and segment performance variables are derived from this information. The last performance period is December 2011.

Figure 1 provides information on the historical values of macroeconomic variables and credit card delinquencies. The macroeconomic variables considered in our study have experienced significant variation during the period of analysis. Unemployment remained relatively stable between 2000 and 2007, with a record low unemployment rate of 4% in year 2000 and a maximum unemployment rate of 6.3% in June 2003. Unemployment increased significantly between 2007 and 2009, from about 4.4% to about 10%, and recovered gradually thereafter. Unemployment and credit card charge-offs historically have moved together, although charge-offs decreased at a more rapid pace in the most recent period.

Table 1. Variable Definitions.

Risk Score (sp; np; p; spp)	*Borrower's Credit score dummies for ranges 250-650, 650-710, 710-770, 770+*
Line (low, medium, high)	*Credit limit dummies for ranges less than $1500, $1500-$10000, and $10000+*
Util (low, medium, high)	*Utilization dummies for ranges between zero and 25%, 25%-90%, and 90%+*
Seasonality	*Indicator for second and fourth quarter*
Ur.	*State-level unemployment rate with a 6 months lag*
Chg. Ur. 12m.	*Change in unemployment rate over the last 12 months with a 6 months lag*

Note: ‘sp’ refers to subprime, ‘np’ refers to near-prime, ‘p’ refers to prime, and ‘spp’ refers to super-prime.

Figure 1 Credit Card 120 days past due balance to outstanding ratio and Unemployment Rate over time.

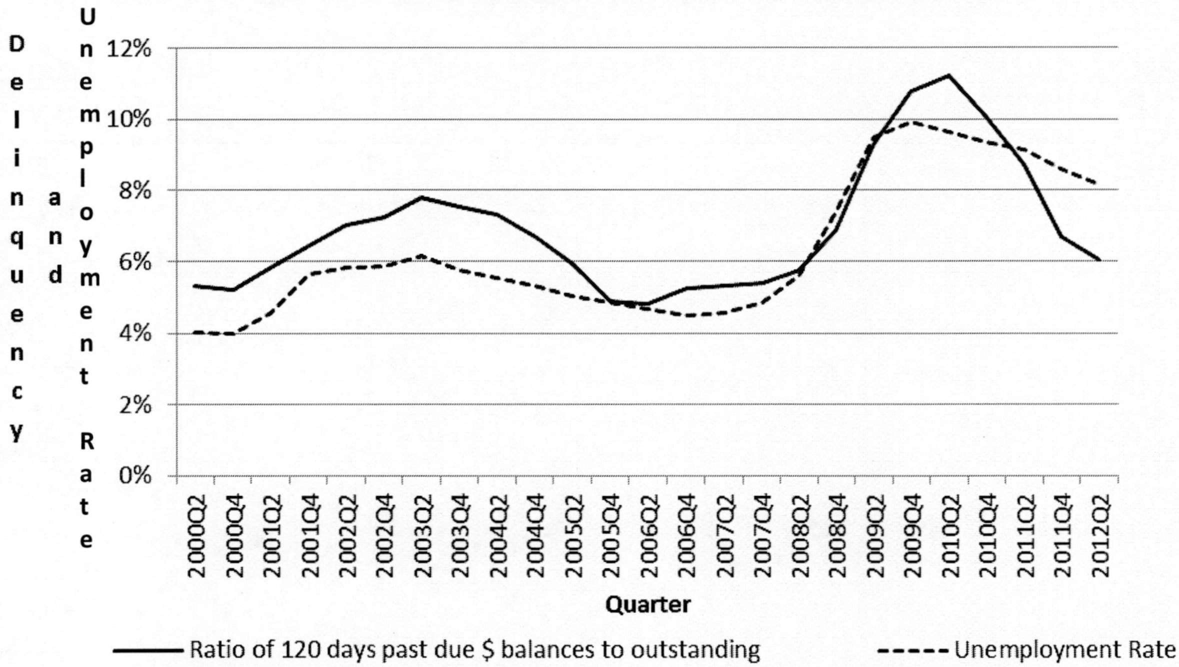

Sources: Aggregated Call Report data for insured commercial banks, Bureau of Labor Statistics.

Table 2a. Default rates across risk segments.

Variable	2001-03	2004-6	2007	2008	2009	2010	2011
Risk Score							
Subprime	15.3%	13.1%	13.6%	16.1%	17.3%	15.5%	11.7%
Near-prime	2.5%	2.4%	2.6%	3.5%	4.8%	4.3%	3.0%
Prime	0.5%	0.6%	0.7%	0.9%	1.6%	1.6%	1.0%
Super-prime	0.1%	0.1%	0.1%	0.1%	0.2%	0.2%	0.2%
Line							
Low	9.9%	8.2%	8.9%	11.2%	11.2%	8.9%	6.0%
Medium	3.8%	3.2%	3.1%	3.8%	4.8%	4.1%	2.8%
High	1.1%	1.1%	1.0%	1.4%	2.1%	2.0%	1.4%
Utilization							
Low	1.3%	1.1%	1.1%	1.2%	1.4%	1.1%	0.8%
Medium	5.5%	4.5%	4.4%	5.2%	5.9%	5.3%	3.9%
High	13.0%	11.6%	12.4%	15.4%	16.4%	13.7%	8.4%

Note: Descriptive statistics are account weighted at the segment level. Data source Equifax.

Table 2b. Loss rates, for 60 days past due balance over outstanding ratio, across risk segments.

Variable	2001-03	2004-6	2007	2008	2009	2010	2011
Risk Score							
Subprime	23.5%	20.4%	22.5%	27.3%	28.4%	21.6%	16.7%
Near-prime	5.4%	5.6%	6.7%	8.2%	9.8%	8.2%	5.7%
Prime	1.4%	1.5%	1.7%	2.4%	3.9%	3.6%	2.1%
Super-prime	0.3%	0.2%	0.2%	0.4%	0.6%	0.7%	0.3%
Line							
Low	11.1%	10.0%	11.3%	14.1%	14.1%	10.7%	7.1%
Medium	6.3%	6.2%	7.0%	8.4%	9.6%	7.2%	5.5%
High	3.7%	3.4%	3.8%	5.8%	7.8%	6.8%	4.7%
Utilization							
Low	6.8%	6.0%	7.1%	9.2%	10.2%	7.0%	4.5%
Medium	5.4%	4.8%	5.4%	6.7%	7.3%	6.3%	5.0%
High	10.9%	10.5%	11.5%	13.9%	15.4%	12.6%	8.5%

Note: Descriptive statistics are account weighted at the segment level. Data source Equifax.

Table 2 presents historical average performance across risk segments for the outcome variables analyzed. Outcome variables of interest considered are measure of default and measure of loss, both represented in the form of ratios. The default rate considered is defined as the ratio of accounts that became 120 days past due within a one-year period for each segment of accounts considered. The loss rate considered is defined as the ratio of account balances that become at least 60 days past due within a one year period for each segment of accounts. We chose to compute the loss rate for accounts that become 60 days past due to avoid potential measurement error problems associated with Bank reporting of account information for more severe delinquencies. While our analysis was conducted at the segment level, any reported statistical results are weighted by the number of accounts per segment.

As expected, default and loss rates are higher for low score segments and low line segments and lower for low utilization segments. Default and loss rates are significantly higher during the most recent recession years. Interestingly, the increase in default and loss rates, from their low values of the 2004-2006 period to their highest values observed in 2009, are proportionally larger for higher risk-score segments. Specifically, default rates for the lowest risk-score, or subprime segment, increased from 20.4% to 28.4%, a 40% increase, while default rates for the higher risk-score, or super-prime segment, increased from 0.2% to 0.6%, or a 300% increase.

Empirical Methodology

The use of loan-level statistical methods for the analysis of credit risk in retail portfolios is of common use in finance. However, the use of portfolio segmentation in the analysis of credit risk in retail portfolios continues to be employed regularly across financial companies, particularly among less sophisticated institutions. Furthermore, risk segmentation represents the basis for analysis of regulatory capital for credit risk in the Basel 2 framework.

In this section, we describe the empirical framework for the analysis of default rate and loss rate defined at the segment level. We highlight technical difficulties associated with the analysis of this type of data and review alternative approaches that can be employed to deal with these problems. In the empirical section of the paper, we compare results from different methods.

As a first step, we begin with analysis of the standard linear regression framework. Specifically, we consider the following linear specification for the relationship between the loss rate, or the rate of default, and a vector of risk drivers, including macroeconomic variables,

$$r_{it} = \beta_0 + \beta_1 X_{it} + \varepsilon_{it}.$$

A problem with this specification is that the regression framework implicitly assumes that the dependent variable is defined in the real line, whereas in our case r_{it} takes values in the unit interval. Specifically, the natural restriction of a ratio taking values in the unit interval is not embedded in the simple linear regression model. As a result, predictions using this specification may fall outside of the unit interval in certain cases. A growing econometric literature proposes applying different types of transformations of the dependent variable as a first step toward resolving this problem. These transformations can be broadly described as non-linear parametric functions from the open unit interval to the space of real numbers. A common example is the logit transformation, where logit(r) = log[r/(1-r)]. Typically the transformations suggested in the literature are not well defined at the 0 or 1 boundaries; this is clearly the case for the logit transformation. To avoid the {0,1} boundary problem, researchers often proceed in two steps: first they consider a transformation from the [0,1] interval into the (0,1) interval and then a transformation from the open-unit-interval to the real line. For example, Smithson and Verkuilen (2006) propose a transformation of the form r' = (r(N-1) + 0.5)/N, with N representing the sample size. In general, if we define the compounded transformation from [0,1] into the real line as R(•), the proposed approach in this literature specifies a linear regression of the form,

$$R_{it} = \beta_0 + \beta_1 X_{it} + \varepsilon_{it},$$

where $R_{it} = R(r_{it})$ represents a transformation of the original rate variable. This regression can be estimated using standard OLS techniques, and predicted values for the transformed dependent variable, denoted $\widehat{R_{it}}$, can be derived from the estimated regression. For the purposes of forecasting the original rate variable, some authors have suggested applying an inversion to the predicted value of the transformed variable after OLS estimation and obtaining a predicted value for the original rate variable as $\widehat{r_{it}} = R^{-1}(\widehat{R_{it}})$. Unfortunately, due to the non-linearity of the original transformation, it is generally the case that $E[R^{-1}(\widehat{R_{it}})|X] \neq R^{-1}E[\widehat{R_{it}}|X]$. As a result, the prediction resulting from applying the transformation in this form is biased and inconsistent.

A review of the relevant literature and a discussion of potential pitfalls can be found in Li, Qi, Xhang, and Zhao (2014). Their paper describes an approach for correcting the bias associated with the transformation estimator by means of Monte Carlo integration techniques. The non-parametric version of this approach will be generally robust to potential non-normality of residuals. However, this approach will not generally be robust to potential heteroscedasticity, or measurement error, of the dependent variable. In contrast, the simple regression estimator without transformation is, by construction, robust to these potential data problems.

In the extensive empirical analysis we have conducted, we observe that naïve predictions using transformations of the dependent variable result in substantial forecasting bias, even for in-sample forecasts. Also, after controlling for bias using a Monte Carlo methodology, we still observe that the results generally underperform those from the simple linear regression model without transformation. Because of these findings, results from the standard linear regression equation are reported in this paper rather than transformations of linear models. Li, Qi, Xhang, and Zhao (2014) also report empirical results broadly supportive of the simple linear regression.

An alternative estimation approach uses parametric or semi-parametric specifications to describe the associated underlying distribution of default, or loss rate, conditional on a finite vector of parameters that can be estimated using maximum likelihood or related estimation techniques. This approach is broadly consistent with the simple linear regression framework because the OLS regression can easily be represented in the form of a maximum likelihood estimator. In this framework, one can consider statistical models specifically designed to accommodate the natural restrictions of a default or loss ratio.

Some of the most flexible statistical models proposed in the recent literature for the analysis of ratios have yet to be incorporated into standard statistical packages. However, there is a well-developed and closely related literature in the area of count models that tackles the same problems that we encounter in our data. Specifically, our data suffers from an excess-zero problem, which is also a typical problem in count data. In simple terms, this problem is identified when the proportion of occurrence concentrated at zero in the data is more than what would be expected in a standard parametric model. In count data, the dependent variable takes on non-negative integer values only. Thus, to take advantage of the extensive suite of statistical models available for the analysis of count data, we transform our continuous default and loss rate data into count data. We accomplish this easily by dividing the unit interval into N separate segments of equal length and assigning an integer value *nit* when the associated *rit* takes a value in the range of (nit -1)/N to nit /N.

Figure 2 presents the empirical distribution of default and loss rates in our data and illustrates the distribution concentration in the vicinity of zero. It is typical when facing an 'excess zero' problem in the data to consider extensions of standard parametric models. One possible approach explores the possibility that the excess zero problem results from the presence of unobserved heterogeneity in the data. A popular count model in this case is the negative binomial regression model. An alternative approach explores the possibility of resolving the excess zero problem by modeling the zero event as a distinctive process. A popular count model in this case is the zero-inflated Poisson regression model. While a detailed description of these models is beyond the realm of this paper, a good source of information about this type of model can be found in Cameron and Trivedi (2013) as well as survey reviews of the literature by these and other authors (e.g., Gurmu and Trivedy, 1994). In our empirical analysis, we present estimation results from linear regression, negative binomial, and zero-inflated Poisson regression models.

Figure 2. Distribution of default and loss rates.

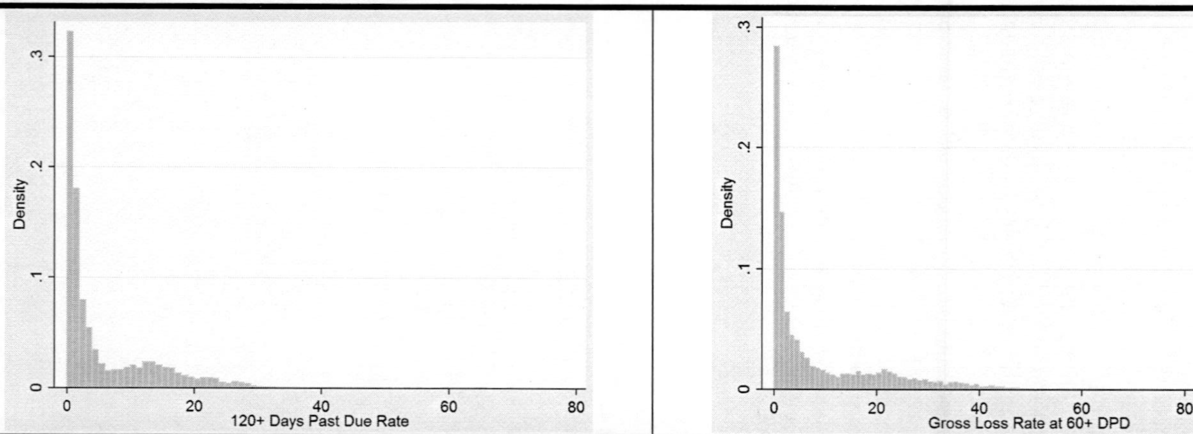

Note: Distributions are account weighted at the segment level. Data source Equifax.

Empirical Results and Analysis

After years of mild and short-lived recessions, a financial crisis led to the 2007-2009 recession and to a rapid increase in the unemployment rate. The national unemployment rate topped at around 10% in October 2009, reaching levels of 14% in Michigan and Nevada and 12% in California. It remained above 8% nationwide until the third quarter of 2012. Using the impact of this recent economic downturn on credit card default and loss rates, we analyze the modeling framework described in the previous section under a variety of model assumptions, model specification assumptions, and sample estimation periods.

With the exception of two measures of unemployment that are treated as continuous variables, other variables included in our model specifications are represented as dummy variables, reflecting specific segment characteristics. For example, credit score is divided into subprime, near-prime, prime, and super-prime, and the segmentation scheme for other relevant variables is as described in Table 1. This approach allows us to estimate the potential nonlinear impact of particular segment characteristics without reliance on specific functional form assumptions. We focus our attention on segments of accounts current at the time of observation and measure the default and loss rate at the segment level over a one-year time interval.

Model Selection

In the empirical methodology section, we discussed a variety approaches for the estimation of models of default and loss rate. We introduced the linear regression as the most simple and straightforward approach and discussed potential weaknesses of this approach. We also discussed possible improvements on the simple linear regression by means of transformations of the dependent variable and discussed naïve applications of this concept as well as more sophisticated applications using Monte Carlo techniques. Finally, we discussed the use of flexible parametric and semi-parametric specifications along with Maximum Likelihood Estimation. In this subsection, we analyze how these techniques perform in our particular application. To achieve this objective, we estimate each of the alternative models described above. In all cases, we employ the same risk drivers and basic model specification structure over the full sample period observed in our data. After that, we compare the model fit performance of different approaches across time, with special focus on the recent period of economic downturn.

Figure 3. In sample model fit, simple regression and negative binomial model.

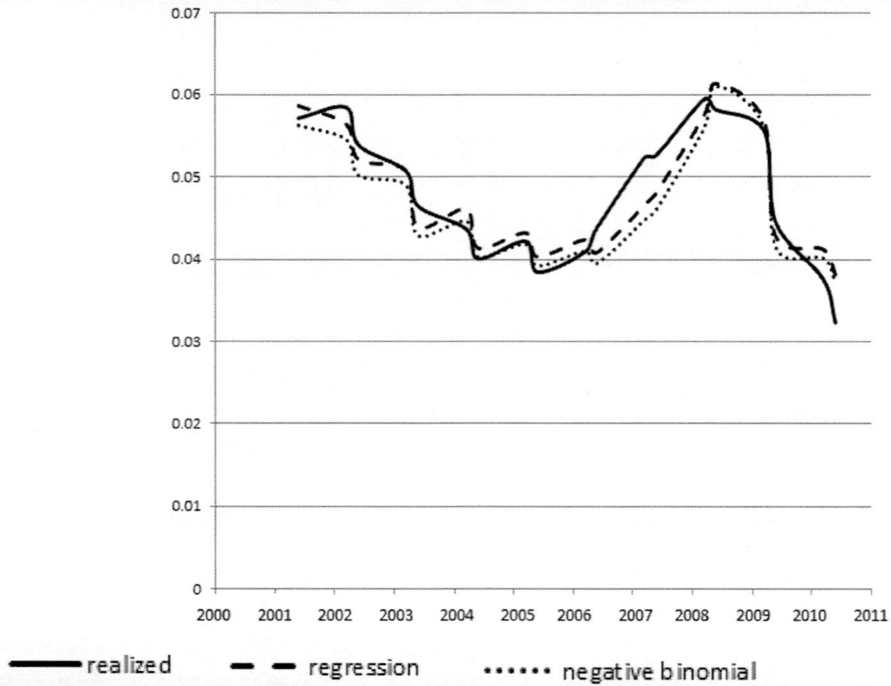

Note: the zero inflated Poisson model provides identical fit to the negative binomial model and has been excluded from the figure. Projections are account weighted at the segment level. Data source Equifax.

Figure 3 presents realized loss rates as well as projected loss rates from a regression model, a negative binomial regression model, and a zero-inflated Poisson regression model. Interestingly, the linear regression projections compare favorably to those of the more sophisticated models. All approaches are able to accurately project the increase in default rates during the last recession, with a small lag. But the regression model seems to have a slight edge in the projection of the initial increase in default rates. In contrast, both the negative binomial regression model and a zero-inflated Poisson regression model seem to have a slight edge in the projection of default rates decreases as the recession subsides. Models using transformations of the dependent variable, even those that explicitly control for potential forecasting bias, generally underperform those from the simple linear regression framework without transformation. Therefore, transformation models are not reported.

From the practitioner's perspective, our investigation suggests that using regression analysis as a benchmark for more complex models is a reasonable and fruitful strategy. Furthermore, a simple regression analysis seems to be able to compete in projection accuracy with more sophisticated methods. These results are also consistent with further analysis of out-of-sample projections not reported in this paper. Comparable findings reported in recent research by Li, Qi, Xhang, and Zhao (2014) in a different context add validity to our analysis.

Model Specification

In this subsection, we analyze the impact of different model specification assumptions on credit card default rates and loss rates. Recent studies have shown that both the level and change in unemployment rate have a significant impact on credit card default rates. However, this impact is not uniform across the portfolio. The impact of a rising unemployment rate environment on prime borrowers is different from its impact on subprime borrowers. Our analysis indicates that models that do not account for this heterogeneous impact are likely to exhibit large forecast errors, especially for sub-segments of the portfolio. Further, these errors can become larger due to portfolio migration during the course of a business cycle.

We analyze model specifications where the impact of macroeconomic factors is homogenous across the entire credit card portfolio. We then compare them with specifications that allow the model parameters to vary across risk-score segments, thus allowing for a heterogeneous impact of the macroeconomic factors. Risk-score segments are based on the Equifax credit score and are defined in Table 1. The lowest segment, referred to as subprime, consists of accounts with scores below 650. The highest segment, referred to as super-prime, consists of accounts with scores above 770. Other intermediate risk-score segments represent the near-prime and prime borrowers, respectively, as identified in Table 1.

Table 3 reports estimation results for the negative binomial regression models that allow for the heterogeneous impact of macroeconomic variables and other risk drivers. The table presents results for both loss rate and default rate models. We report large differences in the impact of utilization and macroeconomic factors across risk-score groups. Low utilized accounts among subprime borrowers are 46% less likely to default, an odds ratio of 0.54, relative to high utilized accounts among the same group of borrowers, but this effect is even stronger among near-prime and prime borrowers, where the likelihood of default for low utilized accounts are 67% and 73% lower, respectively. The heterogeneous impact of utilization is also seen in the loss rate model, where low utilized accounts among subprime borrowers show a mere 1% decline in the likelihood of loss, but has a much stronger effect among prime and super-prime borrowers. In the case of line, there is a greater default probability associated with higher lines, after controlling for score, but this effect is not consistent across risk score segments. However, the most interesting results are related to the level and change in unemployment rate. We find that unemployment rate has almost no impact on default and loss rates in the subprime segment of the portfolio. Looking at the combined impact of an increase in unemployment on the level and change in unemployment rate, a one-unit increase in unemployment rate has a relatively small positive impact on the likelihood of default in the subprime segment when compared with its impact on the near-prime segment. In contrast, the same increase in the level of unemployment rate results in a much larger increase in the likelihood of default in high score segments. These results show that the prime segments of the portfolio are more severely impacted by economic downturn conditions and model specification assumptions relative to the subprime or near-prime segments.

Table 3. Estimated Negative Binomial Regression for the overall sample.

	Default Rate Model				Loss Rate Model			
Credit Score:	SP	NP	P	SPP	SP	NP	P	SPP
Line								
Medium	0.76	0.87	1.11	2.19	0.69	0.86	1.05	1.11
High	0.87	0.90	1.08	2.33	0.73	0.82	1.03	1.28
Utilization								
Low	0.54	0.33	0.27	0.49	0.99	0.90	0.57	0.65
Medium	0.60	0.51	0.48	0.45	0.63	0.60	0.55	0.52
Unemployment								
Ur.	1.00	1.04	1.10	1.09	0.98	1.03	1.08	1.08
Chg. Ur. 12m.	1.07	1.12	1.11	1.04	1.10	1.14	1.16	1.04
Q2 dummy	1.05	1.05	1.05	1.01	1.04	1.06	0.98	1.07
Constant	21.04	4.64	1.22	0.18	34.34	7.37	1.98	0.47

Note: ‘sp’ refers to subprime, ‘np’ refers to near-prime, ‘p’ refers to prime, and ‘spp’ refers to super-prime. Models are estimated using weights for the number of accounts at the segment level. All values reported are statistically significant at the 99% level. Data source Equifax.

In Figure 4, we present results of the relative projection accuracy of both model specifications over the sample period. The solid line at each calendar time shows the realized one-year default rates over the 2001-2011 timeframe. The dotted lines represent model predictions from the two model specifications reported. The Great Recession, or years 2007-09, is of particular interest. We see that both models fit the actual default rates for the overall portfolio well but lag the actual rise in default rates by about six months, especially when the unemployment rate rose rapidly during the 2007-08 period. Furthermore, when we evaluate the relative performance of different model specifications across portfolio segments, we observe that the homogeneous model specification significantly over-predicts in the sub-prime segment while also under-predicting in the near-prime and prime segments of the portfolio. The magnitude of error is particularly severe for the prime segment in 2008 and 2009, where it under-predicts the actual default rates by 45% (1.00% relative to an actual default rate of 1.82%). By contrast, the alternative model specification that allows for a heterogeneous impact of macroeconomic variables across risk segments exhibits a much smaller forecast error on the prime segment of about 10% during the same period. The reverse results are seen for the subprime segment, where the homogeneous model specification over-predicts default rates by 18%, whereas the alternative model specification has a much smaller over-prediction rate of 6%.

Thus, our analysis indicates that the impact of macroeconomic factors is heterogeneous across portfolio risk segments. These results follow naturally from the regression results, where we show that the subprime segment is proportionally less sensitive to changes in macroeconomic conditions than higher-risk-score segments. This finding has important implications for portfolio risk management because it indicates that banks that do not consider heterogeneous responses to macro factors in their models may encounter large loss projection errors, especially during recessions when the portfolio composition changes because of account migration or changes in credit policy.

Figure 4. Portfolio projections and projections across risk-score segments.

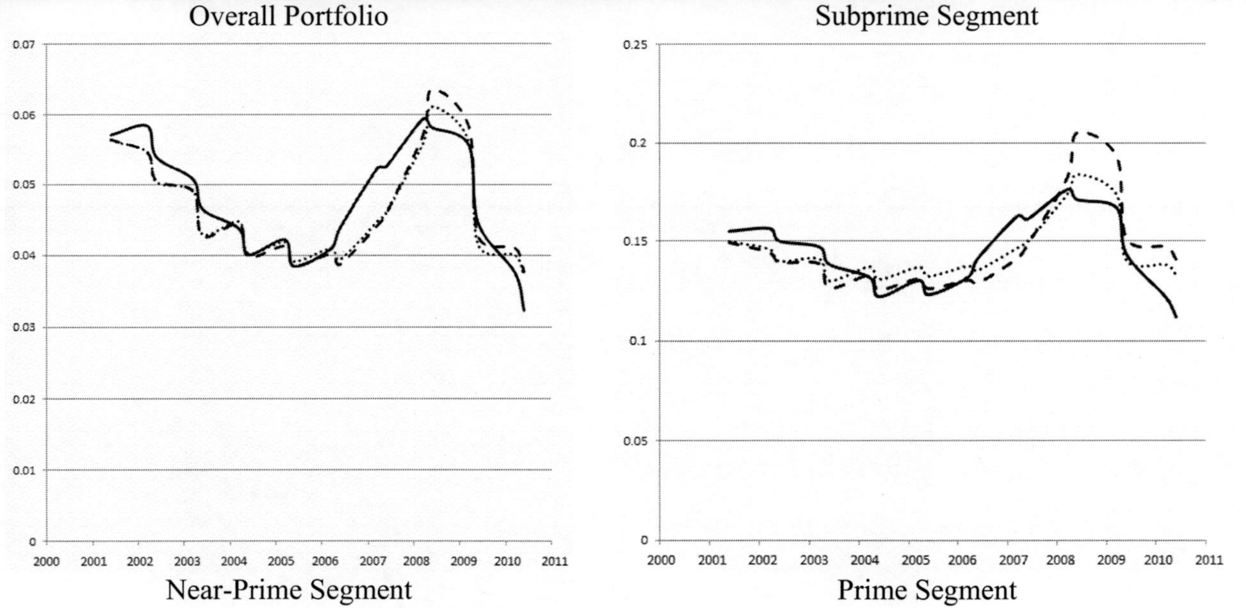

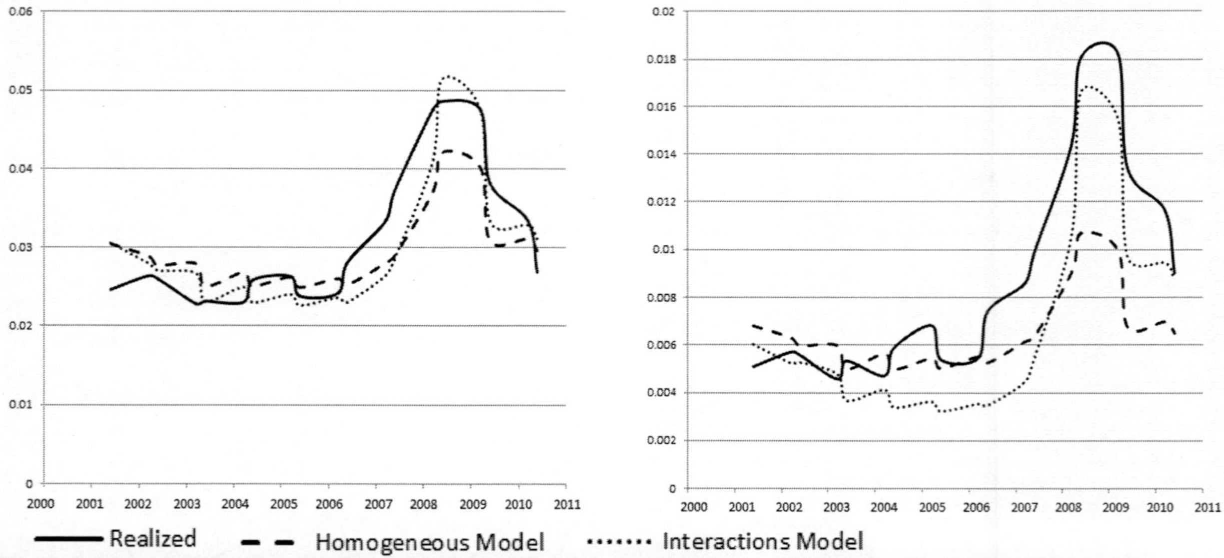

Note: Models are estimated using weights for the number of accounts at the segment level. Data source Equifax.

Sample Selection

Even a well-specified model that accounts for the heterogeneous impact of the macroeconomic variables on portfolio default rates may have large forecast errors if the development sample period is constrained by the lack of a complete business cycle with a significant downturn. This source of model risk can affect the identification and estimation of model parameters and compromise a model's ability to forecast accurately when the postulated stress environment falls outside the stress levels experienced in the data. This potential data shortcoming has been recognized within the Basel II regulatory framework, which requires that banks include at least one economic downturn in their data employed for estimation of regulatory capital.

To illustrate this, in Figure 5, we compare the results from our most general model specification, when it is estimated with data up to 2008, 2010, and 2011. This model specification captures the heterogeneous impact of the macroeconomic variables across portfolio segments. However, it still results in significant over-prediction when estimated with data only up to 2008. The model forecasts default rates that are 16% higher than actual default rates for the overall portfolio during the 2008-11 period,[4] when unemployment rose sharply first and declined thereafter. This over-prediction for the model estimated with data up to 2008 can be attributed to an estimation period that does not capture the complete effect of the downturn because the unemployment rate was still rising during that period. The magnitude of over-prediction falls from 16% to 9% because we expand the estimation sample to include data up to 2010 and to 4% when we include data up to 2011, which contains a more complete business cycle where unemployment has come down to 6.5%. This analysis illustrates that even the most general model specification can have significant forecast errors when estimated over a period that does not include a significant downturn or, conversely, a large enough recovery period. Additional analysis, not reported here, shows that the primary impact of our model specification and sample selection on portfolio loss is channeled through the process of transition to default rather than the drawdown behavior of the borrowers that affects the exposure at default.

[4] The years 2009-11 can be considered as the out-of-time validation sample for this model because it is estimated with data up to 2008.

Figure 5. Default rates model fit.

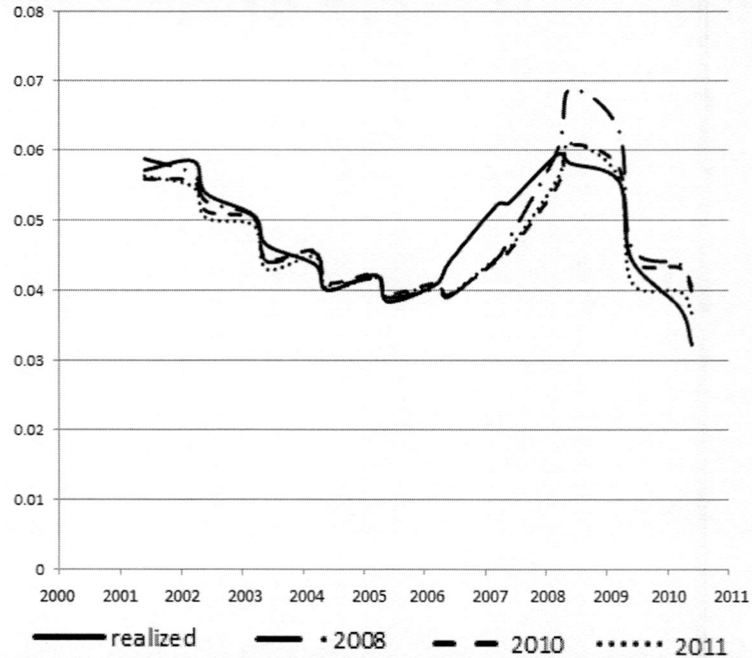

Note: Models are estimated using weights for the number of accounts at the segment level. Data source Equifax.

Figure 6. Loss Rates model fit.

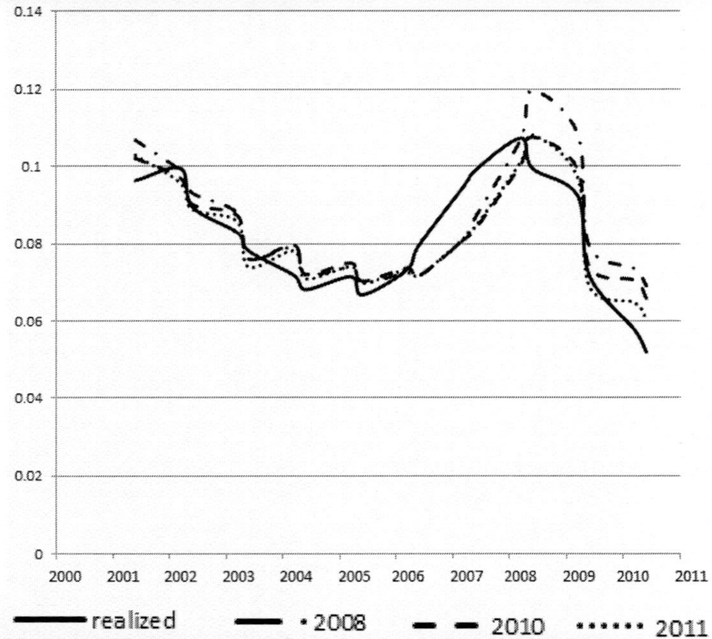

Note: Models are estimated using weights for the number of accounts at the segment level. Data source Equifax.

Loss Rates

For most of the paper we have focused on the impact of model specification and sample selection on forecasting default rates for the portfolio. However, our discussion of default rate models is generalizable to loss rates as well. In Figure 6, we recreate for loss rates the same analysis displayed in Figure 5 for default rates. The most general model specification considered in Figure 6 over-predicts the loss rate by 22% over the 2009-2011 period when the estimation sample is cut off at 2008 and does not include the effect of the complete downturn and recovery. The magnitude of this over-prediction is even greater than the over-prediction seen in the case of default rates. As in the case of default rates, the forecast error declines considerably as the estimation window is expanded to include 2010 and 2011, where over-prediction falls to 14% and finally to 8%. Even after including all the years in our sample, some over-prediction remains; this may be attributed to the model not capturing the entire recovery period.

Conclusions

The focus of this paper is on the impact of model selection, model specification, and sample selection on the relative loss-forecasting performance of credit risk models applied at an aggregated risk-segment level to a representative credit card portfolio. The lessons learned may be applicable more broadly to the modeling of credit risk.

Our loss-projection framework fits the loss experienced in our representative portfolio well when models are estimated over the full sample. The results indicate that macroeconomic conditions have a significant and sizable impact on the default and loss ratios. We observe that the impact of macroeconomic factors is heterogeneous across portfolio risk segments, in particular along the credit score dimension. Segments of accounts classified as subprime according to their low credit score have the highest loss rate in all economic environments considered, but they are proportionally less impacted by changes in macroeconomic conditions than near-prime and prime segments.

The econometric literature offers a variety of alternatives for modeling default and loss rates. Simple regression analysis can be challenging because ratios are naturally defined in the unit interval and because of the prevalence of segments with zero loss or near zero loss. Several alternatives to simple linear regression have been proposed in the literature; we evaluate the performance of dependent variable transformations and parametric models specifically design to ratios and the excess-zero problem observed in the data. Interestingly, the linear regression projections compare favorably to those of more sophisticated models. The naïve application of non-linear transformations generates significant bias; attempts to bias correction using a Monte Carlo approach do not eliminate the problem in our particular application. Of our preferred models, the linear regression model seems to have a slight edge in the projection of the initial increase in default rates at the beginning of the economic downturn. In contrast, parametric, more refined models seem to have a slight edge in the projection of the decrease in default rates as the recession subsides. From the perspective of a practitioner, this analysis suggests that using regression analysis as a benchmark to more complex models is a reasonable and fruitful strategy. Findings are broadly consistent whether the models considered refer to default ratio or loss ratio.

Our analysis indicates that loss projections are significantly impacted by model specification assumptions. Models with controls for macroeconomic variables that do not consider interactions between these variables and measures of creditworthiness can significantly under-predict or over-predict loss under stress for segments of the portfolio. The effect of macroeconomic variables and model specification assumptions is heterogeneous across portfolio segments. In particular, the impact of the significant and rapid increase in unemployment experienced during the Great Recession was proportionally much larger for the near-prime and prime segments in contrast with the subprime segment. The lack of a sufficiently severe stress period in the estimation sample represents another potential source of model risk and results in significant under-prediction of portfolio losses under stressed economic conditions in our application. Model performance improves significantly once a sufficiently large downturn period is included in the data, particularly in the most flexible model specification considered.

References

Agarwal, S., and C. Liu (2003). "Determinants of Credit Card Delinquency and Bankruptcy: Macroeconomic Factors," *Journal of Economics and Finance*, 27(1), 75-85.

Banerjee, P., and J.J. Canals-Cerdá (2012). "Credit Risk Analysis of Credit Cards Portfolios Under Economic Stress Conditions," Federal Reserve Bank of Philadelphia, Working Paper 2012-18.

Canals-Cerdá, J.J. and S. Kerr (2014). "Forecasting Credit Card Portfolio Losses in the Great Recession: A Study in Model Risk" Federal Reserve Bank of Philadelphia, Working Paper 2014-10.

Board of Governors of the Federal Reserve System (2013). "Dodd-Frank Act Stress Test 2013: Supervisory Stress Test Methodology and Results, March 2013," http://www.federalreserve.gov/newsevents/press/bcreg/dfast_2013_results_20130314.pdf.

Cameron A. C. and P. K. Trivedi (2013). "Regression Analysis of Count Data," 2nd edition, Econometric Society Monograph No.53, Cambridge University Press, 1998 (566 pages.)

Ferrari, S.L.P. and Cribari–Neto, F. (2004). "Beta regression for modelling rates and proportions," *Journal of Applied Statistics*, 31, 799–815.

Gross, D. B., and N. S. Souleles (2002). "An Empirical Analysis of Personal Bankruptcy and Delinquency," *Review of Financial Studies*, 15: 319-347.

Gurmu, S. and P. K. Trivedi (1994). "Recent Developments in Event Count Models: A Survey," University of Virginia Thomas Jefferson Center Discussion Paper #261.

Hunt, R. (2013). "Understanding the Model: The Life Cycle of a Debt," prepared presentation for the FTC-CFPB Roundtable.

Li, P., M. Qi, X. Zhang, X. Zhao (2014) "Further Investigation of Parametric Loss Given Default Modeling." Office of the Comptroller of the Currency, Economics WP 2014-2.

Ospina, R. and Ferrari, S.L.P. (2010). "Inflated beta distributions." *Statistical Papers*, 51, 111–126.

Ospina, R. and Ferrari, S.L.P. (2012a). "A general class of zero-or-one inflated beta regression models." *Computational Statistics and Data Analysis*, 56, 1609–1623.

Ospina, R. and Ferrari, S.L.P. (2012b). "On bias correction in a class of inflated beta regression models." *International Journal of Statistics and Probability*, 1(2), 269- doi:10.5539/ijsp.v1n2p269.

Smithson, M. and Verkuilen, J. (2006). "A better lemon squeezer? Maximum-likelihood regression with beta-distributed dependent variables." *Psychological Methods*, 11, 54–71.

CHAPTER FOUR

EFFECTS OF MACROECONOMIC ACTIVITY ON CORPORATE BOND CREDIT RISK: A STUDY BASED ON AN EMERGING COUNTRY

RIMPA SAHA
AND ARUN KUMAR GOPALASWAMY[1]

Abstract

A host of researchers have demonstrated that macro-economic factors have a strong impact on sovereign bond ratings. In this study, this linkage is extended to include corporate bonds. The core objective of this research is to determine the contributing factors behind corporate sector bond downgrades of the top five emerging countries. The study analyses macro-economic factors' (Interest rate, Exchange Rate, Term Spread, GDP growth rate, Industrial Production stock index volatility of individual country, and trade balance) linkages to bond downgrades in five chosen countries (South Korea, China, India, Malaysia, and Taiwan) over a period of 14 years. It is observed that macroeconomic variables significantly impact bond downgrades for each country. However, the differential impact of these factors for each country studied is driven by unique policy measurements and different economic structures.

[1] Rimpa Saha is a research scholar from the Department of Management Studies, Indian Institute of Technology, Madras. Email: rimpa.saha88@gmail.com. Arun Kuma Copalaswamy is a Professor from the Department of Management Studies, Indian Institute of Technology, Madras. Email: garun@iitm.ac.in

Introduction

"Credit risk analysis is an art, not a science. It is impossible to quantify all the elements one must consider in credit analysis" (Langohr and Langohr, 2010). The difficulty in quantifying credit risk lies in capturing the correct factors to measure it. Numerous attempts have been made by a host of researchers to build models that capture the default and credit risk of firms with little improvement. This effort is motivated by credit rating agencies' push to accurately rate firms' borrowing instruments. The significance of rating a firm's debt instrument is to highlight the likelihood of timely debt servicing, which includes repayment of the principal and interest on time. In addition, rating also determines the cost of borrowing for any firm given the established relationship between risk and return.

The growing need for an improved credit rating model coupled with rapid growth of the debt market emphasizes the need for an accurate and robust model. Over the last two decades, credit rating models have attempted to quantify many factors measuring the credit risk associated with debt instruments. Shin and Han (2001) have stressed that the main process of rating starts with reviewing past financial reports to assess free cash flows to the firm. Empirical research suggests that a rating model with strong predictive insights is predominantly based on financial ratios to analyze performance (Altman, 1968, 2000, 2005; Shin and Han, 2001; McKee and Lensberg, 2002; Rus et al. 2009; Bhimani et al. 2010; Li and Sun, 2011). On the other hand, there are some studies (Bensic et al. 2005; Bandyopadhyay 2006) where, in addition to financial ratios, the emphasis on non-financial aspects like the age of the firm, group ownership, and ISO certification are used for credit rating (CR) because these variables are expected to increase predictability. A major departure occurred with Kisgen's study (2006, 2009), where capital structure was considered as the key factor underlining the change in CR.

A long-term debt instrument's rating is used as a proxy for a firm's debt rating. This, in turn, determines the credibility and strength of an enterprise. A plethora of studies have identified and included incremental factors to increase predictability. Despite such development, the problem of default predictability still persists. A few recent studies have attempted to include macro-economic variables as factors of CR to enhance the predicting power, though the method is predominantly used only for sovereign credit ratings.

Cantor et al. (1996) have emphasized that a good sovereign rating not only lowers borrowing cost but also enhances the credit worthiness of a country's firms. The study identified five main country-specific factors

(GDP growth, inflation, external debt, level of economic development, and default history) that play a major role in sovereign rating. Andritzky et al. (2007) have demonstrated that macro-economic data release and policy announcements have a huge impact on the sovereign bond's rating in emerging markets.

Macro-economic factors play a significant role in other assets of capital markets. Studies have linked stock returns and macro-economic factors in both short term and long term relationships (Ahmed, 2008; Barrows and Naka, 1994; Chen, Roll, and Ross, 1986; Gay Jr, 2011; Schwert, 1989). It has also been demonstrated that the volatility of sector index is influenced by macro-economic shocks (Maysami, Howe, and Hamzah, 2004). Studies have also demonstrated that not only stock market returns but also property returns and real estate returns are highly influenced by variation in macro-economic factors (Chan, Hendersh, and Sanders, 1990; Liu and Mei, 1992 ; Brooks and Tsolacos, 1999). However, the impact of the macro-economy on credit risk has been limited to the portfolio of credit assets of banks and financial institutions (Scott and Hashem, 2003; Carling, Jacobson, Lindé, and Roszbach, 2007).

Macro-economic factors and policy announcements have not been considered as important parameters by most studies of non-government bond credit rating. Collin-Dufresne and Goldstein (2001) and Collin-Dufresne and Solnik (2001) have concluded that country specific variables like interest rate may also help in explaining credit risk. In this research, an attempt is made to extend the study of Collin-Dufresne and Goldstein (2001) by including other macro-economic variables like GDP growth, industrial production, exchange rate, term spread, stock index volatility, and trade balance along with interest rate. The core objective of this research is to investigate the impact of changes in macro-economic factors and policy announcements on corporate bond ratings in the context of the emerging economies of South Korea, China, Malaysia, India, and Taiwan.

Proposed Concept

The importance of credit rating (CR) is felt as the debt market matures in a country. Given the pace of growth, investors consider emerging debt markets a prime source for raising funds (Figure 1). In this context, a uniform rating becomes crucial as the nature of the debt market is not only different between the developed and emerging market but also is varied among emerging markets. Andritzky et al. (2007) have reported that the emerging debt market is very volatile due to the prevalence of default risk and constant structural changes in the economy. On the other hand, Kose et al. (2003) have stated that factors affecting business cycle fluctuation are also not the same in developed and developing countries. Therefore, it is very important to distinguish studies related to risk in the debt market separately for emerging economies.

Ferri et al. (2001) have provided evidence that sovereign downgrading and firm downgrading are highly correlated in developing countries, implying that factors of sovereign rating can play a dual role by impacting and determining corporate rating. Kose et al. (2003) have reported that country specific factors like output growth, consumption growth, and investment growth have better explanatory power for the business cycle fluctuation of developing countries when compared to developed countries, where the primary explanation is given by "world factor" (a dynamic factor common to all aggregates, regions and countries). However, the debt market is varied among emerging countries due to different term structures, policies, and economies.

The objective of the current research is to examine the impact of macro-economic variables—interest rate, GDP growth rate, industrial production, term spread, exchange rate, stock index volatility, and trade balance—on corporate bond downgrades in five emerging Asian economies—South Korea, China, Malaysia, India, and Taiwan. The study explores the effect and interaction of each macro-economic factor individually on bond downgrades for each chosen country.

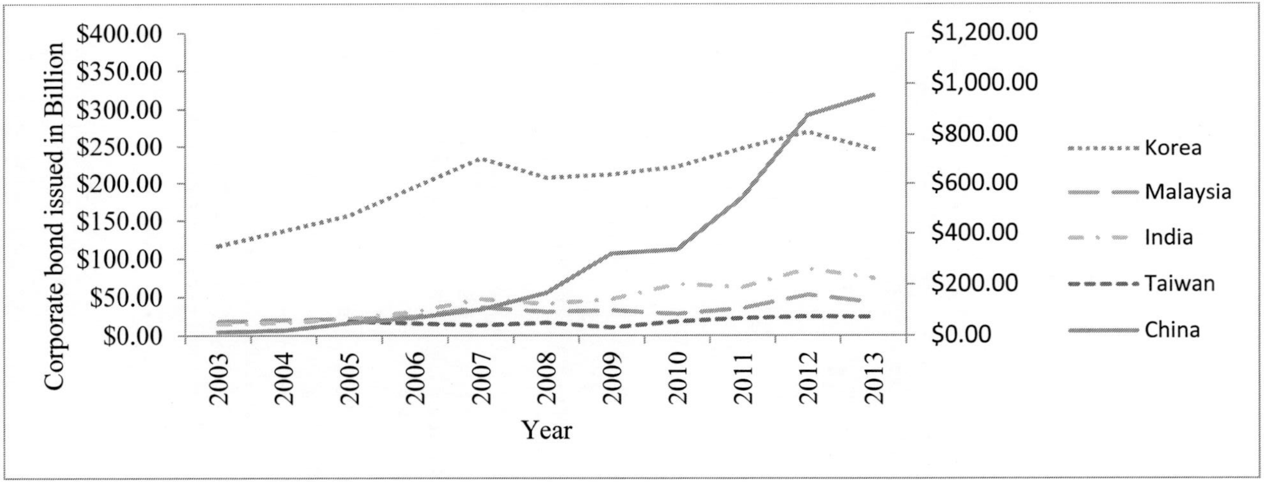

Figure 1. Size of the corporate bond market of top 5 emerging countries in Asia *(Source: Bloomberg Portal).*

Measurement of Credit Risk

Since credit rating provides the relative probability of default risk, any downgrade implies that the instrument's probability of default has increased. In this study, the number of corporate bond downgrades is used as a proxy for measuring credit risk. In recent times the market has witnessed a higher number of new bond issues as well as an increased number of downgrades due to a stricter regulatory mechanism and increased investor participation. Given the level of disparity in new bond issues and the need for analysis standardization, a ratio is arrived at by dividing the number of bond downgrades by the number of corporate bonds issued[2] in each quarter for a given country. This ratio is denoted by 'Down-Issue,' which is the dependent variable in the study.

Macro-economic Variables

The nominal interest rate is an important macro-economic factor because it highlights overall economic conditions and investment opportunities in the country. Interest rate is often altered to control inflation; however, the change in interest rate can increase the credit risk of the firm, leading to the downgrade of its debt instruments. This is driven by the fact that changes in interest rate and credit spread risk are positively correlated. However, the correlation between interest rate factor and the firm's asset value factor decides the magnitude of the downgrade risk (Longstaff and Schwartz, 1995). Following the argument, Collin-Dufresne and Goldstein (2001) have demonstrated that "a negative correlation between firm value and interest rate provides a natural hedge against credit risk. Conversely, when the correlation is positive, the two effects work in the same direction. Hence, one would expect higher credit spreads for positive correlation."

Interest rate is considered to be a potent macro-economic factor because the information content is high and has strong predictive capability (Brooks and Tsolacos, 1999). This strong rationale has forced the inclusion of the interest rate variable, i.e. term spread, in the study. Term spread is the difference between long- and short-term interest rates and is also known as yield curve. A positively slopping yield curve indicates the rise of a future economy, whereas a negatively slopping yield curve signals

---

[2] The quarter-wise ratio of corporate bond downgraded amount in USD to corporate bond issued amount in USD is a better parameter to estimate credit risk. However, as that data is not available, we took the ratio of the number of bonds downgraded to bonds issued.

the down side of an economy (Estrella and Hardouvelis, 1991). Therefore, an increase in the spread will decrease firms' default risk.

Appreciation or depreciation of the exchange rate indicates the country's economic situation with respect to other countries. If the country's economy is booming, the currency will get stronger, which will appreciate the country's exchange rate. This could lead to the downgrade of a firm's debt instrument depending on whether it is an export- or import-oriented firm. Export-oriented firms enhance their profits when the exchange rate depreciates; the converse is true of import driven firms.

Trade balance is the difference between a country's exports and imports. Announcements or change in levy of imports and exports can influence firms' revenues or profits. Therefore, they indirectly affect credit rating through the firm's performance. Change in a country's net export or trade balance can capture the change in trade policy. If there is any policy related change in export like the export duty, the discount on levy will be reflected in the revenue component through forex earnings. If the trade balance decreases, it indicates that the country is losing its revenue from reduced exports or higher imports. Therefore, a positive trade balance is a good economic sign for the country.

Stock index volatility is also a good proxy to measure a country's economic situation and investment position. Volatility can be high because of investment or divestment. Both situations are not favorable for the bond rating.

A positive GDP and Industrial Production are indicators of economic growth. GDP provides the overall image of a country's revenue from all the sectors, including production and service, whereas industrial production measures only the output from manufacturing, mining, and utilities. Both indicators are considered separately to thoroughly check the effect of the country's economic performance on bond downgrade.

Data and Variable

This study aims to test the impact of macro-economic changes and policy announcements on the credit risk of the firms of some leading sectors in a particular country. Sectors have been based on the downgrade data available for the industry of that country.

Data used for the study were obtained from the Bloomberg Portal for the period of 2000 to 2013. Quarterly data for number of corporate bonds issued, number of bonds downgraded, one year yield, and 10 year yield of the zero coupon Treasury bond, GDP growth, growth of industrial production, trade balance of the country, exchange rate of currency of the country with respect to USD, and the country's stock index volatility for

Korea, China, India, Malaysia, and Taiwan have been used throughout the study. The dependent variable is calculated as the ratio of number of bonds issued to number of bonds downgraded in each quarter. Detailed descriptions of the variables used in the study are presented in Table 1.

Table 1. Description of the variables.

Variable Name	Definition
Down-Issue	Ratio of number of corporate bonds downgraded in each quarter to corporate bonds issued in each quarter
10 Year Yield	Percentage change of quarterly average of daily yield of one year zero coupon treasury bond with respect to previous quarter's average yield
One Year Yield	Percentage change of quarterly average of daily yield of 10 year zero coupon treasury bond with respect to previous quarter's average yield
Term Spread	Quarterly average of daily term spread (difference between 10 years' zero coupon yield and three months' zero coupon yield)
Exchange Rate	Percentage change of quarterly average of daily exchange rate (local currency with respect to USD) with respect to previous quarter's average exchange rate
GDP growth rate	Percentage change of quarterly GDP growth rate with respect to its previous quarter
Industrial Production	Percentage change of quarterly average of monthly industrial production with respect to previous quarter's industrial production
Stock Index Volatility	Average quarterly volatility is calculated from daily volatility that is obtained from daily stock index return
Trade Balance	Percentage change of quarterly average of monthly trade balance with respect to previous quarter's trade balance

Methodology

Lags of the variables used in the study are important because they contain powerful information. This is due to the fact that macro-economic shocks take one to three quarters to be reflected in the ratings of corporate bonds. Therefore, the best way to extract information from time series data is either VAR or VECM depending on the presence of cointegration between variables. Most macro-economic variables are stationary at level because changes of variables have been considered in this study instead of raw data. Moreover, the impacts of individual macro-economic factors are considered on bond downgrades, so an unrestricted bivariate VAR framework is set for the analysis.

Variables are required to be stationary to draw a useful inference from VAR analysis. An Augmented Dickey-Fuller Test (Fuller, 2009) has been used to test the presence of a unit root and to identify the order of integration for each variable.

Given the fact that the focus of this research is to assess the causal relationship between each macro-economic factor and bond downgrades in the corporate sector, the Granger causality (Granger, 1988) test has been used followed by variance decomposition. Because some of the variables are not stationary at level, Toda and Yamamoto's (Toda and Yamamoto, 1995) method of the Granger causality test is used.

Apart from the VAR framework setup, the GARCH (1, 1) (Bollerslev, 1986) test has been used to calculate daily conditional variance of daily log return of stock index. We converted daily volatility to quarterly volatility by using the following formula:

$$\sigma_{quarter} = E(\sigma_{daily}) * \sqrt{N} ,$$

where N = No of days in the given quarter

Table 2 Country-wise Granger Causality Result

No.	Null Hypothesis of Granger Causality	South Korea		India		Taiwan		Malaysia		China	
		Chi-Square	p-value	Chi-Square	p-value	Chi-Square	p-value	Chi-Square	p-value	Chi-Square	p-value
1A	10Yld does not GC down	2.876	0.098*	6.705	0.035**	3.202	0.074*	NA	NA	NA	NA
1B	Down does not GC 10Yld	1.512	0.226	1.935	0.380	0.165	0.685	NA	NA	NA	NA
2A	1Yld does not GC down	6.548	0.011***	4.559	0.033**	0.059	0.808	NA	NA	NA	NA
2B	Down does not GC 1Yld	2.423	0.119	0.005	0.942	0.136	0.713	NA	NA	NA	NA
3A	Spread does not GC down	4.080	0.050**	8.630	0.000***	2.523	0.091*	0.274	0.604	NA	NA
3B	Down does not GC Spread	1.318	0.258	2.095	0.114	0.063	0.939	1.195	0.280	NA	NA
4A	TB does not GC down	5.115	0.005***	0.711	0.589	162.1	.000***	0.667	0.519	NA	NA
4B	Down does not GC TB	1.164	0.338	5.074	0.002***	0.000	0.983	0.101	0.905	NA	NA
5A	Ex-Rate does not GC down	2.889	0.068**	0.811	0.372	3.001	0.059**	NA	NA	NA	NA
5B	Down does not GC Ex-Rate	2.284	0.116	1.186	0.281	0.752	0.477	NA	NA	NA	NA
6A	SIV does not GC down	0.843	0.439	4.920	0.031**	1.196	0.279	0.513	0.478	NA	NA
6B	Down does not GC SIV	1.684	0.200	2.054	0.158	0.243	0.624	8.925	0.005***	NA	NA
7A	GDP growth does not GC down	0.780	0.547	0.419	0.52	3.268	0.030**	0.665	0.520	NA	NA
7B	Down does not GC GDP growth	1.624	0.193	0.082	0.776	2.336	0.086	1.130	0.333	NA	NA
8A	IP does not GC down	0.668	0.519	2.281	0.137	50.82	.000***	NA	NA	NA	NA
8B	Down does not GC IP	0.638	0.534	0.471	0.495	4.247	0.044	NA	NA	NA	NA

Note: *, **, *** denotes 1%, 5%, 10% significance level respectively. 10Yld: 10 year zero coupon yield of T-Bond; 1Yld: 1 year zero coupon yield of T-Bond; Ex-Rate: Exchange Rate; IP: Industrial Production; SIV: Stock Index Volatility; TB: Trade Balance; GC: Granger Causes; Down: Bond downgrade. NA denotes none of lag is significant in VAR model. So, Granger Causality test is not possible. It indicates that bond downgrade does not depend on lag of corresponding macro-economic variables.

Results and Implications

This study is an attempt to document the interactions between corporate bond downgrades and individual macro-economic variables in the chosen emerging markets. The results indicate the significant impact of macroeconomic variables on corporate bond downgrades. Out of five chosen countries, all except Malaysia and China are impacted by macro-economic variables on corporate bond downgrades. The country-wise outcomes of the study are presented in table 2.

It is clear form table 2 that that Korea, India, and Taiwan support the hypothesis that changes in macro-economic variables cause bond downgrades. For all three countries, the yield of one year and ten year zero coupon bonds has a significant impact. This corroborates the theory that interest rate change directly changes the credit spread, a key factor in change of bond rating.

Term spread is a significant macro-economic factor in South Korea, India, and Taiwan. Term spread has an effect on the corporate bond downgrade if the 10-year yield has an impact on the same bond downgrade because term spread is the difference between the yields of 10-year and 3-month zero-coupon T-bonds. Therefore, that term spread has a crucial effect on bond downgrade is justified because of the important role of 10-year yield on corporate bond downgrade in those three countries.

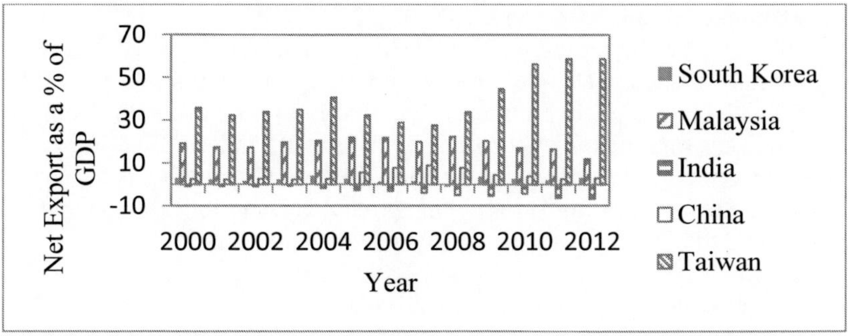

Figure 2. Net Export of South Korea, China, India, Malaysia, and Taiwan (Source: Bloomberg Portal).

Trade balance or the net export of the country has a significant effect on Korea, India, and Taiwan. From Figure 2, it is evident that Taiwan, Malaysia, South Korea, and China have higher positive trade balances. Changes in trade balance Granger cause bond downgrades in Korea and

Taiwan, possibly because both are export oriented countries in Asia, whereas this is not true for Malaysia and China because the structure of the bond market in these countries is different. For India, bond downgrade has an impact on trade balance. From Figure 2, it is very evident that the export of goods and services from India is relatively less when compared to Korea and Taiwan. Therefore, if a firm's forex earnings decrease, the total profit will be affected, leading to a downgrade of its debt instrument. On the other hand, a decrease of forex earnings indicates that a country's revenue from export has come down, which will lead to a decrease in the trade balance.

The recent effect of the exchange rate on corporate bond downgrade is aligned with the logic of the trade balance's impact on the corporate bond downgrade. A significant amount of profit for firms in Korea and Taiwan comes from exports. If firms' profit decreases because of less revenue from forex earnings, it will impact the country's net export (trade balance). This also highlights that exchange rate impacts bond downgrades only in Korea and Taiwan.

Stock market volatility has a significant influence on the corporate bond market only in India. From the literature, it can be argued that there is a strong linkage between the stock and bond market in India (Kolluri and Wahab, 2010) given the relatively nascent nature of the debt market as compared to other markets in the sample. Bond markets of Korea and Taiwan are developed compared to India, signifying the lesser influence of stock market volatility in those countries.

It can also be observed from table 2 that GDP growth rate and industrial production (IP) do not have any impact on bond downgrades for either India or Korea. In addition, GDP and IP do not have a direct impact on bond downgrades for China and Malaysia. IP and GDP both indicate the economic growth of a country. However, GDP growth has an impact on bond downgrades for Taiwan. One possible reason for this exception in Taiwan is the relatively small country size of Taiwan as compared to India and Korea.

None of the macroeconomic variables Granger causes bond downgrades for Malaysia, with the exception of stock market volatility. A plausible explanation is the ideology of the Malaysian bond market: "Islamic bonds based on Shari'a principle play a major role in Malaysia's capital market." [3] Therefore, the term structure of the interest rate and economy may not have a similar impact in comparison to the other countries considered. In addition, the equity market of Malaysia is small and weak. According to the Shari'a principle, a firm's main source of borrowing should be the

[3] Source: Asian Development Bank.

bond market, not the equity market. This could be a potential reason that Malaysian stock market volatility depends on the bond market because a significant portion of the Malaysian capital market is the bond market.

Table 3. Economic Freedom Index for five countries[4]

Country	South Korea	China	India	Malaysia	Taiwan
Economic Freedom Index	71.2	52.5	55.7	69.6	73.9
Worldwide Ranking	31	137	120	37	17

In China, no macroeconomic variables have significant impacts on bond downgrade. One plausible reason is that economic freedom is less in China when compared to the other 5 countries (Table 3). Moreover, the ranking of China according to the economic freedom index is low among the 186 countries[5] for which the index is analyzed. The index of economic freedom consists of the rule of law, limited Government, regulatory efficiency, and open markets. Though the ranking of India and China is not much different, the economic structure and political stability of both countries differ. According to the economic freedom index, India has advanced economic freedom in the last two decades by improving its rules and regulation in trade freedom (free import and export of goods and services), whereas China's economic freedom has remained the same for the last 20 years. The political situation of China is the main hindrance to economic reform. In addition, the literature also supports the claim that the Chinese economy requires more flexibility and should have minimal government intervention (Bénassy-Quéré, Carton, and Gauvin, 2013; Lu, 2004; Xu, 2001). All macro-economic variables are not fully "uncontrolled;" therefore, before arriving at a decisive conclusion, a detailed study of China's corporate bond sector is necessary.

Conclusion

The major findings of this study indicate that macro-economic variables have a significant impact on three of the five chosen countries studied. However, the results vary across countries due to different economic policies or term structure.

---

[4] Source: www.heritage.org.

[5] Source: www.heritage.org.

Of the five countries considered in this study, the results for South Korea, India, and Taiwan indicate macro-economic changes can downgrade corporate bonds. The result differs for Malaysia because it is predominantly driven by the Shari'a principal. Hence, the volatility spillover of the equity market is mainly led by the bond market. Southeast Asian countries like Korea and Taiwan are export dominated countries, which has a significant impact on bond downgrades, but this is not true for China and Malaysia given their different structures.

This study offers insights to help firms anticipate and take appropriate measures to avoid bond downgrades based on macro-economic policies. This may subsequently aid in avoiding excess borrowing costs for the future. This study provides greater insights from the investors' perspective to proactively implement investing strategies based on an understanding of a country's macro-economic variables.

References

Ahmed, S. (2008). Aggregate economic variables and stock markets in India. International *Research Journal of Finance and Economics*, (14), 141–164.

Altman, E. I. (1968). Financial ratios, discriminant analysis and the prediction of corporate bankruptcy. *The Journal of Finance*, 23(4), 589–609.

—. (2000). Predicting financial distress of companies: revisiting the Z-score and ZETA models. Stern School of Business, New York University, 9–12.

—. (2005). An emerging market credit scoring system for corporate bonds. *Emerging Markets Review*, 6(4), 311–323. doi:10.1016/j.ememar.2005.09.007

Andritzky, J. R., Bannister, G. J., and Tamirisa, N. T. (2007). The impact of macroeconomic announcements on emerging market bonds. *Emerging Markets Review*, 8(1), 20–37.

Bandyopadhyay, A. (2006). Predicting probability of default of Indian corporate bonds: logistic and Z-score model approaches. *The Journal of Risk Finance*, 7(3), 255–272.

Barrows, C. W., and Naka, A. (1994). Use of macroeconomic variables to evaluate selected hospitality stock returns in the US. *International Journal of Hospitality Management*, 13(2), 119–128.

Bénassy-Quéré, A., Carton, B., and Gauvin, L. (2013). China and global rebalancing: A two-country approach. *China Economic Review*, 26, 118–139.

Bensic, M., Sarlija, N., and Zekic-Susac, M. (2005). Modelling small-business credit scoring by using logistic regression, neural networks and decision trees. *Intelligent Systems in Accounting, Finance and Management*, 13(3), 133–150.

Bhimani, A., Gulamhussen, M. A., and Lopes, S. D.-R. (2010). Accounting and non-accounting determinants of default: an analysis of privately-held firms. *Journal of Accounting and Public Policy*, 29(6), 517–532.

Bollerslev, T. (1986). Generalized autoregressive conditional heteroskedasticity. *Journal of Econometrics*, 31(3), 307–327.

Brooks, C., and Tsolacos, S. (1999). The impact of economic and financial factors on UK property performance. *Journal of Property Research*, 16(2), 139–152.

Cantor, R., and Packer, F. (1996). Determinants and impact of sovereign credit ratings. *The Journal of Fixed Income*, 6(3), 76–91.

Carling, K., Jacobson, T., Lindé, J., and Roszbach, K. (2007). Corporate credit risk modeling and the macroeconomy. *Journal of Banking and Finance*, 31(3), 845–868.

Chan, K. C., Hendershott, P. H., and Sanders, A. B. (1990). Risk and return on real estate: evidence from equity REITs. *Real Estate Economics*, 18(4), 431–452.

Chen, N.-F., Roll, R., and Ross, S. A. (1986). Economic forces and the stock market. *Journal of Business*, 383–403.

Collin-Dufresne, P., and Goldstein, R. S. (2001). Do credit spreads reflect stationary leverage ratios? *The Journal of Finance*, 56(5), 1929–1957.

Collin-Dufresne, P., and Solnik, B. (2001). On the term structure of default premia in the swap and LIBOR markets. *The Journal of Finance*, 56(3), 1095–1115.

Estrella, A., and Hardouvelis, G. A. (1991). The term structure as a predictor of real economic activity. *The Journal of Finance*, 46(2), 555–576.

Ferri, G., Liu, L.-G., and Majnoni, G. (2001). The role of rating agency assessments in less developed countries: Impact of the proposed Basel guidelines. *Journal of Banking and Finance*, 25(1), 115–148.

Fuller, W. A. (2009). Introduction to statistical time series (Vol. 428). John Wiley and Sons.

Gay Jr, R. D. (2011). Effect of macroeconomic variables on stock market returns for four emerging economies: Brazil, Russia, India, and China. *International Business and Economics Research Journal*, 7(3).

Granger, C. W. J. (1988). Some recent development in a concept of causality. *Journal of Econometrics*, 39(1), 199–211.

Kisgen, D. J. (2006). Credit Ratings and Capital Structure, *Journal of Finance*, 61(3), 1035–1072.

—. (2009). Do firms target credit ratings or leverage levels? *Journal of Financial and Quantitative Analysis*, 44(06), 1323–1344.

Kolluri, B., and Wahab, M. (2010). An Examination of India's Stock and Bond Markets Co-movements, 1–17.

Kose, M. A., Otrok, C., and Whiteman, C. H. (2003). International business cycles: World, region, and country-specific factors. *American Economic Review*, 1216–1239.

Langohr, H., and Langohr, P. (2010). The rating agencies and their credit ratings: what they are, how they work, and why they are relevant (Vol. 510). John Wiley and Sons.

Li, H., and Sun, J. (2011). Empirical research of hybridizing principal component analysis with multivariate discriminant analysis and logistic regression for business failure prediction. *Expert Systems with Applications*, 38(5), 6244–6253.

Liu, C. H., and Mei, J. (1992). The predictability of returns on equity REITs and their co-movement with other assets. *The Journal of Real Estate Finance and Economics*, 5(4), 401–418.

Longstaff, F. A., Schwartz, E. S., Journal, T., and Meeting, P. F. A. (1995). A Simple Approach to Valuing Risky Fixed and Floating Rate Debt, *The Journal of Finance* 50(3), 789–819.

Lu, D. (2004). China's capability to control its exchange rate. *China Economic Review*, 15(3), 343–347.

Maysami, R. C., Howe, L. C., and Hamzah, M. A. (2004). Relationship between macroeconomic variables and stock market indices: Cointegration evidence from stock exchange of Singapore's All-S sector indices. *Journal Pengurusan*, 24(1), 47–77.

McKee, T. E., and Lensberg, T. (2002). Genetic programming and rough sets: A hybrid approach to bankruptcy classification. *European Journal of Operational Research,* 138(2), 436–451.

Russ, R. W., Achilles, W. W., and Greenfield Jr, A. C. (2009). THE ALTMAN Z-SCORE REVISITED. *Journal of International Finance and Economics*, 9(4).

Schwert, G. W. (1989). Why does stock market volatility change over time? *The Journal of Finance*, 44(5), 1115–1153.

Scott, M., and Hashem, M. (2003). Macroeconomic Dynamics and Credit Risk: A Global Perspective.

Shin, K., and Han, I. (2001). A case-based approach using inductive indexing for corporate bond rating.

Toda, H. Y., and Yamamoto, T. (1995). Statistical inference in vector autoregressions with possibly integrated processes. *Journal of Econometrics*, 66(1), 225–250.

Xu, Y. (2001). China's exchange rate policy. *China Economic Review*, 11(3), 262–277.

CHAPTER FIVE

MODEL FOR SOVEREIGN DEFAULT AND RELATIVE VALUE

TERRY BENZSCHAWEL, YONG SU AND ANDREW MORTIMER[1]

Abstract

We combined Euromoney's Country Risk (ECR) scores with default probabilities (PDs) from the Sobehart-Keenan hybrid probability of default (HPD) model to estimate sovereigns' physical default probabilities and the relative values of their credit default swaps. The ECR scorecard ranks sovereigns' credit on a scale of 100 (best) to 0 (default) based on economic, political, structural, and other factors using standardized inputs from economists, government employees, risk managers, and traders. The HPD model is a hybrid structural-statistical model that outputs estimates of corporate default probabilities. Using credit agency ratings to link ECR sovereign scores with HPD PDs, one can impute daily PDs for global sovereign issuers. Analyses of ECR scores prior to agency ratings' changes indicate that changes in Euromoney risk scores lead sovereign downgrades and upgrades. Furthermore, plots of sovereign credit default swap (CDS) spreads against ECR scores are used to identify rich and cheap credits, which converge toward fair value over time, thereby demonstrating the ECR model's use in identifying credit relative value. Finally, we developed an adaptive scorecard, called ECR* by dynamically optimizing the weights on the ECR sub-factors to improve the predictive power of the model.

[1] Terry Benzschawel and Yong Su are from Citi Institutional Clients Group. Andrew Mortimer is at Euromoney. Terry Benzschawel is the corresponding author. E-mail: terry.l.benzschawel@citi.com.

Introduction

Although models for estimating physical default probabilities (PDs) for corporate borrowers abound,[2] estimating PDs for sovereign issuers has proven problematic. Although agency ratings for sovereign debt issues are useful for some applications, their use has several shortcomings. For example, as shown in the left panel of Figure 1, agency ratings tend to lag market perceptions of credit quality as embodied in credit spreads. That is, corporate bond yield spreads over U.S. Treasuries for firms being upgraded and downgraded move toward averages of their target rating categories months before the changes, with spreads already at their target averages at the time of the ratings' change. Second, even if ratings are correct, the fact that default rates vary with the credit cycle (see middle panel of Figure 1) limits the usefulness of rating category historical average default rates for estimating PDs. The aforementioned problems with agency ratings have caused many to favor the use of risk-neutral default probabilities calculated from credit spreads using variants of the formula:

$$PD_d^Q = \frac{e^{-sd}-1}{1-RV} \quad , \tag{1}$$

where PD_d^Q is the cumulative default probability of a bond of duration d, s is the yield spread over the risk-free rate, and RV is the recovery rate in default. The risk-neutral method has gained popularity since, except for the necessity of assuming a value for the recovery value RV one only requires information from credit spreads and bond indicative data to derive obligors' PDs. In particular, the risk-neutral model has proven useful for hedging credit portfolios, especially CDS and structured credit products. Nevertheless, as shown in the right panel of Figure 1, risk-neutral probabilities are consistently higher than historical default rates, as they include the credit risk premium (Elton, Gruber, Agrawal, and Mann, 2001).[3] Furthermore, risk-neutral PDs, being a logarithmic transformation of market-based credit spreads, provide little information as to whether assets are trading rich or cheap given their risk-reward profiles.

---

[2] See Benzschawel (2012) for a detailed treatment of many of those models (and even that list is not exhaustive).

[3] The "credit risk premium" is the excess yield over that required to compensate investors for expected losses from default (i.e., the spread necessary for an expected break-even return with a US Treasury of similar maturity). For example, that is the difference between the two curves in the right panel of Figure 1. See Benzschawel and Lee (2011) for a description of the calculation of the risk premium and Lee and Benzschawel (2013) for its historical time series.

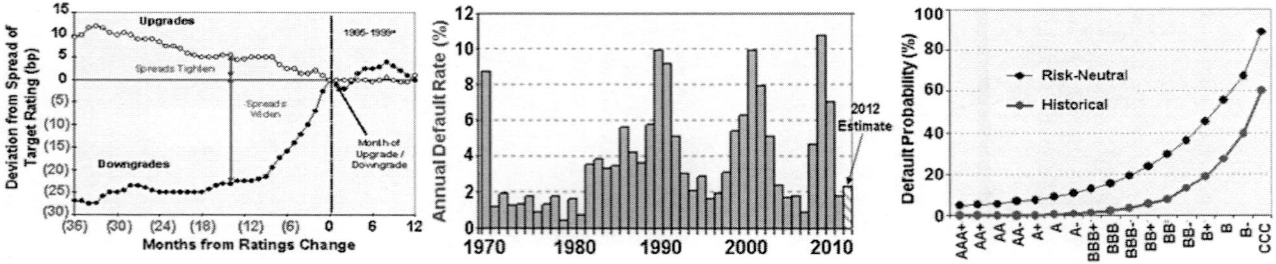

Figure 1. Left: Treasury Yields, Spread Compensation for Default, and Average Investment-Grade Corporate Bond Yields; Right: Average Daily Non-Default Spreads1998-2014.

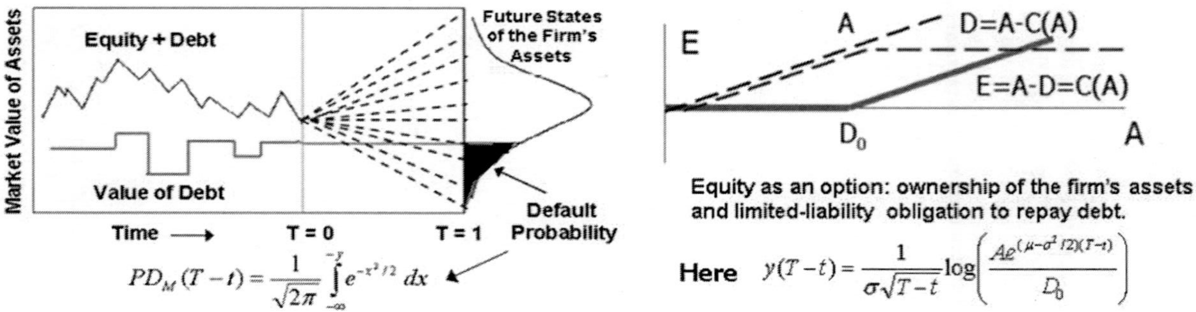

Figure 2. The Merton Structural Model that Characterizes the Risk of the Firm as Future Leverage Scaled in Units of Asset Volatility (Left) and its Interpretation as Calls and Puts on the Value of the Firm (Right).

Merton's (1974) structural model (see Figure 2) has proven useful for assessing credit risk and the relative value of corporate credits (Benzschawel, 2012). Within this view, equity holders are long a call option on the assets of the firm with the strike at the level of the debt. Conversely, debt holders have invested in a risk-free bond equal to the face value of the debt but have sold a put option to equity holders at the par value of the debt, thereby accounting for the spread premium to U.S. Treasuries.[4]

Despite some successes, particularly in signaling credit relative value,[5] the structural model has been criticized as (1) being too simplistic to describe firms experiencing deteriorating credit quality; (2) requiring ad hoc calibration of model outputs to historical default rates, and (3) challenging and modifying each aspect of the Merton model (e.g., estimating the default boundary, asset diffusion process, option pricing, asset volatility, to name a few). Also, despite its influence in academic circles, the Merton framework has not found wide usage in broker/dealer applications, which overwhelmingly favor the risk-neutral approach.

Criticisms and lack of general acceptance aside, structural models are limited in assessing sovereign risk since they require that obligors have public financials and tradable equity. Since sovereigns do not have tradable equity, it is not possible to generate PDs from structural credit models. Gray, Merton, and Bodie (2007) have attempted to extend the structural framework to estimate sovereign PDs. Despite its attractiveness from a theoretical perspective, the assumptions required are numerous, somewhat arbitrary, and complex. Thus far, that model has met with little acceptance by credit practitioners.

Recently, Benzschawel and Assing (2012) proposed a market-implied PD model that can be used for estimating physical PDs from sovereign issuers. The model is an amalgamation of the structural model approach, risk-neutral pricing, the Capital Asset Pricing Model (CAPM), and the Efficient-Market Hypothesis. In the model, the yield spread over U.S. Treasuries, s, for a risky asset of duration d is given as:

$$s = \lambda\sigma - \left\{\frac{1}{d}\ln[1 - (p_d * LGD)]\right\} \quad , (2)$$

where σ is the daily spread volatility of the asset, p_d is the cumulative default probability to time d, LGD is the loss given default, and λ is the

[4] A detailed description of the Merton model framework and many of its variants can be found in Anderson and Sundaresan (2000).

[5] See Benzschawel (2012).

daily risk premium (i.e., the average amount of spread charged by the market per unit of volatility). That is, as shown in the left panel of Figure 3, the yields spread over Treasuries is composed of two parts: the compensation for taking on spread volatility, $\lambda\sigma$ in Equation 2, and the compensation for not receiving the cash flows owing to default (i.e., given by the remainder of the expression on the right-hand side of Equation 2). As described in Benzschawel and Lee (2011), the value of λ is estimated daily by subtracting the spread due to default using values of p_d from Citi's HPD model (Sobehart and Keenan, 2002, 2003), and fitting a line of slope 1.0 to the log of the non-default spread as a function of the log volatility as shown in the middle panel of Figure 3.[6] Given the daily value of λ and a bond's current spread and a three-to-five month series of daily spreads, we can determine the market-implied PD by assuming a value for LGD and solving for p_d in Equation 2.

The main advantage of the market-implied model is that one can estimate physical default probabilities for sovereign and municipal issuers, as well as private firms, from short histories of their bond spreads. There are other attractive features as well. First, as shown Figure 4, the model can be used to track daily levels and changes in the credit risk premium (i.e., the average number of basis points of spread per unit of daily spread volatility), thereby providing information on the current compensation for taking on uncertainty of returns. In addition, by plotting countries' CDS spreads against their market-implied PDs (see Figure 5), CDS with premiums above the best-fit line are suggested as trading wide or cheap, and those trading below are rich or tight. Finally, we have used the market-implied PD model to construct a PD-weighted version of Citi's World Government Bond Index (Benzschawel and Hawker, 2012).

Despite these successes, the market-implied PD framework has not been tested extensively in a relative value context, nor is it optimized for that purpose in its current implementation. Furthermore, since the model takes data from the bond market only, it may not provide the credit spread-leading signals that are provided by structural models, which incorporate information from the equity market. For these reasons, we were anxious to explore alternative methods for estimating sovereign PDs, particularly ones that might provide information not already contained in credit spreads.

---

[6] Although slopes of best fit lines to (log s, log s) are close, but not always 1.0, we impose the 1.0 slope constraint to ensure a constant risk premium per unit of volatility regardless of spread magnitude.

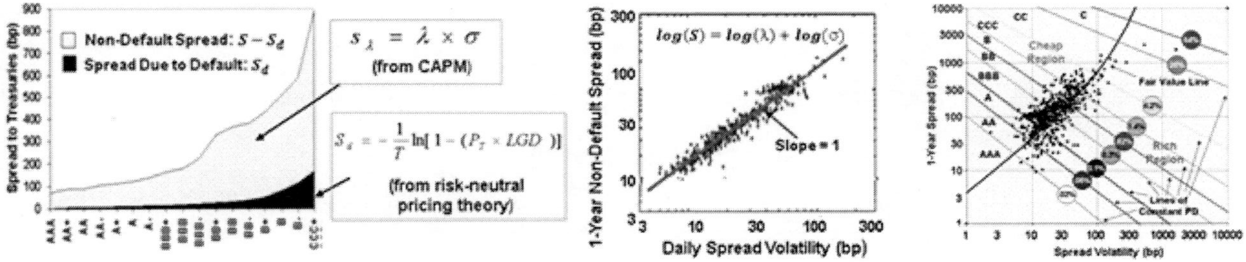

Figure 3. Market-implied PD Model Showing: Left: Separation of Default and Non-Default Related Spread; Middle: Estimation of the Daily Risk Premium; and Right: Determining Market-Implied PD from Bonds Spreads and Volatilities.

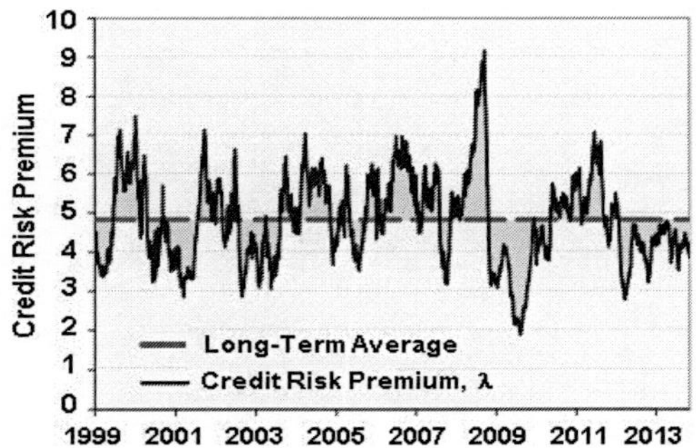

Figure 4. The Credit Risk Premium, Jan-94 to Nov-13.

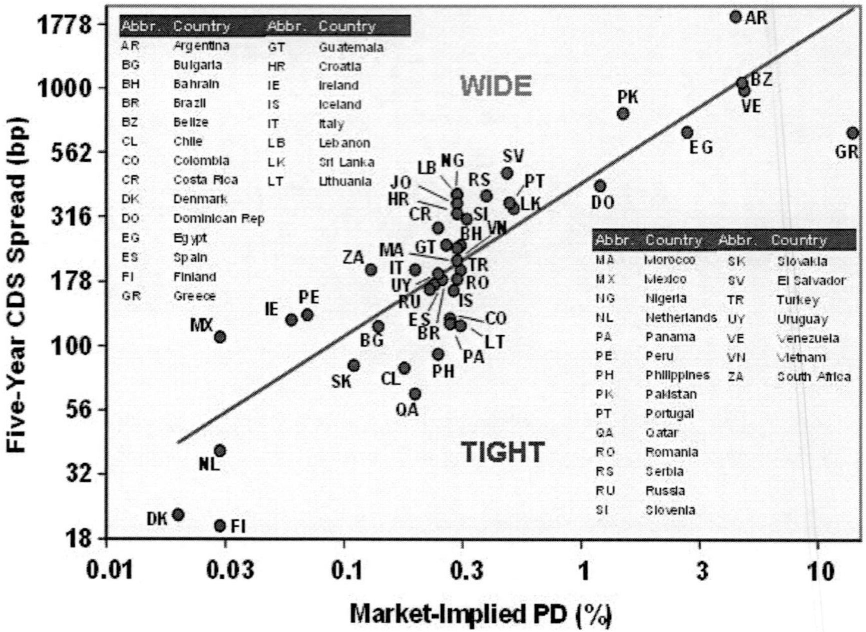

Figure 5. Credit Default Swap Spreads versus Market-Implied PDs for Major Global Sovereign Debt Issuers, 1-Nov-13.

The Euromoney Country Risk Score (ECR)

Our search for a model of sovereign credit risk that can also be used for estimating asset relative value has led us to a new class of credit model, called crowd sourcing, as embodied in the Euromoney's Country Risk Score (ECR).[7] The ECR score was launched in March of 2011, the result of the evolution of Euromoney's Country Risk Rankings, which were introduced in 1994. The ECR score represents the consensus of a network of over 400 economic, political, and country risk experts covering 186 countries. Inputs from those experts along with credit ratings, debt indicators, and access to capital determine the overall ECR score. Examples of experts and their institutions for the Asian-Pacific region along with their locations appear in Figure 6.

The ECR scorecard is presented in Figure 7. The ECR score seeks opinions of over 400 experts worldwide on two main dimensions: country risks and qualitative factors, with each contributing 70% and 30%, respectively, to the total score. The top three sections of Figure 7 show country score categories, which consist of expert scores on 15 variables relating to economic, political, and structural factors. The country scores contribute 70% to the total ECR score, with 30% contributions from economic factors and political factors, and a 10% contribution from structural factors. The items in each factor are as follows:

- **Economic Assessments**: Participants rate each country for which they have knowledge from 0-10 across 5 sub factors, each weighed 6%, for a maximum score of 30%. The categories of economic risk scored are as follows: bank stability/ risk, GNP outlook, unemployment rate, government finances, and monetary policy/ currency stability;
- **Political Risk**: Participants rate each country on which they have knowledge from 0-10 across 6 sub factors, each weighted 5%, for a maximum score 30%. The categories of political risk scored are as follows: corruption, government non-payments/non-repatriation, government stability, information access/ transparency, institutional risk, and regulatory and policy environment;

[7] An overview of the ECR model can be found at www.euromoneycontryrisk.com.

APAC Experts - Institution
APEC Secretariat
Association for International Affairs
Bank of East Asia
Barclays
Barclays Capital
BBVA
Capital Nomura Securities PLC
CIMB Niaga Bank
CIMB
Citibank Taiwan
Credit Agricole
ANZ
CTRISKS Rating Ltd.
Daiwa Securities
Hang Seng Bank

APAC Experts - Institution
HKMA
ICBC
Indian Institute of Foreign Trade
JBIC
KEXIM
Kotak Mahindra Bank
MF Global Sify Securities
Moody's Investors Service
Standard Chartered
Standard Chartered Bank
State Bank of India
EXIM Bank of the Republic of China
Mauritius Chamber of Commerce and Industry
Valuecap

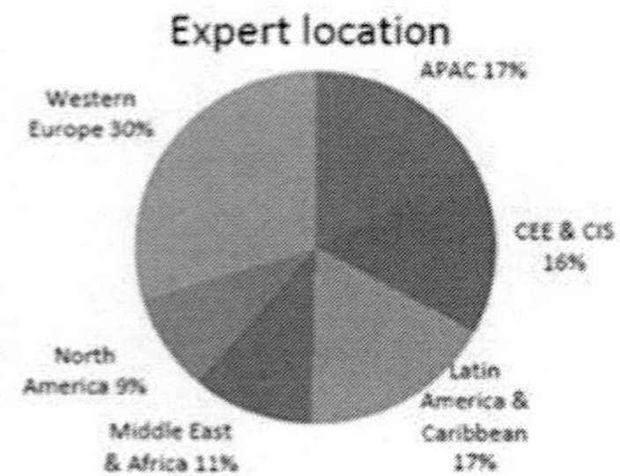

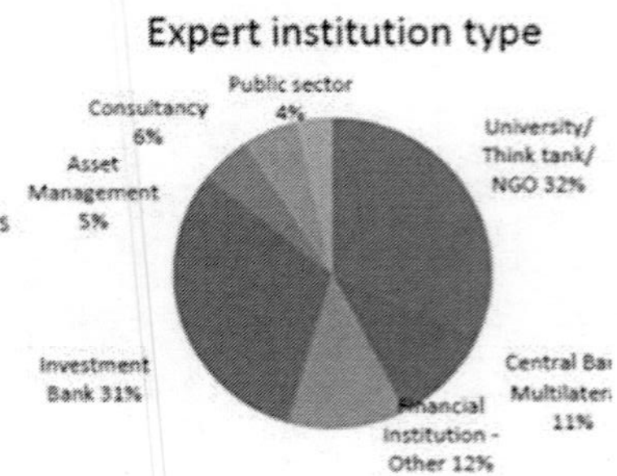

Figure 6. ECR Asia-Pacific Experts: Economists and Country Risk Managers.

- **Structural Risk**: Participants rate each country for which they have knowledge from 0-10 across 4 sub factors, each weighted 2.5%, for a maximum score of 10%. The categories of structural risk scored are as follows: demographics, hard infrastructure, labor market/industrial relations, and soft infrastructure.

The remaining 30% contribution is from three qualitative factors (labeled "Other Inputs" in Figure 7): overall credit ratings,[8] debt indicators, and access to capital, with each contributing 10% to the ECR score. Unlike the country factors on which all experts opine, only star experts have their scores submitted to the qualitative average. The scores on all of these factors are then added to produce a composite ECR score, which can have a value between 100 and 0, with 100 being nearly devoid of any risk, and 0 being completely exposed to every risk (at or near default).

A diagram of the ECR rating system appears in Figure 8. The first stage, the assembling of "experts," appears in the top left panel of the figure. As illustrated in the pie charts at the right in Figure 6, the experts are domiciled all over the globe, not just in major financial centers and their occupations span the financial industry (not just investment banks), government, and academia. This diversification of expert backgrounds is intentional because Euromoney does not wish to capture sentiment within only one sector of interest, such as financial investors. Rather, the objective of the ECR score is to embody as broad a consensus view of countries prospects as is possible. In addition, the backgrounds of the experts and the countries to which they contribute their views are also available.

[8] The credit rating is a composite of the average of ratings from Fitch, Moody's, and Standard & Poor's converted to numerical scales and normalized to the range between 10 (highest) and 0 (default).

ECR EXPERT SCORES		Weights	Sub- Weight
Economic Factors		30%	
Sub Factors	Bank Stability		6.00%
	Economic- GNP Outlook		6.00%
	Employment/ Unemployment		6.00%
	Government Finances		6.00%
	Monetary/ Currency Stability		6.00%
Political Factors		30%	
Sub Factors	Corruption		5.00%
	Govt. Non payment/ Non repatriation		5.00%
	Government Stability		5.00%
	Information Access/ Transparency		5.00%
	Institutional Risk		5.00%
	Regulatory Policy & Environment		5.00%
Structural Factors		10%	
Sub Factors	Demographics		2.50%
	Hard Infrastructure		2.50%
	Soft Infrastructure		2.50%
	Labor Market / Industrial Relations		2.50%
OTHER INPUTS			
Access to Capital		10%	
Credit Ratings		10%	
Debt Indicators		10%	

Access to Capital	A Survey of the "Head of Debt Syndicate" at major global banks on the ease of raising capital for that particular country
Credit Ratings	Credit Ratings of the major credit ratings agencies.
Debt Indicators	World Bank/ IMF debt indicator statistics

Figure 7. The ECR Scorecard for Sovereign Issuers.

The experts input their views into the ECR system using a scorecard rating system. An example of the economic portion of the scorecard appears at the top right in Figure 8. The experts input their views on each sub-factor in a major category using sliders (see figure) to set their ratings on scales of 10 (best) to 0 (worst). A similar procedure is used to input ratings for the other factors. Then, for a given country, scores from all the experts assigned to that country are aggregated to produce a country report. An example of that report for Russia in December of 2013 appears in the lower right portion of Figure 8. That report contains the overall county rating, in this example an ECR score of 51.96, along with changes in ECR score, country rank, and information on the number of expert opinions. In addition, the summary provides information on ratings for each factor (economic, political, and structural) and its momentum as well as rating, access to capital, and debt indicators.

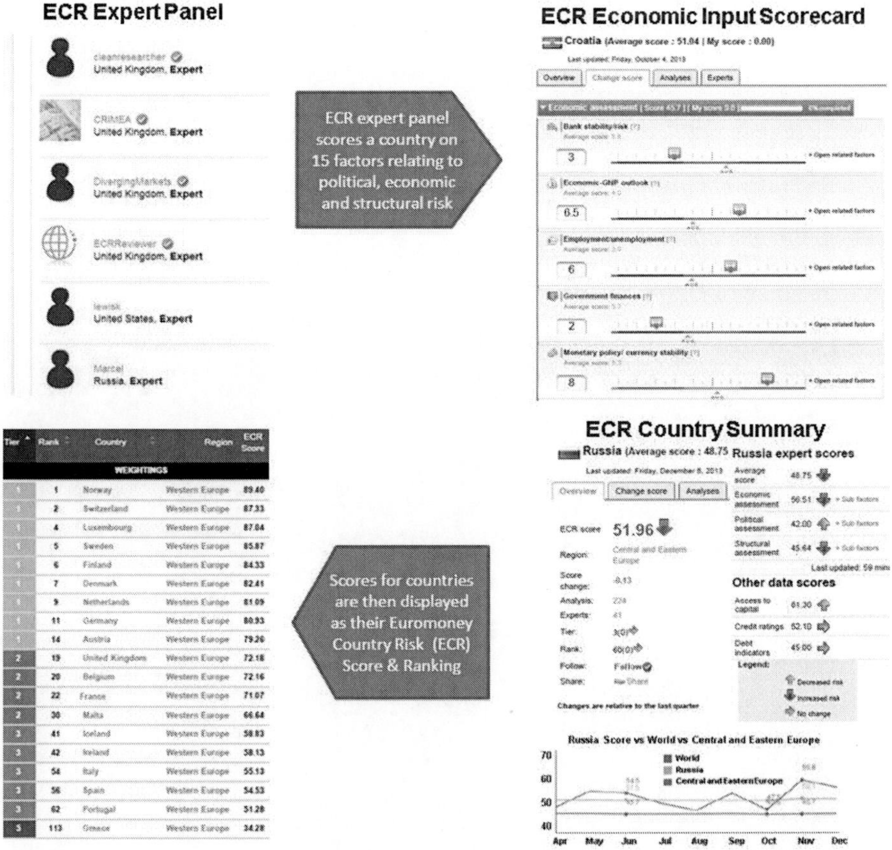

Figure 8. How the ECR System Works: A Panel of Experts (Top Left) Inputs Views via Scorecards (Top Right) that are Aggregated into Country Scores and Summaries (Bottom Right) to Create a Set of Country Scores and Risk Rankings (Bottom Left).

Euromoney Country Risk , December 2011								
Dec-11 Rank		ECR Score	Economic Risk	Political Risk	Structural Risk	Debt Indicators	Credit ratings	Access to Capital
Weightings	Country		30 '(100)	30 '(100)	10 '(100)	10 '(10)	10 '(10)	10 '(10)
1	Norway	91.17	88.17	92.36	82.13	8.88	10.00	10.00
2	Singapore	88.51	79.25	87.94	84.69	10.00	10.00	9.88
3	Switzerland	88.40	82.92	88.42	86.08	8.39	10.00	10.00
4	Luxembourg	87.84	79.88	91.85	83.75	8.76	10.00	9.00
5	Denmark	85.36	73.11	90.71	83.72	8.10	10.00	9.75
6	Finland	85.10	75.36	89.09	78.48	7.92	10.00	10.00
7	Sweden	85.08	78.83	90.15	82.35	8.24	10.00	7.88
8	Netherlands	84.71	75.93	86.79	78.29	8.02	10.00	10.00
9	Canada	84.70	77.40	88.37	77.95	7.24	10.00	9.88
10	Hong Kong	83.68	79.33	82.18	80.11	8.23	9.58	9.00
11	New Zealand	82.33	68.50	89.73	79.94	7.52	9.58	9.75
12	Australia	82.14	73.50	85.59	73.53	7.52	9.79	9.75
13	Germany	82.12	72.55	85.04	78.48	7.59	10.00	9.50
14	Austria	81.59	72.50	82.40	76.21	7.34	10.00	10.00
15	USA	76.28	56.89	83.99	78.68	6.51	9.79	9.92
16	Taiwan	76.19	71.87	73.54	72.32	7.60	7.92	9.67
17	France	76.10	61.20	78.34	73.96	6.58	10.00	10.00
18	Chile	75.24	77.05	78.52	70.14	4.53	7.71	9.00
19	UK	75.20	58.11	82.53	73.33	6.51	10.00	9.08
20	Qatar	73.20	78.43	62.66	57.83	7.34	8.75	9.00

Figure 9. Euromoney Country Score Ranking and Factor Scores as of December 2011.

The final output of the ECR system is a table of country scores and rankings as shown at the lower left panel in Figure 8. A more detailed report by country appears in Figure 9. The figure shows ECR scores and ratings on each of the six factors for the top ranked portion of the 186-country sovereign universe. As mentioned, the ECR score ranges from 100 to 0, with Norway having the highest ECR score of 91.17 (on December 1, 2011). The sum of the sub-factor ratings contributing to each of the three country factor scores are normalized to provide a score on each factor in the range from 100 to 0. The three qualitative factors are expressed on a scale of 10 to 1.

The Euromoney Country Risk Score (ECR)

While useful for a relative ranking of country risks, the ECR does not provide an estimate of likelihood of default (i.e., PDs) and is therefore of limited use for quantifying expected losses on sovereign credit portfolios. For this reason, we devised a method for linking ECR scores with PDs from Citi's HPD model using agency credit ratings as a bridge. Although Citi's HPD model cannot generate PDs for sovereigns because countries do not have tradable equity, each day we construct a map between HPD model PDs and agency ratings such as that shown in the left panel of Figure 10. The map is constructed starting with all triple-A-rated firms that have PDs from the HPD model. For example, say there are 20 firms in the mapping sample with triple-A ratings. We then assign the 20 firms with the lowest PDs from the HPD model to the triple-A bucket and compute their geometric average PD. For the example in Figure 10, that value for the triple-A-rated category is 0.01. Then we proceed to do the same for double-A-plus-rated bonds and so forth, all the way down to single-C. Of course, default is assigned a PD of 100%. Using this method, we can impute a letter rating for all firms scored by the HPD model, and those ratings for a given obligor may or may not correspond to those assigned by the rating agencies.[9]

[9] We tried other mapping schemes prior to arriving at that mentioned above, including assigning the median PD of all firms of a given rating class. Over time, we found that the above method not only preserves the distribution of ratings over the calibration universe of thousands of corporate firms, but also gives rise to the most intuitive set of ratings of all prospective methods.

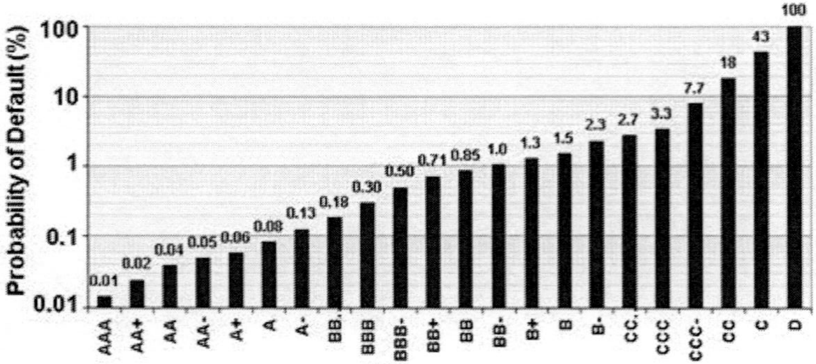

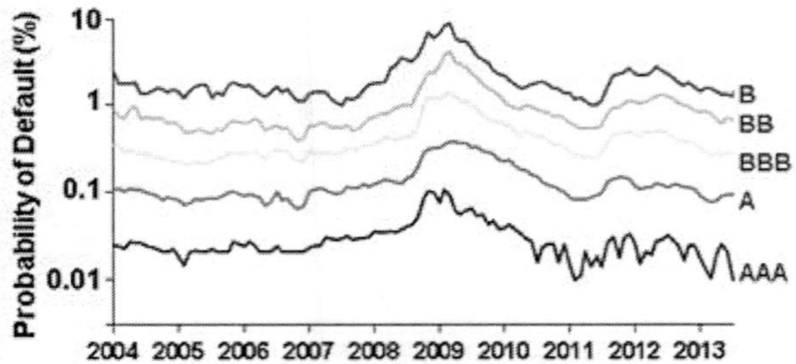

Figure 10. Left: HPD Model PDs and Imputed Ratings; Right: Time Series of Average Default Rates from the HPD Model by Rating Category.

One might ask, "Why not just make a map directly between average ECR scores for firms of a given rating category and their average historical default rates?" The answer, illustrated in the right portion of Figure 10, is that average PDs by rating category vary greatly over the credit cycle.[10] Thus, we decided to use default rates from the HPD model to assign expected default rates to scores from the ECR system.

The first step in the process of mapping ECR scores to default probabilities is to build a map between the ECR scores on a given day and rating categories. For example, the left panel of Figure 11 shows the mapping derived between credit ratings and ECR scores for August 1, 2013. These values are computed using a method similar to that used to construct the HPD PD versus agency ratings map in Figure 10. That is, we determine the number of triple-A-rated sovereigns in the sample and then assemble the same number of sovereigns with the highest ECR scores. Assume that number is 10 countries. Given the upper bound on the ECR score is 100, we need only establish the lower bound. This is given by the average ECR score of the 10th and 11th ranked countries, which, in this example is a score of 81. We proceed similarly down the rating categories scale until we get to single-C rated credits. We set the boundary between single-C and default at the average of the ECR score of the lowest single-C sovereign and 0. The right portion of Figure 11 shows how the mapping between ECR scores and ratings evolves over the period of our test from December of 2011 through August of 2013. That relationship has remained very stable over the period despite the fact that the rating agencies have made dozens of rating upgrades and downgrades of sovereign issuers over that period.

---

[10] Note that, for clarity and consistency, the default rates in Figure 10 are plotted on a logarithmic scale. Although the values shown in the figure are average PDs from the HPD model, they closely mimic average annual default rates provided by the rating agencies.

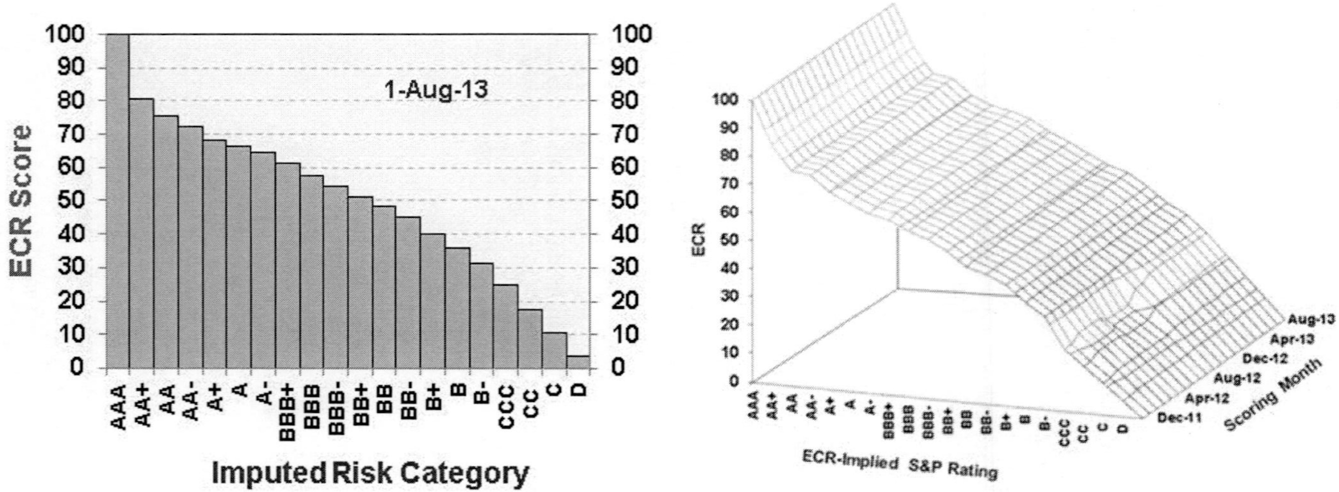

Figure 11. Map of ECR Score Ranges to Implied Credit Risk Categories, 1-Aug-13; Right: Monthly ECR Scores Mapped to Implied Credit Risk Categories, Dec-11 to Aug-13.

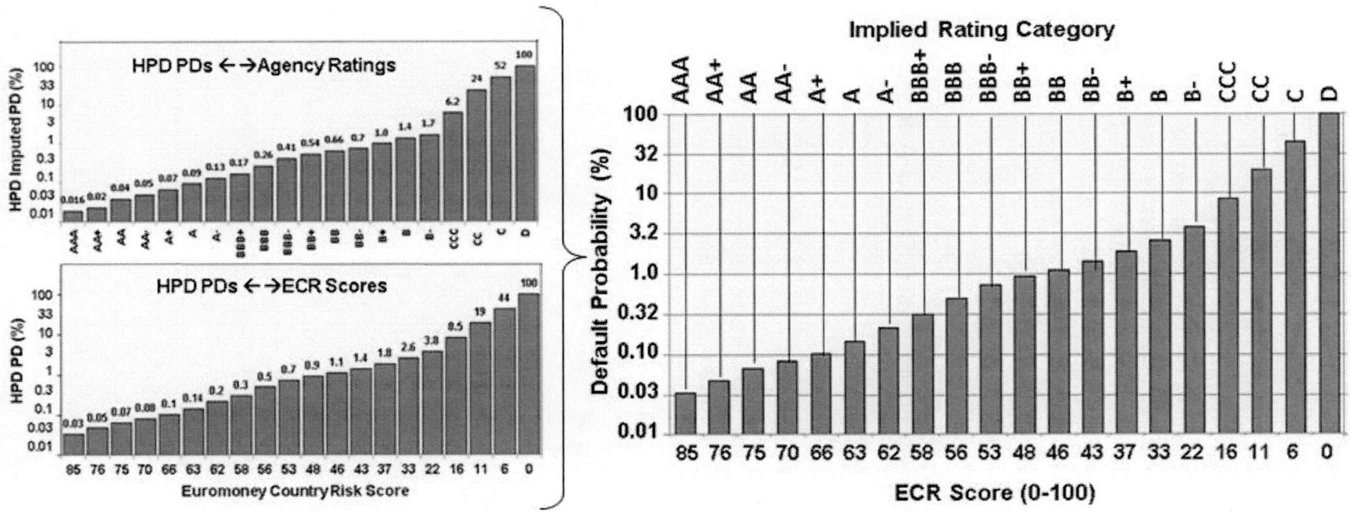

Figure 12. Mapping ECR Scores to Default Probabilities: Left Panels Show Mapping Between HPD and Agency Ratings (Top) and ECR Scores and Agency Ratings (Bottom); Right: A Three-Way Plot between ECR Scores, HPD PDs and Implied Rating Categories, 1-Aug-11.

At this point, we have a mapping between ECR scores and implied ratings, but we wish to map ECR scores to PDs. The process of inferring PDs for ECS scores proceeds similarly to the ratings' mapping. That is, we determine implied ratings from Figure 11 from our assumed 10 sovereigns with the highest ECR scores. Then, we assign each sovereign a PD based on its imputed rating from the HPD PD ←→ agency ratings map. Next, we take the geometric average of the 10 PDs and assign that PD to the average ECR score of the ten sovereigns. Hence, we associate a PD of 0.03% with the ECR value of 85 and an implied credit rating of triple-A. We call this the ECR-HPD PD. Of course, the fact that the average rating for triple-A is not identical to the 0.016% value of HPD's triple-As is due to the fact that some non-triple-A sovereigns are ranked in the top 10 of the ECR score universe. The process of assigning PDs to ECR scores is summarized in Figure 12.

ECR Scores and Agency Rating Changes

Given that ECR scores are meant to capture experts' forward-looking views on the credit prospects of the various sovereigns, we were interested in examining if changes in ECR scores would anticipate sovereigns' upgrades and downgrades by credit rating agencies. To that end, we acquired monthly agency credit ratings for the 143 sovereigns in the ECR scoring system over the sample period from December 2011 through August 2013.[11] The sample contained 44 upgrades and 69 downgrades. For each month preceding the upgrade/downgrade for each sovereign, we computed the difference between each sovereign's ECR score and the average ECR score of its target-rating category (i.e., the average ECR of the category to which it was being upgraded or downgraded).

Figure 13 displays the differences in ECR scores for the upgrades and downgrades in months relative to that of the upgrade and downgrade (0 on the x-axis).[12] The ECR model scores lead agency ratings' changes: average ECR scores for upgrades increase prior to the upgrade and scores for downgrades decrease prior to the downgrade. (Note that the method used to derive the relationship between credit spreads and agency ratings

[11] A rating change could be triggered by any of the major rating agencies: S&P, Moody's, or Fitch. To avoid double counting, we kept only the scores related to the first ratings' change for sovereigns having similar ratings' changes in subsequent months.

[12] Note that because the various upgrades and downgrades took place over different periods in the 19-month ECR score sample, their histories do not overlap completely on the graph in Figure 13.

in Figure 13 is analogous to that used for the left panel of Figure 1.) Furthermore, as for corporates in Figure 1, in the month of the ratings' change, the average sovereign ECR scores for both upgrades and downgrades are at the averages of their target rating categories. Clearly, the ECR scores begin to reflect changes in sovereign credit quality as early as ten months prior to agency ratings' changes. Notice also that the predictive power of ECR scores tends to be asymmetric; ECR scores appear to predict rating downgrades more effectively than upgrades.

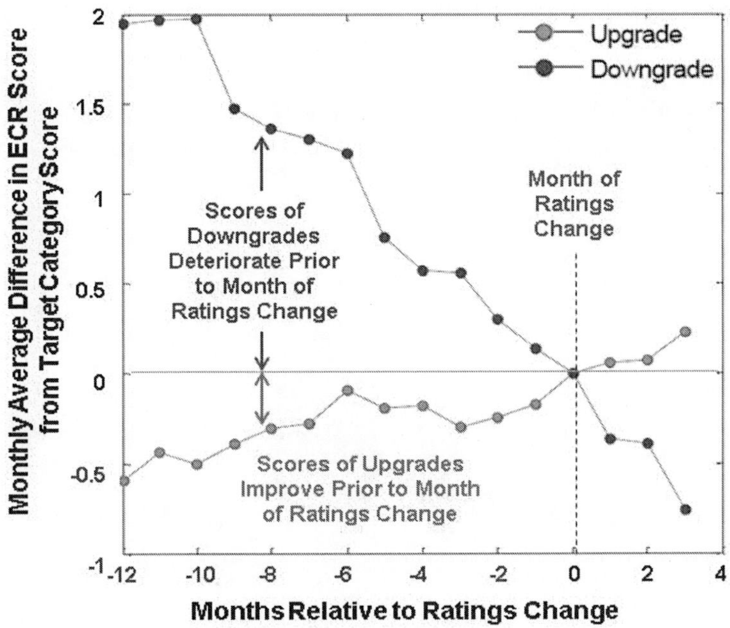

Figure 13. Time Series of Average ECR Scores for Sovereigns That Were Upgraded (N=44) and Downgraded (N=69) Relative to Averages of their Target Rating Categories Before and After the Ratings' Change.

There are several plausible reasons for the asymmetry between upgrades and downgrades. First, since ECR scores and PDs are logarithmically related, the absolute ECR score difference between a given rating category and its neighbors will be greater for the lower rating than for the higher one. Thus, upgrades should have smaller changes in ECR scores than downgrades. Also, note that for corporate upgrades and downgrades in the left panel of Figure 1, ratings' upgrades are evident in market spreads 12-24 months before downgrades become evident. Given the small interval (average of nine months) around the upgrades of the sample in Figure 13, it is possible that much of the ECR score improvement for the upgrades has already occurred prior to our sampling period. Finally, note that there is a tendency for some persistence of improving and deteriorating credit quality (persistence of changing ECRs after the upgrade or downgrade), but our sample is too small to test this reliably.

Another way to assess the ability of ECR scores to anticipate ratings' changes is to track differential changes in ECR scores for upgrades and downgrades prior to the month of the upgrade. For example, Figure 14 shows averages of three-month changes in ECR scores for upgrades (blue bars) and downgrades (red bars). The average of the three-month changes for upgrades is 0.6 and for downgrades is 0.0. The fact that the average of three-month ECR changes' prior downgrades is zero, yet for upgrades is 0.6, implies that the average ECR scores for global sovereigns improved slightly over the sample period. This is also reflected in the trend in narrowing credit spreads (see below).

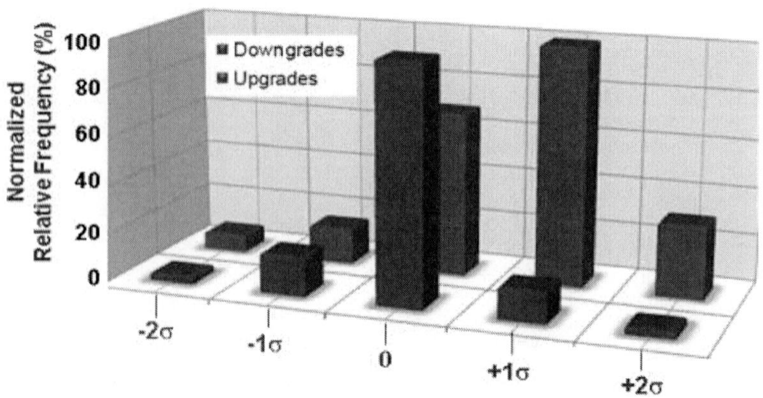

Figure 14. Densities of Three-Month Changes in ECR Scores Prior to Ratings' Upgrades and Downgrades.

We also tracked the dispersion of ECR scores over time for upgraded and downgraded sovereigns relative to their target categories. Those results are displayed in Figure 15 as a time series of distributions relative to target category averages as they approach the date of their ratings' changes. For both upgrades (left panel) and downgrades (right panel), the distributions of scores are very widely dispersed in the months prior to the ratings' change, but they converge upon the target rating category average (i.e., 0 in the figure) as they near the date of the ratings' change.

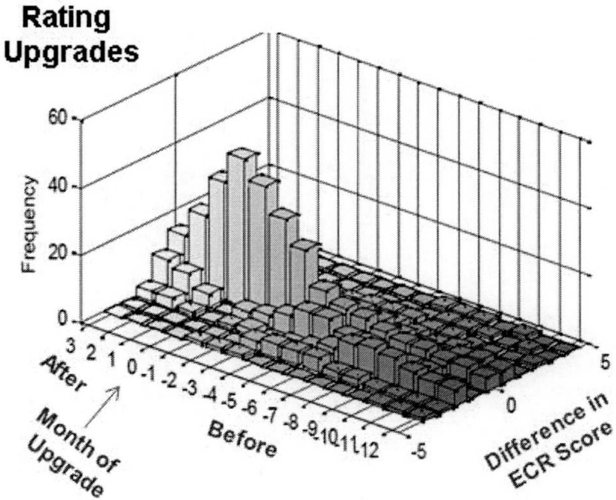

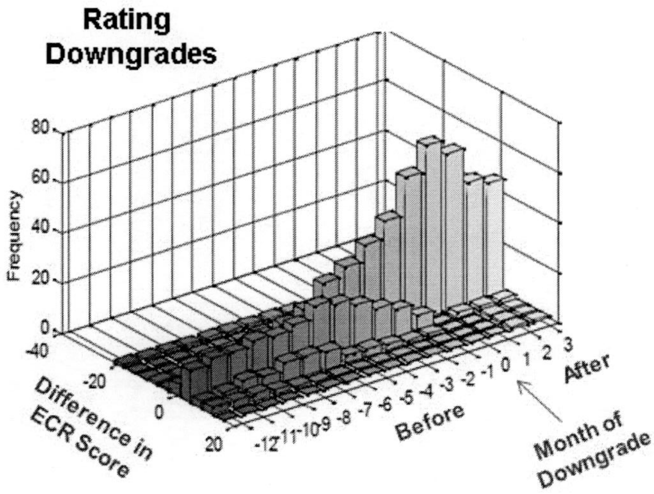

Figure 15. Pattern of Difference in ECR Scores and Target Rating Categories Relative to Months of Agency Ratings' Upgrades (Left) and Downgrades (Right).

Receiver operating characteristic (ROC) analysis is a powerful tool for assessing the discriminatory power of a system. A ROC is a two-dimensional plot where the proportion of the correct detections or "hits" is plotted on the y-axis as a function of the rate of errors, called "false positives," on the x-axis. As such, a ROC depicts relative trade-offs that a classifier makes between detecting an event and errors of incorrectly identifying events when none occurs. (A description of the important features of ROC analysis is provided in Appendix I.) In this case, we applied ROC analysis to measure the ability of three-month changes in ECR scores to predict a ratings' change within the subsequent three months. Thus, we define the independent variable, the three-month change in ECR score, as:

$$\Delta_{3m\_ECR} = ECR_t - ECR_{t-3} \tag{3}$$

with the dependent variable being whether or not a ratings' change occurred between t and $t+3$. If a ratings' change occurred, we associate a value of 1 with that Δ_{3m_ECR}; otherwise, the dependent variable is assigned a value of 0.

To generate the ROCs for upgrades, we first rank the Δ_{3m_ECR} values from largest positive to largest negative. For the ROCs for downgrades, we rank values of Δ_{3m_ECR} from most negative to largest positive. Then, say for upgrades, we go through the ranked population of Δ_{3m_ECR} scores starting from the largest and, for each population criterion, calculate the fraction of "hits." The hit rate is calculated as the fraction of sovereigns having a value of 1 (an upgrade) associated with values of Δ_{3m_ECR} below the criterion to the total upgrades in the sample. Percentages of "hits" are plotted as a function of the rate of "false positives." The false positive rate for upgrades is calculated as the fraction of all sovereigns having values of 0 (i.e., no ratings' change) associated with Δ_{3m_ECR} values for a given criterion in the ranked population with respect to the total of Δ_{3m_ECR} values for sovereigns that are not upgraded.[13]

[13] Note that for these ROCs, the dependent variable is binary: for sovereigns with ratings' changes in the subsequent three months the dependent variable associated with each Δ_{3m_ECR} is a "1" and for cases of no ratings' change, the variable is a "0."

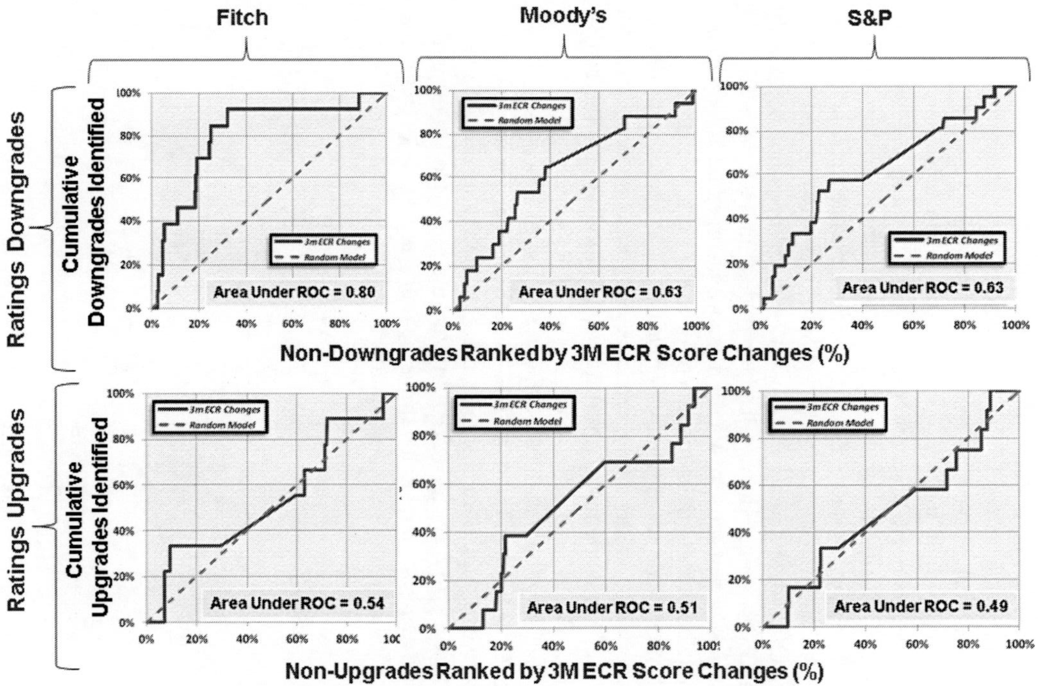

Figure 16. ROC Analysis of Ranked Δ_{3m_ECR} Predictions of Subsequent Ratings' Downgrades and Upgrades in the Following Three Months for Fitch, Moody's, and Standard & Poor's.

The ROC analysis of changes in ranked Δ_{3m_ECR} values to predict ratings' changes within the following three months appears in Figure 16. ROCs are shown for downgrades (top panels) and upgrades (lower panels) and by rating agency (Fitch, Moody's, and Standard & Poor's, respectively), from left to right. The areas under the curves (AOCs) are also shown, with areas above 0.50, indicating discriminatory power of the ECR score. Both visual inspection and areas under the ROC curves indicate that changes in ECR scores better anticipate ratings' downgrades than upgrades. While AOCs for downgrades range from 80% for Fitch to 63% for both Moody's and S&P, AOCs for upgrades are just above chance for Fitch and Moody's at 54% and 51%, respectively, and 49% for S&P. That AOCs for upgrades are close to chance does not necessarily indicate that ECR scores do not lead upgrades. In fact, inspection of Figure 13 indicates that most of the ECR score changes for upgrades are already completed prior to three months prior to the ratings' change

Finally, we evaluate the predictive power of ECR scores with respect to each of the major credit rating agencies. Figure 17 shows AOCs for downgrades (left) and upgrades (right) for Fitch, Moody's and Standard & Poor's ratings. For downgrades, changes in ECR scores better predict changes in ratings by Fitch at 80%, with anticipation of Moody's and S&P changes at 63%. Although the pattern is roughly similar for upgrades, the difference between AOCs for agencies are small, ranging from 51% for Fitch and Moody's to 49% for S&P. In fact, the ability to better predict Fitch ratings suggests that Fitch ratings actually lag those of S&P and Moody's, particularly for credit downgrades.

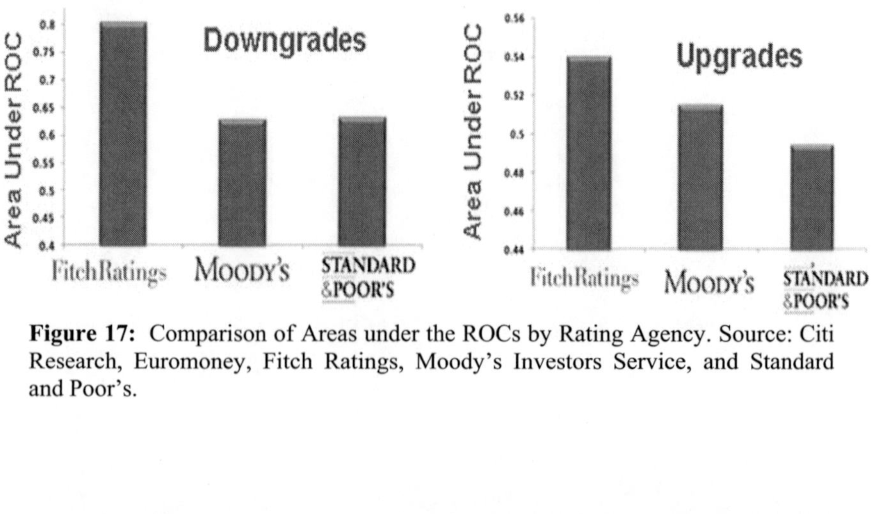

Figure 17: Comparison of Areas under the ROCs by Rating Agency. Source: Citi Research, Euromoney, Fitch Ratings, Moody's Investors Service, and Standard and Poor's.

ECR Scores and CDS Relative Value

In this section, we present returns from simulated long/short sovereign CDS trades constructed from ECR score-based measures of relative value. The procedure for these trades is similar to that we devised for long/short investment-grade corporate CDS trades based on the HPD model (Benzschawel and Lee, 2012). For example, consider Figure 18, which plots CDS spreads versus ECR scores for sovereigns in Citi's World Government Bond Index (Citigroup Index, 2012) on January 31, 2012. Corresponding ECR-based inferred PDs from the HPD, denoted PDS for imputed sovereign PD, are plotted on the top axis. Each month, we fit a regression line to five-year CDS spreads versus ECR scores (and/or) PDS, which we define as the "fair value" line. Although points deviate from the line, a linear function provides a good functional form for the relationship between ECR scores or PDS and CDS premiums.

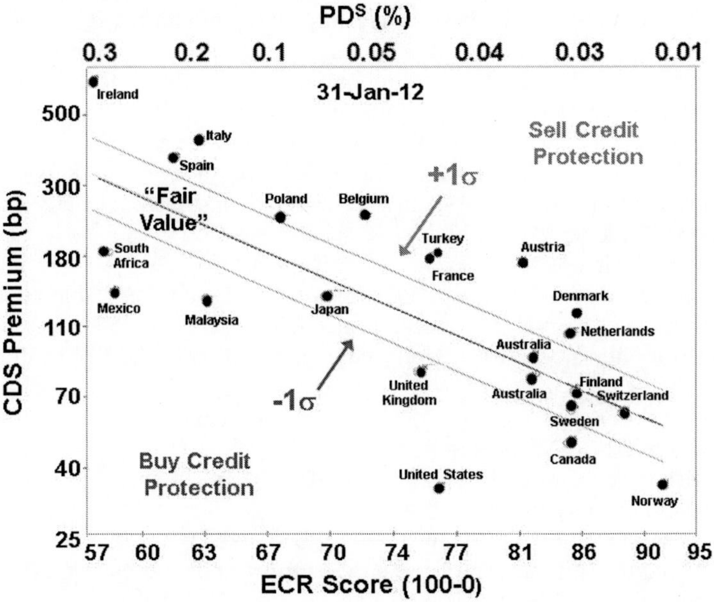

Figure 18: Plot of Five-Year WGBI Sovereign CDS Premiums Versus ECR Scores and ECR-HPD PDs, Illustrating "Cheap" and "Rich" CDS Defined by +/- 0.5σ from the "Fair Value" Regression. Source: Euromoney, Citi Research, and Markit Partners.

Having defined fair value, CDS spreads that plot above fair value in Figure 18 are inferred to be cheap, offering investors above average compensation for their credit risk. Conversely, sovereign CDS spreads below the line are rich. Lines of +/ 0.5σ are chosen to define sell/buy boundaries for short/long CDS trades. In each month, we simulate a long/short CDS trade by:

1. Eliminating from the trade the 10% of eligible credits with the largest PD^S;
2. Selling protection on all CDS above given criterion (e.g., +0.5σ or a fixed number of CDS in other studies);[14] and
3. Buying credit protection on sovereign CDS below the given criterion (e.g., -0.5σ or, for other studies, a fixed number of CDS).

In any given month, our strategy is to buy and sell protection on an equal number of sovereign CDS, all with the same assumed notional amount. We hold each monthly trade for a three-month period, such that after an initial three months, there are three long/short CDS trades active at any one time. Each month, one three-month trade rolls off to be replaced by another. We ran the long/short strategy on various subsets of the sovereign CDS universe over the period from December 2011 through August 2013 with similar results. These included trades on CDS available for all sovereigns, the countries in Citi's WGBI, and separate analyses for investment-grade rated and high yield sovereigns.

Consider first results of the long short CDS trades on the entire universe for which five-year CDS are available. We were able to find monthly spread premiums for five-year CDS contracts on 84 sovereigns. For each month in the test period, we construct a long/short portfolio by the following steps:

1. Convert ECR scores to PD^S;
2. Remove from consideration the 10% of sovereigns that have the largest one-year implied PDs;
3. Regress log PD^S against log CDS spreads of the remaining sovereigns in the sample by solving for y_0 and y_1 in the equation:

$$log(CDS_i) = y_0 + y_1 * log(PD_i) + \varepsilon_i \quad , \qquad (4)$$

[14] If there are more trades above or below +/-1σ, we add the next "cheapest/richest" credits within the "fair value" band to have an equal number of CDS on each side of the trade. Also, for some tests, we used a fixed number of long/short bonds on each side of the trade, rather than the criterion of +/-1σ.

where the subscript i stands for individual countries. The results of that regression for December 1, 2011, appear in Figure 19;

4. Calculate the relative value for each CDS as a z-score using the following:

$$z_i = \frac{log(CDS_i) - y_0 + y_1 * log(PD_i)}{\sigma_\varepsilon}, \quad (5)$$

which describes the deviation of each country's CDS from fair value. The higher a country's z-score, the cheaper its CDS, and vice versa;

5. Construct a long/short portfolio of CDS by selling protection for the cheapest 30% of CDS and buying protection on the richest 30%;
6. Finally, for comparison, construct a benchmark portfolio on which we sell protection on the middle 30% names, which is equivalent to long being those sovereigns.

After eliminating from consideration the CDS from the 10% riskiest sovereigns, we formed a portfolio of long 23 CDS and short 23 CDS with equal weights. Here we designate \$1 million (MM) notional for each CDS. So the total notional for the long/short strategy is \$23MM on each side, with the benchmark portfolio having sold \$23MM of protection.

There are two sources of profit-and-loss (P/L) from the long/short CDS trades. First, the trades have positive carry that results from buying protection on credits with narrow premiums (i.e., the rich CDS) and selling protection on CDS with higher average premiums (i.e., the cheap CDS). The carry from each long/short trade is:

$$P/L_t^{Carry} = N * \left(\sum_{i=1}^{n} c_{S_i} - \sum_{i=1}^{n} c_{B_i}\right) * 0.25t, \quad (6)$$

where N is the notional, which is the same for each CDS, n is the number of CDS, and cB and cS are the annual premiums buying and selling protection, respectively. Premiums on the CDS are paid quarterly (hence the coefficient of 0.25). The other source of P/L is from spread convergence, which is the amount that market premiums increase for CDS on which protection is bought and amount of spread tightening for CDS on which protection is sold. That is, convergence P/L for a single long/short CDS trade on which we buy protection on one CDS and sell protection on one other is calculated as:

$$P/L_{Convergence,t+0.25} = \{dV01_S * (c_{S,t} - c_{S,t+0.25})\} + \{dV01_B * (c_{B,t+0.25} - c_{B,t})\}, \quad (7)$$

where $dV01$ is the price value of a 1 basis point (bp) change in CDS spread for a given contract over the three-month period of the trade.[15] Of course, for a long/short trade of n contracts, the total convergence is:

$$P/L_{Convergence} = \sum_{i=1}^{n} \left(P/L_{Convergence,t+0.25}\right)_i \tag{8}$$

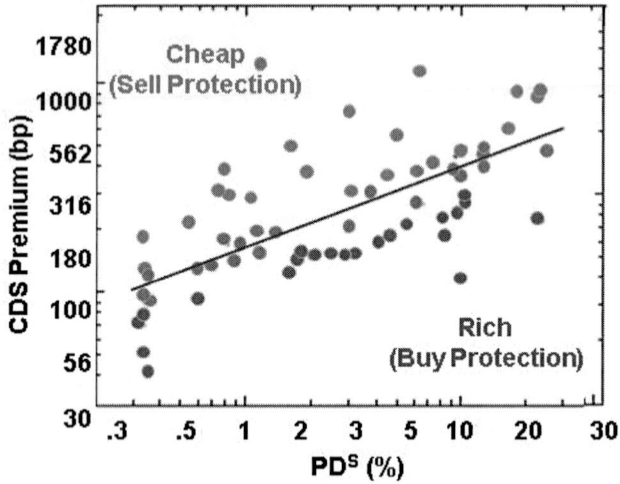

Figure 19. CDS Premiums versus ECR-HPD Default Probabilities, 1-Dec-11. Source: Euromoney, Citi Research and Markit Partners.

As mentioned, each month we construct a new long/short portfolio and hold that position for three months. Thus, after three months, there will be three overlapping trades, and we calculate the total performance of the ensemble of three-month long/short rolling trades from December 2011 to August 2013.

A summary of the results of the simulated long/short trades on the universe of sovereign CDS and the benchmark long-only strategy is presented in Figure 20. The left panel shows averages of total cumulative P/L over all trades since December 2011 normalized to the start of each trade at 0. That figure also shows average P/L broken out by carry and convergence. Although our actual strategy is to unwind each trade after a three-month holding period (the vertical dashes in Figure 20), the plot

[15] Since all the CDS in the simulation are on-the-run five-year contracts, they will have similar, but not identical, values of dV01.

tracks P/L for the trades beyond their termination date.[16] First, it is clear that the long/short CDS trades are profitable: the average terminal value at three months is positive. In addition, the plot at the left shows that, although the trades continue to be profitable beyond the three-month holding period, most of the P/L from convergence occurs within the first couple months. This pattern of P/L over time is similar to what we find for long/short CDS trades on corporate issuers and supports our choice of a three-month holding period for each trade.

The middle panel of Figure 20 displays the cumulative P/L from the series of three-month long/short CDS trades initiated monthly (solid lines). Cumulative P/L from the analogous set of long-only CDS trades (i.e., just sell protection) in the middle 30% of the relative value diagram is shown using dashed lines. P/L for both long/short and long-only strategies is broken out by total P/L carry and convergence, where convergence for the long-only strategy is from spread tightening only. Consider first, the total P/L. Given improvement in the global economy over our test period, the long-only benchmark portfolio is highly profitable, generating roughly 6.5% from December 2011 to August 2013.[17] However, total P/L from the long/short CDS trades is almost double the long only, topping 10% over the period.

Both long/short and long-only CDS trades produce consistent positive carry as indicated by the carry line and dashes, respectively, in the middle panel of Figure 20. For the long only strategy, the 2.2% return from carry comes from premiums on the 30% of CDS nearest to fair value. In comparison, positive carry from the three-month long/short CDS trades is 4.0% over the period, reflecting the difference between premiums received from selling protection on cheap CDS over those paid for protection on rich CDS.

---

[16]Since the maximum length of each subsequent monthly trade will decrease, each point on the graph at successively later months is the average of one less trade.

[17] Recall that at any given time after an initial two months period, there will be three overlapping monthly CDS trades from each strategy. This accounts for the relatively large returns. If the contracts were non-overlapping three-month trades, the long-only trades would have returned roughly 1.5% per annum and the long/short CDS trades would have returned 2.3% per annum.

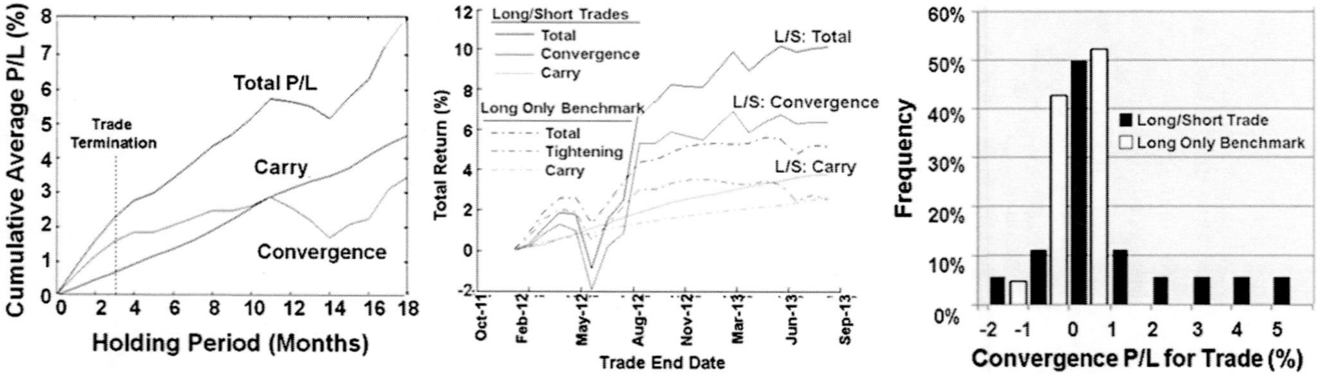

Figure 20. P/L Analysis from Long/Short ESBI Trades: Left: Average P/L of All Trades Over Time; Middle: Cumulative P/L for Long/Short Trades and Long-Only Benchmark with 3-Month Holding Periods; Right: Distribution of Convergence P/L for Long/Short Trades and Spread Tightening for the Long Only Benchmark Trades.

The middle panel of Figure 20 also shows P/L from convergence for long/short and long-only strategies. As mentioned, convergence on the long-only trades (dashes) corresponds to the overall spread tightening of CDS. For a long-only portfolio, over the long run, one would expect little P/L from spread tightening because CDS premiums should fluctuate around their average value. The fact cumulative P/L from spread tightening on the long only trades is 2% (roughly equal to the carry) is indicative of the rally in sovereign CDS spreads over the relatively small sample period available for testing. Cumulative P/L from convergence for the long/short CDS trades (the line) is just over 6%, topping the total P/L for the long only strategy. Notice that, during the late May selloff in emerging markets, both the long-only and long/short strategies were unprofitable, but both rebounded rapidly, catching up to trend P/L growth shortly thereafter.

The right panel of Figure 20 presents frequency distributions of convergence P/L for the long/short (dark bars) and long-only (white bars) CDS trades. First, note that the distribution of convergence P/L is centered on the interval between 0% and 1% for both long/short and long-only strategies. However, the long-only trades have negative skew to their convergence P/L, whereas the long/short trades have positive P/L skew. Also, the largest returns from convergence for the long-only strategy are less than 1%, whereas three of the 16 long/short CDS trades returned more than 2% from convergence over their three-month tenors.

Investment-Grade and High Yield CDS Trades

In related simulations, we split our sample of sovereign CDS into investment grade-rated (IG) sovereigns and high yield (HY) sovereigns. We examined the performance of the long/short CDS trading paradigm on each subset of the sample. As before, portfolios were constructed each month and each trade was unwound after three months. For these strategies, we used the paradigm for long and short CDS shown in Figure 18. That is, for IG and HY sovereigns, we divided the population of CDS into four groups based on their z-scores in Equation 5:

1. CDS with z-scores >= $+0.5\sigma$ (sell protection);
2. CDS with z-scores < -0.5σ (buy protection);
3. CDS with 0 < z-scores < $+0.5\sigma$ (sell protection); and
4. CDS with -0.5σ < z-scores < 0 (buy protection).

Then, for both IG and HY sovereigns, we simulated monthly long and short CDS trades between groups 1 and 2, respectively, and similarly between groups 3 and 4. Although, by design, the positive carry from the long/short trade on groups 1 and 2 will be greater than carry for 3 and 4, we can compare the differential convergence P/L between those trades. Presumably, if PDS predicts CDS spread moves, then convergence between CDS farther away from fair value (i.e., groups 1 and 2) ought to be greater than those inside the +/-0.5σ band.

The results of our simulated trades are summarized in Figure 21, which presents returns from the long/short CDS trades on IG sovereigns on the top and the analogous results for HY below. The left graphs in Figure 21 present cumulative returns for long/short trades, where we sell protection on CDS with z-scores above and below +/-0.5σ (case 1 versus 2) or within the +/-0.5σ band on both sides of z-scores = 0 (cases 3 versus 4). For both IG (top) and HY (bottom), P/L is much greater for long/short trades on CDS outside +/-0.5σ bands, suggesting that larger rich/cheap signals based on PDS are predictive of larger CDS moves. The middle panels display those results as average annual returns and Sharpe ratios, demonstrating that there is virtually no convergence for CDS within +/-0.5σ of fair value; annual P/L is actually negative for IG (and this is a positive carry trade), whereas annual P/L for HY long/short trades is just barely positive at 42bp, a factor of ten below the CDS trades outside the +/-0.5σ band.

Finally, the graphs at the right in Figure 20 display monthly average (of the three, three-month overlapping trades) P/L from convergence (dark bars) and carry (light bars) for IG (top) and HY (below). Clearly, for IG, the major source of P/L in the IG long/short trades is convergence: rich CDS becoming cheaper and cheap CDS richening. Interestingly, for HY, the carry plays a larger role in P/L than convergence most months, with convergence P/L being roughly equivalent to that for IG, but much more volatile.[18]

[18] Note that the P/L axes for results from IG and HY are on different scales.

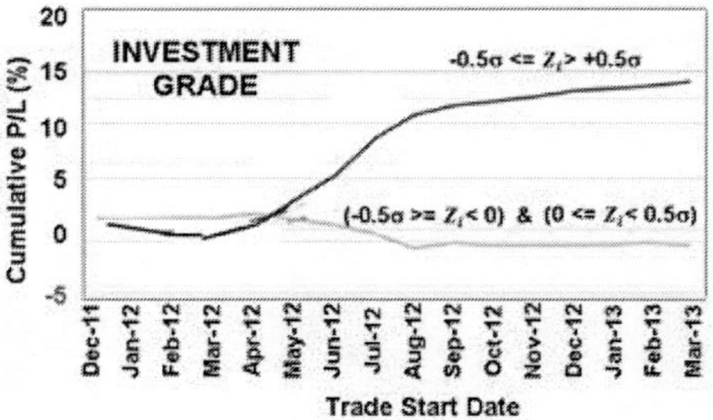

Investment Grade		
	L/S +/-0.5 Out	L/S +/-0.5 In
Ann. Return	2.81%	-0.32%
Volatility	1.87%	0.87%
Sharpe Ratio	1.50	-0.37%

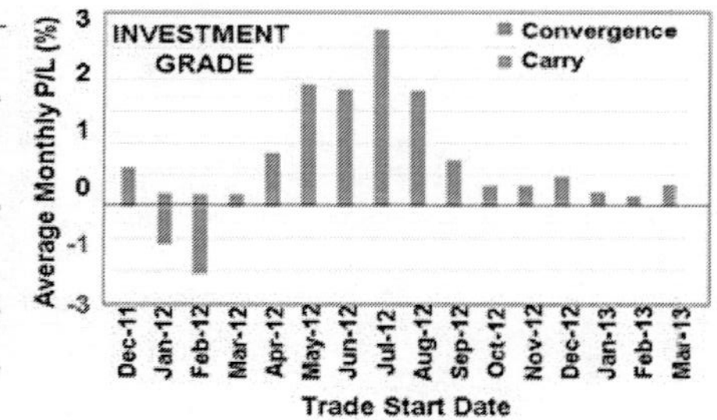

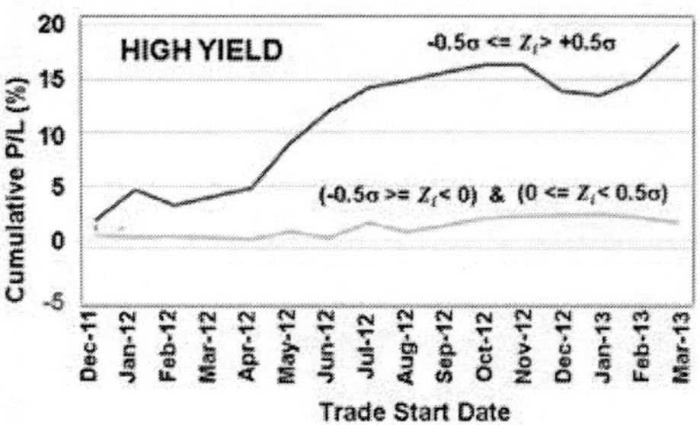

High Yield		
	L/S +/-0.5 Out	L/S +/-0.5 In
Ann. Return	4.51%	0.42%
Volatility	3.48%	1.07%
Sharpe Ratio	1.30	0.39%

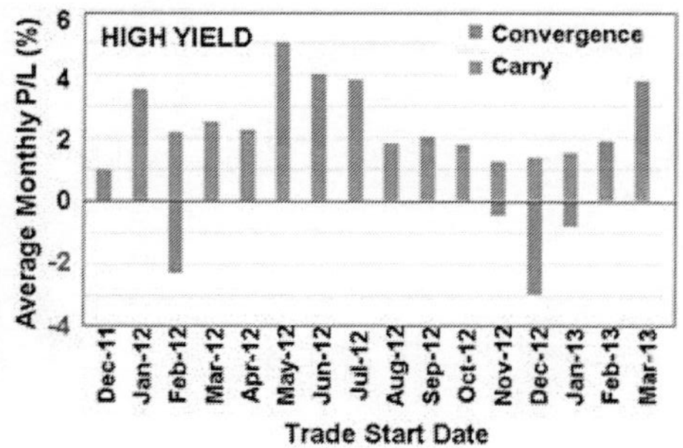

Figure 21. Analysis of Returns from Sovereign Long/Short Investment-Grade CDS (Top) and High Yield CDS (Bottom) Trades: Left: Total P/L for L/S Trades Inside (Dark) and Outside (Light) +/-0.5σ Cheap/Rich Bands; Middle: Sharpe Ratios for Those Trades; Right: Analysis of Contributions to Trade P/L from Carry and Convergence.

Long/Short CDS Trades on WGBI Sovereigns

We performed a similar analysis on CDS trades for the sovereigns in Citi's World Government Bond Index, the WGBI. Recall that Figure 18 presents the rich/cheap plot of CDS of the WGBI credits relative to +/-0.5σ, which defines the region of fair value. Although the CDS for WGBI credits was in our earlier samples, we isolate their performance here owing to the popularity of that index.[19]

The results of WGBI simulated trades are summarized in Figure 22, and the pattern is similar to that of individual IG and HY CDS. That is, P/L and Sharpe ratios are much greater for long/short CDS outside +/-0.5σ bands than inside (3.30% and 1.44 versus 0.67% and 0.86), suggesting that larger rich/cheap signals from the PD^S are predictive of larger CDS moves. However, for the WGBI, CDS within the region from 0 to +/-0.5σ display slightly greater convergence (not shown) than for IG and HY long/short trades, thereby contributing greatly to its 0.86 Sharpe ratio (versus -0.37 and 0.39 in Figure 21). This might be due to the greater liquidity in the WGBI CDS. The right panel of Figure 22 breaks monthly average P/L into P/L from convergence (dark bars) and carry (light bars) and, as for IG, the major source of P/L in the long/short WGBI trade is convergence: rich CDS becoming cheaper and cheap CDS richening.

[19] The World Government Bond Index (WGBI), Citigroup's flagship fixed income index, is comprised of investment-grade sovereign debt from 23 countries denominated in 14 currencies (see Citigroup Index Guide, 2013).

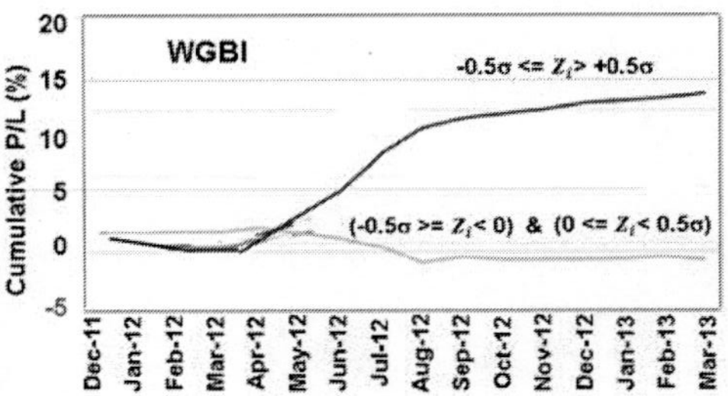

WGBI		
	L/S +/-0.5 Out	L/S +/-0.5 In
Ann. Return	3.30%	0.67%
Volatility	2.30%	0.78%
Sharpe Ratio	1.44	0.86%

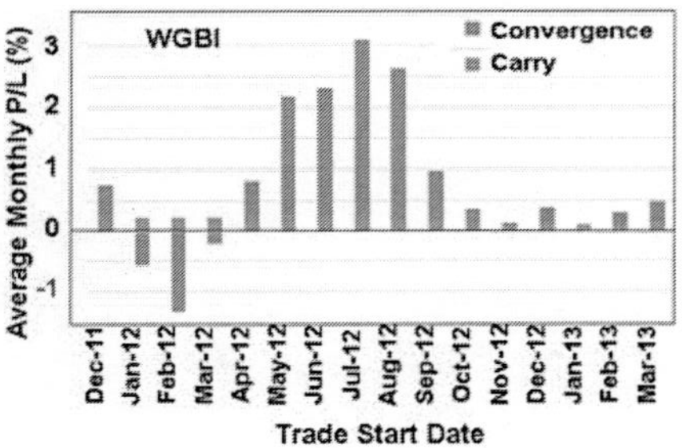

Figure 22. Analysis of Returns from WGBI Sovereign Long/Short Trades: Left: Total P/L for L/S Trades Inside (Dark Line) and Outside (Light Line) +/-0.5σ Cheap/Rich Bands; Middle: Sharpe Ratios for Those Trades; Right: Analysis of Contributions to Trade P/L from Carry and Convergence.

Toward An Adaptive ECR Score, ECR*

The weights applied by Euromoney to the major factors and sub-factors that comprise the ECR score have evolved over several decades. Nevertheless, they were assigned using subjective criteria. That is, Euromoney factor weightings are not based on quantitative studies of their ability to predict defaults or market prices. We decided to examine if, by changing the weights on the sub-factors in the model, we could improve the predictive power of ECR scores. Since there are very few sovereign defaults because the model was introduced in December 2011, adjusting model weights by optimizing on defaults is not practical. Although one might choose to optimize model weights using results of the long/short CDS trades, it seemed more expeditious, at least for this proof-of-concept, to calibrate the weights in the model to best predict ratings' changes.

Sub Factor	Weight
Bank stability/risk	2.90%
Economic-GNP outlook	9.50%
Monetary policy/ currency stability	9.58%
Employment/unemployment	8.26%
Government finances	7.64%
Government non-payments / non-repatriation	8.19%
Corruption	4.03%
Information access/transparency	3.15%
Institutional risk	8.81%
Regulatory and policy environment	2.94%
Government stability	5.71%
Soft infrastructure	3.06%
Demographics	3.71%
Hard infrastructure	4.59%
Labour market/industrial relations	4.33%
Debt indicators	2.12%
Credit ratings	10.98%
Access to capital	0.50%

Figure 23. ECR Sub-Factor Weights.

Recall that the ECR score is a weighted average of 18 sub-factors that contribute to aggregate scores arranged into 6 main factors. A list of the current weights of the sub-factors appears in Figure 23. We define our objective function for the optimization as the discriminatory power of the Euromoney score measured as the sum of the areas under the ROC curves for upgrades and downgrades. That is, we chose the weights of the sub-factors to maximize the function $f(\vec{w})$, where

$$f(\vec{w}) = \max_{w1,w2,\dots,w18}\left(Area_{Downgrades} + Area_{Upgrades}\right)$$
$$Subject\,to\colon \textstyle\sum_{i=1}^{18} w_i = 1; w_1 \geq 0, \dots, w_{18} \geq 0 \quad (9)$$

Initial attempts to apply algorithmic optimization methods resulted in problems with local minima affecting our solutions. This caused us to adopt a "brute force" optimization, whereby we sampled a large portion of the solution space at random. As shown in the pseudo code in Figure 24, we ran 100,000 simulations with weights chosen at random, computing the sum of areas under the ROCs for upgrades and downgrades for each. We then selected the 10 simulations that produced ROCs with the largest areas and took the average of their weights as our best estimate of the new ECR weights. We designate the adaptive score as ECR* to distinguish it from the original ECR score.

```
For i=1 to 100,000

  MyRand = RandToOne(18)

  % Draw 18 random numbers between 0 an 1 whose sum equals one

  Area_Down = ROC(MyRand,Downgrade_Data)
  Area_Up = ROC(MyRand,Upgrade_Data)

  Tot(i)= sum(Area_Down, Area_Up)

Next i

Optimal=max(Tot)
```

Figure 24. Pseudo Code for Optimizing ECR Sub-Factor Weights.

The results of the optimization are presented in Figure 25. The left panels show the weights of the major factors before and after the optimization. (Note that the factor weights are sums of sub-factors on which the optimizations are performed.) In general, the ordering of the major factors is not affected much; the "optimal" economic and political factor weights are only slightly larger than their original 30% values, at 37.9% and 32.8%, respectively. Slight increases in weights also occur for structural factors (15.7% versus 10%) and agency credit ratings (11.0% versus 10%). Finally, weights in debt indicators and access to capital have large decreases from their original ECR weights of 10%, with optimized weights of 2.1% and 0.5%, respectively.

Factor	Weight Original	Optimal	Change
Economic Factors	30.0%	37.9%	7.8%
Political Factors	30.0%	32.8%	2.8%
Structural Factors	10.0%	15.7%	5.7%
Credit Ratings	10.0%	11.0%	1.0%
Debt Indicators	10.0%	2.1%	-7.9%
Access to Capital	10.0%	0.5%	-9.5%

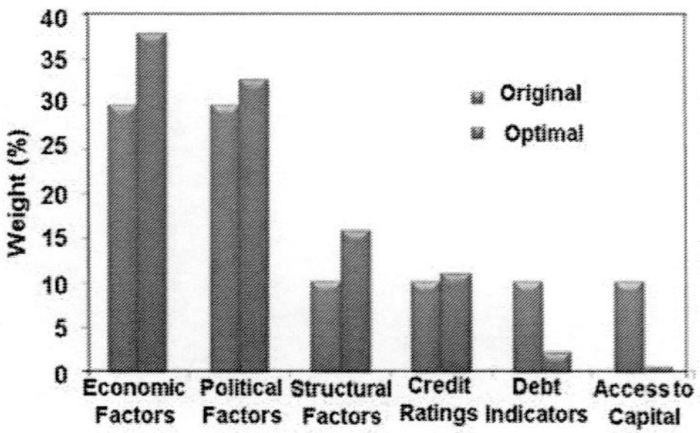

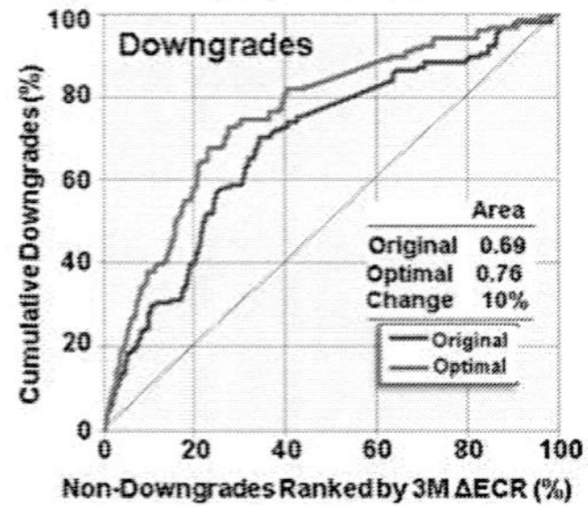

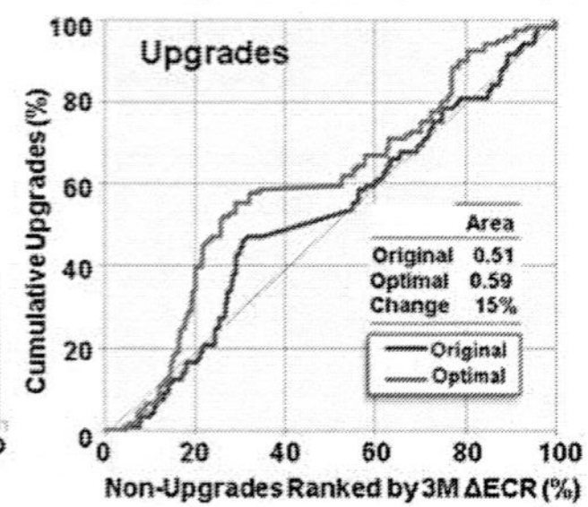

Factor/Sub-Factor	Weight Original	Optimal	Change
Credit Ratings	10.0%	11.0%	1.0%
Monetary Policy / Currency	6.0%	9.6%	3.6%
Economic GNP Outlook	6.0%	9.5%	3.5%
Institutional Risk	5.0%	8.8%	3.8%
Employment / Unemployment	6.0%	8.3%	2.3%
Gov't Non-Payment / Repat.	5.0%	8.2%	3.2%
Government Finances	6.0%	7.6%	1.6%
Government Stability	5.0%	5.7%	0.7%
Hard Infrastructure	2.5%	4.6%	2.1%
Labor Mkts / Industrial Rel.	2.5%	4.3%	1.8%
Corruption	5.0%	4.0%	-1.0%
Demographics	2.5%	3.7%	1.2%
Information Access / Transp.	5.0%	3.2%	-1.9%
Soft Infrastructure	2.5%	3.1%	0.6%
Regulatory & Policy Environ	5.0%	2.9%	-2.1%
Bank Stability / Risk	6.0%	2.9%	-3.1%
Debt Indicators	10.0%	2.1%	-7.9%
Access to Capital	10.0%	0.5%	-9.5%

Figure 25. Effect of Optimization on ECR Weights and Predictions: Left: Changes in ECR Factors; Middle: ROC Curves and Areas under Curves for Original ECR Model and ECR*; Right: Factor and Sub-Factor Weights Before and After Optimization.

The middle panel of Figure 25 shows the amount of improvement in predicting ratings' upgrades and downgrades that result from brute force optimization. That is, optimization improves ROCs for both upgrades and downgrades, with areas under the ROCs increasing by 10% and 15% on the full sample.

The right panel of Figure 25 shows the results of the optimization at the sub-factor level, whereas the factors of credit rating, debt indicators, and access to capital (which have no sub-factors) are also included. Agency credit ratings are the most important single variable, contributing 11% to the ECR* scores, but similar to their contribution in the original ECR score. The greatest overweights relative to ECR resulting from the optimization are for monetary policy/currency stability, economic outlook, employment, and various aspects of government policy. Greatest underweights of ECR* scores relative to ECR occur for regulatory and policy environment, bank stability, and the aforementioned debt indicators and access to capital. These latter underweights are somewhat surprising, but may be the result of their co-linearity with other variables.

To examine the stability and robustness of the optimized weights, we performed the optimization on an early portion of the sample, from December 2011 until August 2012, and tested the improvement on the remaining twelve months. Results of the out-of-sample testing appear in Figure 26, indicating a much-reduced improvement in predictability over in-sample optimization and testing. That is, as opposed to a 10% and 15% improvement in the areas under the ROCs for downgrades and upgrades, respectively, the out-of-sample optimization improved performance by only 4% for downgrades and was actually slightly worse for upgrades. It is worth noting that the sample size of ECR* scores and ratings' changes are now much smaller (roughly 20 upgrades and 30 downgrades in optimization and test samples). Despite the loss of predictability of upgrades in the out-of-sample testing, we find that the optimized weights are stable across in-sample and out-of-sample optimizations.

It is important to remember that this optimization is only intended as a proof of concept. As we go forward, we will re-optimize the weights with the objective of not only maximizing ROC areas for upgrades and downgrades, but also maximizing returns on long/short CDS trades. In addition, as we have demonstrated for our bank model (Benzschawel, Li, and Lee, 2013), we would optimize using adaptive methods based on a Bayesian Information Criterion as applied to the selection of scores both within and among major factor groups.

	Area Under the ROC	
	Downgrade	Upgrade
Original	0.80	0.45
Optimal	0.83	0.45
Change	4%	-1%

Figure 26. Results of Out-of-Sample Testing on Optimized ECR Score.

Analyzing Risk and Relative Value of Sovereign Portfolios

In this final section, we present an example of how ECR scores and PDS can be applied for analyzing the risk and relative value of a portfolio of sovereign CDS. Figure 27 displays a sample of a risk and relative value report for a subset of sovereigns in the ECR scoring universe patterned after reports that we have developed over the past decade for use in analyzing client portfolios. We present herein only a small portion of our typical portfolio report, with the analysis focusing on individual credits. A more detailed description of our portfolio analysis methods can be found in Benzschawel (2012).

As mentioned, the analysis in Figure 27 is patterned after our standard portfolio analysis, but illustrates only a small portion of our analytic system. Our reports provide an overall summary of portfolio risk, both from agency ratings and our PD models (i.e., HPD and market-implied) along with measures of average spread in the portfolio relative to fair value. That is, average market spreads in the portfolio are compared with what the market is paying on average for the overall default risk, duration, and recovery value. In addition, our reports provide measures of one- and three-month credit momentum, highlighting those obligors whose credit quality is improving the most and those whose credit quality is deteriorating the most. The reports also highlight bonds or CDS, which offer the best and worst relative value, and we highlight credits with the largest discrepancies between PD models and agency ratings as reflect default risk. Finally, our reports provide estimates of expected losses from default over one-, three-, and five-year horizons using our copula model of default correlation and use that method to compute distributions of expected losses and portfolio value-at-risk (VaR).

Soverign Bond Portfolio

Monday, December 31, 2012

Indicative Data				Credit Analytics											
Sovereign		Notional ($)	5-yr CDS Spread (bp)	ECR Score	ECR Implied Rating	S&P Rating	Moody's Rating	Fitch Rating	ECR 1Y PD^S (%)	S&P 1Y Implied PD (%)	Moody's 1Y Implied PD (%)	Fitch 1Y Implied PD (%)	Relative Value (Rich / Cheap)	Relative Value (Z-score)
ANGOLA	AO	1,000,000	417	39	BB	BB-	Ba3	BB-	0.62	0.52	0.42	0.71	RICH	(0.17)
ARGENTINA	AR	1,000,000	1464	34	BB	B-	B3	CC	0.91	1.14	1.13	17.32	RICH	(0.64)
AUSTRIA	AT	1,000,000	44	78	AAA	AA+	Aaa	AAA	0.07	0.08	0.08	0.05	CHEAP	0.40
AUSTRALIA	AU	1,000,000	47	81	AAA	AAA	Aaa	AAA	0.07	0.07	0.08	0.05	CHEAP	0.36
BELGIUM	BE	1,000,000	86	72	AAA	AA	Aa3	AA	0.10	0.10	0.12	0.08	CHEAP	0.18
BULGARIA	BG	1,000,000	97	51	BBB-	BBB	Baa2	BBB-	0.30	0.27	0.24	0.37	CHEAP	0.33
BAHRAIN	BH	1,000,000	201	55	BBB	BBB	Baa1	BBB	0.25	0.27	0.21	0.30	RICH	(0.03)
BRAZIL	BR	1,000,000	108	60	BBB	BBB	Baa2	BBB	0.19	0.27	0.24	0.30	CHEAP	0.19
CANADA	CA	1,000,000	38	82	AAA	AAA	Aaa	AAA	0.07	0.07	0.08	0.05	CHEAP	0.45
CHILE	CL	1,000,000	73	74	A+	AA-	Aa3	A+	0.09	0.11	0.12	0.12	CHEAP	0.22
CHINA	CN	1,000,000	64	60	A+	AA-	Aa3	A+	0.19	0.11	0.12	0.12	CHEAP	0.42
CHINA-HK	HK	1,000,000	44	82	AAA	AAA	Aa1	AA+	0.07	0.07	0.09	0.06	CHEAP	0.38
COLOMBIA	CO	1,000,000	96	59	BBB+	BBB-	Baa3		0.21	0.31	0.28		CHEAP	0.26
COSTA RICA	CR	1,000,000	230	50	BBB-	BB+	Baa3	BB+	0.32	0.37	0.28	0.46	RICH	(0.04)
CROATIA	HR	1,000,000	253	53	BBB-	BB+	Baa3	BBB-	0.27	0.37	0.28	0.37	RICH	(0.11)
CZECH REP	CZ	1,000,000	68	70	AA	AA	A1	A+	0.12	0.10	0.14	0.12	CHEAP	0.30
DENMARK	DK	1,000,000	32	83	AAA	AAA	Aaa	AAA	0.07	0.07	0.08	0.05	CHEAP	0.52
DOMINICAN REP	DO	1,000,000	403	36	B+	B+	B1	B	0.78	0.68	0.59	1.54	RICH	(0.11)
EGYPT	EG	1,000,000	480	33	B-	B-	B2	B+	0.96	1.14	0.81	1.05	RICH	(0.15)
EL SALVADOR	SV	1,000,000	410	44	BB-	BB-	Ba3	BB	0.45	0.52	0.42	0.57	RICH	(0.22)
ESTONIA	EE	1,000,000	69	70	AA-	AA-	A1	A+	0.11	0.11	0.14	0.12	CHEAP	0.28
FINLAND	FI	1,000,000	30	85	AAA	AAA	Aaa	AAA	0.07	0.07	0.08	0.05	CHEAP	0.55
FRANCE	FR	1,000,000	92	73	AA+	AA+	Aa1	AAA	0.10	0.08	0.09	0.05	CHEAP	0.14
GUATEMALA	GT	1,000,000	202	37	B+	BB	Ba1	BB+	0.68	0.44	0.32	0.46	CHEAP	0.16

Figure 27. Sample of Risk and Relative Value for Selected Sovereigns from ECR-CITI Model and Comparison of Risk with Rating Agency Ratings and Implied PDs. Source: Citi Research, Euromoney, Fitch Ratings, Moody's Investors Service, and Standard & Poor's.

Summary

We combined Euromoney's Country Risk (ECR) scores with default probabilities (PDs) from Citi's corporate HPD model to measure sovereigns' credit risk and the relative values of their credit default swaps. The ECR scorecard ranks sovereigns' credit on a scale of 100-0 (best-to-worst) based on economic, political, structural, and other factors using standardized inputs from economists, government employees, risk managers, and traders. Using credit agency ratings to link ECR sovereign scores with HPD PDs, we impute daily values of PDS for global sovereign issuers. The daily values of PDS allow us to track sovereigns' credit momentum over time. In examining the predictive power of the ECR scores, we find that changes in Euromoney country risk scores lead sovereign downgrades and upgrades. Our tests suggest that ECR scores better predict ratings' downgrades than upgrades, but the small size of our test sample, the mostly positive performance of global sovereigns over the period, and the typically earlier market recognition of improving credits limits our confidence in that result.

Regressions of sovereigns' credit default swap (CDS) spreads against their implied PDS are used to identify rich and cheap credits by their deviations above and below the line, respectively. Based on that measure, we constructed long/short CDS trades on various sets of sovereign CDS. For investment-grade, high yield, and WGBI sovereigns, we find that rich and cheap credits converge toward fair value, with most of that convergence taking place within the first three months after inception. To improve the predictive power of the ECR scores, we developed an adaptive model, called ECR*, by dynamically optimizing the weights on the ECR sub-factors. Although our current optimization is little more than a proof-of-concept, with some limitations, it at least suggests that adjusting ECR scores to better predict market data may improve the predictive power of ECR measures. Finally, we show how the PDS based on ECR scores and HPD PDs can be used to produce a risk and relative value report on portfolios of sovereign credits.

References

Anderson, R. and Sundaresan, S. A Comparative Study of Structural Models of Corporate Bond Yields: An Exploratory Investigation, *Journal of Banking and Finance* 24, pp. 255-269, 2000.

Benzschawel, T. *Credit Risk Modeling: Fact, Theory and Applications, Incisive Media*, London, U.K., 2012.

Benzschawel, T. and Hawker, B. PD-Weighted WGBI Performance, Citi, March 12, 2013.

Benzschawel, T., Li, J. and Lee, M. Predicting Bank Failure: An Adaptive Statistical Model for Estimating Banks' Default Risk, Citi, September 11, 2013.

Benzschawel, T. and Assing, A. Inferring Default Probabilities from Credit Spreads, *Journal of Fixed Income* 21 (4), pp. 13-24, Spring 2012

Benzschawel, T. and Lee, M. Market-Implied Default Probabilities: Update, Citi, September 8, 2011.

Benzschawel, T. and Lee, M. A Rule-Based Long/Short CDS Strategy, Citi, April 30, 2012.

Citigroup Index, Citigroup Global Fixed-Income Index Catalog – 2012 Edition, Citi, January 17, 2012.

Citi Fixed Income Indices, Index Guide – 2013 Edition, Citi, January 2013

Elton, J., Gruber, M., Agrawal, D. and Mann, D. Explaining the Rate Spread on Corporate Bonds, *Journal of Finance* 56, pp. 449-470, 2001.

Fama, E. The Behavior of Stock Market Prices, *Journal of Business* 38, pp. 34 105, 1965.

Gray, D., Merton, R., and Bodie, Z. Contingent Claims Approach to Measuring and Managing Sovereign Credit Risk, *Journal of Investment Management* 5 (4), pp. 5-28, 2007.

Lee, M. and Benzschawel, T. Corporate Markets Quantitative Review, Citi, November 7, 2013.

Markowitz, H.M. *Portfolio Selection: Efficient Diversification of Investments*. New York: John Wiley & Sons, 1959.

Merton, R. A. On the Pricing of Corporate Debt: The Risk Structures of Interest Rates, *Journal of Finance* 29, pp. 449-470, 1974.

Sobehart, J. and Keenan, S. Hybrid Contingent Claims Models: A Practical Approach to Modeling Default Risk, Credit Ratings: Methodology, Rationale and Default Risk, M. Ong (ed.), Risk Books, 2002.

Sobehart, J. and Keenan, S. Hybrid Probability of Default Models: A Practical Approach to Modeling Default risk, Quantitative Credit Analyst 3, Citigroup Global Markets Inc., pp. 5-29, October 2003.

Appendix I: The ROC

A ROC is a two-dimensional plot, where the variable of interest, say the likelihood that the sovereign was downgraded in the following three months, is plotted against the predictive variable, the ranked magnitude of the previous three-month change in ECR score. The ROC at the top of Figure 28 illustrates some important features:

- The negative diagonal shown by dashes is the “chance line,” where the likelihood of detecting a subsequent ratings’ change is unrelated to the previous change in ECR score; the “hit” and “false positive” rates are the same;
- The ROC “curve,” the solid curved line in Figure 28, the plot of “hits” versus “false positives” as one goes through the entire set of ranked predictors (in this case, three month changes in ECR scores from largest to smallest); and
- The dashed area under the ROC curve is an important measure of performance, whose value is the percentage of area above the negative diagonal.

The bottom portion of Figure 28 provides descriptions of the points labeled in the ROC. For example, the “star” in the plot at (hit, false alarm) = (0.0, 1.0) is indicative of a perfect predictor; all target cases are ranked above the first “false positive” in the sample. That is, all sovereigns with ratings’ changes in the following three months have larger previous three-month changes in ECR scores than those without ratings’ changes. A point along the chance line, “E”, is also shown. The point “A” is said to plot at a “conservative” criterion, as the false positive rate is very low. Points “B” and “C” illustrate more permissive criteria than “A.” Finally, the point “D” is on the ROC curve for a given level of discrimination. Note that points A, B, and C could intersect the same ROC, which would indicate superior predictability to that shown through point “D.”

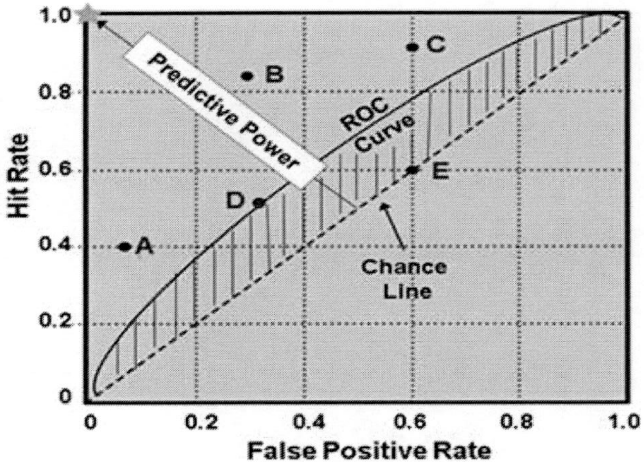

Point	Description
★	Perfect Classification
E	Poor Classification (Equivalent to Guessing)
A	Conservative Classification
B	More Permissive Classification than A, More Conservative than C
C	More Permissive than A and B
D	Worse Classification Than B (Hit Rate is Lower and False Positive Rate is the Same

Figure 28. Left: ROC Plot with Points to Illustrate Various Features; Right: Descriptions of Points on the ROC.

CHAPTER SIX

RISK MODELS FOR CMO WITH CREDIT TRANCHING

DROR PARNES AND MICHAEL JACOBS[1]

This chapter reviews our recent study, composed of two credit risk models that assess the expected time to default for senior bond classes of Collateralized Mortgage Obligation (CMO) while supported by other subordinate tranches. Although our schemes can serve a broad spectrum of structured financial instruments, we have illustrated the mathematical derivations over common hazards and retreats within the U.S. housing market, thus, in the context of CMOs. We have designed the models to be as adaptable as possible to resolve real problems in gauging the dynamic credit quality of senior bond tranches. As an important derivative of our analyses, we have discovered the limitations of these structured financial products when exposed to relatively modest probabilities of a widespread economic crisis. In particular, we have revealed that, despite their inherently supportive structures, CMOs are not as protective when a broad housing calamity advances as originally assumed.

Prior to discussing the results of our study, we wish to briefly describe the economic and the legal environments in which CMOs operate. In 1983, Lewis S. Ranieri, along with the mortgage-trading desks at Salomon Brothers and First Boston, formed the first CMO. Formally, a CMO is a Special Purpose Entity (SPE) that assembles numerous mortgage loans (also known as "collaterals") from their legal owner (the "entity") and securitizes these collaterals into "pools" of Mortgage Backed Securities (MBS). It then repackages and sells these pools to prospective investors as bond "tranches," based on a predetermined set of rules (the "structure"). In practice, many pools are clustered, based on the geographic regions in

---

[1] Dror Parnes is from University of South Florida. Email: parnesdror@yahoo.com. Michael Jacobs is from Price Waterhouse Coopers.
Email: mike.jacobs@yahoo.com.

which their respective mortgages are distributed. The entity, collaterals, and structure are collectively referred to as the "deal." In the case of agency deals, MBS pools are purchased or retained by the agency issuing the CMO. Conversely, non-agency deals are customarily funded by individual mortgage loans instead of shares of pools. CMOs supported by tranches from other CMOs are typically called Re-Remics.

While many CMOs these days contain as many as 20,000 mortgage pools, investors in CMOs often include banks, mutual funds, hedge funds, pension funds, insurance companies, and even governmental institutions and central banks. CMOs may have different structures, including sequential pay bonds, Planned Amortization Classes (PAC), or Targeted Amortization Classes (TAC). Sequential pay bonds remove principal debt from subsequent tranches only after higher-priority tranches have been retired. Many of these offerings aim for their first tranche to have an average life of 2-3 years, the second tranche to have an average life of 5-7 years, a third tranche to have an average life of 10-12 years, and so forth. PACs are amortized based on a defined schedule, as long as prepayments reside within a specific band ("collar"). TACs track an amortization schedule when prepayments approach a certain threshold. With PAC and TAC tranches, the yield, the average life, and the lockout periods are usually estimated at the CMO initiation. Overall, these diverse structures are meant to satisfy different return, risk, liquidity, and maturity profiles for investors, as well as regulatory capital requirements for banks and financial institutions alike.

Although CMOs are subject to various types of hazards, including prepayment risk, extension risk, contraction risk, reinvestment risk, and interest rate risk, they are primarily exposed to credit risk, and, in particular, to default risk. Throughout the recent U.S. housing crisis, these credit threats have become prevalent, more than ever before. Nevertheless, there are several techniques of credit enhancement that can protect CMOs' investors to different extents. These methods include cash reserve accounts, excess servicing spread accounts, overcollateralization, and various external ("third party") means of insurance. Nonetheless, the most common protective practice is ordinarily accomplished through "credit tranching."

Generally, a credit tranching mechanism requires that credit losses are absorbed first by the most subordinate class of bondholders. This procedure continues until the principal amount of the respective investment is completely eradicated. Only then does the next class of bonds engage with further credit losses and so forth until the most senior class of bondholders realizes shortfalls itself. In practice, these deals are habitually designed with specific delinquency or default "triggers" that activate sequential transfers of funds among the different bond tranches. In this case, the CMO is said to have "support tranches."

A common problem with the structure of credit tranching is that the protection given to the senior class of bondholders constantly changes as the "level of subordination" (the weight of support tranches within the entire CMO) varies over time due to either prepayments or defaults. Consequently, credit quality assessment for CMO senior classes becomes exceptionally difficult in practice. Moreover, the relative sizes of tranches and the degrees of support among these classes may diverge across different CMOs. These factors noticeably add great complexity to the credit risk appraisal of the senior bond tranches. We therefore aim our risk models to mitigate these complications by allowing ordered tranches to sequentially default and by permitting credit analysts to calibrate transition likelihoods accordingly.

In our study, we have concentrated on feasible defaults among the securitized mortgage pools and presented two relatively simple and highly intuitive risk models that assist investors in capturing the expected time to default of CMOs' senior bond tranches when supported by any number of junior debt classes. To shape universal paradigms that correspond to various economic settings, we have outlined two schemes. While the second model essentially serves as an extension of the first one, our first model requires that at least a single tranche collects debt interest to support the senior class of bondholders. The second scheme commands that at least m out of n support tranches remain operative to allow the senior class of bonds to service its corresponding debt. These models can serve institutions trading CMOs, respective investors, and credit rating agencies that attempt to grade the risks involved in these relatively complex financial instruments.

In our models, we have considered that a CMO is constructed from n supporting tranches, all linked to the same pool of MBS and clustered based on their geographic region. We have assumed that at initiation, hence at time $\tau = 0$, all n supporting tranches within the CMO start collecting interest. However, the CMO's structure requires that at least some tranches (one in the first model and any $m \leq n$ in the second scheme) endure their debt collection for the CMO's senior class to continue paying its debt-holders. In addition, we have presumed that the tranches may default due to either a major economic shock to the entire housing market at the corresponding district or because of a series of minor economic tremors within the geographic region where the underlying pool of mortgages is issued. Essentially, we allow the CMO to fold either at once or in light of progressive defaults of supporting tranches. We have also allowed for two general types of government interventions in the form of either minor assistance for singular distressed housing submarkets (one at a time) or more comprehensive regulatory changes that can salvage the entire geographic region at once. Yet, upon a full-blown housing crisis or a complete set of economic tremors that crumple all supporting tranches, we have allowed the CMO to reach its final states of default.

After deploying sets of differential equations and composing the necessary derivations of the models, we have turned to examine the functionality of the two proposed models. Nonetheless, since no databases of CMOs were available to us, and due to the lack of pertinent records of regional housing submarkets and ad hoc regulatory propensities (which are rather subjective in their nature), we have directed this authentication toward notional computer simulations with presumably realistic quantities.

We have decided to demonstrate the models over two representative CMOs. The first contains up to four supporting tranches, hence $n \leq 4$, but a single mandatory active tranche. To portray a credible scenario, we have selected transition rates sorted in a descending order, based on their credit qualities or potential absorptions of aggregated losses within the underlying pool. In light of the sluggish nature of many housing markets, we have elected relatively low transition rates and a reasonably lengthy period of time (one month) as our standard time-unit τ.

In addition, we have nominated homogeneous probabilities for a severe economic shock to the entire housing market at the underlying district. This allocation has simplified the presentations, yet it has also substantiated our early assumption for statistical independence between minor economic tremors and a major regional housing crisis. We have therefore allowed uniform likelihoods for a regional housing calamity to vary within the range of $\{0, 0.005, 0.01, \dots, 0.10\}$ and subsequently tested how the Expected Time to Default (ETD) changes with respect to fluctuations in the probabilities for a widespread economic shock to the broader housing market.

We have conducted another set of simulations for the second model over CMOs that include up to six supporting tranches, hence $n \leq 6$, but two mandatory active tranches. Once again, we have assigned relatively low transition rates and a reasonably lengthy period of time (one month) as our standard time-unit τ, and we have further arranged transition rates in descending orders within their respective groups to better depict different tranches, which are already sorted based on their distinct credit-loss capacities. Again, we have allowed identical likelihoods for a regional housing crisis to alter within the interval of $\{0, 0.005, 0.01, \ldots, 0.10\}$ and consequently tested how the ETD varies with respect to changes in probabilities for a widespread economic shock to the entire housing market.

The combined results of the above simulations were rather striking. In light of arbitrarily selected figures, relatively low probabilities (up to 5%) for a widespread housing crisis have evidently yielded significant differences in the creditworthiness of CMOs that contain different numbers of supporting tranches. Conversely, relatively moderate likelihoods (from 5% to 10%) for a widespread housing calamity have produced only minor differences in the creditworthiness of CMOs that hold diverse levels of supporting tranches. Moreover, for the above designated quantities, even slightly higher chances for such a macroeconomic shock (more than 10%) have generated negligible transformations in the creditworthiness of CMOs that comprise any number of supporting tranches. These findings exhibit robust economic meaning for credit agencies that, according to many, have disappointed investors and granted higher-than-necessary credit ratings to numerous CMOs with supporting tranches during the recent U.S. housing crisis.

Throughout an array of robustness tests with other arbitrarily selected values for the models' parameters, we have confirmed that the above phenomenon sustains.

In our simulations, we have decided to demonstrate the impact of homogeneous likelihoods for a severe macroeconomic shock to a regional housing market on the expected time to default of CMOs' senior tranches. Within these experiments, we have unified all respective probabilities (within diverse states of nature) for major economic shocks. This characterization has complemented our primary presumption for statistical independence between minor economic tremors and a major widespread housing crisis. Nevertheless, our two models sustain, both mathematically and economically, more heterogeneous allocations among these likelihoods. When the economic circumstances promote some levels of dependency across specific submarkets and regional markets, one can straightforwardly adjust the models and further calibrate them with binding functions that associate the models' parameters. For instance, when the likelihoods for minor economic tremors are known to be positively (negatively) correlated with the probabilities of major economic shocks, one can link these sets of parameters through some positive (negative) coefficients.

Furthermore, one can also tune the probabilities for minor federal bailouts or major regulatory changes to respond to various economic settings. Therefore, the suggested models can add binding functions that link either some or all transition rates. Clearly, the models can also remove any one of these parameters by setting them equal to zero. These possible alterations make our models well adaptable to diverse economic settings and sufficiently flexible to various assumptions.

CHAPTER SEVEN

A SUMMARY OF "THE RELATION BETWEEN COUNTER-PARTY DEFAULT AND INTEREST RATE VOLATILITY AND ITS IMPACT ON THE CREDIT RISK OF INTEREST RATE DERIVATIVES"

GEOFFREY R. HARRIS, TAO L. WU AND JIARUI YANG[1]

According to the Triennial and Semiannual survey by the Bank for International Settlement, by the end of 2010, there were $647.762 trillion outstanding gross notional of over-the-counter (OTC) derivatives of which more than 77% (approximately $432.657 trillion) are interest rate contracts. Meanwhile, large financial institutions are linked by their mutual derivatives' agreements, which are usually collateralized to prevent huge losses caused by the default of a derivative's counterparty. The collateral amounts are typically adjusted based on the mark-to-market value of the derivative portfolio. Usually, the amount of the collateral is updated daily as the value of interest rate derivative agreements change. Therefore, a large interest rate movement in a short period, which is more likely when interest rate volatility is high, can potentially cause a huge credit loss arising from a shortfall between the value of the collateral and

[1] Harris is with the Federal Reserve Bank of Chicago. Wu is with the Illinois Institute of Technology. Yang is with FactSet Research Systems. Wu is the corresponding author. Email: twu5@iit.edu. The views expressed in this article are those of the authors and do not reflect the views of the Federal Reserve Bank of Chicago or its staff. Tao L. Wu would like to acknowledge the financial support from the Stuart School of Business at IIT and IFSID. We thank Darrell Duffie and J. Austin Murphy for very helpful comments. All errors remain our own responsibility.

the value of the derivative contracts. For example, the counterparty may default and fail to post collateral one day. Then, it may still take several days to make sure that the counterparty has absolutely defaulted and then to unwind or replace the trades. During this period, the difference between the value of derivative contracts when the portfolio is liquidated and the value of the collateral posted the4 day before the counterparty defaulted could be large. Actually, this will become even worse when big financial institutions are linked together with interest rate contracts. The default of one institution will cause losses in other institutions, which may cause them to default.

Therefore, it is important to study the relationship between interest rate volatility and the default likelihood of financial institutions and how this relationship influences the credit risk of interest rate derivatives. We take three steps to achieve this goal:

1. Model interest rate volatility to consistently match the observed yield curve and prices of interest rate derivatives in the cross section as well as historical time series.
2. Quantify the correlation between interest rate volatility and default likelihood of different counterparties using information from both credit risk markets and the interest rate market.
3. Evaluate this correlation's impact on the cost of credit default for different counterparties.

We want to specify an interest rate model that captures the following characteristics of interest rates. First, the volatility of interest rates is stochastic and is driven by unspanned factors. (See for example, Li and Zhao, 2006; Collin-Dufresne, Goldstein, Jones, 2002; Casasus, Collin-Dufresne, Goldstein, 2005). Second, the term structure of interest rate volatility is hump-shaped. (See for example, Dai and Singleton, 2000). Reno and Uboldi (2005) show that a model with hump-shaped volatility could improve the performance of the interest rate model by presenting unspanned volatility factors and in terms of the model's specification for terms of yield curve estimation errors and cap pricing performance. Third, changes in interest rate volatility are correlated with changes in interest rates. For instance, both Andersen and Lund (1997) and Ball and Torous (1999) study the dynamics of the short-term interest rate. They show that relative interest rate volatility is negatively correlated with interest rates while absolute interest rate volatility is positively correlated with interest rates. Based on the above reasons, we adopt the stochastic volatility multifactor model developed by Trolle and Schwartz (2009) to model interest rates. They also provide an analytical formula of the zero-coupon bond option in terms of a finite number of state variables, which enables us to price more complex interest rate derivatives. To quantify the correlation between interest rate volatility and the credit spread, we start by selecting an appropriate credit model. To keep the default rate (or hazard rate) positive, we use the square root process proposed by Feller (1951), which has been widely used in finance, appearing in the term structure model of Cox, Ingersoll, and Ross (1985). In the square-root process, a state variable follows a diffusion in which both the drift and the diffusion coefficients are affine functions of the state variable itself. This allows us to directly make use of all the closed form pricing formulas and statistical properties of interest rates for pricing the CDS spread and to simulate credit events. Another reason that we choose the CIR model is because we want the variance of the CDS spread to grow with its magnitude rather than to remain constant. Moreover, we assume that interest rate is correlated with the credit spread. Finally, we estimate the correlation between interest rate volatility and credit spread using an unscented Kalman filter. Last but not least, we use the Monte Carlo method to simulate the default event of 14 counterparties given the estimated interest rate and hazard rates. Then, by controlling the correlation parameter between interest rate volatility and default spread and by repeating the above process, we can study the impact of this correlation on the loss and likelihood of a credit default event for different counterparties.

Using the estimated interest rate dynamics, we can compute the loss caused by counterparty default. In order to study the influence of the correlation between interest rate volatility and credit risk on credit loss, we compute credit loss in two different situations. In the first case, we allow the interest rate to be correlated with default intensities. In the second case, interest rate volatility is assumed to be independent from default intensities. Then, by comparing results for the two cases, we can see if it makes a difference by ignoring the correlation between interest rate volatility and credit risk.

According to our numerical results, potential credit losses computed by allowing interest rate to be correlated with default intensities are always greater than the ones computed by assuming they are independent. Our estimate for the correlation between interest rate volatility and hazard rate is always positive for all counterparties. Therefore, when default happens (usually caused by a high hazard rate), we are more likely to get a higher interest rate volatility, which results in a larger credit loss. Our result indicates that ignoring the correlation between interest rate volatility and hazard rate will lead one to underestimate the expected credit loss of interest rate derivatives due to counterparty default.

References

Andersen, T.G., and J. Lund. Estimating continuous-time stochastic volatility models of the short-term interest rate. *Journal of Econometrics*, 77:343-377, 1997.

Ball, C.A., and W. N. Torous. The stochastic volatility of short-term interest rates: Some international evidence. *Journal of Finance*, 54:2339-2359, 1999.

Casassus, J., P. Collin-Dufresne, and R. Goldstein. Unspanned stochastic volatility and fixed income derivatives pricing. *Journal of Banking and Finance*, 29, 2005.

Collin-Dufresne, P., R. Goldstein, and C. Jones. Identification and estimation of 'maximal' affine term structure models: an application to stochastic volatility. Working Paper, 2002.

Cox, J. C., J. E. Ingersoll, and S. A. Ross. A theory of the term structure of interest rates. *Econometrica*, 53:385-408, 1985.

Dai, Q., and K. Singleton. Specification analysis of affine term structure models. *Journal of Finance*, 55:1943-1978, 2000.

Duffee, G. Term premia and interest rate forecasts in affine models. *Journal of Finance*, 57:405-443, 2002.

Feller, W. Two singular diffusion problems. *Annals of Mathematics*, 54:173-182, 1951.

Harris, G., T. Wu and J. Yang. The Relation between Counter-Party Default and Interest Rate Volatility, and its Impact on the Credit Risk of Interest Rate Derivatives, working paper.

Li, H., and F. Zhao. Unspanned stochastic volatility: Evidence from hedging interest rate derivatives'. *Journal of Finance*, 61:341-378, 2006.

Reno, R., and A. Uboldi. On the presence of unspanned volatility in European interest rate options. *Applied Financial Economics Letters*, 1:15-18, 2005.

Trolle, A. B., and E. S. Schwartz. A general stochastic volatility model for the pricing of interest rate derivatives. *Review of Financial Studies*, 22:2007-2057, 2009.

CHAPTER EIGHT

LIQUIDITY AND CORPORATE GOVERNANCE: EVIDENCE FROM FAMILY FIRMS

LIANG FU[1]

In this presentation, Liang Fu of Oakland University presents research by Ran Lu-Andrews, Yin Yu-Thompson, and herself, which establishes a direct link between quality of corporate governance and level of liquidity by focusing on a set of family firms. In particular, their major findings indicate that family firms have higher corporate liquidity and stock liquidity, which are consistent with the literature and the perception that, as organizations with effective corporate governance structure, family firms are more liquid than non-family firms.

Family firms, in this research, are defined as those whose "founders or their descendants are CEO or serve as the chairman of the board or have the majority holdings." Given the unique characteristic that a family is at the apex of the firms' governance institutions, family firms are suggested to suffer less severe agency problems between managers and shareholders, thus leading to superior firm performance, more conservative investment decisions, and lower audit risks than their non-family firm counterparts. The corporate governance literature has documented that stronger corporate governance improves firm liquidity. This research bridges two lines of research together and investigates directly the link between liquidity and corporate governance in the context of family firms.

The authors focus on Standard & Poor's 500 firms as of 12/31/2013 for their classification of family firms. They first present evidence from univariate analysis that family firms have a higher level of stock liquidity and corporate liquidity and that family firms are better financially positioned and tend to have lower financial leverage than their peer non-family firms. Both ordinary least squares and two-stage least squares regression analyses show that family firms hold substantially higher cash,

[1] Liang Fu is with Oakland University. Email: liangfu@oakland.edu.

short-term investments, cash from operations, and work capitals than non-family firms. Family firms also have a higher cash ratio, quick ratio, and current ratio. The tendency of family firms to hoard more corporate liquid assets is an indication of their low-risk, precautionary saving behavior. On the stock liquidity dimension, family firms also show a higher level of stock liquidity and lower liquidity risk, where the latter is proxied by the LM12 measure (Liu, 2006), which emphasizes trading speed; turnover, which emphasizes trading liquidity; and effective bid-ask spread, which captures transaction costs.

As sensitivity analysis, the authors also further partition family firms based on their different ownership structures. The founder is identified as CEO, chairman on the board, internally promoted, or with majority holdings of the firm. The analyses indicate subtle differences within family firm structure though.

This research is not only consistent with the literature that their unique ownership structure provides family firms a platform with a close monitoring mechanism and, thus, a relatively less severe agency problem, but also it helps to explain the apparent superior performance of family firms.

References

Liu, W. (2006). A liquidity-augmented capital asset pricing model. *Journal of Financial Economics* 82, 631-671.

CHAPTER NINE

CAN BALANCE SHEET DIVERSIFICATION SUBSTITUTE FOR BANK CAPITAL?

MATJAZ STEINBACHER AND MITJA STEINBACHER[1]

Abstract

We construct a structural model of credit risk to examine the relationship between bank balance sheet diversification and bank capital in terms of the stability of the banking system. By using the α-criticality index, we demonstrate that balance sheet diversification reduces the probability of a bank failure much more than diversification across the interbank market, which works only for weak shocks. Bank capital improves the bank's ability to absorb shocks and substitutes balance sheet diversification. Large systemic shocks are highly detrimental in all network topologies. Even for moderate shocks, connectivity works contagiously. The system's microstructure importantly affects the consequences of shock. In a stable banking system, banks would primarily diversify their exposure across different systemic events, if possible, and not only across the interbank market, as well as maintain adequate levels of capital. Finally, we have found an extremely nonlinear characteristic in the effects of shock.

Introduction

What is the appropriate level of capital for a bank? Should bigger banks have more capital than smaller ones? Should low-capitalized banks have more diversified balance sheets than well-capitalized banks, and

[1] Matjaz Steinbacher is a research affiliate with the Kiel Institute for the World Economy, Kiel. Email: matjaz.steinbacher@gmail.com. Mitja Seinbacher is with the Faculty of Business Studies, Ljubljana. Email: mitja.steinbacher@gmail.com.

should poorly-diversified banks have more capital than others to cover risks that arise from non-diversification? How does the system's microstructure matter?

Since the seminal work of Markowitz (1952), there has been a widespread belief that diversification of risky assets across various dimensions of time and space is beneficial. For a bank, diversification benefits are assumed to come from the smaller importance of a single asset within a diversified portfolio of assets (Beale et al. 2011; Battiston et al. 2012a). Others suggest that diversification can increase capital requirements (Lang and Stulz, 1994; Berger and Ofek, 1995; Acharya et al. 2006). Diversification can direct the bank to put resources toward less liquid and valuable assets (Rajan et al. 2000) or to increase highly volatile noninterest income (Stiroh, 2004; Stiroh and Rumble, 2006). Battiston et al. (2012b) find ambiguous effects of diversification on systemic stability. Wagner (2010) argues that diversification increases the likelihood of systemic crises.

We build a structural credit risk model on a banking network and run a series of simulation-based experiments under different circumstances to address the question of whether more diversified banks default less frequently than less diversified ones and to determine the effect of bank capital on system stability. Early credit risk models include structural and reduced-form models (see Duffie and Singleton, 2012, for an overview of these models). The network-based approach attributes a great part of the credit risk to counterparty risk and factors that arise from the network of interconnected banks (Rochet and Tirole, 1996; Allen and Gale, 2000; Furfine, 2003; Boss et al. 2004; Leitner, 2005; van Lelyveld and Liedorp, 2006; Egloff et al. 2007; Nier et al. 2007; Degryse and Nguyen, 2007; Iori et al. 2008; Allen and Babus, 2009; Schweitzer et al. 2009; Gai and Kapadia, 2010; Blume et al. 2011; Haldane and May, 2011; Caballero and Simsek, 2013; Craig and von Peter, 2014; Fricke and Lux, 2014; Steinbacher et al. 2014a,b). In such a constellation, banks as debtors affect the balance sheets of their creditors, while they are affected by their debtors. We use heterogeneous banks, which differ in size and balance sheet structures. Then, we stress the banking system with a systemic shock. It is introduced as a reduction in the value of mortgage assets by a certain percent. A bank defaults when its capital is wiped out; then its creditors are repaid the recovery rate proportion to the exposure at default. We assume that troubled banks cannot raise additional capital or be bailed out, while credit events do not exacerbate uncertainty or loss of confidence or a panic. Two different measures of diversification are used. First, we run the model on several different networks to examine the effects of interbank market diversification on the bank credit risk. The second measure is through non-interbank market diversification. The α-criticality index, as defined in Steinbacher et al. (2014a), is then used to assess the costs of shock to the banking system.

We show that shock propagation is determined by the interplay between systemic and bank-specific components. We find that interbank market diversification works only for weak shocks and promotes contagion for higher magnitudes. On the other side, bank capital improves banking system stability, ceteris paribus. Hence, a stable banking system would consist of well-capitalized banks that primarily diversify their exposure across different systemic events and not only across the interbank market. We can explain the default clustering and demonstrate that defaults are highly concentrated within the very short post-default period, even for moderate magnitude. The probability of subsequent defaults increases if a defaulted bank is linked to poorly capitalized banks or if a substantially bigger bank is heavily exposed to poorly-capitalized smaller banks. When the banking system reaches a critical point, even a small change in parameter values can cause large changes in the outcomes. This reflects the nonlinear character of the shock effects.

The paper proceeds as follows. The next section describes the model, and section 3 presents our data. Section 4 presents the results and a discussion, while the last section offers our conclusions.

The Model

The model is run in a discrete and finite time, defined on an interval $t = \{0,1,2,\ldots,252\}$. The banking network consists of a finite set of banks, which are modeled through their balance sheets. They are linked with one another through mutual exposures on the interbank market. The resulting network is a complex structure of interdependent and intertwined balance sheets (Figure 1).[2]

[2] Wasserman and Faust (1994) and Jackson (2010) provide overviews of social networks; Steinbacher et al. (2014c) examine characteristics of these models in economics and finance.

Figure 1. Graphical representation of a network.

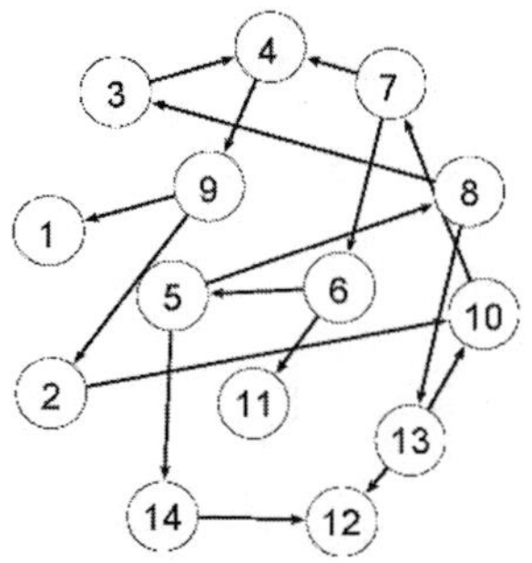

In a simplified balance sheet, total assets of bank i, $A_{i,t}$, consist of mortgage loans $H_{i,t}$, trading assets $B_{i,t}$, non-trading assets $N_{i,t}$ and the interbank market assets denoted $IB_{i,t}^{j}$:

$$A_{i,t} = H_{i,t} + B_{i,t} + N_{i,t} + \sum_{ij=1} IB_{i,t}^{j} \tag{1}$$

$$A_{i,t+1} = A_{i,t} + \Delta H_{i,t} + \Delta B_{i,t} + \Delta N_{i,t} + \sum_{ij=1} \Delta IB_{i,t}^{j} \tag{2}$$

Condition $ij = 1$ marks the link from bank j to i, while $ij = 0$ if there is no link. Directed and weighted links indicate the exposure of bank j to i with the strength given by the weight $IB_{i,t}^{j}$. By definition, an incoming link from bank i to j is an outgoing link from bank j to i representing the debt.

Banks act in both roles, as creditors and debtors. The number of incoming links denotes the number of affected banks due to the bank default. The number of outgoing links signifies the number of banks whose defaults affect a single bank. Of course, the affected banks can become the sources of affection in subsequent periods if they default. Risk propagation is illustrated in Figure 2 and shows how an initial default of bank 1 spreads along the network over time.[3] The figure demonstrates that connectivity can either share the risk across adjacent banks or induce subsequent bank defaults.

---

[3] Bright circles denote banks that were not affected by the shock, semi dark circles denote affected banks, and dark circles denote defaulted banks, while arrows denote exposures.

Figure 2. Risk propagation over time.

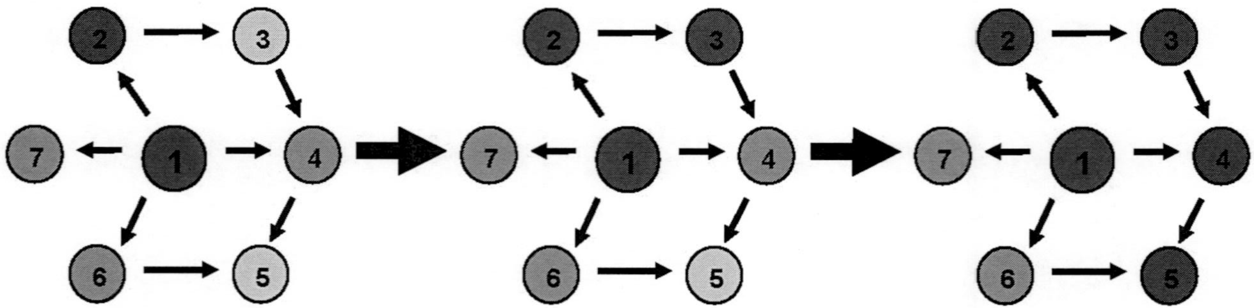

The initial value of mortgage loans is randomly assigned to each bank, while the value can only be changed by the mortgage shock in $t=10$; hence $\Delta H_{i,t=10}=\gamma H_{i,t=10}$. γ denotes the shock magnitude. We start with a zero shock ($\gamma=0$) and increase the level by a percentage point in additional runs up to the magnitude of 50% ($\gamma=0.5$). We assume that the mortgage market remains at the post-shock level and that it does not affect other parameters. Each bank is assigned a random proportion of trading assets, which consists of a random combination of 6 stocks from the DJIA. Banks keep the initially assigned portfolios throughout the runs and scenarios. We use real data for the corresponding stocks by which the market risk is treated as a part of the credit risk. Other non-trading assets are included as a residual category to keep the value of each bank's total assets intact. Its initial value is defined as the difference between the bank's initial total assets and the sum of initial values of the bank's other assets.

Bank liabilities are reduced down to bank capital $C_{i,t}$, which refers to Tier 1 capital. Its initial value for each bank $C_{i,0}$ refers to the bank's real data, while the bank capital evolves over time as:

$$C_{i,t+1}=C_{i,t}+\Delta H_{i,t}+\Delta B_{i,t}+\Delta N_{i,t}+\sum_{ij=1|C_j\le 0}\left(\left(RR_j-1\right)\cdot IB_{i,t}^{j}\right) \tag{3}$$

At the end of each period, any change in bank assets is transformed into bank capital, and the new value represents its level in the subsequent period, and so on. A bank can incur losses either from the mortgage shock or from the drop in the asset prices (market risk) or the interbank market (counterparty risk). A bank defaults when its capital is wiped out and $C_i\le 0$. Following the bank default, creditors are paid the recovery rate (RR) proportion of EAD in the subsequent period. The recovered amount increases the creditor's amount of non-trading assets N. We assume no debt subordination, collateral, security held, or debt settlement. Instead, RR levels are independent of balance sheets and assigned to each bank from the uniform distribution on an interval (0.3, 0.6). They are the same for all runs.

We impose the following supporting assumptions. There is no liquidity condition. Bankruptcies do not induce intra-industry effects, which may be the case as argued by Lang and Stulz (1992). A troubled bank can neither be bailed out nor raise additional funds to avoid a default. Banks are not allowed to form new links or intentionally sever existing ones. The link ceases to exist if and only if an adjacent bank defaults.

Data

We have 150 arbitrarily selected real banks. As our initial data, we use the banks' data on total assets and Tier 1 ratios, which we extracted from the banks' 2011 Annual Reports as of December 31, 2011. Table 1 reports some descriptive statistics.

Table 1. Descriptive statistics of banks' initial positions.

	Assets	Capital	Tier 1 ratio
Mean	388.77	45.66	12.57
Median	187.10	20.60	11.85
Max	2800.00	361.20	25.57
Min	0.20	0.02	6.60
Std. Dev.	553.16	66.84	3.51
Skewness	2.31	2.55	1.36
Kurtosis	8.47	10.06	5.28
Obs.	150	150	150

Banks are heterogeneous in both size and balance sheet structure, which has important implications for credit risk analysis (Iori et al. 2006). Generally, bank heterogeneity implies nonlinearity. The distribution of bank assets exhibits a power law characteristic ($y = Cx^{-\lambda}$) with the exponent of $\lambda = 1.75$ ($R^2 = 0.67$). This means that there are a few big banks, some medium-sized banks, and a vast majority of smaller banks (Figure 3).

The initial value of total assets of the banking system sums to 58,314.9 billion USD. Banks have 15,634 billion USD in mortgage loans, 18,037.8 billion USD in trading assets, and 6,894.5 billion USD of Tier 1 capital. The correlation between banks' initial assets and corresponding Tier 1 ratios is -0.17. The correlation coefficient between the proportion of mortgage loans and initial assets is 0.38, indicating that larger banks have a higher proportion of mortgage loans than smaller ones. The corresponding correlation between the proportion of mortgage loans and the initial Tier 1 ratio is -0.14. Initial amounts of the interbank market and other non-trading assets depend upon the network topology.

Figure 3. Initial values of banks' assets against (a) the corresponding Tier 1 ratios, (b) proportions of banks' mortgage loans, and (c) capital ratio.

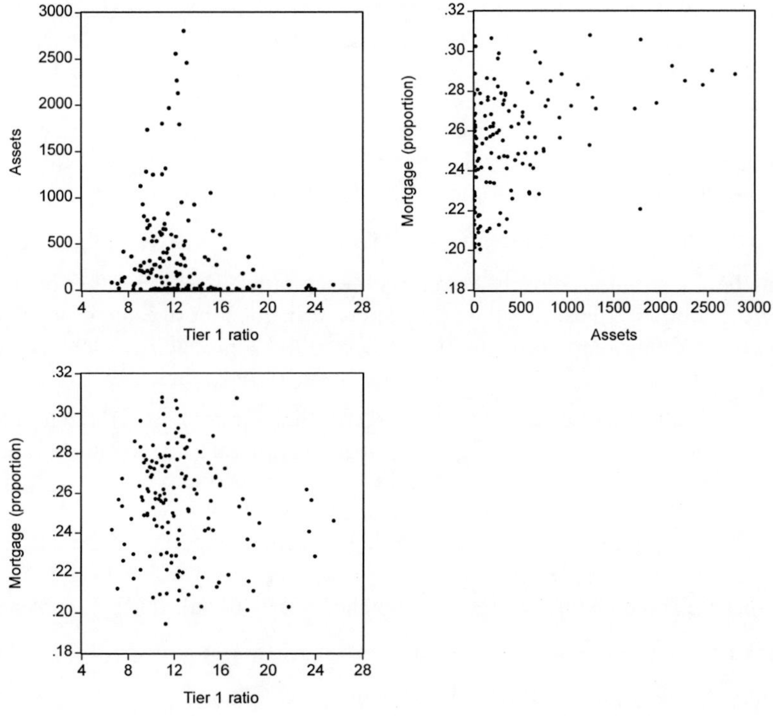

The alternative measure of diversification is represented through the occurrence of a shock. In the first scenario, each bank is affected by the shock. In the second, 100 randomly selected banks are affected by the shock, while only five of the largest banks are affected by the shock in the third scenario. The number of mortgage loans affected by the shock reaches 9,122.3 billion USD in the second scenario and 3,512.6 billion USD in the third.

For each scenario, the model is simulated on nine different network topologies, reflecting interbank diversification. The rule for link formation in the complex network is the following: if $A_{i,0} > 1700$ and $A_{j,0} > 1700$ then $\Pr(ij = 1) = 0.75$, else $\Pr(ij = 1) = 0.05$. In this network, the largest nine banks are more closely linked with each other than with other banks, representing a cohesive subgroup. There are no cohesive subgroups in other random networks, in which the link probability is set at $\Pr(ij = 1) = \varphi$ for all $i \neq j$. Links are formed independently from one another with identical probability. Here, link probability reflects the degree of interbank diversification, with the bigger the probability the bigger the diversification. PL signifies a complex banking network, in which formation depends upon the size of the two banks.

The cost of the shock to the banking system is measured through the α-criticality index. By definition, the shock is α-critical if it collapses α-part of the banking system (Steinbacher et al. 2014a). If $C_{i,t}^{b}$ represents a capital of bank i over time in a benchmark model and $C_{i,t}^{k}$ the capital with a shock of magnitude k, then the index is defined as

$$\alpha_{i,t}^{k} = \frac{C_{i,t}^{b} - C_{i,t}^{k}}{C_{i,t}^{b}} \tag{4}$$

The value of $\alpha = 1$ denotes a default of the entire banking system, while $\alpha = 0$ when the shock induces no additional effects to the system. A shock that would increase the after-shock level of capital would improve the stability of the banking system, hence $C_{i,t}^{k} > C_{i,t}^{b}$ and $\alpha < 0$. Such a scenario is not possible in our case because we neither have growth parameters nor bank bailouts. To measure pure network effects of a shock for a given magnitude, we subtract direct costs of the shock at this magnitude ($\gamma H_{i,t=10}$) and the zero-shock run from criticality values of a run at a given shock magnitude.

Results

α -criticality indices

In what follows, we present the results. In this subsection, we focus on α -criticality indices and continue with bank defaults in the next.

Throughout Figures 4-6, panel (a) presents α -criticality indices in terms of banking capital, panel (b) presents α -criticalities in terms of banking assets, panel (c) represents the differences in α -criticalities in terms of banking capital against the corresponding values in the network with $\varphi = 0.05$, and panel (d) represents pure network effects. Results refer to end-states in $t = 252$. Shock magnitudes are shown on horizontal lines.

The baseline network appears resilient for weak shocks, which do not exceed 5% (Figure 4). Shocks that do not lead to bank defaults do not induce indirect costs for which the effects are linear in magnitude and small. Along with the first defaults, the linear part of costs is increased by a discrete jump, which occurs between the magnitude of 5% and 20%. The jump can be explained by the fact that moderate shocks drastically reduce the system's capital level, making the banks highly susceptible to the counterparty risk. When banks run on minimum capital, even a small additional disturbance can initiate contagion, leading to an avalanche of bank defaults, and can turn the entire system from stability to default in a very short period of time. In such a situation, the default of a bigger bank would be particularly detrimental for the system. Figures demonstrate that network effects are the main cause of the system's fragility. For magnitudes ranging between 10% and 20%, pure network effects are the largest and vary across networks. Criticality levels increase in shock magnitude, but as the shock increases, network effects are subordinated to the shock that destroys a larger fraction of the banking capital. Network effects are the smallest in a poorly connected random network in which $\varphi = 0.05$. Because $c_{i,t} < 1$, the criticality values in terms of the banking capital are larger than in terms of the assets, ceteris paribus.

Figure 4. α -criticality indices across shock magnitudes for different network topologies within the baseline scenario.

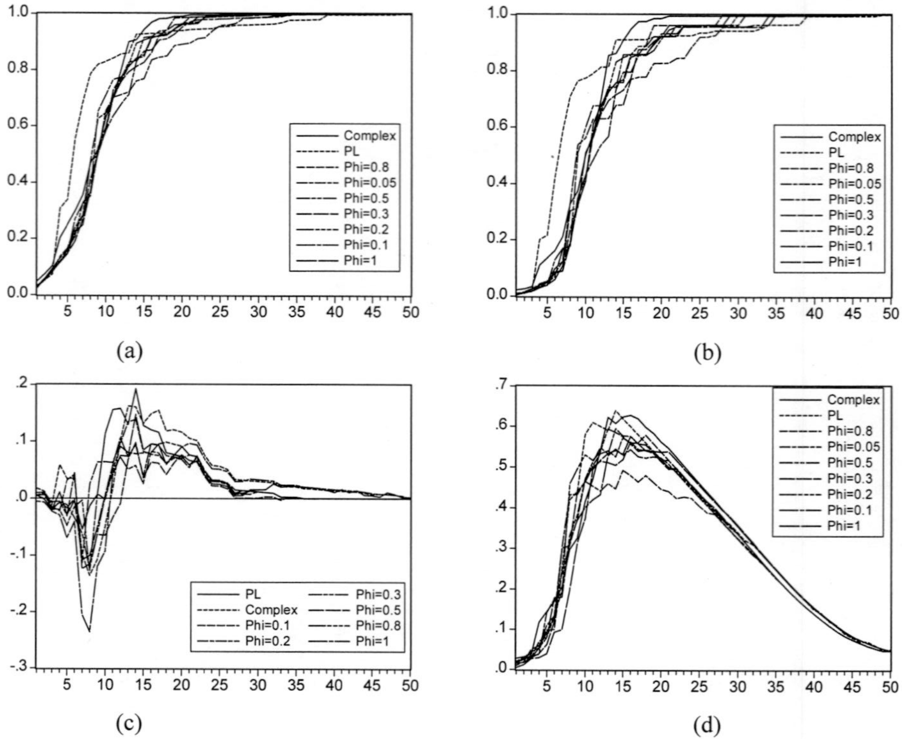

Figure 5. α -criticality indices across shock magnitudes for different network topologies within the random scenario.

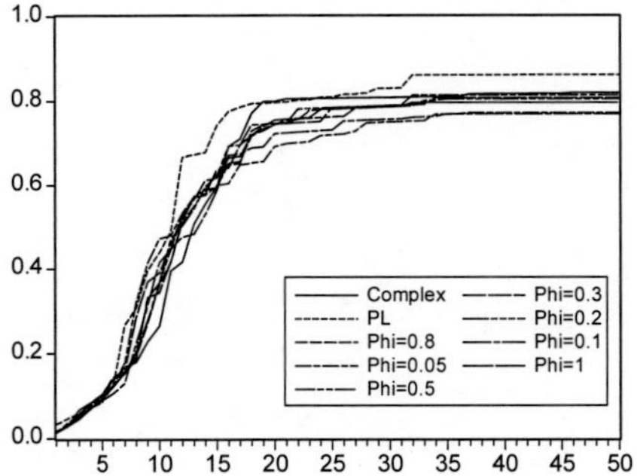

(a)

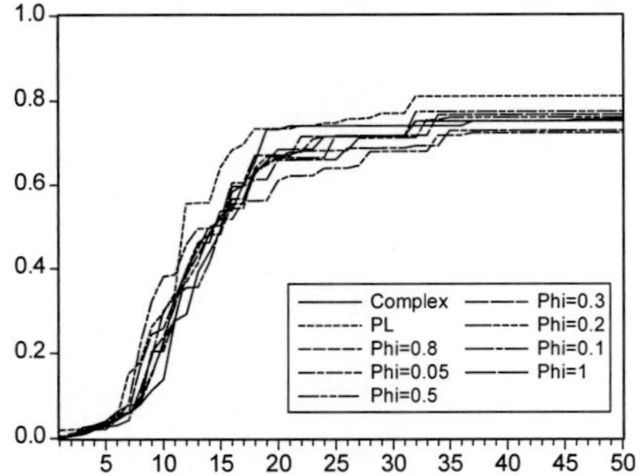

(b)

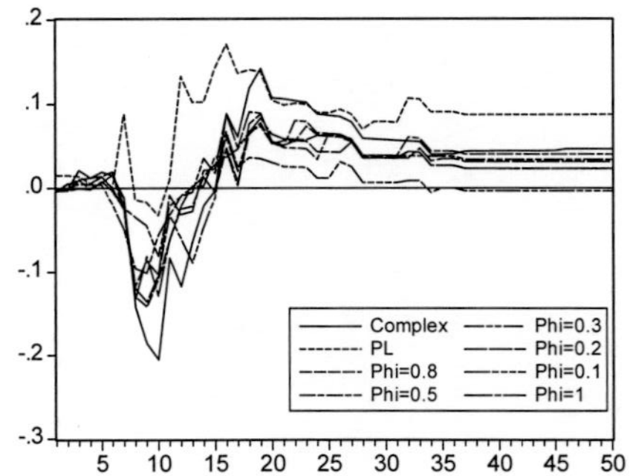

(c)

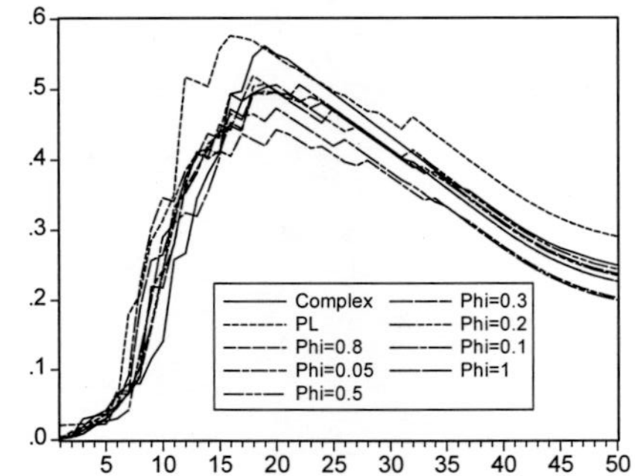

(d)

Figure 6. α -criticality indices across shock magnitudes for different network topologies within the big banks scenario.

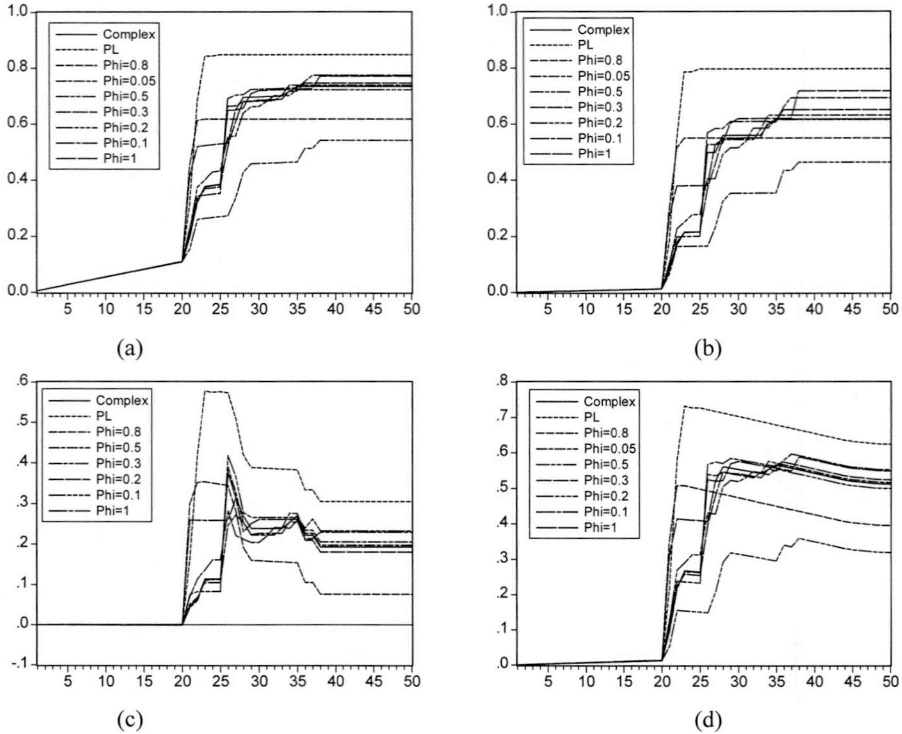

In the second scenario, 100 randomly selected banks are stressed by the mortgage shock of magnitude γ. Implicitly, we assume that the remaining 50 banks have diversified balance sheets and avoid systemic shock, but they still face the counterparty risk and, through trading assets, also face the market risk.

Criticality values are smaller than in the previous scenario (Figure 5). The smaller values can be explained by the fact that 50 banks that were not hit by the shock have higher capabilities to sustain the counterparty risk. As a consequence, they default less frequently and impose a smaller contagious potential to the system. As such, these banks are more likely to stop contagion rather than to promote it. Stability of the system is improved if some medium-sized and large banks are also protected against the shock because these banks have higher detrimental potential on one side and capabilities to stop contagion on the other. The system stabilizes at a shock of around 35% at high criticality levels.

In the last scenario, only the largest five banks are stressed by the mortgage shock. The intuition for this scenario is based on a common presumption that big banks are too-big-to-fail-institutions because it is believed that a default would induce large negative externalities to the banking system and the economy. Figure 6 plots the results.

Consequences of a targeted shock, which hits the biggest banks, substantially differ across the networks. In particular, they are determined by the specifics of stressed banks and their positions within the banking system. None of these banks default until a shock of 21%, which makes shock effects proportional to the magnitude and equal across networks. A sharp increase in criticality values from $\alpha = 0.11$ to $\alpha = 0.84$ occurs between the magnitudes of 20 and 23%. A combination of 21% shock and market risk collapse bank 42 in $t = 190$. With 2800 billion USD in assets, bank 42 is the largest of the sample. In a complex network, in which the biggest banks form a cohesive subgroup, while five of the biggest are affected by the shock, default of bank 42 collapses, among others, two other big banks—22 and 24—while they jointly collapse other banks from their neighborhood and further propagate across the network. The system stabilizes at the shock magnitude of 23% at very high criticality levels. Not surprisingly, a poorly connected random network, in which single banks are weakly integrated into the fragile banking system, exhibits the lowest criticality values. Note that the bank can contribute to the contagious dynamics if and only if it has links with other banks. When $\varphi = 0.05$, there is a high probability that banks either have no incoming links and are not affected by defaults of other banks or have no outgoing links and do not pass their defaults on to others. Generally, a small number of links limits the contagious potential of poorly connected banks.

As expected, a great majority of criticality effects result from the contagion and not the shock itself. Network effects are the largest in a complex network (for the shock of 23%) and the smallest in a poorly connected network.

Defaulted banks

In this last part, we turn to the number of bank defaults within the three scenarios across the networks. The aggregate perspective may fail to adequately capture defaults of smaller banks. This is much more relevant in the presence of a systemic shock, which weakens the banking system and thus makes banks more likely to default (Acharya and Yorulmazer, 2007).

Figure A1 in the Appendix depicts how bank defaults evolve over time for different shock magnitudes across scenarios and networks. In each figure, the color represents the number of defaulted banks in a given time period, while the color palette propagates from blue (<20 defaulted banks) to white, which signifies a default of all 150 banks. Figures show that the number of defaulted banks is increasing in shock magnitude, while banks collapse earlier in single runs as the magnitude increases.

The effects of connectivity are ambiguous. For weak shocks, it transfers losses across neighboring banks. As the shock magnitude increases, connectivity promotes contagion because the number of affected banks is higher. Note that banks are more likely to default in an under-capitalized system. Hence, highly connected banking systems are inferior to poorly connected ones when the shock is large, and vice versa. In addition, when a bigger bank defaults in a distressed system, connectivity works contagiously.

In Figure 7, we plot frequencies of bank defaults against their size and capitalization level within the three scenarios. For each bank, frequency is calculated as the average number of its defaults across the nine network topologies in a given scenario. A bank that does not default in any network topology for any shock level has a value of zero, while a maximum value of 50 is attributed to the bank that defaults in every topology for each shock magnitude. The frequency is the inverse of the magnitude at which a bank fails on average within the given scenario. The line represents a linear regression line.

Figure 7. The average frequencies of bank defaults in three scenarios against bank size (upper figures) and capitalization level (bottom figures).

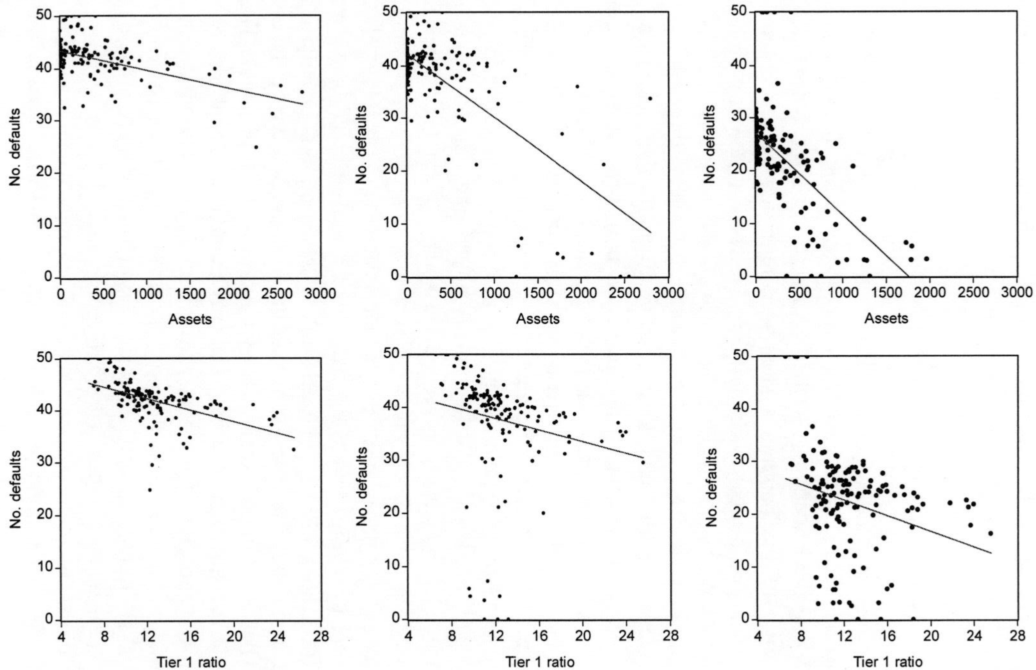

(a) baseline (b) random (c) big banks

In all three scenarios, we find a negative correlation between the average frequency of bank defaults and bank size (-0.53, -0.69, -0.64) and the capital ratio (-0.51, -0.20, -0.27), respectively. This suggests that bigger and more capitalized banks default less frequently than others. In all three scenarios, the correlation is stronger for bank size than for capital ratio, which points to the importance of big banks to system stability.

Concluding Remarks

The paper presents a network-based structural model of credit risk to examine the effects of bank capital and diversification on bank credit risk.

By using the effective α-criticality index, we have demonstrated that the stability of the banking system is determined by a combination of systemic and bank-specific components. Network structure plays a crucial role in shock propagation. Generally, networks that we used have been very vulnerable even to weak shocks. Therefore, to keep the banking system stable, banks would need to primarily diversify their exposure across different systemic events, if possible, and not only across the interbank market as well as maintain adequate capital levels. Because a banking system that is weakened by systemic shock is very susceptible to contagion, even a small perturbation in parameter values can easily turn the banking system from stability to default when the critical point is reached.

Interbank market diversification distributes the risk for weak shocks only. As shock increases, it becomes a source of contagion because the banks, weakened by shock, are correlated with one another. Diversification across non-interbank market assets decreases the probability of a bank default but may not prevent the default of a non-infected bank, which is highly integrated into the infected banking system. Homogeneity in banks' balance sheets may increase the probability of contagion within the clustered group when a common factor is hit by a moderate to large shock. There is a negative correlation between the number of defaults and bank size as well as between the number of defaults and initial Tier 1 ratio. Further, as the shock magnitude increases, the post-shock time until the banking system collapses shortens. This is consistent with historical evidence, which shows that banks are under distress in recessions.

The paper has demonstrated how single shocks can propagate across the banking system and how they can easily transform into a crisis. When the first bank defaults, the linear part is increased by a discrete part due to writedowns, which make the shock consequences nonlinear in magnitude. If different markets are correlated or co-integrated with one another and the shock initiates large changes in other markets, the shock may be followed by another systemic event with additional widespread writedowns. Such a combination of events would make the shock consequences enormous. From a methodological perspective, the paper has demonstrated that banking system stability analysis requires a network-based approach because the complex network structure of a banking system has a profound contagious potential, leading to nonlinear effects. By relaxing assumptions, the model could easily be extended in many directions.

References

Acharya, V. (2009). A theory of systemic risk and design of prudential bank regulation. *Journal of Financial Stability* 5: 224-255.

Acharya, V., I. Hasan, and A. Saunders (2006). Should Banks Be Diversified? Evidence from Individual Bank Loan Portfolios. *Journal of Business* 79(3): 1355-1412.

Acharya, V., and T. Yorulmazer (2007). Too Many to Fail: An Analysis of Time-inconsistency in Bank Closure Policies. *Journal of Financial Intermediation* 16: 1-31.

Albert, R., H. Jeong, and A.L. Barabasi (2000). Error and attack tolerance of complex networks. *Nature* 406, 378-382.

Allen, F., and A. Babus (2009). Networks in finance. In: Kleindorfer, P., Wind, Y., Gunther, R. (Eds.). *The Network Challenge: Strategy, Profit, and Risk in an Interlinked World*. Prentice Hall Professional, pp. 367-382.

Allen, F., A. Babus, and E. Carletti (2012). Asset Commonality, Debt Maturity and Systemic Risk. *Journal of Financial Economics* 104: 519-534.

Allen, F., and D. Gale (2000). Financial contagion. *Journal of Political Economy* 108(1): 1-33.

Battiston, S., D. Delli Gatti, M. Gallegati, B. Greenwald, and J. Stiglitz (2012a). Liaisons dangereuses: Increasing connectivity, risk sharing, and systemic risk. *Journal of Economic Dynamics and Control* 36: 1121-1141.

Battiston, S., D. Delli Gatti, M. Gallegati, B. Greenwald, and J. Stiglitz (2012b). Default cascades: When does risk diversification increase stability? *Journal of Financial Stability* 8: 138-149.

Beale, N., D. Rand, H. Battey, K. Croxson, R. May, and M. Nowak (2011). Individual versus systemic risk and the regulator's dilemma. *Proceedings of the National Academy of Sciences* 108: 12647-12652.

Berger, P., and E. Ofek (1995). Diversification's Effect on Firm Value. *Journal of Financial Economics* 37: 39-65.

Blume, L., D. Easley, J. Kleinberg, R. Kleinberg, and E. Tardos (2011). Network formation in the presence of contagious risk. Proceedings of the 12th ACM Conference on Electronic Commerce.

Boss, M., H. Elsinger, M. Summer, and S. Thurner (2004). Network topology of the interbank market. *Quantitative Finance* 4: 677-684.

Caballero, R., and A. Simsek (2013). Fire Sales in a Model of Complexity. *Journal of Finance* 68(6): 2549-2587.

Craig, Ben, and Goetz von Peter (2014). Interbank tiering and money center banks. *Journal of Financial Intermediation* 23(3): 322-347.

Degryse, H., and G. Nguyen (2007). Interbank Exposures: An Empirical Examination of Contagion Risk in the Belgian Banking System. *International Journal of Central Banking* 3(2): 123-171.

Duffie, D., and K. Singleton (2012). *Credit risk: pricing, measurement, and management.* Princeton: Princeton University Press.

Egloff, D., M. Leippold, and P. Vanini (2007). A simple model of credit contagion. *Journal of Banking and Finance* 31: 2475-2492.

Freixas, X., B. Parigi, and J.C. Rochet (2000). Systemic risk, interbank relations, and liquidity provision by the central bank. *Journal of Money, Credit and Banking* 32: 611-638.

Fricke, Daniel, and Thomas Lux (2014). Core-Periphery Structure in the Overnight Money Market: Evidence from the e-MID Trading Platform. *Computational Economics* (in press).

Furfine, C. (2003). Interbank exposures: Quantifying the risk of contagion. *Journal of Money, Credit and Banking* 35: 111-128.

Gai, P., and S. Kapadia (2010). Contagion in financial networks. *Proceedings of the Royal Society A: Mathematical, Physical and Engineering Science* 466: 2401-2423.

Iori, G., S. Jafarey, and F. Padilla (2006). Systemic risk on the interbank market. *Journal of Economic Behavior and Organization* 61: 525-542.

Iori, G., G. De Masi, O. Precup, G. Gabbi, and G. Caldarelli (2008). A network analysis of theItalian overnight money market. *Journal of Economic Dynamics and Control* 32: 259-278.

Jackson, M. (2010). *Social and economic networks*. Princeton: Princeton University Press.

Kindleberger, C., and R. Aliber (2011). *Manias, panics and crashes: a history of financial crises*. New York: Palgrave Macmillan.

Lang, L., and R. Stulz (1992). Contagion and Competitive Intra-Industry Effects of Bankruptcy Announcements: An Empirical Analysis. *Journal of Financial Economics* 32: 45-60.

Lang, L., and R. Stulz (1994). Tobin's Q, Corporate Diversification and Firm Performance. *Journal of Political Economy* 102(6): 1248-1280.

Leitner, Y. (2005). Financial networks: Contagion, commitment, and private sector bailouts. *Journal of Finance* 60: 2925-2953.

van Lelyveld, I., and F. Liedorp (2006). Interbank contagion in the Dutch banking sector: A sensitivity analysis. *International Journal of Central Banking* 2: 99-133.

Markowitz, H. (1952). Portfolio Selection. Journal of Finance 7(1): 77-91.

Merton, R. (1974). On the pricing of corporate debt: The risk structure of interest rates. *Journal of Finance* 29: 449-470.

Nier, E., J. Yang, T. Yorulmazer, and A. Alentorn (2007). Network models and financial stability. *Journal of Economic Dynamics and Control* 31(6): 2033-2060.

Rajan, R., H. Servaes, and L. Zingales (2000). The Cost of Diversity: The Diversification Discount and Inefficient Investment. *Journal of Finance* 55(1): 35-80.

Reinhart, C., and K. Rogoff (2009). *This Time is Different: Eight Centuries of Financial Folly*. Princeton: Princeton University Press.

Rochet, J.-C., and J. Tirole (1996). Interbank Lending and Systemic Risk. *Journal of Money, Credit and Banking* 28(4): 733-762.

Schweitzer, F., G. Fagiolo, D. Sornette, F. Vega-Redondo, A. Vespignani, and D. White (2009). Economic networks: The new challenges. *Science* 325: 422-425.

Steinbacher, M., M. Steinbacher, and M. Steinbacher (2014a). Robustness of banking networks to idiosyncratic and systemic shocks: A network-based approach. *Journal of Economic Interaction and Coordination. DOI: 10.1007/s11403-014-0143-3*.

Steinbacher, M., M. Steinbacher, and M. Steinbacher (2014b). Banks and their contagion potential: How stable is banking system? In: Leitner, S., Wall, F. (Eds.). *Artificial Economics and Self Organization*. Springer International Publishing, pp. 161-175.

Steinbacher, M., M. Steinbacher, and M. Steinbacher (2014c). Interaction-based Approach to Economics and Finance. In: Faggini, M., Parziale, A. (Eds.). NEW Series book: *Complexity in Economics: Cutting Edge Research*. Springer International Publishing, pp. 161-203.

Stiroh, K. (2004). Diversification in Banking: Is Noninterest Income the Answer? *Journal of Money, Credit and Banking* 36(5): 853-882.

Stiroh, K., and A. Rumble (2006). The dark side of diversification: The case of US financial holding companies. *Journal of Banking and Finance* 30(8): 2131-2161.

Wagner, W. (2010). Diversification at Financial Institutions and Systemic Crises. *Journal of Financial Intermediation* 19(3): 373-386.

Wasserman, S., and K. Faust (1994). *Social Network Analysis: Methods and Applications*. Cambridge: Cambridge University Press.

Figure A1. Number of defaulted banks over time for different shock magnitudes.

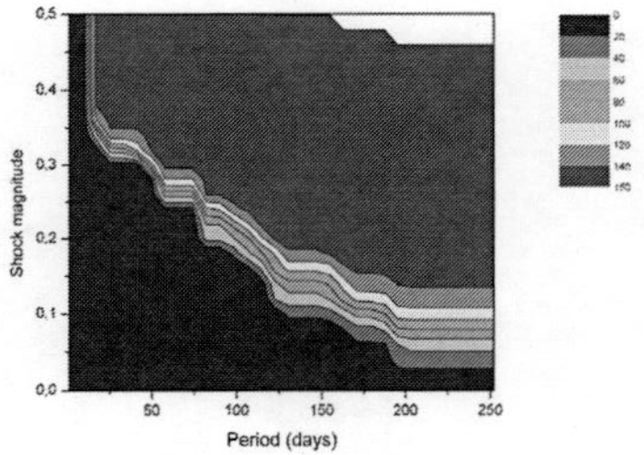

(Aa) complex, baseline

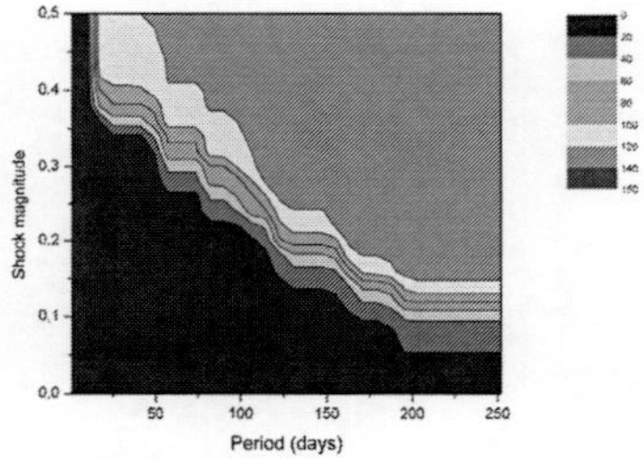

(Ab) complex, random

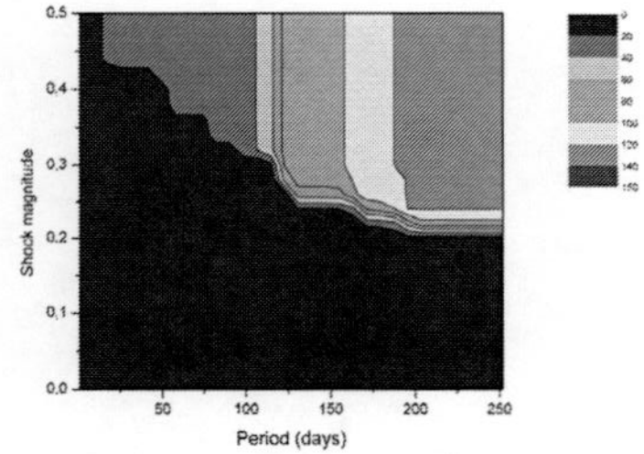

(Ac) complex, big banks

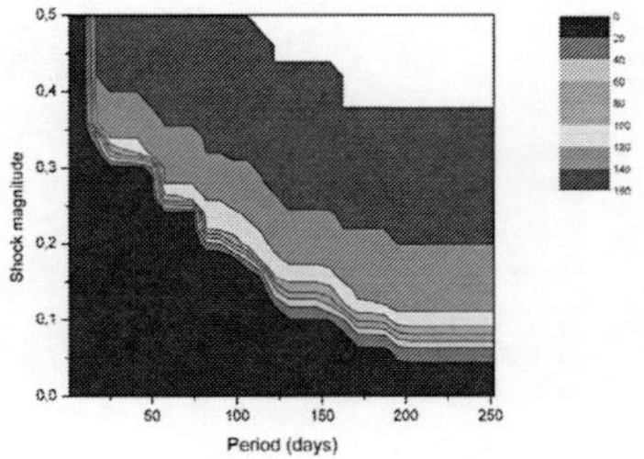

(Ba) Phi = 0.05, baseline

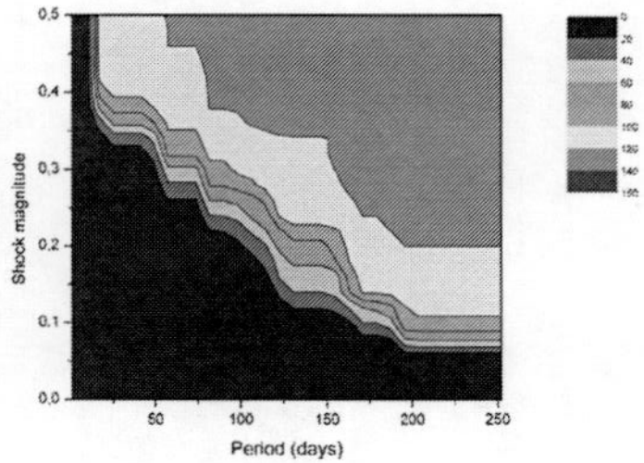

(Bb) Phi = 0.05, random

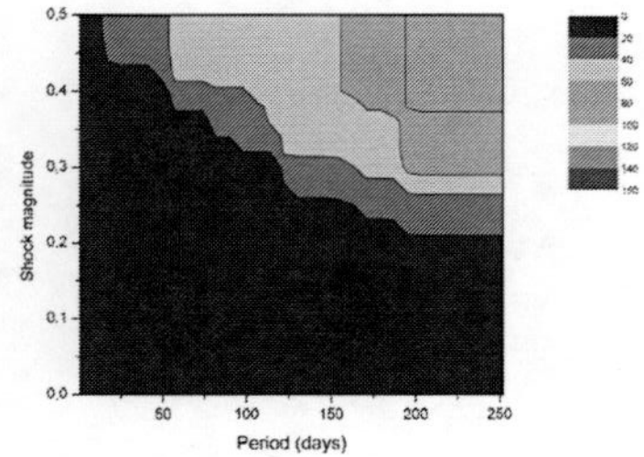

(Bc) Phi = 0.05, big banks

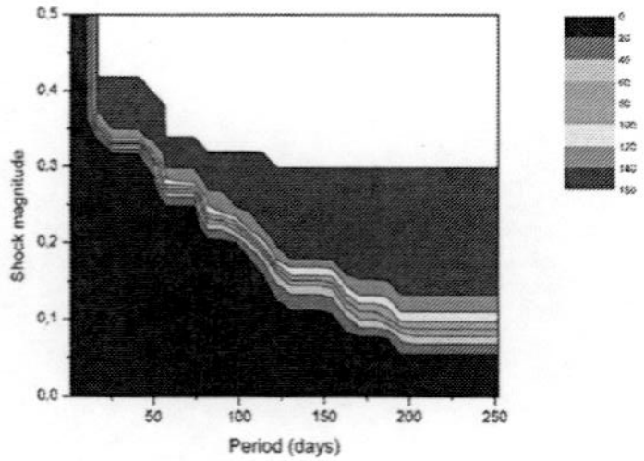

(Ca) Phi = 0.8, baseline

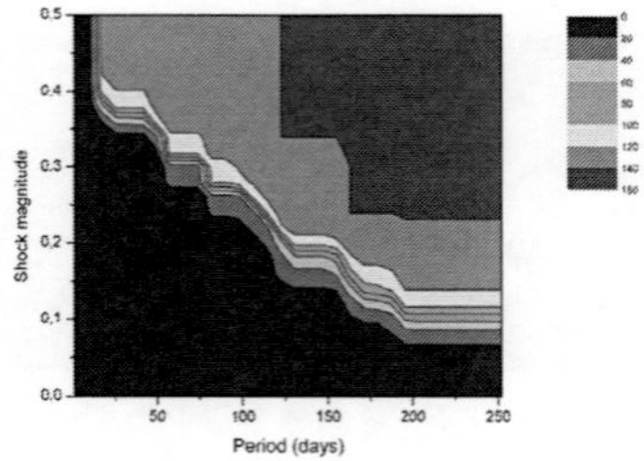

(Cb) Phi = 0.8, random

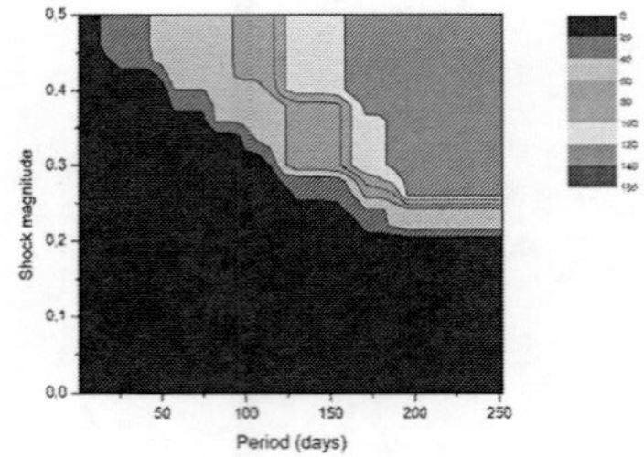

(Cc) Phi = 0.8, big banks

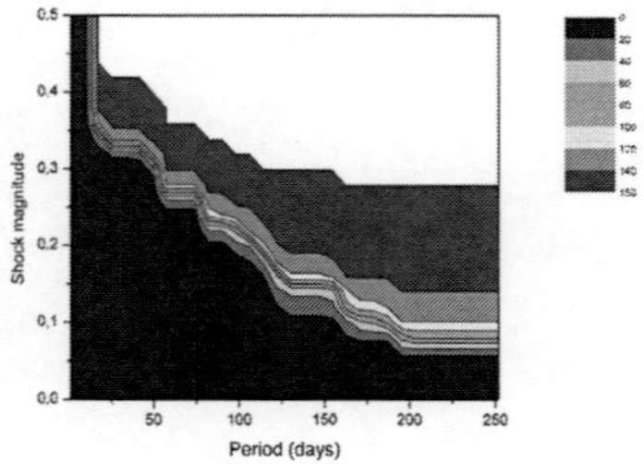

(Da) complete, baseline

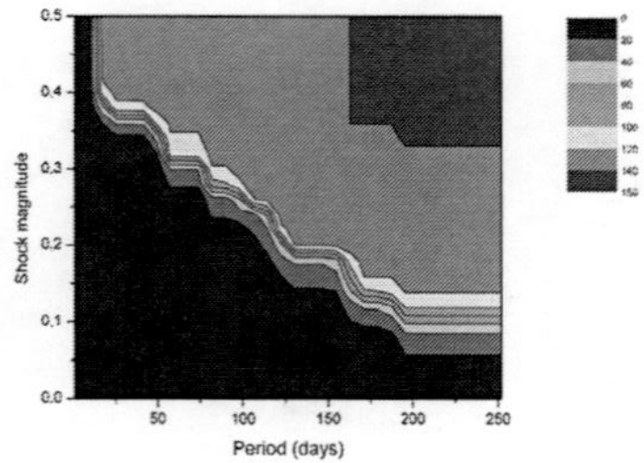

(Db) complete, random

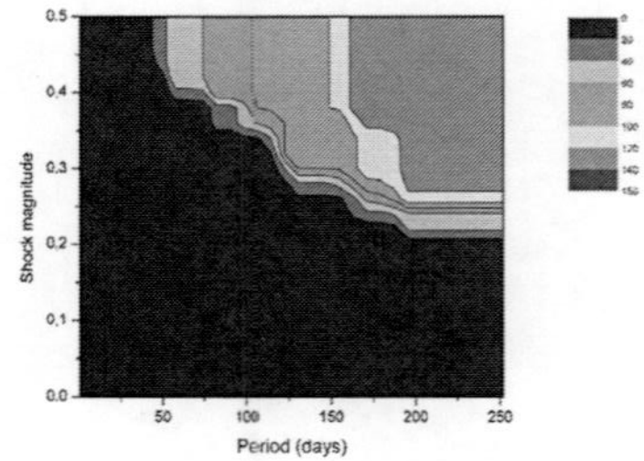

(Dc) complete, big banks

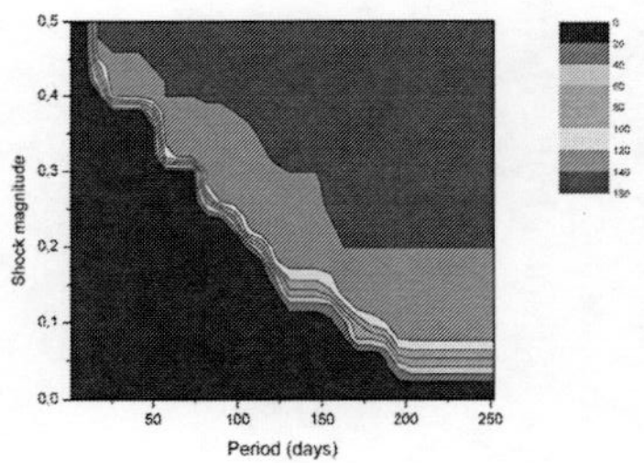

(Ea) PL, baseline

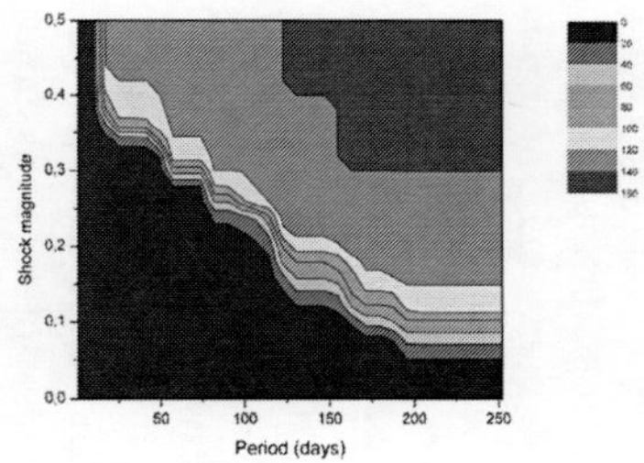

(Eb) PL, random

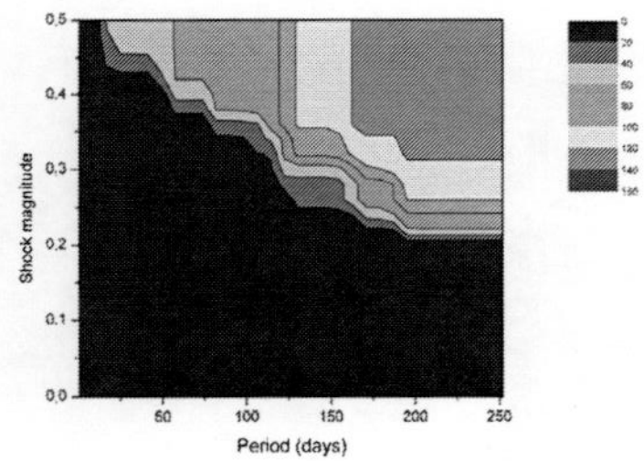

(Ec) PL, big banks

CHAPTER TEN

JOINING RISKS AND REWARDS

HARVEY J. STEIN[1]

Abstract

The dichotomy between risk analytics and pricing is well known among financial practitioners and researchers. For risk analysis, such as computing value at risk and credit exposures, expectations for future values must be computed under the real world measure. For pricing, expectations are computed under a risk neutral measure. This means that for calculations such as value at risk (VaR) and credit exposures (EEs, EPEs, etc) on derivative portfolios, risk factors are evolved to the horizon date under the real world measure, at which point the portfolio is re-priced under a risk neutral measure.

Simulation under the real world measure followed by re-pricing under a risk neutral measure is computationally intensive, especially when the re-pricing requires Monte Carlo. Because of the computational effort involved, shortcuts are often taken. One common shortcut is to assume the real world measure is the risk neutral measure, so calculations can be done under one measure. This shortcut is especially problematic because it leads to wildly varying results depending on the numéraire chosen (Stein 2014).

Here we detail methods of avoiding this problem by combining the real world measure with a risk neutral measure. We present an application for risk analytics, which speeds up calculations by orders of magnitude, changing $O(n^2)$ calculations to $O(n)$ with a far smaller scaling constant. This allows the computation of exposures under the real world measure, obviating the need for the dangerous practice of computing exposures under a risk neutral measure.

This chapter is a summary of Stein (2013).

[1] Harvey Stein is the head of Regulation and Credit Risk, Quantitative Risk Analytics Group. Email: hjstein@bloomberg.net.

Introduction

The dichotomy between risk analytics and pricing is well known among financial practitioners and researchers. For risk analysis, such as computing value at risk and credit exposures, expectations of future values must be computed under the real world measure. For pricing, expectations are computed under a risk neutral measure (Markowitz, 1952; Morgan, 1996; Dash, 2004; Stein, 2013).

According to (a loose statement of) the first fundamental theorem of arbitrage pricing theory, a market is arbitrage free if and only if an equivalent martingale measure exists with respect to a numéraire under which the price processes in units of the numéraire become martingales. An equivalent martingale measure is also known as a risk neutral measure and must be equivalent to the real world measure, meaning that there must exist change of measures that convert the real world measure into the risk neutral measure (Harrison and Kreps, 1979; Harrison and Pliska, 1981; Delbaen and Schachermayer, 1994)

In practice, the real world measure is not well known, and a risk neutral measure is chosen without regard to its equivalence to the real world measure. In general, this is disturbing because it means the risk neutral measure will typically exhibit behavior quite different from that observed in the real world.

For example, it is common to price equity call and put options at Black-Scholes' implied volatilities that are a function of strike and maturity and different from observed historical volatility even though the instantaneous volatility of a geometric Brownian motion is preserved under measure changes. Similarly, the observed dynamics of swap rates bear little resemblance to the dynamics they are given in common pricing models.

The rift between observed real world dynamics and risk neutral models leads to much financial research that attempts to reconcile the two. A large and growing body of financial research on ever more complex pricing models is motivated in part by the search for this "holy-grail" — a pricing model that exhibits real world dynamics. This paper does not address the issue, although it offers a canonical method for combining real world and risk neutral measures.

Another consequence of this rift is that it greatly complicates risk analytics. When computing the value at risk (VaR) for a portfolio of derivatives, one must evolve market factors to the horizon date under one model and then re-price derivatives using a different model. As VaR is typically computed using some form of Monte Carlo, and complex derivatives are often priced using Monte Carlo, this leads to performing a

Monte Carlo within a Monte Carlo, an extremely computationally heavy prospect. This becomes worse by orders of magnitude for credit exposure computations because they require doing the same thing for a variety of horizon dates.

To address this inefficiency, practitioners take a number of shortcuts, such as reducing the number of horizons used to estimate exposures, using simplified pricing models, using very small numbers of paths, applying various sorts of variance reduction schemes, using adaptive Monte Carlo techniques and interpolation methods, and resorting to the use of experimental high performance computing platforms, such as clusters of GPU and FPGA equipped computers. This leads to tremendous development effort, duplication of effort, and loss of accuracy. Even with these efforts, calculations often can only be done by harnessing a battalion of computers to run the computations overnight (Dixon et al., 2009; Weston et al. 2012; Chinchalkar et al. 2006; Stein et al. 2011).

One especially disturbing shortcut taken is to compute exposures under a risk neutral model. As shown in Stein (2013), this is quite dangerous because a risk neutral measure can be chosen to minimize exposures. Even with common models and numerical methods, one can observe differences in exposures of a factor of 2 or larger. It is important to the industry to be able to compute exposures efficiently and without resorting to such shortcuts.

Here we describe a methodology that can be used to circumvent the need to compute exposures under a risk neutral measure. We develop a partial reconciliation of risk neutral and real world measures by combining models. We demonstrate one simple, practical way to apply this methodology to arbitrary risk neutral and real world measures. We show that by using this reconciliation, VaR and credit risk calculations can be done with just one set of Monte Carlo paths, thus speeding up these calculations by many orders of magnitude and drastically reducing developmental efforts.

Risk Valuation

Let $S = \langle S_i \mid 0 \leq i < n \rangle$ be a vector of price processes of tradable securities with real world measure P with respect to filtration $\mathscr{F}$. Suppose we are pricing our contingent claims using the martingale measure Q with respect to the filtration $\mathscr{F}$ and numéraire N.

Consider a portfolio $\pi = \langle \pi_i \mid 0 \leq i < m \rangle$ of derivatives with payoff at maturity T, so that at time T the holder receives $\pi_i(T, S)$. For example, if π_1 is a call option on S_1 with strike K, then $\pi_1(T, S) = \max(S - K, 0)$. For brevity of exposition, we also express positions in the underlying securities as positions in derivatives that pay the underlying security, so, if π_1 is a position a in S_1, then $\pi_1(T,S) = aS_1$.

The value at time t of these positions is given by:.

$$V(t) = \sum N(t) E^Q \left[\frac{\pi_i(T)}{N(T)} \,\middle|\, \mathcal{F}_t \right]$$

The c percentile value at risk for portfolio π at time horizon h is the c percentile loss on $V(h)$ relative to $V(0)$ under P. This is the largest X such that

$$P(V(h) - V(0) < -X) = 1 - c/100$$

The value at risk of a portfolio can be computed once the real world distribution of $V(h)$ is known, as can other risk measures, such as the potential future exposure, the expected exposure, and profiles.

If there exists a change of measure weighting $dP/dQ = M(h)$ from Q to P, calculations can be done entirely under the risk neutral measure Q, in that

$$E^P[V(h)] = E^Q[V(h)M(h)]$$

So

$$P(V(h) - V(0) < -X) = E^P[1_{V(h)-V(0)<-X}] \quad (1)$$
$$= E^Q[1_{V(h)-V(0)<-X^{M(h)}}] \quad (2)$$

Monte Carlo Analysis and Measure Change

Risk calculations amount to calculating variants of equation (1). For complex portfolios, this is often done using a Monte Carlo analysis. A set of scenarios consisting of evolutions of the risk factors to the horizon time h under the risk neutral measure are generated. For each scenario, $V(h)$ is computed under the risk neutral measure conditional on the evolution of the risk factors. If $V(h)$ itself must be computed by Monte Carlo, this leads to an inefficient Monte Carlo within a Monte Carlo.

If a change of measure exists, then equation (2) can be used for risk calculations. Only one Monte Carlo under the risk neutral measure that evolves the portfolio from time zero would be needed. The prices $V(h)$ would be computed using an American Monte Carlo technique (such as least squares Monte Carlo (Longstaff-Schwartz), stochastic mesh, or stochastic grid) applied to time h. The above indicator function could then be computed. Its average weighted with the change of measure $M(h)$ would yield the desired expectation.

The computational effort saved by using equation (2) can be substantial. If m real world scenarios and n paths for each pricing are used, the computational effort is $O(mn)$ versus $O(n)$ for the one Monte Carlo method. In a case where we do not have a closed form for the distribution of $S_1(h)$ or $S_2(h)$, each path has many time steps (say k, and l, respectively) and the computational effort is $O(km+mln)$, versus $O(ln)$ for when we use the change of measure, and these expressions would have constants of similar magnitude. The minimal combined model of the next section would arguably require twice the number of paths for the same error level, which is still a small price to pay for replacing $km + mln$ with ln.

The savings is even greater when computing an exposure profile as a function of horizon time. For u horizons, the two Monte Carlo approach requires m real world scenarios and mu pricings using n paths (one for each scenario at each horizon). Instead, we have n scenarios and u applications of a regression approach, such as in least squares Monte Carlo.

It is worthwhile to note that care should be taken with the dual Monte Carlo technique. Rather than doing all of the calculations under the risk neutral measure, it would be worthwhile to do the calculations under a change of measure that ensures that we sample the relevant part of $V(h)$ under both sets of paths.

In practice, the recursive Monte Carlo required for using equation (1) is so computationally intensive that its calculations can only be done by commandeering a legion of computers to work all night. And even with this much computing power, shortcuts are needed. It is a common practice to reduce the number of paths, simplify the pricing models so that positions contributing to $V(h)$ can be computed without Monte Carlo, interpolate $V(h)$ from its values on a reduced set of paths, use simplified pricing models for positions that do not require Monte Carlo pricing, and even compute exposures in a risk neutral measure. Each of these approaches leads to substantial drops in accuracy, and the results of computing exposures in a risk neutral measure can be misleading (Stein 2013), so being able to use one Monte Carlo for both pricing and the risk neutral calculation has the potential to be quite valuable.

Minimal Model Extensions

In practice, estimates of the real world measure differ so much from the risk neutral measure that there is no change of measure from one to the other, making the above procedure impossible to follow. For example, for a stock price process, the real world measure is often inferred from historical prices, with the stock price process assumed to be a geometric Brownian motion with fixed drift and volatility. But for pricing options on this stock process, the price process is tailored to fit observed option prices and may be a local volatility model, a stochastic volatility model, or even a geometric Brownian motion with a fixed volatility different from the historically observed volatility. In all of these cases, there is no change of measure from one to the other.

To take advantage of a change of measure between the risk neutral measure and the real world measure, we need a model for which such measure changes exist. In the full paper, we show how to create such a model by combining the two models.

Let $U = (\Omega,\sigma,P,F)$ be a probability space with sample space Ω, sigma algebra σ, probability measure P, and filtration F. Suppose $S_1 =< S_{1,i} >$ are the security price processes in the real world measure, and $S_2 =< S_{2,i} >$ are the security price processes in the risk neutral measure.

Let $\Omega' = \Omega \sqcup \Omega = \Omega \times \{1,2\}$ be the disjoint union of Ω with itself, with p_1 and p_2 being the two coordinate maps. Every $A \subset \Omega'$ can be decomposed uniquely into a disjoint union, which we will write as $A = A_1 \sqcup A_2$, where $A_1 = A \cap p_2^{-1}(1)$ and $A_2 = A \cap p_2^{-1}(2)$ (i.e. A_1 consists of the elements of A with second coordinate 1, and A_2 consists of the elements of A with second coordinate 2).

Let σ' be a family of subsets of Ω' defined by $A = A_1 \sqcup A_2 \in \sigma'$ iff $A_1 \in \sigma$ and $A_2 \in \sigma$. Then σ' is a sigma algebra on Ω'. Similarly, use F to induce a filtration F' on σ'. Let the probability measure P' on the measurable space (Ω',σ') be given by $A = A_1 \sqcup A_2 \rightarrow aP(A_1) + (1 - a)P(A_2)$, where a is a constant between zero and one.

Then $p_1 : \Omega' \rightarrow \Omega$ is a probability preserving surjective map, and hence the filtered probability measure space $U' = (\Omega',\sigma',P',F')$ extends $U = (\Omega,\sigma,P,F)$.

Define the security price process vector $S' =< S_i' >$ on U' by $S'((w,j)) = S_j(w)$. Then S' is adapted, and its paths are the unions of the paths of S_1 and S_2.

We have a larger family of equivalent measures in (U',S') than in (U,S_i). In addition to the set of measure changes on the underlying space U (e.g., drift changes that come from Girsanov's theorem if U is induced by a vector of Brownian motions), we also have measure changes induced by changing a, which essentially weights the model more toward S_1 as a tends towards 1 and weights the model towards S_2 when a tends towards zero. In fact, $S' = S_1$ a.e. when $a = 1$, and $S = S_2$ a.e. when $a = 0$, so we have (non-equivalent) changes of measures that take us from the measure induced by S' on the path space (e.g. — $C[0,T]^n$, the space of vectors of continuous functions on the interval $[0,T]$ in the case that the paths are continuous) to the measures induced by S_1 and S_2, but not back to that induced by S', as S' has sets of positive measure that are of measure zero under S_1 and has positive measure sets that are of measure zero under S_2.

More generally, (U',S') is the minimal model extending both (U,S_1) and (U,S_2) in the sense that any model for which there exists a measure change to both (U,S_1) and (U,S_2) must factor through (U',S'). As such, in some sense, it is the model with the least additional assumptions that contains both path sets.

Within (U',S') we can compute risk measures with one Monte Carlo via a measure change, as equation (2) would hold, with change of measure $M(T)$ being given by varying a between zero and one to get as close as desired to each model. One can in fact also set $a = 1$ to work exactly in the real world measure, and set $a = 0$ to work exactly in the risk neutral measure, although these would not yield equivalent martingale measures.

Another way to view (U',S') is in terms of the measure induced on the path space by the process. A process S can be viewed as a function S: $\Omega\times[0,T] \rightarrow R$ given by (w,t) 7⟶ $S_t(w)$, where we denote the value of S at time t on sample space point w by $S_t(w)$. If S is a continuous process, it can be viewed as a function $S : \Omega \rightarrow C[0,T]$ to the space of continuous functions on the interval $[0,T]$ given by w 7⟶ f, where $f(t) = S_t(w)$. Viewed in this way, it induces a measure S^* on $C[0,T]$ given by $S^*(B) = P(S^{-1}(B))$ for Borel sets $B \subset C[0,T]$.

If S_1 and S_2 are both continuous processes, then

$$S'^* = aS_1^* + (1-a)S_2^*.$$

In words, the measure induced by the S' process on the space of continuous functions is a weighted average of the measures induced by the S_i processes. As such, its marginals will be the same weighted average of the marginal of the S_i processes, and its joint distributions will be the corresponding weighted averages, etc.

In the paper, we go on to compare the minimal model extension to regime switching models, such as Bollen (1998), Hamilton (2008), and White and Rebonato (2008). We show that there is an important difference between the two. In Stein (2015), we show a way of interpreting this in terms of a "pseudo-change of measure".

Example

Working with (U',S') in practice is straight forward. In the paper, we outline how one least squares Monte Carlo could be used to compute the c percentile VaR for a horizon time h for a call option with strike K and maturity T. We detail this using the stochastic processes $dS_i = \mu_i S_i dt + \sigma_i S_i dW$, where S_1 is the real world process and S_2 is the risk neutral process under the money market numéraire and assuming fixed interest rates, so that $B(t) = e^{rt}$, and $\mu_2 = r$.

We also show that it is straight forward to generate the sample set M of m scenarios in the minimal model extension (U',S') with real world paths occurring with probability a. We randomly generate the first $a \times m$ scenarios following the risk neutral dynamics $dS_1 = \mu_1 S_1 dt + \sigma_1 S_1 dW$, and randomly generate the remaining $(1-a)\times m$ scenarios following the real world dynamics $dS_2 = \mu_2 S_2 dt + \sigma_2 S_2 dW$ (see figure 1). We can then do the above calculations within the minimal model extension. If a is chosen close to zero, then the result will be a good approximation of the result within the risk neutral model.

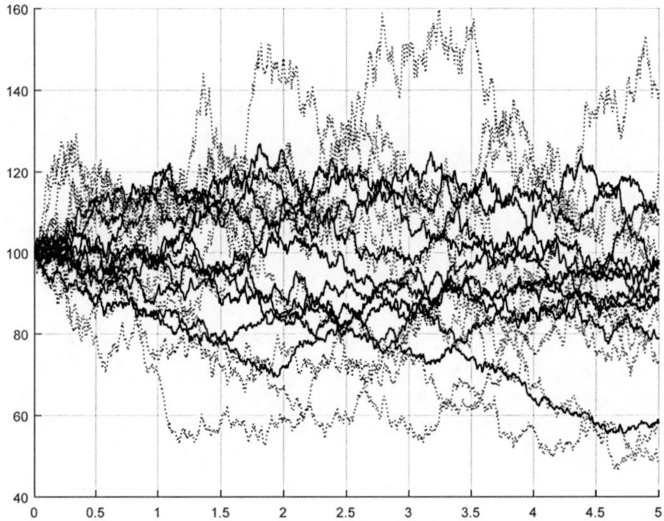

Figure 1. Sample paths for $(U^{\square},S^{\square})$ model with 10 real world paths (solid) and 10 risk neutral paths (dotted). The stock processes are given by geometric Brownian motion with zero drift. The real world paths have $\sigma_1 = 0.10$, and the risk neutral paths have $\sigma_2 = 0.20$.

We can also write down the probability density function of $S'(t)$. In the full paper, we derive $f_{Si}(x)$, the probability density function of $S_i(t)$. Since the marginals of S' are the weighted averages of the marginals of the S_i processes, $f_{S'}(x)$, the probability density function of $S'(t)$, is given by

$$f_{S'}(x) = af_{S1}(x) + (1 - a)f_{S2}(x) \quad (3)$$

This is illustrated in figure 2.

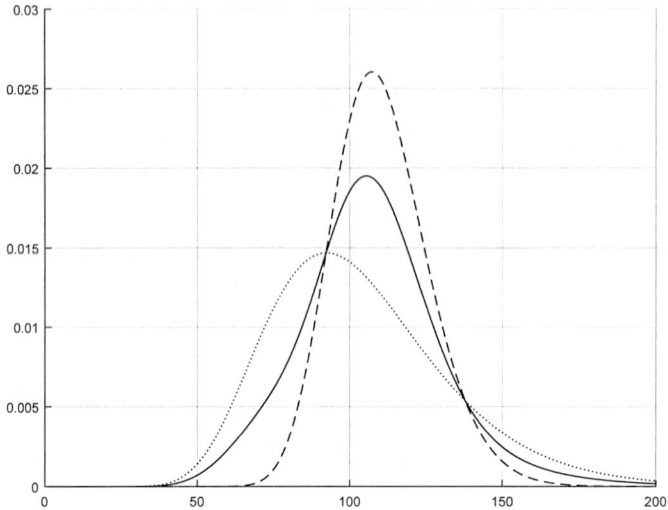

Figure 2. Probability density functions of the S_i and S' at $t = 2$, when the real world paths have parameters $\mu_1 = 0.05$ and $\sigma_1 = 0.10$ and the risk neutral paths have parameters $\mu_2 = 0.02$ and $\sigma_2 = 0.2$, with $a = 1/2$ and $S(0) = 100$. The real world density is shown as a dashed line, the risk neutral density is shown as a dotted line, and the minimal model's density is shown as a solid line.

To compute risk statistics via equation (2), we use the distribution generated from the same set of scenarios but change the measure to be close to the real world process. The change is merely giving the real world paths from the sample set M high weights and those from the risk neutral model low weights.

In the paper, we go on to discuss efficiency considerations regarding the choice of a in the simulation because it has an important sampling impact. We conclude that it may be advantageous to simulate with $a = 1/2$ and switch a both for pricing and for risk calculations, or even to select an a that optimizes accuracy.

We close with a discussion of software engineering implications of this model, concluding that including all paths and modifying a when needed is likely simpler than modifying separate Monte Carlos and combining the results.

Future Work

It would be interesting to further investigate the dynamics of the combined minimal model and to investigate calibrating it or extensions of it simultaneously to both observed prices (risk neutral calibration) and historical dynamics (real world measure). It would also be interesting to further systematically explore the category of financial market models and, in particular, operations that combine, extend, and decompose models in this category.

Summary

We described a methodology that can be used to achieve a partial reconciliation of risk neutral and real world measures. We showed a way to construct a minimal model extension that contains both path processes. The construction yields a simple, practical way to apply this methodology to arbitrary risk neutral and real world measures. And, we showed that by using this reconciliation, VaR and credit exposure calculations can be done with just one set of Monte Carlo scenarios, potentially speeding up these calculations by many orders of magnitude. This obviates the need to do exposure calculations under a risk neutral model, which is a dangerous practice, as noted in Stein (2013).

References

Bollen, Nicholas P. B. Valuing options in regime-switching models. *The Journal of Derivatives*, 6(1): 38–49, 1998.

Chinchalkar, Shirish, Thomas F. Coleman, and Peter Mansfield. Cluster computing for financial engineering. In Jack Dongarra, Kaj Madsen, and Jerzy Waniewski, editors, *Applied Parallel Computing. State of the Art in Scientific Computing*, volume 3732 of *Lecture Notes in Computer Science*, pages 395–403. Springer Berlin Heidelberg, 2006. doi:10.1007/11558958_47.

Dash, Jan W. *Quantitative Finance and Risk Management: A Physicist's Approach*. World Scientific Pub., 2004.

Delbaen, Freddy, and Walter Schachermayer. A general version of the fundamental theorem of asset pricing. *Mathematische Annalen*, 300(1): 463–520, 1994.

Dixon, Matthew, Jike Chong, and Kurt Keutzer. Acceleration of market value-at-risk estimation. In *Proceedings of the 2nd Workshop on High Performance Computational Finance*, page 5. ACM, 2009.

Hamilton, James D. Regime-switching models. *The New Palgrave Dictionary of Economics*, 2, 2008.

Harrison, Michael J., and David M. Kreps. Martingales and arbitrage in multi-period securities markets. *Journal of Economic Theory*, 20(3): 381–408, 1979.

Harrison, Michael J., and Stanley R. Pliska. Martingales and stochastic integrals in the theory of continuous trading. *Stochastic Processes and Their Applications*, 11(3): 215–260, 1981.

Markowitz, Harry. Portfolio selection. *The Journal of Finance*, 7(1): 77–91, 1952.

Morgan, J.P. *Riskmetrics: Technical document*. Morgan Guaranty Trust Company of New York, 1996.

Stein, Harvey J. Two measures for the price of one. *RISK MAGAZINE*, 02 March 2015.

Stein, Harvey J. Fixing Underexposed Snapshots – Proper computation of credit exposures under the real world and risk neutral measures. Technical report, Bloomberg LP, January 2014. http://ssrn.com/abstract=2365540

Stein, Harvey J. Joining Risks and Rewards. Technical report, Bloomberg LP, December 2013. http://ssrn.com/abstract=2368905

Stein, Harvey J. Alexander Belikoff, Kirill Levin, and Xusheng Tian. Analysis of mortgage backed securities: Before and after the credit crisis. In Tomasz Bielecki, Damiano Brigo, and Fr´ed´eric Patras, editors, *Credit Risk Frontiers: Subprime Crisis, Pricing and Hedging, CVA, MBS, Ratings, and Liquidity*, volume 138. Wiley.com, New York, 2011.

Weston, Stephen, James Spooner, Sebastien Racaniere, and Oskar Mencer. Rapid computation of value and risk for derivatives portfolios. *Concurrency and Computation: Practice and Experience*, 24(8): 880–894, 2012.

White, Richard, and Riccardo Rebonato. A swaption volatility model using markov regime switching. *Journal of Computational Finance*, 12(1): 79, 2008.

CHAPTER ELEVEN

THE CREDIT RISK PREMIUM: MEASUREMENT, HEDGING, AND PREDICTION

TERRY BENZSCHAWEL AND YONG SU[1]

Abstract

Although fixed-for-floating rate swaps have proven effective for hedging volatility in interest rates, neutralizing price changes from changes in credit spreads has remained challenging. To address this problem, one can estimate the fraction of bonds' yield spreads to U.S. Treasuries due to default from their overall spread, thereby revealing their non-default spreads. On any given day, bonds' non-default spreads are roughly a constant fraction of their spread volatilities. That ratio is the credit risk premium, whose historical series is presented herein. Given quantitative estimates of the credit risk premium, one can hedge systematic moves in bond spreads due to changes in investors' risk appetites and/or market volatility as expressed by changes in the credit risk premium. Three-month changes in the North American investment-grade CDS index, CDX.IG.NA, generally track changes in values of bonds' credit risk premiums, suggesting trailing three-month changes as the basis for computing the hedge ratio. We compared a simple beta hedging strategy with a dynamic beta strategy whereby the hedge ratio is based on the slopes of regression analyses on a rolling window of changes in non-default spreads and changes in the CDX.IG.NA. Although the simple beta hedge works well in all years except during the liquidity crisis of late 2007 to 2009, the dynamic hedge works well over the entire test period since 2004. Finally, we demonstrate that the ratio of current risk premium to predicted annual default rate can predict subsequent annual changes in the credit risk premium with an accuracy of 80% in historical back testing since 2004.

---

[1] The authors are from Citi Institutional Clients Group, 388 Greenwich St., New York, NY 10013. E-mail: terry.l.benzschawel@citi.com.

Introduction

With the introduction of interest rate swaps in the early 1980s, lenders and investors were able to minimize their exposure to changes in interest rates, even for very long-dated commitments.[2] Arguably, the interest rate swap may be the most useful innovation produced using financial engineering. No longer must long-term investors worry about fluctuations in interest rates; they can hedge that exposure by choosing to swap fixed-rate for floating-rate debt. Unfortunately, investors in credit spread products have no such option for hedging their exposure to systematic changes in credit spreads. In fact, these changes can be large. Consider, for example, the left panel of Figure 1, which displays the average 4.5-year U.S. Treasury yields and the corresponding average investment-grade bond yields from 1998 to 2014. The yield compensation for default is estimated using average default probabilities (PDs) for the bonds from Sobehart and Keenan's (2002, 2003) Hybrid Probability of Default (HPD) mode as input to:

$$s_d = -\frac{1}{T}\ln[1 - p_T \cdot LGD]\,, \tag{1}$$

where T is 4.5 years, the average duration of the bonds, p_T is the average cumulative default probability to time T, and LGD is the expected loss in default.[3]

The right panel of Figure 1 presents the time series of average investment-grade non-default spreads and its average level. As elaborated below, it is clear that the majority of the yield spread to U.S. Treasuries for corporate bonds results from something other than not receiving the cash flows from default. In particular, the right portion of Figure 1 shows that this compensation, which averages about 150 bp, has been as large as 800bp during times of stress, such as in 2008. Although default risk was large in 2008, default risk was also relatively large in 2002, when the non-default spread was near its long-term average. Of course, during the credit crisis, bond investors incurred large mark-to-market losses on their portfolios, while, at least in general, they still received their promised cash flows.

---

[2] Salomon Brothers brokered the first currency swap in 1981 between IBM and the World Bank and interest rate swaps followed shortly thereafter.

[3] As explained in Appendix I, Equation 1 is simply a rearrangement of the price versus yield formula combined with the notion from risk neutral pricing theory that the spread value is the expectation of the nominal cash flows adjusted for default probability and discounted at the risk-free rate.

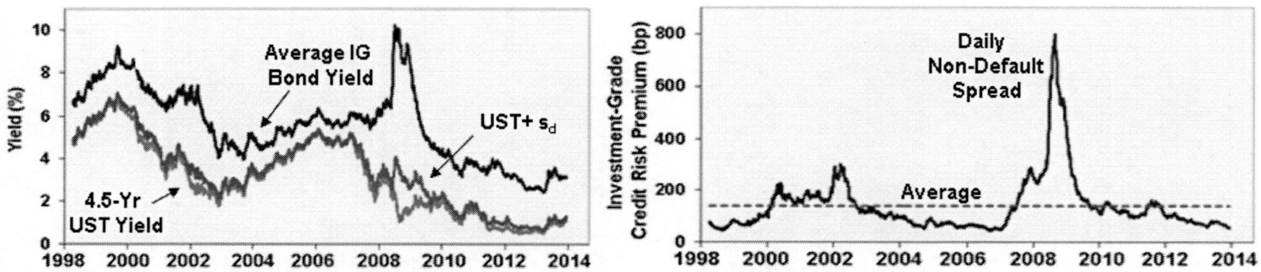

Figure 1. Left: Treasury Yields, Spread Compensation for Default, and Average Investment-Grade Corporate Bond Yields; Right: Average Daily Non-Default Spreads, 1998-2014.

At least one reason for the failure of financial engineers to develop a product to hedge systematic credit risk is the lack of understanding necessary to isolate and study the determinants of credit spread risk. However, as we point out in detail in several recent studies (Benzschawel and Assing, 2012; Benzschawel and Lee, 2012) and as described below, one can understand the credit spread as the sum of two major components:

- Yield compensation for not receiving the cash flows due to default, which can be valued under risk neutral pricing theory given an estimate of default probability and an assumed recovery value in default; and
- The remaining yield spread to Treasuries being compensation for credit spread volatility.[4]

We call the former the *spread compensation for default* and the latter *the credit risk premium,* and we explain their relationship to credit spreads below. In this report, we also show that, based on the ability to decompose credit spreads into default and non-default components, short positions in the CDX.IG.NA provide very good hedges for changes in the credit spread premium.

Understanding the Credit Risk Premium

Only recently have market participants begun to unravel the components that underlie spread compensation for investing in default-risky assets. Although the early work of Jones, Mason, and Rosenfeld (1984) suggested that compensation for default accounts for only a small fraction of the credit spread, it was Elton, Gruber, Agrawal, and Mann (2001) who first documented the role of the credit risk premium in corporate bond spreads.[5] Using the logic embedded in Equation 1, Elton et al. decomposed the credit spreads of single-A-rated corporate bonds into their compensation for default and the remaining portion, which they interpreted as the credit risk premium. We designate the spread compensation

[4] This is ignoring for the moment the effects of relative marketability of securities and the "embedded leverage effect." We elaborate on those effects later in this report.

[5] It may also contain a premium for liquidity/illiquidity. For now, we use the term *credit risk premium* to refer to the entire spread compensation over and above that necessary for the present value of expected cash flows to equal that of an equal-duration US Treasury security.

for default as s_d and the credit risk premium as s_λ. The value of s_d can be viewed as the spread compensation necessary to account for the loss of cash flows due to default. That is, an investor who receives a yield spread to U.S. Treasuries equal to s_d receives only an amount equal to the expected return from an equivalent-duration U.S. Treasury security. For this reason, s_d could be called a *rock bottom spread.*

To demonstrate the existence of a risk premium, Elton et al. used historical default rates from the rating agencies for double-A rated corporate bonds and assumed a recovery value in default of 40%. Benzschawel (2012) reported a more systematic study of the credit risk premium for corporate bonds by rating; those results are summarized in Figure 2. The figure shows average cumulative 4.5-year default probabilities by rating category from the HPD model for corporate bonds in Citi's Broad Investment Grade (BIG) and High Yield Indexes over the period from 1994-2010.[6] 4.5-year cumulative default rates were used as they correspond roughly to the average duration of the bonds in those indexes. The figure also shows average monthly spreads by rating category over the 17-year period along with the spread compensation for default using Equation 1, depicts average PDs by rating from the HPD model, and assumes a 40% recovery value in default. The last column of the table presents differences by rating category between average spreads and spread due to default.

The right portion of Figure 2 graphically presents by rating category average values of the default spread (dark area) and the non-default spread (lighter area). The dark area corresponds to average values of s_d, over the period, with the light area representing average values of the credit risk premium, s_λ. The average value of the credit risk premium ranges from 69bp for triple-A-rated bonds to 727bp for triple C-rated ones, but is five-to-ten times larger than the average compensation for default regardless of rating category.

---

[6] See Citigroup Index (2013) for descriptions of Citigroup's BIG Index and High Yield Index.

S&P Credit Rating	4.5 Year Implied PD	Average Spread (bp)	Spread Due to Default (bp)	Non-Default Spread (bp)
AAA	0.3%	70	1	69
AA+	0.3%	87	4	82
AA	0.4%	88	5	83
AA-	0.5%	104	6	98
A+	0.6%	113	8	105
A	0.7%	122	9	112
A-	0.9%	137	11	126
BBB+	1.0%	160	14	146
BBB	1.3%	178	17	161
BBB-	1.6%	223	21	201
BB+	1.9%	326	25	301
BB	2.3%	366	30	336
BB-	2.7%	383	36	347
B+	3.8%	438	51	386
B	5.7%	511	77	433
B-	8.2%	588	113	476
CCC+	11.8%	891	164	727

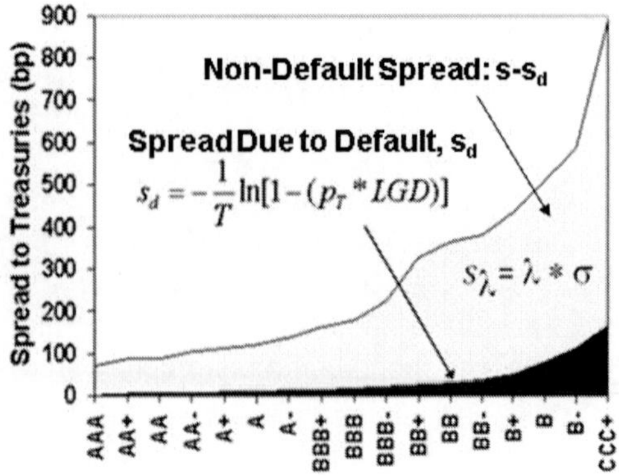

Figure 2. Average Credit Spreads Due to Default and Non-Default Spreads by Agency Rating Category, 1994-2010. Left: Treasury Yields, Spread Compensation for Default, and Average Investment-Grade Corporate Bond Yields; Right: Average Daily Non-Default Spreads 1998-2014.

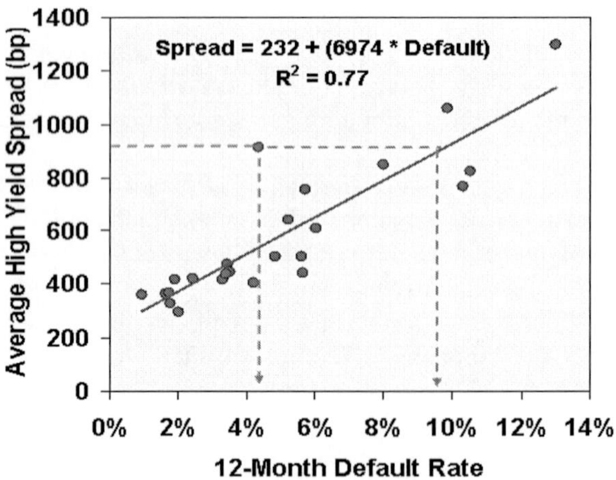

Figure 3. Annual Average High Yield Credit Spreads and Annual Default Rates, 1986-2009.

Although Figure 2 shows average values of the risk premium, default rates vary over the credit cycle as do credit spreads. Perhaps by determining the relationship between credit spreads and default rates, one could make inferences as to PDs from current values of credit spreads or vice versa. Then, applying this knowledge to individual credits, one could determine what a given difference in credit spread implies regarding probability of default or how a change in default probability would impact a bond's credit spread. Unfortunately, this has not proven possible as illustrated in Figure 3, which displays annual average high yield credit spreads against comparable default rates over the period from 1986 to 2009. That is, even though overall spread levels and defaults are correlated (R^2=0.77), that relationship is not sufficient to be useful for accurate prediction of overall spread levels, much less credit spreads for individual firms. The dashed lines in Figure 3 show that errors can be large. For example, in 2008, the average spread was 912bp, but the default rate was only 4.4% as opposed to the predicted value of 9.7%.

increasing both the spread and volatility simultaneously, at least on average.

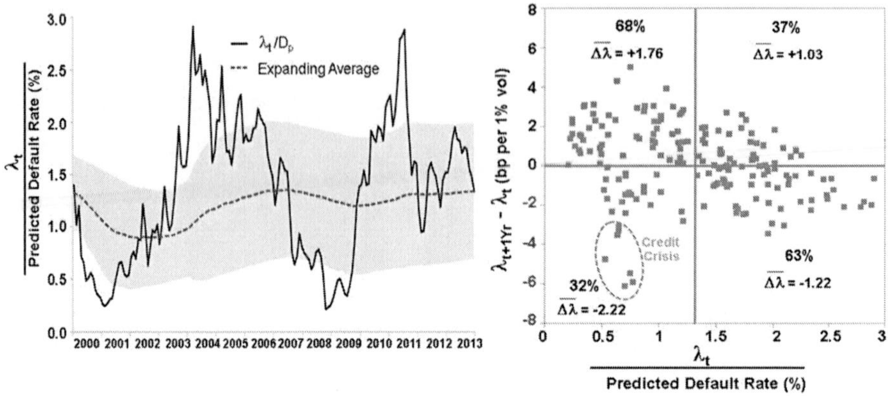

Figure 18. Left: Monthly Values of λt-to-Dp from 1998 to 2014 along with its Expanding Average; Right: One-Year Changes in the Credit Risk Premium (λ) as a Function the Ratio of the Current Risk Premium to the Predicted Default Rate. Percentages and Average Changes in the Risk Premiums are also shown for each.

Although the S_{HY}-to-D_p ratio fails to predict one-year changes in λ, we examined if the ratio of the current risk premium to predicted default (i.e., λ_t-to-D_p) could predict subsequent one-year changes in the risk premium, λ_{t+1Y} - $\lambda_{t.}$. To do this, we first calculated the series of monthly values of λ_t-to-D_p from 1998 to early 2014. The time series of λ_t-to-D_p ratios from 2000 to 2014 appears along the expanding average ratio in the left panel of Figure 18.[11] The right panel of Figure 18 displays one-year changes in the credit risk premium as a function of the λ_t-to-D_p ratio. The vertical line in the figure is the average λ_t-to-D_p ratio as of April 2014. The figure reveals that, unlike the S_{HY}-to-D_p ratio, the λ_t-to-D_p ratio has significant predictive power as regards subsequent one-year changes in the compensation per units of credit spread volatility. That is, when the ratio of λ_t-to-D_p is below average, the risk premium one year later tends to increase by an average 1.76 bp per unit of volatility with a 68% probability. Conversely, when the

[11] Although we began computing the λ_t-to-D_p series in 1998, we display it beginning in 2000 to allow two years of history in order to compute the first value of the expanding trailing average. Thus, the trailing average on a given month is computed from all the monthly ratios beginning in 1998 through the month prior to the date in the plot.

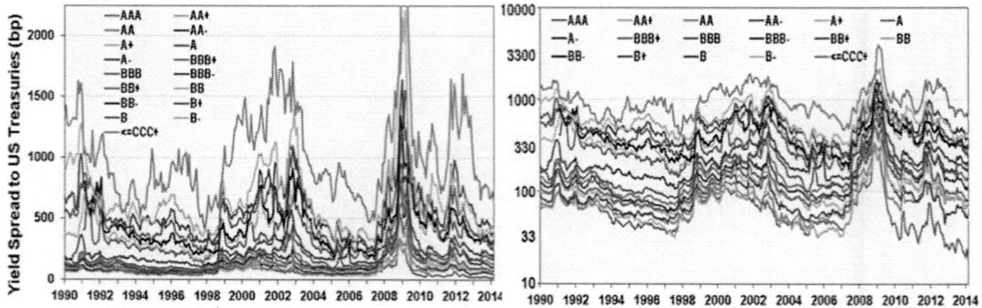

Figure 4. Monthly Average Yield Spreads to US Treasuries by Rating Category on Linear (Left) and Logarithmic (Right) Axes, 1990-2014.

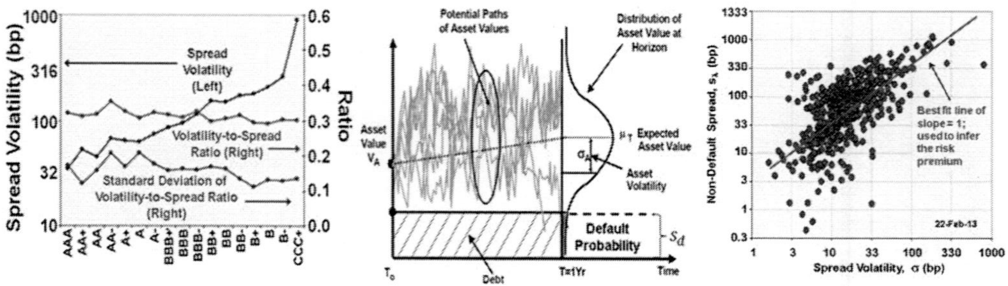

Figure 5. Left, Spread Volatility by Rating (Left Axis) and Ratio of Volatility to Spread (Right Axis) and the Volatility of Rolling Volatility-to-Spread Ratio; Middle: Merton-type Structural Model Used to Estimate Default Probabilities to Compute Default Spreads, s_d; Right: Non-Default Spreads by Volatility for the Calibration Universe using HPD PDs.

A key to understanding the credit risk premium comes from observations of historical credit spreads by rating categories over time. The left panel of Figure 4 shows monthly average yield spreads to U.S. Treasuries by rating category. Clearly, spread values vary widely over the credit cycle. However, when plotted on logarithmic axes, as in the right panel of Figure 4, one sees that credit spreads by rating seem to move in tandem at a constant ratio across rating categories. This suggests that although default rates and the credit risk premium may not be perfectly correlated, spread moves for default-risky credits, regardless of rating, are all linked by changes in a single common factor.

Another insight into the factor underlying the non-default spread, sλ (i.e., the credit risk premium), comes from examination of the volatility of credit spreads over time. For example, the diagonal points in the left panel of Figure 5 show that average monthly spread volatility as a function of rating category is roughly linear when plotted against the logarithms of average credit spreads. Furthermore, the middle function referenced to the right axis, is the ratio of spreads to volatilities by rating and is roughly 0.3 for all rating categories. Importantly, this implies that the market charges, on average, the same amount of credit spread per unit of volatility regardless of credit quality of the bonds. Finally, we find that the volatility of the rolling spread-to-volatility ratio (the lower function) is also constant across rating categories.

The results in the left panel of Figure 5 suggest that the credit risk premium might be related to the ratio of bonds' non-default spreads to their spread volatilities. To test this, we first computed values of default spreads, sd, for bonds in Citi's Investment-Grade and High Yield Indexes using PDs from the HPD model. As shown in the middle panel of Figure 5, one can think of pT in the structural framework of Merton (1974) as the likelihood that a given firm is insolvent at time T. Then, given pT and an assumed value for LGD, in this case 60%, one can use Equation 1, the risk-neutral spread formula, to determine the spread value of default for each bond. By subtracting the value of sd from the bond's overall spread, s, one can determine value of the non-default spread sλ as shown in Figure 2. The resulting values of sλ for the bonds in our sample appear on a logarithmic scale as a function of log spread volatility in the right panel of Figure 5. If the market charges the same amount on average per unit of volatility regardless of its source, then the relationship between non-default spread and spread volatility should have a slope of 1.0 in log-log coordinates. In fact, the line in Figure 5 with slope equal to 1.0 fits values of sλ well, although there is considerable variability around that line. Note that, all points on the line have the same ratio of spread to volatility and we call this ratio λ and designate $\lambda\sigma = s\lambda$ as the value of the daily risk premium for a given bond.[7]

Historical analyses of plots of non-default spreads versus volatility as in Figure 5 indicate that, at least to a first approximation, lines of slope equal to 1.0 fit the data well. Accordingly, following the methods described above, we can compute historical values of the daily ratio of spread-to-volatility (i.e., λ). The left panel of Figure 6 shows values of λ since 1999, whereas the right panel shows λ over the past year. The dashed line in each plot is the average value of λ, which is 4.8bp per unit of spread volatility. The plots also show that, as of the past year or so, the spread value of volatility has been consistently below average and trending downward. That is, investors have been increasingly willing to accept less spread per unit of volatility than average, presumably in the quest for yield amid the U.S. Federal Reserve's qualitative easing program.

Finally, we calculated the distribution of daily values of λ since 1999, and it appears in the left panel of Figure 7. Summary statistics of the distribution of λ values reveal it to be near Gaussian. That is, the mean and median are roughly the same value, with little skew or kurtosis. We also tracked the average non-default spread of our sample; it appears along with average spread volatility in the right panel of Figure 7.

[7] For simplicity, we presented an abbreviated description of how the points in Figure 5 were determined. In fact, as described in Benzschawel and Lee (2011), we use a Nelson-Siege (1987) procedure to determine one-year equivalent spreads (i.e., T=1) for all firms in our sample; these values appear in Figure 5. Also, we compute spread volatility on the trailing 100 daily spread values, but impose an exponential decay with a half-life of three months (i.e. 66 days) on trailing spread values.

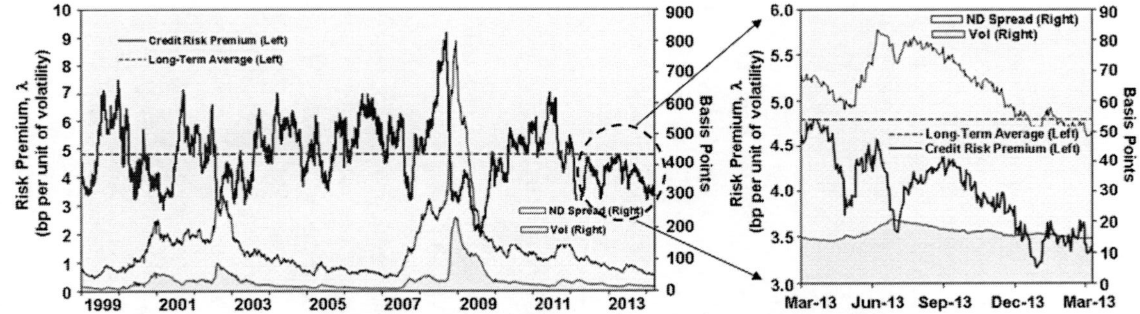

Figure 6. Historical Values of the Credit Risk Premium, λ from 1999 to 2014 (Left) and from Mar-13 to Mar-14 (Right).

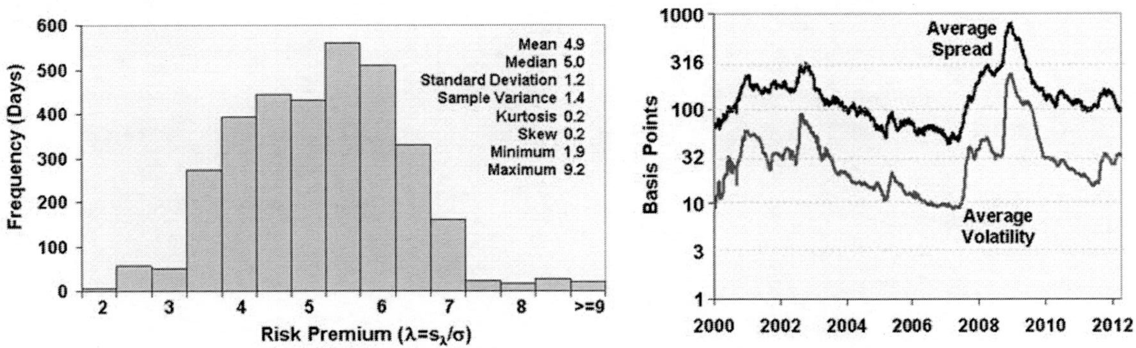

Figure 7: Distribution of Values of the Credit Risk Premium, λ, Since 1999; Right: Average Non-Default Spreads and Average Spread Volatilities Since 2000.

We are now in a position to summarize our formulation and measurement of the credit risk premium. That is, we first decompose bonds' credit spreads into the compensation for default s_d and into compensation for spread volatility s_λ where

$$s_d = -\frac{1}{T}\ln[1 - p_T \cdot LGD] \text{ and } s_\lambda = \lambda_t \sigma \ , \tag{2}$$

where T is the duration of the bond, p_T is the cumulative default probability up to time T, LGD is the expected loss from default, σ is the spread volatility, and λ_t is the current price of spread volatility (i.e., the "Sharpe ratio"), which on any given day is assumed to be the same for all credits. Putting those two expressions together, we can express the overall yield spread to US Treasuries on day t as:

$$s = \lambda_t \sigma - \frac{1}{T}\ln[1 - p_T \cdot LGD] \quad . \tag{3}$$

Thus, the model of spreads presented in Equation 3 embodies physical probabilities of default (PDs) from the HPD structural/statistical model, risk neutral theory to convert physical PDs and estimates of LGD to spread compensation for default, and the Sharpe ratio from Capital Asset Pricing Theory (CAPM) to estimate the daily spread value of volatility, λ_t, from non-default spreads and their trailing volatilities.

Hedging the Credit Risk Premium

The default component of risky bonds, s_d, is issuer specific, depending on obligors' credit qualities. For example, an investor may be comfortable bearing an obligor's default risk, but may be concerned about mark-to-market risk owing to changes in the credit risk premium. This concern is reasonable since, as demonstrated by the average spread decomposition in Figure 2, the spread value of volatility, λ_t, dominates all obligors' bond spreads. Changes in the risk premium and its near-perfect correlation among corporate bonds pose additional challenges over considerations of default risk for managers of credit portfolios. That is, values of their securities may rise or fall dramatically due to changes in s_λ and those changes may be largely unrelated to the default risk of their holdings.

Given our understanding of the credit risk premium, we sought the possibility of hedging the changes in investors risk appetites and market volatility as reflected in changes in the credit risk premium, s_λ. A successful and timely implementation of the hedge can both help investors preserve compensation from a suitable level of default risk and protect their portfolios against tail risk. In the following sections we first develop a hedging strategy for mark-to-market changes in non-default spreads using the North American Investment-Grade CDX index (CDS.IG.NA) followed by an extension of that hedging strategy to a portfolio of bonds.

Market NDS and the CDX Index

We calculate the market volatility on day t, designated as σ_t^M, as the mean of all bonds' volatilities.[8] The superscript M is used to denote that it represents the market. With the value of λ_t calibrated daily, the market non-default spread is defined as:

$$NDS_t^M = s_\lambda^M = \lambda_t \cdot \sigma_t^M \quad . \tag{4}$$

The left panel of Figure 8 displays the daily spread levels of NDS_t^M and the five-year $CDX.IG.NA$ since 2004 and the right panel of displays the cumulative changes of each of the two series. The figure shows that both series remain relatively stable prior to 2008, and they tend to co-move when the credit environment deteriorates, suggesting that it might be possible to hedge ΔNDS_t^M with $\Delta CDX.IG.NA$.

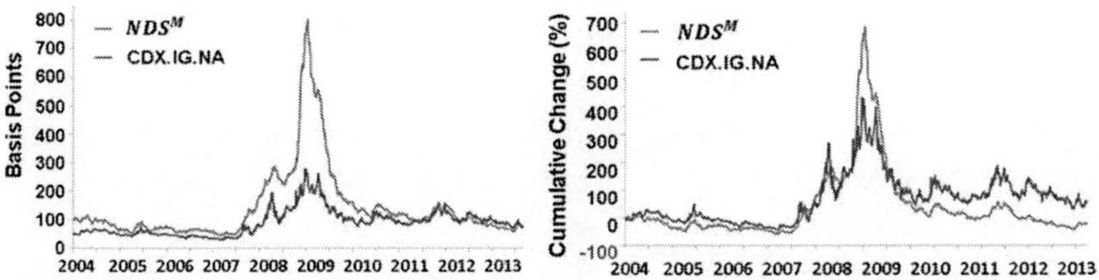

Figure 8. Left: Daily Values of the Market Non-Default Spread, $\boldsymbol{NDS_t^M}$ and the CDX.IG.NA; Right: Cumulative Percentage Changes of the Market Non-Default Spread, $\boldsymbol{NDS_t^M}$ and the CDX.IG.NA.

Since the goal is to hedge changes in market NDS (ΔNDS_t^M) by simultaneous changes in CDX.IG.NA (ΔCDX), one would expect a large value of ΔNDS_t^M to be accompanied by a large value of ΔCDX of the same sign. This is consistent with the trailing one-month and three-month correlations between the two series in Figure 9, which spike upward during the credit crises of 2007-2008. Given the positive correlation under times of stress, it appears that the CDX.IG.NA provides at least an approximate hedge against tail risk in corporate bond spreads. In the next

[8] For each single bond, its volatility is calculated as the standard deviation of exponentially weighted bond spreads over the past 100 days.

step, we determine the optimal interval over which to determine the hedging parameters.

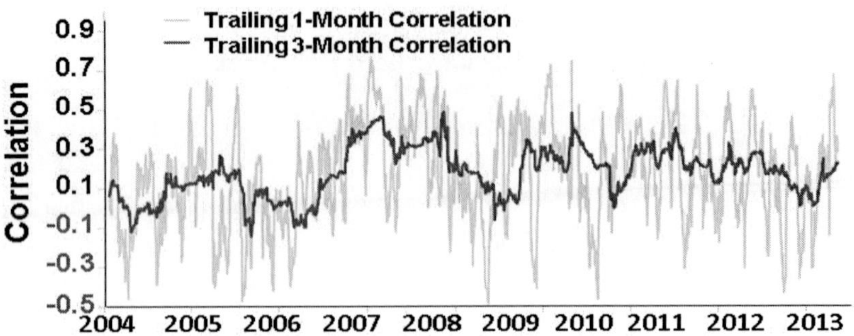

Figure 9. Trailing One- and Three-Month Correlations Between the Market Non-Default Spread, $\boldsymbol{NDS_t^M}$ and the CDX.IG.NA.

Market NDS and the CDX Index

The usefulness of $CDX.IG.NA$ as a hedge for NDS_t^M depends on how well ΔCDX tracks ΔNDS_t^M. The left set of panels in Figure 10 displays scatterplots of daily (top left), weekly (top right), monthly (bottom left), and three-month (bottom right) changes in spread levels for market NDS_t^M and $CDX.IG.NA$ from 2004 to 2013. Each set of changes is evaluated daily. In these plots, the upper right and lower left panels contain points whose values of ΔCDX and ΔNDS_t^M are of the same sign, positive and negative, respectively. These cases we call hits, as P/L from a short CDX position would at least partially hedge P/L from changes in the NDS_t^M. Conversely, the upper left and lower right panels contain points whose values of ΔCDX and ΔNDS_t^M have opposite signs. In the statistical literature, these cases are called false alarms or false positives, cases for which short/long CDX positions would add to gains/losses from long/short exposures to NDS_t^M, respectively.[9] Visual inspection is sufficient to

[9] The term *false alarm* originated with the literature on statistical decision theory, whereby the original development of ROC analysis was applied to detection of signals in noise and an incorrect response would be to indicate a signal when none was present. We use it here for consistency, but it is synonymous in this case with inconsistent P/L from changes in CDX and NDS.

reveal that on a daily basis there is little relationship between ΔCDX and ΔNDS_t^M and the correlation between those two series is only 20%. Thus, hedging $\Delta NDS_{t=1}^M$ with $\Delta CDX_{t=1}$ would be relatively ineffective, even counterproductive. However, as the tenor of the hedging frequency increases from one day to three months, there is a concomitant increase in the relationship between ΔCDX_t and ΔNDS_t^M such that there are very few false positives for three month changes. In fact, the correlations increase to 38%, 54%, and 74% as the hedging interval increases to one week, one month, and three months, respectively.

The relationships between ΔCDX and ΔNDS_t^M on the various time scales are further characterized in the ROC curves in the right panels of Figure 10. To construct the ROC curve, daily values of $\Delta NDS_{\Delta t}^M$ for a given hedging frequency Δt (i.e. ,$\Delta NDS_{\Delta t}^M = NDS_t^M - NDS_{t-\Delta t}^M$) are ranked from largest positive to largest negative and paired with their corresponding values of $\Delta CDX_{\Delta t}$ on that day. Then, as one goes through the sample of paired values of $\Delta NDS_{\Delta t}^M$ and $\Delta CDX_{\Delta t}$ ranked by $\Delta NDS_{\Delta t}^M$ one notes the percentage of $\Delta CDX_{\Delta t}$ that are of the same sign as the ranked values of $\Delta NDS_{\Delta t}^M$ (i.e., the percentage of hits as described above). We also note as we go through the ranked sample the percentage of $\Delta CDX_{\Delta t}$ that are of the opposite sign as the ranked values of $\Delta NDS_{\Delta t}^M$ (i.e., the false alarms). Note that as we go through the sample of $\Delta CDX_{\Delta t}$ based on ranked $\Delta NDS_{\Delta t}^M$, for each successive false alarm, we can calculate an increasing false alarm rate. Furthermore, for each increasing false alarm rate, there will be an associated fraction of hits, the cumulative percentage of $\Delta CDX_{\Delta t}$ values having the same sign as the $\Delta NDS_{\Delta t}^M$ within the range of false alarms. The ROC is constructed by plotting the fraction of hits as a function of the false alarm rate. These are the values displayed on the ROC curves in Figure 10.

The ROCs for values of Δt equal to one day, one week, one month, and three months appear in the right panels of Figure 10. The ROCs confirm that daily and weekly changes in ΔCDX and ΔNDS are only weakly correlated and are therefore not suitable for the hedge. On the other hand, monthly and three-month ΔCDX and ΔNDS appear to move much more closely in tandem, with the three-month Δt being best. As a result, we suggest using three-month changes as the appropriate hedging frequency. Moreover, a less frequent hedging has the added bonus of reducing transaction costs.

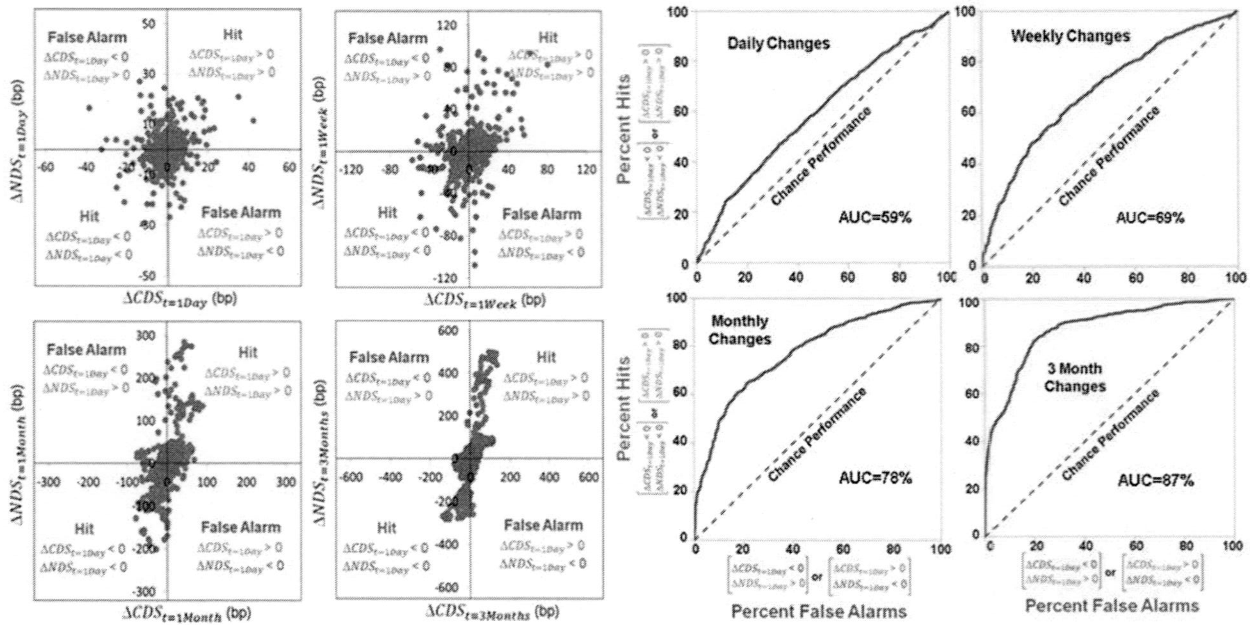

Figure 10. Left Panels: Scatterplots of Daily, Weekly, Monthly and Three-Month Changes in Spread Levels for Market $\boldsymbol{NDS_t^M}$ and the CDX.IG.NA; Right Panels: ROC Curves for Daily, Weekly, Monthly, and Three-Month Changes in Spread Levels for Market $\boldsymbol{NDS_t^M}$ and the CDX.IG.NA.

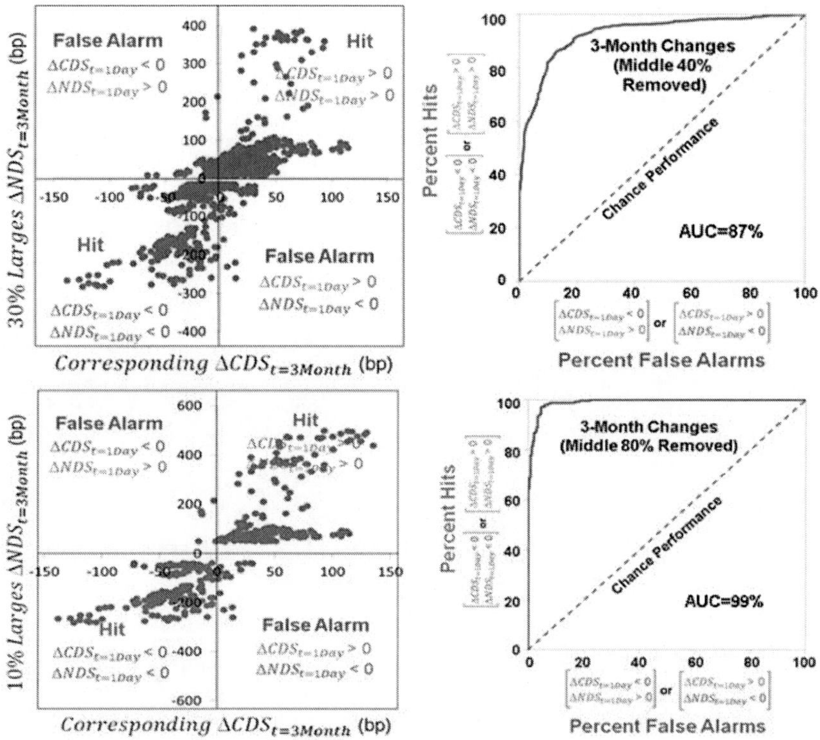

Figure 11. Left Panels: Scatterplots of the 30% (Top) and 10% (Bottom) Largest Changes in Three-Month Market $\boldsymbol{NDS_t^M}$ Against the Largest Values of three-month $\boldsymbol{\Delta CDX}$; Right Panels: ROC Curves the 30% (Top) and 10% (Bottom) Largest Changes in Three-Month Market $\boldsymbol{NDS_t^M}$ Against the Largest Values of three-month $\boldsymbol{\Delta CDX}$.

Having decided upon a three-month hedging frequency, we evaluated the likelihood that the largest values of $\Delta NDS^M_{\Delta t=3M}$ would correspond to the largest values of $\Delta CDS_{\Delta t=3M}$. That is, the analysis in Figure 10 examined only the correspondence in signs of changes in CDX and NDS and not their magnitudes. To that end, we selected the 30% largest positive and 30% largest negative three-month changes in NDS (i.e., $\Delta NDS^M_{\Delta t=3M}$) and plotted those changes against the corresponding values of $\Delta CDX_{\Delta t=3M}$. Thus, for this study, the sample excluded 40% of the cases having the smallest absolute values of three-month changes in $NDS^M_{\Delta t=3M}$.

The upper left panel of Figure 11 presents a scatterplot of $NDS^{M}_{\Delta t=3M}$ versus $\Delta CDX_{\Delta t=3M}$ after removal of the smallest 40% of absolute changes in $NDS^{M}_{\Delta t=3M}$ and their associated values of $\Delta CDX_{\Delta t=3M}$. The corresponding ROC curve appears at the upper right. The ROC curve was constructed in a similar manner to that for the three-month changes in Figure 10, except that the ROC in Figure 11 excludes the values of $\Delta CDX_{\Delta t=3M}$ associated with the 40% of the smallest absolute changes in $NDS^{M}_{\Delta t=3M}$. Eliminating the 40% of the smallest changes in $NDS^{M}_{\Delta t=3M}$ improves the performance of the hedge, as evidenced by increasing the AUC3 to 93% from its value of 87% with the full sample of $NDS^{M}_{\Delta t=3M}$ and $\Delta CDX_{\Delta t=3M}$.

The lower panels of Figure 11 illustrate the performance of $\Delta CDX_{\Delta t=3M}$ as a hedge for $\Delta NDS^{M}_{\Delta t=3M}$ when the smallest 80% of the changes in $NDS^{M}_{\Delta t=3M}$ are excluded. The scatterplot of only the largest and smallest 10% of the changes in $NDS^{M}_{\Delta t=3M}$ and corresponding $\Delta CDX_{\Delta t=3M}$ values reveals only a few false alarms and in those cases, the magnitudes of the changes in $CDX_{\Delta t=3M}$ are relatively small. The usefulness of $\Delta CDX_{\Delta t=3M}$ for hedging large absolute values of $\Delta NDS^{M}_{\Delta t=3M}$ is further quantified by the corresponding ROC whose AUC is near perfect at 99%.

Hedging Strategy and Optimal Hedge Ratio

Given the foregoing, we wish to determine the optimal hedge ratio β such that the hedged portfolio, which earns a spread difference of $[\Delta NDS - (\beta \cdot \Delta CDX)]$, minimizes risk as measured by the variance of the hedging portfolio. We call the case where $\beta = 1$, the naïve hedging strategy. Also, for the simple case in which β is a constant, since the minimum-variance linear predictor of ΔNDS based on ΔCDX is given by:

$$E(\Delta NDS) + \frac{Cov(\Delta NDS,\ \Delta CDX)}{Var(\Delta CDX)} \cdot [\Delta CDX - E(\Delta CDX)] \quad , \tag{5}$$

we can show that $Var(\Delta NDS - \beta \cdot \Delta CDX)$ is minimized by the optimal hedge ratio:

$$\beta^* = \frac{Cov(\Delta NDS,\ \Delta CDX)}{Var(\Delta CDX)} \quad . \tag{6}$$

This is called the minimum-variance (MV) hedge ratio (Johnson, 1960) and it is equivalent to the slope of the best-fit line from a least squares regression of ΔNDS on ΔCDX.

Dynamic hedging strategies, on the other hand, use $\beta = \beta_t$ and make frequent adjustments to the hedging portfolio. A simple method is to perform a linear regression based on a rolling window of time-series data, where the optimal hedge ratio is found by estimating the time-varying slope. We carry out the hedging strategy according to the following steps:

1. Trigger the dynamic hedge at date t only when the level of NDS_{t-1}^{M} is greater than 200bp. This threshold will not be breached under most market conditions but is necessary in times of market stress. If the dynamic hedge is not triggered, we default to using the naïve hedge ratio $\beta = 1$;
2. Find the previous 20 trading days' trailing 3-month changes in levels of NDS and CDX.IG.NA (i.e., $\Delta NDS_{\Delta t=3M}$ and $\Delta CDX_{\Delta t=3M}$). For notational convenience, we express the daily series of three-month changes as:

$$N = (N_{t-20}, N_{t-19}, \dots, N_{t-1})$$
$$\text{and } C = (C_{t-20}, C_{t-19}, \dots, C_{t-1}) \quad , \tag{7}$$

accordingly, where

$$N_i = NDS_i - NDS_{i-3M}, \quad C_i = CDX_i - CDX_{i-3M} \; ; \tag{8}$$

3. The optimal hedge ratio is given by $\beta^{*M} = \hat{\beta}_{t|t-1}^{M}$ from the fit of the regression:

$$N = \beta_{t|t-1} C + \epsilon \quad , \tag{9}$$

where $\beta_{t|t-1}$ means the hedge ratio is based on all information up to date $t-1$.

Analysis of Hedging Performance

Based on the hedging strategy discussed in the previous section, in Figure 12 we plot the estimated dynamic hedge ratio over time where our portfolio is examined every three months. Again, when the dynamic hedge is not triggered, β_t is assumed to be the naïve hedge ratio of 1.

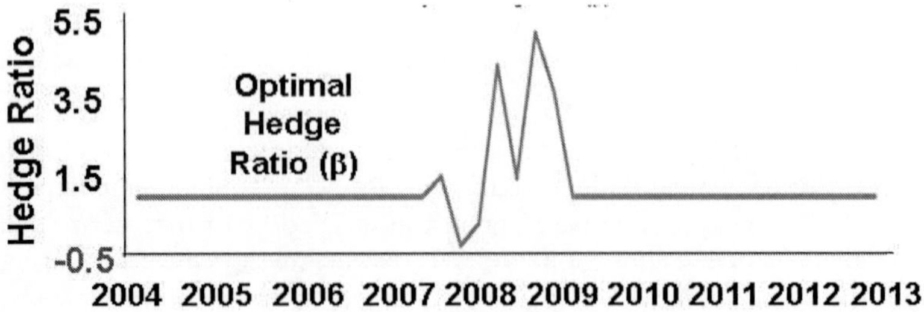

Figure 12. Optimal Dynamic Hedge Ratio with Threshold Trigger of $\boldsymbol{NDS^{M}_{t-1}}$ Greater Than 200bp.

We use the naïvely hedged NDS as a benchmark. One way to judge the hedging performance is by the amount of variance reduction in P/L (VR) produced by the hedge when compared with an unhedged portfolio. That is,

$$VR = \frac{Var(\text{Unhedged Portfolio}) - Var(\text{Hedged Portfolio})}{Var(\text{Unhedged Portfolio})} \quad (10)$$

For the naïve hedge with a constant $\beta = 1$, we find that VR = 35%. For the dynamic hedge, VR = 85%, a significant improvement over the naïve hedge. This is confirmed in Figure 13, which displays much flatter differences for the dynamically hedged portfolio. In fact, Figure 13 shows that the dynamic hedge reduces changes in spread value between NDS and CDX to nearly zero.

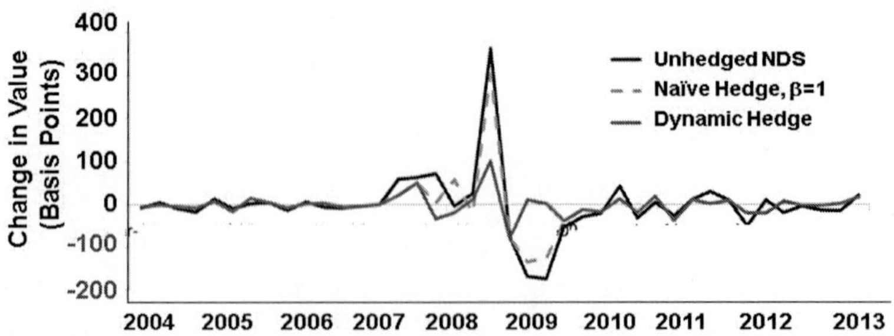

Figure 13. Three-Month Spread Changes for the Unhedged Portfolio, the Naïve Hedge of $\boldsymbol{\beta = 1}$, and the Dynamic Hedge.

Finally, we evaluate the hedging performance of the $CDX.IG.NA$ in terms of cumulative P/L of hedged and unhedged credit portfolios. A perfectly hedged portfolio will be P/L neutral and will have a constant value of zero for the cumulative change in portfolio Value. Assume the spread level of portfolio at the previous balancing period is S_{t-1} (in basis points) and the current spread level is S_t, the change in portfolio value from V_{t-1} to V_t, is:

$$V_t = V_{t-1} \cdot \frac{1+S_{t-1}/10000}{1+S_t/10000}. \tag{11}$$

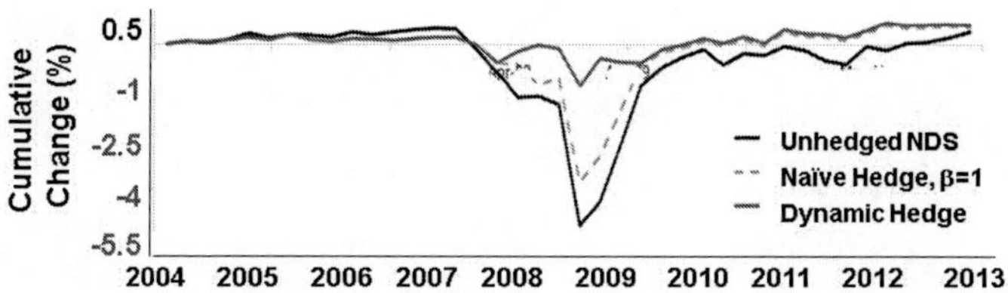

Figure 14. Cumulative Changes in Hedged and Unhedged Portfolio Value.

Figure 14 displays cumulative portfolio changes for hedged and unhedged portfolios. The plot shows the effectiveness of the dynamic hedge at reducing the tail risk from large moves in the credit risk premium. The fact that even the unhedged NDS position (dark line in Figure 14) has a cumulative P/L of roughly zero over the ten-year test period illustrates the mean reverting characteristic of the credit risk premium, s_λ. However, the unhedged portfolio has larger deviations from zero P/L during the period than either the naïve hedge or the dynamic hedge. Although the static hedge matches well the performance of the dynamic hedge over much of the period between 2004 to 2007 and 2010 to 2013, it fails nearly as badly as the unhedged portfolio during the liquidity crisis of 2008 and 2009. Meanwhile, the dynamic CDX hedge, while performing its worst during the crisis, still provided a good hedge for the changes in NDS during that period.

Another advantage of the dynamic hedge is illustrated in Figure 15, which displays distributions of a daily series of three-month changes in basis points for the unhedged portfolio and three-month hedged P/L. Both the unhedged and hedged portfolios have mean P/L values near zero. However, the standard deviation of the three-month unhedged P/L is 75bp, whereas the naïve hedge reduces it to 61bp. But the 28bp volatility of three-month spread changes for the dynamic portfolio is about one-third that of the unhedged portfolio and under half that of the static portfolio.

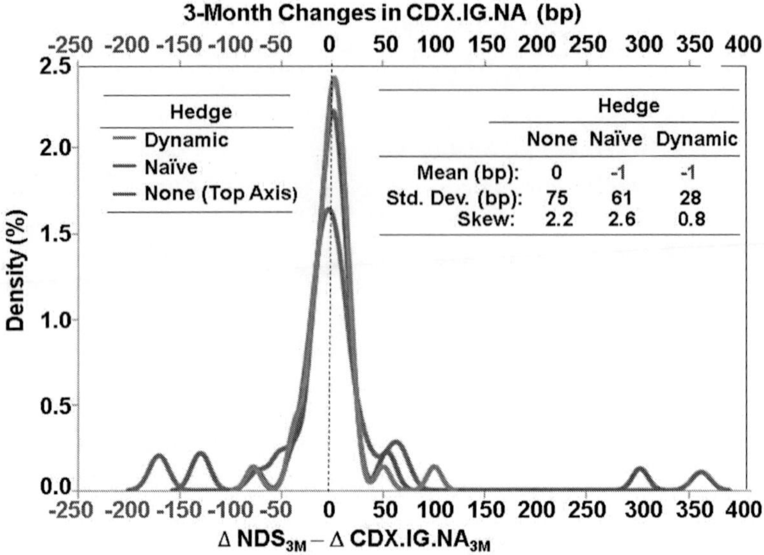

Figure 15. Distributions of Unhedged Three-Month P/L for the Unhedged Portfolio (Top Axis) and the Naïve and Dynamic Hedges (Bottom Axis) from 2004 to 2013.

Hedging the Risk Premium for a Portfolio of Bonds

Recall that a key finding in our model of the credit risk premium is that, at least on average, the market charges roughly the same amount of spread per unit of volatility regardless of the underlying credit quality. In other words, λ_t, calculated from market every day, does not depend on credit ratings or spread volatility, per se. In light of this, assume we have a bond portfolio consisting of N bonds: $B_1, B_2, \dots B_N$ with weights in the portfolio indicated by $w_1, w_2, \dots w_N$ such that $\sum_{i=1}^{N} w_i = 1$. Then, the non-default exposure of this portfolio can be characterized by:

$$NDS_t^P = \sum_{i=1}^{N} w_i \cdot (\lambda_t \cdot \sigma_{i,t}) = \lambda_t \sum_{i=1}^{N} w_i \cdot \sigma_{i,t} \quad , \qquad (12)$$

where $\sigma_{i,t}$ is the spread volatility for bond i calculated on date t. Consequently, the optimal hedge ratio for this portfolio, P, is given by

$$\beta^{*P} = \frac{Cov\,(\Delta NDS^P,\ \Delta CDX)}{Var(\Delta CDX)} = \frac{Cov\,(\sum_{i=1}^{N} w_i \cdot \Delta NDS_i,\ \Delta CDX)}{Var(\Delta CDX)}$$

$$= \frac{\sum_{i=1}^{N} w_i \cdot Cov\,(\Delta NDS_i, \Delta CDX)}{Var(\Delta CDX)} \quad . \tag{13}$$

Because for each individual bond in the portfolio, the optimal hedge ratio for that bond is

$$\beta_i^* = \frac{Cov\,(\Delta NDS_i, \Delta CDX)}{Var(\Delta CDX)} \quad , \tag{14}$$

which we estimate by following the same steps as described above. We now have

$$\beta^{*P} = \sum_{i=1}^{N} w_i\, \beta_i^* \quad . \tag{15}$$

That is, the optimal hedge ratio for the whole portfolio is the weighted average of the optimal hedge ratio for each member bond in the portfolio. In the extreme case when the portfolio contains all bonds in the market in equal weights, the optimal hedge ratio becomes exactly the optimal hedge ratio β^{*M} for the market NDS as demonstrated in the previous sections.

Predicting the Credit Risk Premium

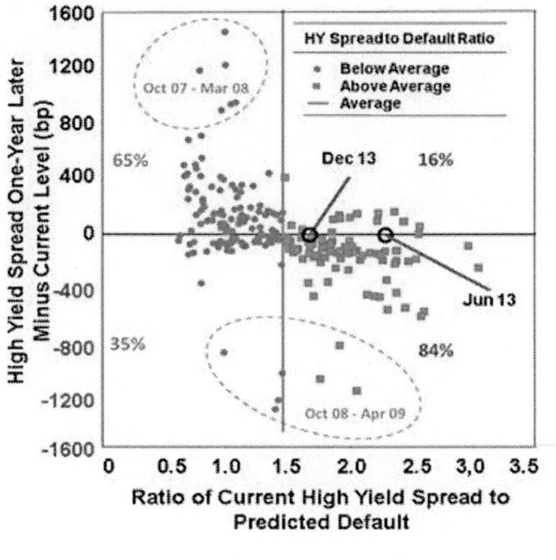

Figure 16. Predicting One-Year Changes in Average High Yield Bond Spreads using the Ratio of Current Average High Yield Spread to Predicted Default Rate.

Figure 16 from Benzschawel and Su (2014b) demonstrates that one can predict well above change one-year changes in the average high yield bond spread based on the ratio of the current average high yield spread to the predicted default rate from their HT-2.0 model. Accordingly, to the extent that the majority of the fluctuations in high yield spreads are due to changes in the credit risk premium, one ought to be able to predict the credit risk premium as well by knowing its current level relative to the predicted one-year default rate. We examine that hypothesis in this section.

We first examined if, as for one-year changes in high yield spreads, the average high yield spread to predicted default rate can predict one-year changes in the credit risk premium. Those results appear in the left panel of Figure 17 in which one-year changes in the credit risk premium λ are plotted versus the ratio of the current high yield average spread to predicted default rate.[10] Points in the figure are generated at monthly intervals from January 2000 through December 2014. As before, average high yield spreads are those from Citigroup's High Yield Market Index (Citi Index Group, 2013) and predicted default rates are from Citi's HT-2.0 model. Contrary to our expectations, the data in the left panel of Figure 17 indicate that there is very little relationship between the ratio of the average high yield spread to the predicted default rate (SHY-to-Dp) ratio and changes in the credit risk premium. That is, when the SHY-to-Dp ratio is below average there is a 52%/48% chance of the risk premium widening/tightening. When the SHY-to-Dp ratio is above average, there is a slight tendency (58%/42%) for the risk premium to widen. However, this is the reverse pattern of that observed for the CDX.HY index in the right panel of Figure 8. That result is somewhat paradoxical in that one might expect the risk premium to decrease when its value is higher than relative to the default rate that occurs over the following year.

[10] Because Citi's HT-2.0 model is able to generate monthly values of predicted default rates and average high yield spreads and the credit risk premium are updated daily, we are able to generate monthly sets of points on the graphs in Figure 17.

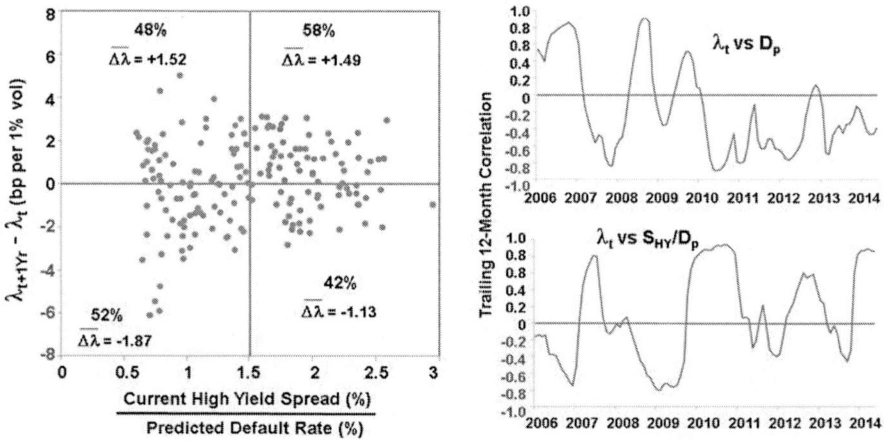

Figure 17. One-Year Changes in the Credit Risk Premium (λ) as a Function of the Ratio of the Current High Yield Average Spread to the Predicted Default Rate, SHY-to-Dp (Left Panel) with Percentages and Average Changes in the Risk Premiums are Also Shown. Right: Trailing 12-Month Correlations between λ and Predicted Default from the HT-2.0 Model (Top); and λ Versus the Ratio of CDX.HY to Predicted Default (Bottom).

The failure of the S_{HY}-to-D_p ratio to predict changes in the credit risk premium suggested that, perhaps, the lack of correlation between the effects of changes in spreads and volatilities resulting from changes in perceived default risk and changes in the spread compensation for default (i.e., the risk premium). To examine this, we calculated 12-month trailing correlations between the current credit risk premium, λ_t, and the predicted default rate, D_p, from 2006 to 2014. The time series of that correlation appears in the top right panel of Figure 17. The lower right plot is the analogous time-series of the trailing correlation between λ_t and the S_{HY}-to-D_p ratio. Although values of λ_t and D_p are highly correlated at times, that correlation can be either positive or negative; in fact, it is rarely near zero. The same is true for λ_t and the S_{HY}-to-D_p ratio. However, the patterns of changes in the correlations over time differ between the two series. These results suggest that the ability to predict changes in high yield index spreads is due to investors increasing their expected compensation for not receiving the cash flows owing to default (i.e., not related to the credit risk premium). Still, that compensation is greater than the increase in spread owing to the non-receipt of cash flows, suggesting that the default rate is

ratio of λ_t-to-D_p is above its average, the spread compensation for volatility tends to decrease, averaging -1.2bp per unit of volatility with a 63% probability.

Figure 19 presents further analysis of the relationship between the λ_t-to-D_p ratio and one-year changes in the risk premium. The left panel displays average one-year changes in λ and probabilities of correct directional moves as predicted by deviations of the λ_t-to-D_p ratio from average values. The results are binned by buckets of standard deviations from the average. Although for all buckets, λ_t-to-D_p ratios predict directional changes at above chance (50%) levels, the predictive power for decreases in the risk premium are better and more monotonic for decreases in the credit risk premium than for increases. This is true both for average changes in λ as well as the probability of a correct directional change. In fact, the probabilities of being correct for signals the extreme bins (λ_t-to-$D_p < 0.75$ and λ_t-to-$D_p > 1.0$) are 83% for increases in the risk premium and 100% for decreases. This pattern is also visible in the scatterplot of Figure 18.

The right panel of Figure 19 displays the value of the credit risk premium as of May 19, 2014 and its expected value one year later based on the ratio of the current value of λ to the predicted default rate form the HT-2.0 model (i.e., λ_t-to-$D_{p.}$). The figure shows the current value of λ is 3.5cbp per unit of spread volatility. This corresponds to -0.26σ below its average value and implies that the current risk premium is 0.4 bp lower at 3.9 bp per unit of volatility than implied by the current λ_t-to-D_p ratio.

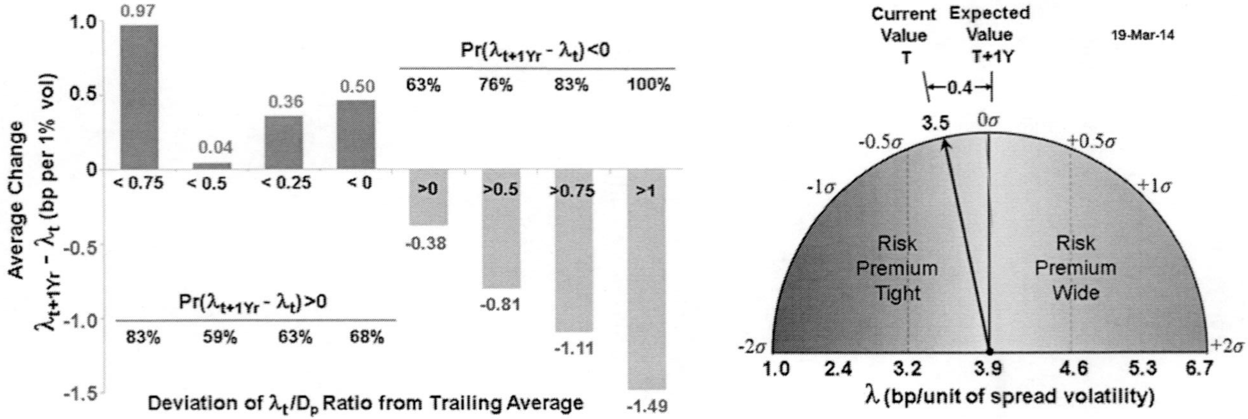

Figure 19. Left: Average One-Year Changes and Probabilities Correct for Changes in the Credit Risk Premium, λ as a Function of Standard Deviations from the Average Ratio of λ to Predicted Default, Dp; Right: Current and Expected Value of the Credit Risk Premium.

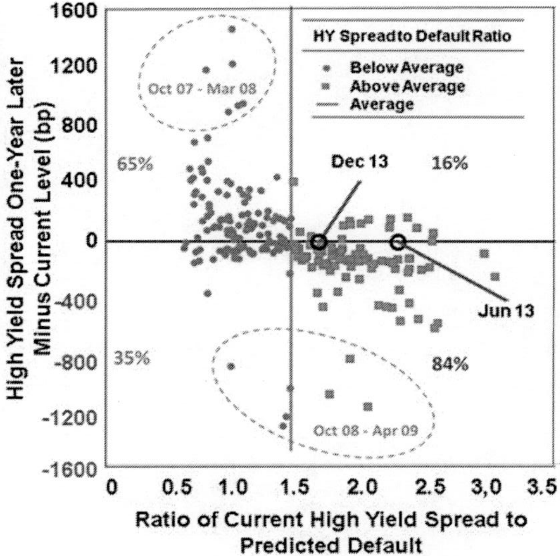

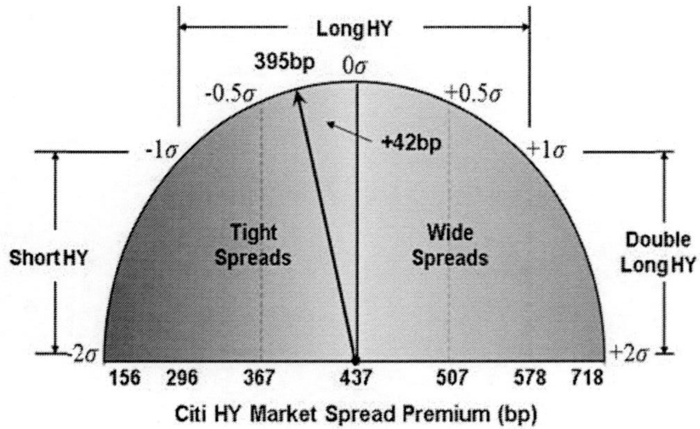

Figure 20. Left: Predicted Changes in High Yield Spreads Based on Ratios of Current High Yield Spreads to Predicted Default Rates; Right: Current and Expected Value of the Average High Yield Spread.

Implications for Investors

The results presented above demonstrate that one can predict one-year changes in the credit risk premium at above-chance levels. That result, along with our earlier demonstration of the ability to hedge changes in the risk premium and to predict spread changes in the investment-grade and high yield markets, has implications for investors in the credit markets.

Consider first, the left panel of Figure 20 that displays results of Benzschawel and Su (2014b), who demonstrated that the ratio of Citi's current High Yield Index spread to the HT-2.0 model's predicted default rate can predict one-year changes in average high yield spreads. (Note that a similar effect holds for investment grade spreads.) Furthermore, the right panel of Figure 20 indicates that the high yield index spread of 395 bp as of May 19, 2014 would be expected to be wider by +42 bp based on the difference between the current SHY-to-Dp ratio and its historical average. In general, this is not a large spread widening, and our long/short high yield CDX index strategy, superimposed in the right panel of Figure 20, would recommend that investors remain long credit exposure (Benzschawel and Su, 2014c).

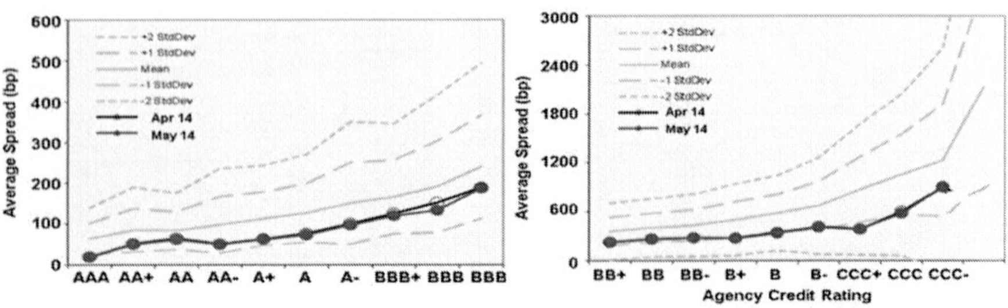

Figure 21. Average Credit Spreads by Rating for Investment Grade (Left) and High Yield Bonds (Right), 30-Apr-14.

Although our models predict only moderate widening of high yield spreads and less than a 1bp per unit of volatility increase in the credit risk premium, the current tightness of credit spreads and the very low levels of the credit risk premium suggest that there remains little room for further spread tightening. For example, Figure 21 shows average investment-grade (top panel) and high yield (lower panel) spreads by rating category for bonds in Citi's Broad Investment Grade (BIG) and High Yield Indexes, respectively (Lee and Benzschawel, 2014). The figure demonstrates that, for high quality investment-grade bonds, spreads are nearly two standard deviations tighter than average. However, spreads widen to only one standard deviation below average for credit rated below single-A.[12] Furthermore, the expected high yield default rate for 2014 is about 2.3%, near cyclical lows, and the credit risk premium at 3.5 bp per unit of volatility is way below its average of 4.8 bp, which also suggests little room for further spread rallies.

Against this backdrop, investors are worried about a rapid backup in credit spreads, particularly in response to impending Fed actions regarding quantitative easing (QE). The results provided herein offer some insight for investors. Assuming agreement on the general asymmetric risk of spreads widening relative to tightening, it would seem reasonable for investors to lock in gains from previous spread tightening by buying protection on the CDX.NA.IG. As demonstrated above, the CDX.NA.IG can be an effective hedge for changes in spreads owing to increases in the credit risk premium. In fact, given little room for credit spreads to tighten significantly and the mean-reverting characteristic of the risk premium shown in Figure 6, one might consider over-buying protection on the CDX.NA.IG (i.e., going short the credit risk premium), at least until the risk premium reaches average levels. In fact, our results suggest a general strategy for outperforming the market by over-buying protection when the risk premium is below average and over-selling protection (i.e., going even longer) via CDX.NA.IG when the risk premium is above average.

Summary

The purpose of this report is to describe the credit risk premium, to derive a suitable hedge for changes in the credit risk premium, and to determine if it can be predicted. We began by providing empirical evidence for a constant daily credit risk premium across agency rating categories. We then showed how bonds' credit spreads can be conceived as consisting of two parts: a spread compensation for default and compensation for spread volatility. We also demonstrated that the default-related spread can be modeled in accordance with risk neutral pricing theory. Also, we showed that the non-default spread, which is not obligor-specific, can be modeled within the framework of the CAPM as the product of bonds' spread volatilities times the daily price of risk. This risk

[12] The tightness of spreads is even more remarkable when one considers that the distribution of spreads for a given rating category is generally skewed toward higher spreads when plotted on linear y-axes.

premium is the excess yield per unit of volatility over similar duration U.S. Treasuries that investors receive after accounting for losses from default.

After presenting some historical aspects of the credit risk premium and its properties, we explored the possibility of hedging changes in the non-default spreads using the North American credit default swap index, the CDX.IG.NA. We find that three-month changes in the CDS index generally track changes in bonds' non-default spreads over three-month periods, which suggests using trailing three-month changes as the basis for computing their hedge ratio. We compared a naïve one-for-one hedging strategy between the CDX and non-default spread with a dynamic strategy, whereby the hedge ratio is determined by regression analyses based on a rolling window of changes in the CDX index versus changes in non-default spreads. We find that the constant hedge works well in all years except during the liquidity crisis of late 2007 and 2008, whereas the dynamic hedge works well over the entire test period since 2004. Finally, we demonstrated that changes in the ratio of the credit risk premium to the predicted default rate can predict changes in the credit risk premium at above chance levels.

We then considered implications for investors in corporate bonds of expected changes in credit spreads and the risk premium in the context of the current market environment. Noting that current levels of corporate credit spreads and the credit risk premium are at relatively tight levels, we argued that there is little opportunity for further spread tightening. Given that and the fact that our predictive models indicate that spreads and the risk premium should increase slightly, we argue that investors should consider hedging their exposure to credit spreads by using the five-year CDX.NA.IG. Furthermore, considering the historical mean-reverting pattern of the credit risk premium, we suggest that investors might even consider short credit spreads via the CDS index, at least until bond spreads and the risk premium revert back to their historical average levels.

References

Benzschawel, T. and Lee, M. Market-Implied Default Probabilities: Update: Inferring Credit Risk from Bond Prices, Citi, September 9, 2011.

Benzschawel, T. and Assing, A. Inferring Default Probabilities from Credit Spreads, *Journal of Fixed Income* 13, pp. 16-24, Spring 2012.

Benzschawel, T. *Credit Risk Modeling: Facts, Theory and Applications, Incisive Media*, London, 2012.

Benzschawel, T. and Su, Y. Hedging the Credit Risk Premium, Citi, January 22, 2014a.
Benzschawel, T. and Su, Y. Predicting Annual Default Rates, Citi, February 2, 2014b.
Benzschawel, T. and Su, Y. CDX.NA 5Y OTR Index Trades, Citi, February 25, 2014c.
Citi Index Group, Index Guide – 2013 Edition, Citigroup, January 2013.
Elton, J., Gruber, M., Agrawal, D. and Mann, D. Explaining the Rate Spread on Corporate Bonds, *Journal of Finance* 56, pp. 449-470, 2001.
Johnson, L.L. The Theory of Hedging and Speculation in Commodity Futures, *Review of Economic Studies* 27(3): 139–151, 1960.
Jones, E. Mason, S. and Rosenfeld, E. Contingent Claims Analysis of Corporate Capital Structures, *Journal of Finance* 39, pp. 611-625, 1984
Lee, M. and Benzschawel, T. *Corporate Markets Quantitative Review – May 2014*, Citi, May 5, 2014.
Merton, R. A. On the Pricing of Corporate Debt: The Risk Structures of Interest Rates, *Journal of Finance* 29, pp. 449-470, 1974.
Nelson, C. R. and Siegel, A. F., Parsimonious Modeling of Yield Curves, *Journal of Business* 60(4), 1987, pages 473-89.
Sobehart, J. and Keenan, S. *Hybrid Contingent Claims Models: A Practical Approach to Modeling Default Risk, Credit Ratings: Methodology, Rationale and Default Risk*, M. Ong (ed.), Risk Books, 2002.
Sobehart, J. and Keenan, S. Hybrid Probability of Default Models: A Practical Approach to Modeling Default Risk, *Quantitative Credit Analyst* 3, pp. 5-29, 2003.

Appendix: The Spread Value of Default

As described briefly in the text, the spread value of default can be derived from the price-yield formula with the assumption from risk-neutral pricing theory that the present value of a set of cash flows is their expected likelihood of receipt discounted at the risk-free rate. To illustrate this as applied to the yield value of risky security, consider a single cash flow of \$1 to be received at time T in the future as shown in Figure 22. From bond math, we know that we can find a discount factor y_T applied to the \$1 such that, when discounted back from T to the present, it will equal the market value PV. That is,

$$PV = 1 * e^{y_T T} \quad . \qquad \text{(A-1)}$$

If the cash flow at T will be received with certainty, then according to risk-neutral pricing theory, the fair value of PV is the value of \$1 discounted at the risk-free rate, r_T between time 0 and T. That is, for a certain cash flow, we can substitute r_T for y_T in Equation A1-1.

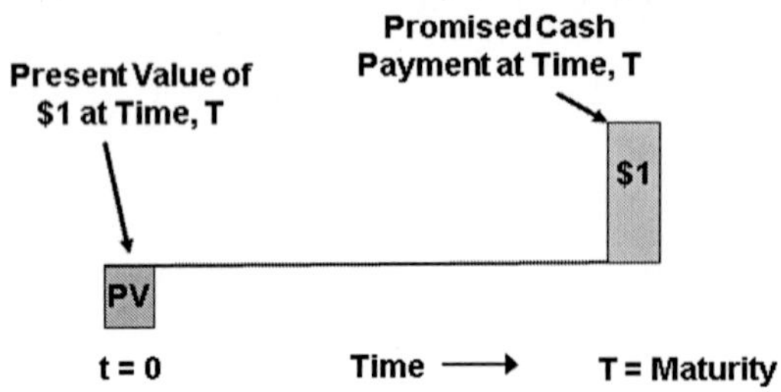

Figure 22. Present Value at Time *t=0* of \$1 Promised at Time *T*.

For discounting uncertain cash flows, we add a factor to r_T, call it s_T, such that $y_T = r_T + s_T$, when discounting. In addition, we represent the uncertain cash flow as an expected value, $E[1]_T$ in this case. If the obligor does not default, we receive \$1 at time T with the probability $1 - p_T$; otherwise, we receive the recovery value R with probability p_T. Thus, we can express the expected value of the \$1 to be received at time T as the weighted sum of receiving the \$1 or the recovery value R. That is,

$$E[1]_T = [(1 - p_T) * 1 + p_T R] \quad . \qquad \text{(A-2)}$$

Based on the foregoing and risk-neutral pricing theory, we can rewrite Equation A1-1 for a default-risky cash flow as:

$$e^{-T(r_T+s_T)} = e^{-Tr_T}[(1 - p_T) * 1 + p_T R] \quad , \qquad \text{(A-3)}$$

where s_T reflects that additional yield required to compensate for the likelihood of not receiving the full \$1 at T. By taking the natural logarithms of both sides of Equation A1-3 and rearranging, we can express the spread compensation owing to default as:

$$s_T = -\frac{1}{T} ln[1 - (p_T * LGD)] \quad , \qquad \text{(A-4)}$$

which is the expression in Equation 1 of the text. Note that in the text, for simplicity, we represent a stream of cash flows from a bond as a single cash flow to be received at the duration of the bond.

CHAPTER TWELVE

FIXING UNDEREXPOSED SNAPSHOTS: PROPER COMPUTATION OF CREDIT EXPOSURES UNDER THE REAL WORLD AND RISK NEUTRAL MEASURES

HARVEY J. STEIN[1]

Abstract

As per regulations and common risk management practice, the credit risk of a portfolio is managed via its potential future exposures (PFEs), expected exposures (EEs), and related measures, such as the expected positive exposure (EPE), the effective expected exposure (EEE), and the effective expected positive exposure (EEPE). Notably, firms use these exposures to set economic and regulatory capital levels. Their values have a big impact on the capital that firms need to hold to manage their risks.

Due to the growth of CVA computations and the similarity of CVA computations to exposure computations, firms find it expedient to compute these exposures under the risk neutral measure.

Here we show that exposures computed under the risk neutral measure are essentially arbitrary. They depend on the choice of numéraire and can be manipulated by choosing a different numéraire. Even when restricting attention to commonly used numéraires, exposures can vary substantially. As such, it is critical that these calculations be done under the real world measure, not the risk neutral measure.

This chapter is a summary of Stein (2014).

[1] Harvey Stein is head of Regulation and Credit Risk, Quantitative Risk Analytics Group. Email: hjstein@bloomberg.net.

Introduction

Based on the principle that one cannot manage what one cannot measure, to manage credit risk, one needs some way to measure it. The common way to measure the credit risk of a portfolio is via its potential future exposures (PFEs), expected exposures (EEs), and related measures, such as the expected positive exposure (EPE), the effective expected exposure (EEE), and the effective expected positive exposure (EEPE). See the Basel Committee on Banking Supervision (2011) or the Basel Committee on Banking Supervision (2009), for example.

The PFE of a portfolio measures the loss that could be realized in the future in the event of a counterparty default (Canabarro and Duffie, 2003). Specifically, for a portfolio *V*, a PFE of *X* at a horizon time of *T* and a confidence level of *p* is defined by

$$P[V_T < X] = \mathrm{E}^P[1_{V_T<X}] = p,$$

where *P* is the real world measure, and V_T is the value of the portfolio at time *T*. For example, a 1 year 95% PFE of $1,000,000 means that there is a 95% chance that the portfolio will be worth $1,000,000 or less in a year, or in other words, a 95% chance that the exposure will not exceed $1,000,000.

The expected exposure at a time *T* is the average expected loss if default occurs at time *T*, assuming no recovery:

$$\mathrm{EE}(V,T) = \mathrm{E}^P[\max(V_T,0)] = \mathrm{E}^P[V_T 1_{V_T \geq 0}]$$

The expected positive exposure (the average loss over a time period):

$$\mathrm{EPE}(V, t_1, t_2) = \frac{1}{t_2 - t_1} \int_{t_1}^{t_2} \mathrm{EE}(V, s) ds$$

The effective expected exposure is the maximum effective exposure over a time period:

$$\mathrm{EEE}(V,t_1,t_2) = \max_{t_1 \leq s \leq t_2} (\mathrm{EE}(s))$$

The effective expected positive exposure is the average of the EEE over a time period:

$$\mathrm{EEPE}(V, t_1, t_2) = \frac{1}{t_2 - t_1} \int_{t_1}^{t_2} \mathrm{EEE}(V, t_1, s) ds$$

Banks use PFEs, along with the related expected exposures (EEs) and expected positive exposures (EPEs), to set credit limits. Basel II and III use the EEPE(*V*,0,1) to determine capital charges. There are many regulations addressing how to compute these and how to set capital limits based on them, such as the Basel Committee on Banking Supervision (2005), the Comptroller of the Currency, Treasury (2012), and the Basel Committee on Banking Supervision (2011). There is also a large body of literature on the use of exposures in risk management. See, for example, Canabarro et al. (2003) and Canabarro and Duffie (2003).

For CVA calculations, we need to calculate the value of call options on the portfolio that mature at different times (Stein and Lee, 2011). This means computing, under the equivalent martingale measure Q with respect to a numéraire N, the value

$$\mathrm{E}^{Q}\left[\frac{\max(V_t,0)}{N_t}\right]N_0.$$

The details of such calculations are also widely covered in the literature and in regulations. References include Stein and Lee (2011), Pykhtin and Zhu (2007), Brigo and Capponi (2009), and Jarrow and Yu (2001)

Once one is able to compute CVAs, it is appealing to repurpose the same software to compute the above credit exposure measures by computing them under the equivalent martingale measure Q instead of under the real world measure P. Doing so tacitly assumes that using the risk neutral measure will not have a substantial impact on the PFE when compared to using the real world measure. This is in fact becoming common practice in banks and is even being requested by some regulators.

However, the risk neutral measure Q is not unique. It depends on the choice of numéraire N, so, in fact, an additional assumption is being made, namely that the choice of numéraire also has little impact on exposure calculations.

Here we explore this assumption. We will look at how changing numéraires (and corresponding risk neutral measures) change exposure measures while leaving option prices unchanged.

Exposure Exploration

In the full paper, we consider a number of ways of expressing exposures under a change of numéraire. We relate exposures and numéraires to cumulative density functions and to Radon-Nikodym derivatives, and we express risk neutral exposures as option values.

In particular, consider two risk neutral measures Q and Q' with respect to numéraires N and N', respectively. A PFE of X for a horizon time T with confidence level p under Q satisfies:

$$p = \mathrm{E}^{Q}[1_{V_T<X}]$$

Under Q', this corresponds to a PFE with confidence level

$$p' = \mathrm{E}^{Q'}[1_{V_T<X}] = \mathrm{E}^{Q}\left[X\frac{N'_T/N'_0}{N_T/N_0}\right]$$

This shows that a change in confidence level corresponds to the impact of multiplying by the ratio of the numéraires involved. In fact, this ratio is the Radon-Nikodym derivative of Q' with respect to Q for time T measurable random variables:

$$\frac{N'_T/N'_0}{N_T/N_0} = \frac{dQ'}{dQ}$$

We then show the confidence level for a PFE of X with respect to Q at a horizon time T is the current price of the following time T payoff:

$$1_{V<X}\frac{N_T}{N_0}$$

We conclude that the confidence level associated with a PFE of X at a horizon T with respect to a risk neutral measure Q and numéraire N is the price of an option to purchase $1/N_0$ shares of the numéraire when the portfolio value is less than X. As such, changing risk neutral measures changes the payoff and changes the probability of experiencing an exposure exceeding X.

Constructing Numéraires

In the paper, we go on to show how to construct a numéraire that yields a specific PFE at a specific confidence level. This allows a nefarious institution using "the risk neutral measure" to adjust its PFE to whatever it chooses.

Suppose a PFE of X with a confidence level p at a horizon T is desired. Let Q be the time T forward measure. Let

$$A = \frac{p}{\mathrm{E}^{Q}[1_{V<X}]}$$

$$B = \frac{1 - A\mathrm{E}^{Q}[1_{V<X}]}{\mathrm{E}^{Q}[1_{V\geq X}]}$$

$$N'_T = A\,1_{V<X} + B\,1_{V\geq X}$$

$$N'_t = \mathrm{E}[N'_T/N_T]N_t$$

We show that N' is a numéraire with respect to a corresponding equivalent martingale measure Q', and that under Q',

$$\mathrm{E}^{Q'}[1_{V<X}] = A\,\mathrm{E}^{Q}[1_{V<X}] = p,$$

so under Q', the PFE for a confidence level of p is X.

More generally, the full PFE profile can be sculpted. The full PFE profile under Q is given by $F^{-1}(p)$, where

$$F(X) = \mathrm{E}^{Q}[1_{V<X}].$$

Consider a desired PFE profile F'. If F' is an increasing, continuous function of X, then by using the same approach along with the inverse function theorem, we can find a numéraire N' and corresponding measure Q' such that

$$\begin{aligned} F'(X) &= \mathrm{E}^{Q}[1_{V<X} N'_T] \\ &= \mathrm{E}^{Q'}[1_{V<X}]. \end{aligned}$$

So, in general, a numéraire can always be chosen to make a portfolio's time T PFE profile match any desired target PFE profile. EEs can be adjusted by selecting the PFE profile necessary to achieve the desired target EE profile and by using the above method to pick a numéraire that yields this PFE profile.

Moreover, one can in fact match any exposure profile at a discrete set of times T_i by applying the same process inductively, first to T_1 and then to T_2 conditional on T_1, etc.

Examples

While this shows that, in general, exposures under risk neutral measures are essentially arbitrary and meaningless from a risk management perspective, it is interesting to consider how much exposures vary for typical models and commonly or easily selected numéraires.

In the paper, we explore the impact on equity exposures, zero coupon bond exposures, and swap exposures. We compare the differences in stock portfolio PFEs and EEs when using the money market numéraire versus using the stock itself as a numéraire, and find differences as large as 60%. Similar results are seen for equity option portfolios.

We also compare zero coupon bond and interest rate swap exposures using the Hull-White model with the money market numéraire, forward numéraires of different maturities, and the LGM numéraire. Here we observe PFEs and EEs for zero coupon bonds differing by as much as 30%.

For interest rate swaps, we observe that a high coupon pay fixed swap can have a PFE of zero under the LGM measure, while exhibiting a PFE of over 1.3 million under the money market measure (see figure 1). Similarly, swap EEs can differ by as much as 200%

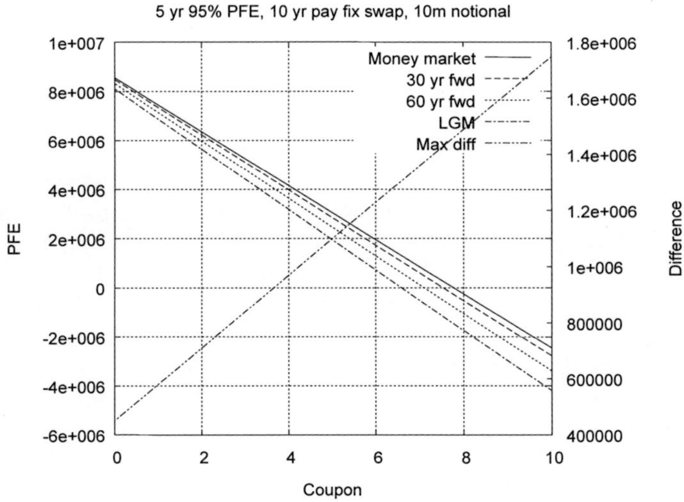

Figure 1. Five-year 95% PFE for a 10-year pay fixed swap on a 10 million notional as a function of the swap coupon.

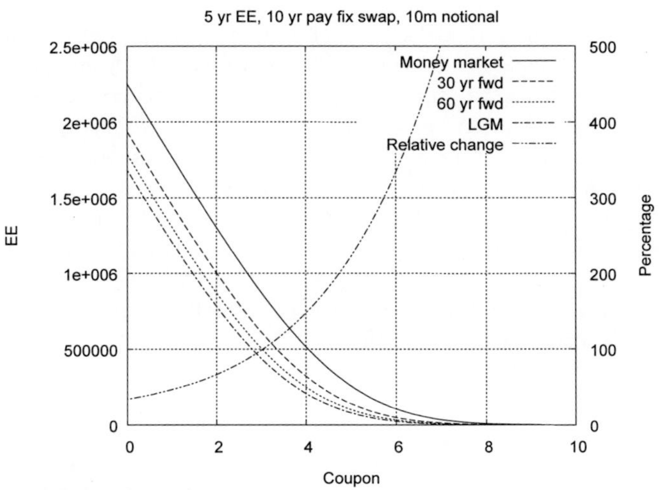

Figure 2. Five-year EE for a 10-year pay fixed swap on a 10 million notional as a function of the swap coupon.

Under the money market measure, an at-the-money receive-fixed swap has twice the EE under the money market measure as it does under the LGM measure. Pay-fixed swaps show larger differences, with an at-the-money swap having an EE three times as large under the money market measure as under the LGM measure (figure 2).

Better than Neutral

The use of risk neutral exposures was prompted by the existence of a risk neutral computational infrastructure. However, we have seen that this is of limited utility because risk neutral exposures are arbitrary in general and can vary widely depending on the numéraire used in the computations.

The situation can be salvaged. By identifying the change of measure between the risk neutral measure and the real world measure and using the above change of measure techniques, one can compute real world exposures using the risk neutral computational infrastructure.

More generally, the technique used to generate arbitrary PFEs at a given horizon can be used to compute real world exposures using a risk neutral framework even when there is no change of measure from the risk neutral to the assumed real world measure.

For a systematic treatment of this, see Stein (2015).

Conclusions

Even for complete models, the risk neutral measure is not unique; it depends on the choice of numéraire. Change of measure techniques can be used to investigate the impact of changing the risk neutral measure/numéraire pair on the values produced by exposure measures such as PFEs and EEs.

We find that without changing the model, picking different numéraires can substantially change PFEs. In fact, the numéraire can be chosen in such a way as to make the PFE profile fit almost any arbitrary distribution.

Even among commonly used numéraires, we see that PFEs and EEs for swaps can vary by large factors.

As a result, it is extremely ambiguous, if not dangerous, to compute exposures under the risk neutral measure used for pricing. The only way to get meaningful exposures is to compute them under the real world measure.

Finally, Stein (2015) shows various ways of leveraging a risk neutral valuation framework to compute real world exposures, thus circumventing the need for risk neutral exposure calculations. We expect that this would be a fruitful direction to pursue.

References

Basel Committee on Banking Supervision. The application of Basel II to trading activities and the treatment of double default effects. Technical report, Bank of International Settlement, June 2005. URL http://www.bis.org/publ/bcbs116.pdf.

—. Enhancements to the Basel II framework. Technical report, Bank of International Settlement, 2009. URL http://www.bis.org/publ/bcbs157.htm.

—. Basel III: A global regulatory framework for more resilient banks and banking systems. Technical report, Bank of International Settlement, June 2011. URL http://www.bis.org/publ/bcbs189.htm.

Brigo, D., and A. Capponi. *Bilateral Counterparty Risk Valuation with Stochastic Dynamical Models and Application to Credit Default Swaps*. SSRN, 2009. URL http://ssrn.com/abstract=1318024.

Eduardo Canabarro and Darrell Duffie. Measuring and marking counterparty risk. *Asset/Liability Management of Financial Institutions, ed. Leo M. Tilman, Institutional Investor Books*, 2003. URL http://www.darrellduffie.com/uploads/surveys/DuffieCanabarro2004.pdf.

Eduardo Canabarro, Evan Picoult, and Tom Wilde. Counterparty credit risk analysing counterparty risk. *RISK-LONDON-RISK MAGAZINE LIMITED-*, 16(9): 117–122, 2003.

Comptroller of the Currency, Treasury. Risk-based capital guidelines: Market risk. *Code of Federal Regulations*, 77(169): 530060–53115, August 2012. URL https://federalregister.gov/a/2012-16759.

Jarrow, R. A., and F. Yu. Counterparty risk and the pricing of defaultable securities. *Journal of Finance*, LVI (6), October 2001.

Pykhtin, M., and S. Zhu. A guide to modelling counterparty credit risk. *Global Association of Risk Professionals*, July/August 2007.

Stein, Harvey J. Two measures for the price of one. *RISK MAGAZINE*, 02 March 2015.

Stein, Harvey J. Fixing Underexposed Snapshots – Proper Computation of Credit Exposures Under the Real World and Risk Neutral Measures. Technical report, Bloomberg LP, January 2014. URL http://ssrn.com/abstract=2365540.

Stein, Harvey J., and K. P. Lee. Counterparty valuation adjustments. In Tomasz Bielecki, Damiano Brigo, and Frederic Patras, editors, *Credit Risk Frontiers: Subprime Crisis, Pricing and Hedging, CVA, MBS, Ratings, and Liquidity*, volume 138. Wiley.com, New York, 2011.

CHAPTER THIRTEEN

MEASURING AND CORRECTING FOR THE UNDERESTIMATION OF THE SYSTEMATIC RISK OF FIXED-INCOME SECURITIES

AUSTIN MURPHY[1]

In this presentation, Austin Murphy of Oakland University presents research by Liang Fu, Terry Benzschawel, and himself, which demonstrates that existing techniques underestimate systematic risk in fixed-income instruments and shows mathematically how to correct for the biases in such underestimates. Empirical investigation of that research finds strong evidence in favor of the model. In particular, the model's adjusted measures of systematic risk are found to be highly related to yield spreads (above yields on Treasury bonds with the same duration) in a large sample of bonds. In addition, the new measures of systematic risk are also shown to have strong predictive power in estimating market risk premiums. These findings are very important for purposes of enabling avoidance of future calamities, such as those that occurred in the credit boom leading up to the financial crisis of 2007-2009.

The proof that standard measures of systematic risk, such as market betas, underestimate systematic risk doesn't require specification of any particular distribution for returns to debt instruments. The finding applies to virtually any existing fixed-income security that has never defaulted. As long as the past time-series of price data for a debt instrument doesn't include defaults, and as long as the covariance between market returns and the return on a fixed-income instrument is higher in the case of a default (as should be expected even without observing such a possible eventuality), estimates of systematic risk will be significantly biased

[1] The author is with Oakland University. Email: jamurphy@oakland.edu.

unless an adjustment is made for this greater unobserved but feasibly larger return co-movement in the case of an actual future bankruptcy. Without such an adjustment for estimation bias, measures of systematic risk are shown to be underestimated by approximately 80% for average fixed-income securities with a 1-year maturity and 30% for those with a 10-year maturity.

The mathematics also indicate quite conclusively that, unlike the standard accepted theory, the co-movement of fixed-income instruments with overall market portfolio returns as measured by a beta are not a precise linear function of the duration of the debt. In particular, by avoiding unrealistic assumptions of standard theories of bond prices that specify a specific distribution, which typically is continuous, the model shows how a bond's beta can be higher for a short-term bond than for a long-term bond under reasonably normal circumstances. Even though longer-term bonds might usually have higher betas, the model shows the ratio of bond betas to be far less than the ratio of their durations. A mathematical proof is provided, demonstrating that arbitrage would prevent priced systematic risk to be an exact linear function of duration.

Analytically assuming various reasonable parameter values for the model variables, an exact estimate of betas is derived that specifies a precise relationship between true measures of systematic risk and beta estimates based on past bond return data that include no defaults. The exact relationship is derived to be

$$\text{True beta} = \text{Beta Estimate x } (1 + \{H/T\}), \tag{1}$$

where T is the bond's maturity in years, and H is a parameter to be estimated empirically. Further calculations show H can be estimated by regressing bond beta estimates on estimates of the expected values of bond default losses.

Using estimates of bond default losses based on their credit ratings, which imply specific average default losses for bonds of each quality, H is estimated to be 1.18 for a sample of 126,733 observed bond observations over the 2003-2011 interval (from data provided by Citibank).[2] This finding indicates

$$\text{True beta} = \text{Beta Estimate x } (1 + \{1.18/T\}). \tag{2}$$

Using this adjustment to bond beta estimates, systematic risk is computed for the sample of bonds. The results indicate no positive relationship between bond betas and duration. In addition, a regression of yield spreads on various estimates of bond systematic risk as well as on

[2] Bond betas were estimated by regressing monthly returns on each bond over the prior 60 months on the monthly excess returns of a market portfolio proxy consisting of 60% equities and 40% bonds.

duration and several estimates of default losses indicated strong positive statistical significance in the relationship of spreads with betas estimated using (2). On the other hand, no positive relationship whatsoever was found between spreads and duration in this regression. In fact, spreads were found to be negatively correlated with duration even when measuring the correlation directly. Thus, evidence is found in favor of (2) being a viable measure of systematic risk, while the results reject standard estimates of bond betas.

Findings using H=1.18 indicate that bond betas are underestimated by about 20% on average. A higher estimate for H of 4.0, which is also theoretically feasible, indicates a bias of approximately 50% in the sample. For example, bond betas for BBB bonds are estimated to be 0.37, 0.27, and 0.23 for H=4, H=1.18, and H=0, respectively. The 0.27 estimate here is identical to that estimated by Murphy (1988) from observed bond spreads in excess of those that would be expected given past default losses on bonds of that type.

A regression is then run to estimate the premium for systematic risk in any month. The dependent variable in this regression is each sample bond's yield spread less the estimate of past default losses based on its credit rating, whereas the independent variable is the bond's beta estimated with H=1.18. The regression indicated very low market risk premiums except during the financial crisis of 2007-2009, when the extra yield per unit of beta risk rose to an average of over 4%.

The time-series ex-post returns on a market portfolio proxy consisting of 60% equities and 40% bonds are then measured above the risk-free short-term Treasury bill rate over the 2003-2011 interval and regressed on ex-ante market risk premiums estimated by applying the H=1.18 estimate to the sample of bonds. Results indicated a statistically significant relationship that is immaterially different from a 1:1 relationship. This finding implies that estimates of systematic risk result in reasonable estimates of systematic risk premiums that can be useful in forecasting market returns. Thus, the model is useful not only for estimating systematic risk more precisely but also for forecasting market returns.

References

Murphy, A. "A Discounted Cash Flow Model of Fixed Income Securities Subject to Multiple Calls." *Southern Economic Journal* 55 (1988), 21-36.

CHAPTER FOURTEEN

ANALYSIS OF LOSS GIVEN DEFAULT: A LITERATURE REVIEW AND CLASSIFICATION

ABDOLREZA NAZEMI, MARYAM MIRZAEI, AND MARKUS HOECHSTOETTER[1]

Abstract

As of now, a vast variety of approaches exist for quantifying the recovery of defaulted debt or, alternatively, the loss-given-default (LGD). This study presents the first systematic academic literature review of how empirical benchmark studies assess loss given default. The contribution of this study is multiple-fold. First, it analyzes 47 comparative studies' endeavors to give a comprehensive account of existing recovery rate models. Second, this study provides a systematic overview of assessment-related decisions based on a classification framework. Finally, the assessment criteria of LGD data validation, consistency, application fit, and transparency are introduced to analyze observed assessment-related decisions. It becomes obvious that there are a multitude of definitions of recovery, rendering it almost infeasible to directly compare different results.

Introduction

The terms LGD and recovery rate have become widely used as of late. In light of the recent crisis, sufficient energy has to be committed to the assessment of these quantities. According to Standard & Poor's (2011),

[1] Abdolreza Nazemi and Markus Hoechstoetter are with School of Economics and Business Engineering, the Karlsruhe Institute of Technology (KIT). Maryam Mirzaei is with the Department of Management, Universiti Teknologi Malaysia, Malaysia. Abdolreza Nazemi is the corresponding author.
Email: abdolreza.nazemi@kit.edu.

between 2007 and 2011, a total of 496 rated institutions, mostly from the U.S., have defaulted, representing over one trillion in outstanding debt and dwarfing anything seen so far. Moreover, due to the current crisis, even entire countries have found themselves on the brink of bankruptcy, which still provides for daily headlines. The impact has not only been felt across the corporate and sovereign world but also on the consumer side. The fear of any repetition of the current crisis in the future may be founded in light of the seemingly increasing occurrence of financial crises as brought to attention by Stiglitz (1998) already one decade ago. Support for this hypothesis is provided by the fact that in the USA alone, public sector and corporate consumer debt have reached dizzying levels.

According to the Board of Governors of the Federal Reserve System (2011), public sector debt amounts to over 14 trillion dollars, while U.S. corporate and privates have both accumulated similarly shocking amounts. This trend is by no means unique to the USA, however. Thomas (2009) presents equivalent tendencies for Europe, especially in the private sector. Loss related quantities, such as the probability of default, the amount of potential loss, and the amount recovered in case of a default are stated by the Basel II accords. Even though not mandatory for all lenders, the terminology and definitions are used widely in the context of credit risk. However, the definitions, in particular with respect to recovery, are not unique. Here, we present a variety of studies that refer to different interpretations of the definition of the recovery rate, such as, for example, in the context of market recovery versus ultimate recovery. We endeavor to provide an extension of well-known references, such as Schuermann (2004) or Altman et al. (2005a).

Although these studies discussed different interpretations of the recovery rate definition, the discussions differ primarily on a theoretical basis. Therefore, the question arises regarding how published studies have addressed the performance assessment of loss given default analysis. It is argued here that assessment-related decisions face several challenges. First, researchers should implement stable models, which work for a long period of time without many alterations. A stable model adequately represents the cause-effect relationship between loss given default and its parameters. Therefore, a stable model gives stable outcomes for loss estimations given default parameters because it is not affected by incidental correlations in the data set Deutsche Bundes bank (2003). Second, researchers must employ a sequence of performance perspectives, which represent discriminatory power. Assessment-related decisions must fit the characteristics of the classification circumstances because these characteristics have a great influence on assessment results. Third, calibration is a part of determining goodness of fit. LGD calibration means verifying whether the predicted loss corresponds to the realized losses (Van Gestel and Baesens, 2009). Finally, researchers should offer a maximum level of precision and simplicity to enable the reader to understand each assessment decision and to evaluate the assessment's results.

This study analyses how published studies that benchmark loss given default have dealt with performance assessment on a practical level. Therefore, this study attempts to provide a useful and applicable reference for researchers regarding loss given default analysis. To achieve this aim, we analyze studies published on assessment-related decisions in academic journals between 2000 and 2014 based on the following approaches. First, we developed a framework to classify the reviewed studies on the basis of methods and performance assessment. Second, assessment criteria considering stability, calibration, and precision are employed to discuss observed assessment decisions.

The paper is organized as follows. Section 2 presents the methodological framework, which analyses chosen studies according to the methodological framework and classifies the reviewed studies based on the performance perspective. In section 3, the results are summarized and implications and recommendations are discussed.

Methodological Framework

Research classification scheme

Various assessment options are documented among different research studies. The choice of performance indicator varies among studies, and the usefulness of the indicator choice depends on data validation, given degree of information, chosen performance perspective, and indicator dimensionality. To classify the research, this study points out these relationships.

Study setting and performance perspective

A variety of performance indicators are selected based on the implementation of different performance criteria among reviewed studies and the available information on loss given default analysis. In terms of a discriminative approach to estimate loss given default, historical data accessibility is essential. As such, the degree of available information on loss given default is differentiated into two study settings: “low level” and “high level.” It is obvious that determining the comprehensive information to assess loss given default might be difficult. Thus, the “low level” study setting is specified by the ambiguity of the available information. Given the number and nature of variables thought to affect recovery outcomes, this is an important advantage if one wants to simultaneously use all available information and to understand the marginal effects of included variables. Therefore, in a "high level" situation, information on some circumstances, including conditioning information, might be known. As well, in a "high level" situation, information on out-of-sample and out-of-time testing is mostly approximated. Empirical studies have demonstrated that evaluating the methods, efficiency and robustness is essential because in-sample results can be misleading. Most studies in this field have reported in-sample findings but not out-of-sample results, although the latter are crucial for proper risk management and are required for regulatory purposes (See Table 1).

Performance perspective and indicator choice

In supervised learning, finding a model that could predict the true underlying probability for each test case would be optimal. Several performance metrics are available for the assessment of loss given default analysis performance. According to Caruana and Niculescu-Mizil (2004), these indicators can be divided into three main types: threshold, order-related, and probabilistic indicators. Threshold metrics measure the true positive rate in the fraction of cases that fall above the threshold. In the case of threshold metrics, it is not important how close a prediction is to a threshold but only whether the predicted value is above or below the threshold. Order related metrics look at predictions from a different viewpoint. Order related metrics measure how well the ordering ranks positive cases above negative cases. Alternatively, probability metrics depend on predicted values, not on how the values fall relative to a threshold or relative to each other.

Suboptimal models vary from the one true model in different ways. Various performance metrics reflect these differences. For instance, ordering metrics, such as the area under the ROC curve, can be used to address an error minimization perspective, while probabilistic indicators are an expression of discriminatory power. These performance metrics may be used to minimize errors. Therefore, it is worth mentioning that the minimization of error seems to be an important object among most studies.

Performance perspective and indicator dimensionality

Based on the literature, various regression methods are benchmarked for loss given default modeling, and their most important purpose is error-minimization. In this regard, some studies choose a one-dimensional performance perspective, which is expressed by a single scalar measurement (i.e., Qi and Yang, 2009; Renault and Scaillet, 2004; Thomas et al., 2012; Leow et al. 2014). However, using a one-dimensional performance perspective might present a challenge to situations that cannot be readily characterized by a single scalar value. Some studies represent different results using various performance indicators. According to results by Zhang and Thomas (2012), linear regression always achieves the lowest MSE, whereas the results for MAE are very consistent, except that the linear regression is poor. A multi-dimensional performance perspective can improve model accuracy evaluation. Thus, model performance evaluation requires a multi-dimensional performance perspective, which must be expressed by different indicators or by a graphical instrument. In general, researchers are likely to use several indicators for their investigations (e.g., Bastos, 2010; Bellotti and Crook, 2012; Grunert and Weber, 2009; Loterman et al., 2012; Zhang and Thomas, 2012; Tong et al., 2013; Leow and Mues, 2012).

The performance assessment criteria

Major financial institutions with unstable credit portfolios increasingly require measuring the performance of multiple loss-given-default in a straightforward and reliable approach. In accordance with the regular default and recovery data collection process and availability of data, the potency to estimate LGD models turns out to be an essential element of any such institution's credit risk management. Based on reviewed studies, a multiplicity of potential combinations of performance assessment criteria can be made. Focusing on the performance of model validations that make transaction-level LGD predictions, three important aspects should be considered among reviewed studies, including: LGD validation dataset, performance indicator consistency, and robustness over the time. This study attempts to analyze different performance criteria through previous empirical studies. Therefore, the assessment criteria are examined below.

The LGD validation dataset

It is assumed that definite loss data are readily available at the time of application. Whereas precise requirements for the definition of loss, default, and workout LGD may differ from firm to firm, a reliable definition, applied across all business units, is essential in terms of desired centralized model validation. Based on the literature, a variety of datasets and different variables have been employed to LGD analysis. It is arguable whether one should employ all available variables. One should recognize the marginal effects of included variables. In terms of the data sample, the exact amount of indispensable and appropriate data needs to be determined on a case-by-case basis. Furthermore, it seems that by using several datasets in comparative research, at least one dataset may provide more precise information. Thus, it should be noted that dataset validation is an important factor affecting model performance.

Consistency

Constant with the decision-making mechanism, researchers need to follow a consistent set of assessment-related steps. Its degree of information with respect to assessment conditions provides obstinate grounds for the choice of a performance perspective. The greater the magnitude of available and included information guides the chosen performance perspective to more reliable results and relevant decision support. Thus, the choice should operationalize LGD assessment with the orientation of available information, the greater feasibility of the chosen perspective, and the multi-inference aspects of the performance in question.

Application fit

It is assumed that the chosen performance indicators should provide reliable decision support and consider the available degree of information. In this context, researchers employ a variety of performance indicators to evaluate LGD models. It is obvious that the selected indicators should be relevant and capable to compare estimated to observed LGD accurately. Application fit can be determined based on characteristics of the measurement circumstances that are incorporated into the study setting. This is part of determining goodness of fit. Therefore, it is remarkable that performance indicators chosen by various researchers should hold two aspects: a credible assortment of included information and probable parameter incorrectness.

Transparency

Based on the literature, various performance indicators are available. Therefore, it warrants providing transparent performance indicator records that include explicit description, estimation, and records of the parameter set that is imposed for the loss given default analysis performance.

Research Analysis

Study setting and performance perspective

In this section, an analysis of selected research studies is provided based on performance indicators, study setting, and assessment-related decisions. In this regard, an overview of all reviewed studies is afforded in Table 1. Among 37 of 47 reviewed studies, less information of debtors is available for the dataset used. Nevertheless, when using several datasets in comparative research, at least one dataset provides more precise information. According to Thomas et al. (2012), the information available in each case is quite different. However, these studies analyze loss given default based on in-sample testing. In the outstanding 10 studies, a higher degree of information is provided. As summarized in table 1, 43 studies chose in-sample testing and only 4 studies chose both in-sample and out-of-sample testing.

Indicator choice and dimensionality

In this section, an overview of performance indicator choice and dimensionality for in-sample and out-of-sample testing is provided. As summarized in figure 5, most studies of loss given default analysis used various types of error minimization indicators, which measure how much an estimate differs from realized value. Just a few studies have employed order-related indicators. In this regard, the mentioned studies have mainly used AUC followed by ROC curve to estimate model accuracy in order to loss given default assessment. AUC refers to the area under the ROC curve (Fawcett, 2006), which is used to plot how good the model is at distinguishing values that are higher than average from those that are lower than average (Jacobs and Karagozoglu, 2011; Loterman et al., 2012; Tong et al., 2013; Leow and Mues, 2012; Gurtler and Hibbeln, 2013; Loterman et al., 2012; Bonini and Caivano, 2014). A probabilistic indicator, rarely used in loss given default analysis, is the Kolmogrov-Smirnov value (Jacobs and Karagozoglu, 2011). Based on the literature, the reviewed research accounts for the multidimensionality of error perspectives (Fig.6). It is clear that various indicators provide a different dimensionality of the LGD analysis performance, which could provide a variety of advantageous evaluation dimensionalities.

The LGD validation dataset

A correct and sufficiently large data history is a prerequisite for the development of any reliable model. Attention should be paid to data integrity and consistency. There is doubt whether the choice of variables used in the model is optimal. This is in line with expectations of the Risk Management department, which expects that different variables could be useful in predicting LGD. Also, because of dataset errors, there may also be different relationships between the variables and LGD. Therefore, researchers should employ a correct and sufficiently large data history, which covers different types of variables thought to affect LGD.

In terms of variable type, most studies use account variables to assess loss given default. Some other variables, like macroeconomic factors affecting loss given default, have been analyzed in a group of studies (Altman et al., 2005a; Bastos, 2010a; Bellotti and Crook, 2012; Qi and Zhao, 2011). Alternatively, Altman and Kalotay (2014) provide clarity on the role and importance of economic influence on recovery outcomes and provide a richer characterization of how conditioning variables affect recovery outcomes.

Consistency

As noted, researchers need to follow a consistent set of assessment-related decision steps. To reach this aim, a variety of performance indicators have been employed to assess loss given default models. Fourteen studies consider one dimensional indicator choice to operationalize the error minimization perspective; of these, R^2 is the most used indicator among reviewed studies. In contrast, the remaining studies speculate multidimensional indicators. Summarizing performance indicator choice, RMSE, MAE and R2 are the most preferable mixture of indicators among reviewed studies. Furthermore, conventional measures, including the area under the receiver operating characteristic curve (AUC and ROC), are adopted to assess LGD model performance (e.g., Jacobs and Karagozoglu, 2011; Loterman et al., 2012; Tong et al., 2013; Gürtler and Hibbeln, 2013; Bonini and Caivanoa, 2014). The other performance indicator, rarely used in LGD assessment, is Kolmogrov Smirnov (Jacobs and Karagozoglu, 2011).

Moreover, most of the reviewed research assesses LGD model performance using a variety of indicators, between 2 and 6 indicators. It has not been proven that a multidimensionality of indicators generates more reliable results, but each indicator provides information on different aspects of model performance (See Table 1).

Application fit

In terms of application fit, model reliability is considered. This quality is another measure to assess loss given default models by examining how accurate their LGDs are in predicting actual loss rates. The goodness of fit is chosen as the criteria for the methodology performance analysis. The combination of R^2 and MSE indicators appears to be an especially acceptable method of assessing LGD performance. The majority of reviewed studies used these metrics to analyze model performance. It has been observed that 35 of the 47 considered studies chose these indicators to operationalize error minimization (R^2, MSE, MAE or a combination of these indicators). Therefore, the majority of studies noted the importance of goodness of fit between chosen performance indicators.

On the point of order-related indicators (i.e., ROC curve and AUC indicator), no noticeable information in terms of application fit can be observed. Probabilistic indicators only express statistical dimensions. In addition, the majority of studies are likely to use error minimization indicators to evaluate loss given default analysis performance.

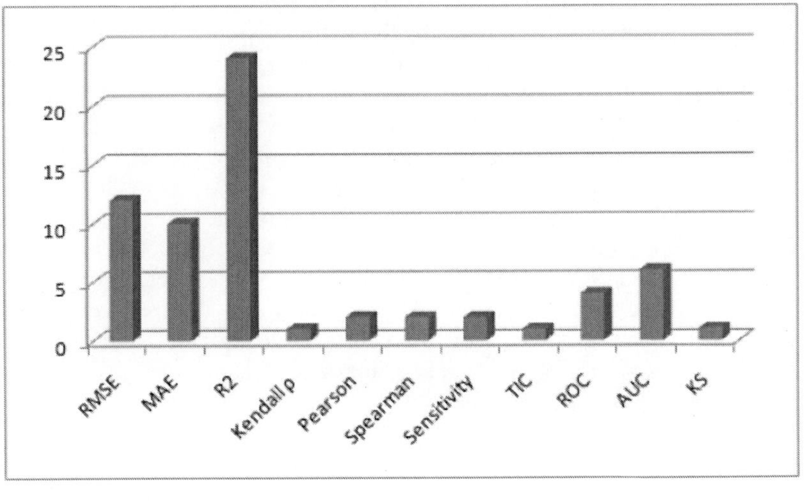

Figure 1. In-sample/out-of-sample testing, indicator choice, and dimensionality (y-axis: number of studies; x-axis: performance indicators).

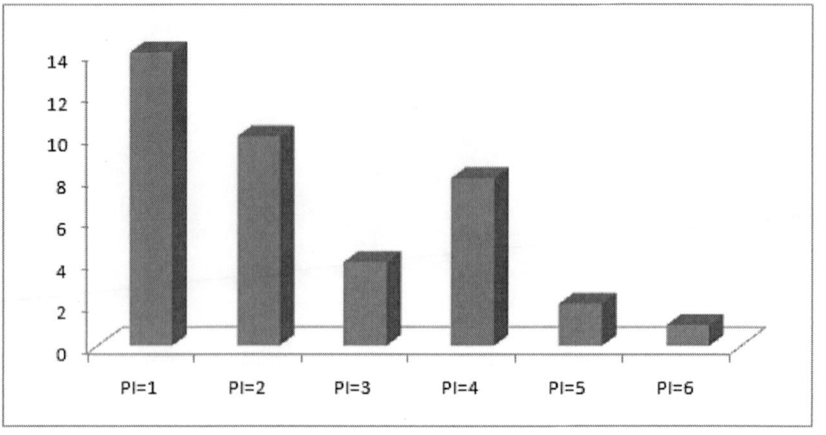

Figure 2. Dimensionality indicator (y-axis: number of performance indicators (PI) used per study; x-axis: number of studies).

Transparency

Several performance metrics can be used to evaluate the extent to which the models produce accurate predictions for the dependent variable. Each metric has its own method of quantifying model performance. These performance metrics are differentially defined. Some studies present a sensitivity analysis to improve discriminatory power. Ando (2014) presents a sensitivity analysis to investigate the effects of market factors as well as the downgrading of the credit rating. Sensitivity tests assess the impact of made-up large movements in financial variables (Rösch and Schule, 2007). Various indicators are used in the literature to evaluate LGD models performance. Therefore, interpreting these results cannot be simple and might be problematic due to a wide span of indicators.

Moreover, various methods have been employed to model LGD in the literature. Loterman et al. (2012) compared 24 different regression techniques, such as OLS, B-OLS, BR, BC-OLS, RiR, RoR, RT, and MARS, to evaluate LGD model performance. Tang and Yuan (2013) propose a new structural model for loss given default, which takes into account the severity of default. Alternatively, Bonini and Caivano (2014) evaluate an alternative method of modeling LGD using a technique based on advanced credibility theory. Recently, Altman and Kalotay (2014) proposed a relatively simple, accurate, and flexible approach to forecasting the distribution of defaulted debt recovery outcomes. A variety of techniques have been employed to provide an accurate and simple approach in terms of LGD modeling. For all these models, the performance indicator choice depends on the subjective choice of the researcher. Therefore, it is obvious that no approach has been established to clearly set performance indicators.

Conclusions

This study fulfilled a literature review and classification of comparative studies in the field of loss given default assessment. To reach this aim, the selected studies on LGD were analyzed and classified to model performance. In this regard, the selected studies were classified and various performance indicators were identified. Based on the reviewed studies, the choice of performance perspective is dependent on the degree of available and included information. It is observed that for the performance perspective, the usage of error minimization indicators seems to be widely accepted. The higher degree of available and included information leads to performance perspective choices that provide relevant decision support. Therefore, researchers attempt to implement a supreme conservable performance perspective, which uses a mixture of various performance indicators in literature.

It is noteworthy that the reviewed studies frequently used a combination of performance indicators to evaluate loss given default. This combination did not always lead to the desired decision support, and it is unclear whether frequently used combinations of performance indicators provide managerially-relevant decision support for loss given default analysis. However, each performance indicator examines a different aspect of LGD model performance. Further, it has been observed that researchers have not systematically implemented a specific performance perspective. In sum, the reviewed studies are differentiated by a great variety of performance indicators developed for decision support. As a result, the mentioned studies considered loss-given default assessment expansion. Furthermore, it should be noticed that in the LGD assessment context, the deficiency of a consistent LGD assessment might lead to obscure results for model performance. Thus, it is recommended that researchers implement a specific performance perspective systematically. This research serves as a basis for future studies in terms of loss given default analysis.

Table 1. Study settings and performance.

Reference	Setting	Perspective	Performance Indicator
Altman & Kalotay (2014)	HL	In- & Out-of-sample	R^2
Hartmann et al. (2014)	HL	In- & Out-of-sample	RMSE, MAE
Tobback et al. (2014)	HL	In- & Out-of-sample	MSE, MAE, ME, R^2
Chava et al. (2011)	HL	In- & Out-of-sample	-
Qi and Yang (2009)	HL	In-sample	R^2
Thomas et al. (2012)	HL	In-sample	R^2
Tong et al. (2013)	HL	In-sample	AUC, HI, RMSE, r, R^2
Loterman et al. (2012)	HL	In- & Out-of-sample	RMSE, MAE, AUC, R^2,r
Ando (2014)	HL	In-sample	Sensitivity analysis
Bastos (2010)	LL	In-sample	RMSE, MAE,
Bastos (2013)	LL	In-sample	MSE, MAE, RSE, RAE
Bonini & Caivano (2014)	LL	In-sample	AUC, ROC
Bellotti & Crook (2012)	LL	In-sample	R^2, MSE
Bellotti & Crook (2008)	LL	In-sample	RMSE, R^2
Bijak and Thomas (2014)	LL	In-sample	MSE, MAE, Pearson, Spearman
Caselli et al. (2008)	LL	In-sample	RMSE, R^2
Calabrese (2010)	LL	In-sample	-
Chen and Chen (2010)	LL	In-sample	Pearson
Das & Hanouna (2009)	LL	In-sample	RMSE
Dermine et al. (2006)	LL	In-sample	R^2,RMSE, MAE, AUC, r
Grunert & Weber (2009)	LL	In-sample	RMSE, R^2
Gupton and Stein (2002)	LL	In-sample	RMSE, R^2

Gurtler & Hibbeln (2013)	LL	In-sample	AUC, ROC, R^2
Han & Jang (2013)	LL	In-sample	MAE, MSE, R^2
Hanouna (2009)	LL	In-sample	RMSE
Hoechstoetter et al. (2012)	LL	In-sample	R^2, SS Error, misclassification, ROC
Jacobs et al. (2011)	LL	In-sample	KS, ROC
Khieu et al. (2012)	LL	In-sample	R^2
Leow & Mues (2012)	LL	In-sample	ROC, AUC, MAE, RMSE
Leow et al. (2014)	LL	In-sample	R^2
Park & Bang (2014)	LL	In-sample	R^2
Qi and Zhao (2011)	LL	In-sample	Cross validation, R^2
Renault & Scaillet (2004)	LL	In-sample	R^2
Rösch & Scheule (2014)	LL	In-sample	R^2
Thomas et al. (2012)	LL	In-sample	R^2
Tangy & Yuan (2013)	LL	In-sample	RMSE, MAE, AUC, R^2,r
Zhang & Thomas (2012)	LL	In-sample	R^2, Spearman, MAE, RMSE

References

Altman E. I., A. Resti, and A. Sironi. Loss given default: A review of the literature in recovery risk. In E. I. Altman, A. Resti, and A. Sironi (Eds.), *Recovery risk: The next challenge in credit risk management*, 2005a.

Altman, Edward I., and Egon A. Kalotay. Ultimate recovery mixtures. *Journal of Banking and Finance*, 2014.

Ando, R. Bayesian corporate bond pricing and credit default swap premium models for deriving default probabilities and recovery rates. *Journal of the Operational Research Society*, 65: 454-465, 2014.

Bastos, J. Forecasting bank loans loss-given default. *Journal of Banking and Finance*, 34(10): 2510-2517, 2010a.

Bastos, João A. Ensemble predictions of recovery rates. Springer, *J Finance Serv Res*, 2013.

Bellotti, T., and J. Crook. Modelling and predicting loss given default for credit cards. Technical Report, 2008.

Bellotti, T., and J. Crook. Loss given default models incorporating macroeconomic variables for credit cards. *International Journal of Forecasting*, 28: 171-182, 2012.

Bonini, S. and G. Caivanoa. Estimating loss-given default through advanced credibility theory. *The European Journal of Finance*, 2014.

Calabrese, R. Regression for recovery rates with both continuous and discrete characteristics. Proceedings' of the 45th Scientific Meeting of the Italian Statistical Society (SIS), Italy, 2010.

—. Downturn loss given default: Mixture distribution estimation. *European Journal of Operational Research*, 2014 (In press).

Caruana, R., and A. Niculescu-Mizil. Data mining in metric space: An empirical analysis of supervised learning performance criteria. In Proceedings of the tenth ACM SIGKDD international conference on Knowledge discovery and data mining, Seattle, WA, USA. ACM, 2004.

Caselli, S. Gatti, and F. Querci. The sensitivity of the loss given default rate of systematic risk: new empirical evidence on bank loans. *Journal of Financial Services Research*, 34(1): 1-34, 2008.

Chen, T. H., and C. W. Chen. Application of data mining to the spatial heterogeneity of foreclosed mortgages. *Expert Systems with Application*, 37(2): 993-997, 2010.

Das, S. R., and P. Hanouna. Implied recovery. *Journal of Economic Dynamic and Control,* 33: 1837-1857, 2009.

Dermine, J., and C. Neto De Carvalho. Bank loan losses-given-default: A case study. *Journal of Banking and Finance*, 30(4): 1219-1243, 2006.

Deutsche Bundesbank. Monthly report: Approaches to the validation of internal rating systems. Working Paper, 2003.

Dragomir, Tudor A. E. An exercise of stress-testing for the fleet usage and the loss-given-default in an operating leasing business. *International Journal of Mathematical Models and Methods in Applied Science*, 6(6), 2012.

Fawcett, T. An introduction to roc analysis. *Pattern Recognition Letters*, 27: 861-874, 2006.

Gürtler, M., and M. Hibbeln. Improvements in loss given default forecasts for bank loans. *Journal of Banking and Finance*, 37: 2354-2366, 2013.

Gupton, G. M., and R. M. Stein. Losscalc: Model for predicting loss given default. Moody, February, 2002.

Han Ch., and Y. Jang. Effects of debt collection practices on loss given default. *Journal of Banking and Finance*, 37: 21-31, 2013.

Hartmann-Wendels, T., P. Miller, and E. Töws. Loss given default for leasing: Parametric and nonparametric estimations. *Journal of Banking and Finance*, 40: 364-375, 2014.

Hoechstoetter, M., A. Nazemi, S.T. Rachev, and C. Bozic. Recovery rate modeling of non-performing consumer credit using data mining algorithms. RMI Working Paper, 2012.

Jacobs, M., and A. Karagozoglu. Modeling ultimate loss-given-default on corporate debt. *Journal of Fixed Income*, 21(1): 6-20, 2011.

Jokivuolle, E., and M. Virén. Cyclical default and recovery in stress testing loan losses. *Journal of Financial Stability*, 9: 139-149, 2013.

Khieu, H., D. Donald, J. Mullineaux, and H. C. Yi. The determinants of bank loan recovery rates. *Journal of Banking and Finance*, 36: 923-933, 2012.

Loterman, G., I. Brown, D. Martens, C.H. Mues, and B. Baesens. Benchmarking regression algorithms for loss given default modeling. *International Journal of Forecasting,* 28: 161-170, 2012.

Park. Yun W., and D.W. Bang. Loss given default of residential mortgages in a low LTV regime: Role of foreclosure auction process and housing market cycles. *Journal of Banking and Finance*, 39: 192-210, 2014.

Qi, M., and X. Zhao. Comparison of modeling methods for loss given default. *Journal of Banking and Finance*, 2011.

Renault. O., and O. Scaillet. On the way to recovery: A nonparametric bias-free estimation of recovery rates densities. *Journal of Banking and Finance*, 28 (12): 2915-2931, 2004.

Rosch, H., and D. Scheule. Stress-testing credit risk parameters: an application to retail loan portfolios. *Journal of Risk Model Validation*, 2007.

Rosch, H., and D. Scheule. Forecasting probabilities of default and loss rates given default in the presence of selection. *Journal of the Operational Research Society*, 65: 393-407, 2014.

Schuermann, T. What do we know about loss given default? in D. Shimko (ed.). *Credit Risk Models and Management* (2 ed.), 249-274, 2004.

Standard & Poor's. Standard & Poor's financial services llc. http://www.standardandpoors.com, 2011.

Stiglitz, J. Must financial crises be this frequent and this painful? Technical report, McKay Lecture, Pittsburgh, Pennsylvania, 1998.

Tang, Q., and Z. Yuan. Asymptotic analysis of the loss given default in the presence of multivariate regular variation. Working Paper, 2013.

Thomas, L. C. *Consumer credit models*. Oxford, UK: Oxford University Press, 2009.

Thomas, L. C., A. Matuszyk, and A. Moore. Comparing debt characteristics and lgd models for different collections policies. *International Journal of Forecasting*, 28: 196-203, 2012.

Tobback, E., D. Martens, T. Van Gestel, and B. Baesens. Forecasting loss given default models: impact of account characteristics and the macroeconomic state. *Journal of the Operational Research Society*, 65: 376-392, 2014.

Edward N.C. Tong, Ch. Mues, and L. Thomas. A zero-adjusted gamma model for mortgage loan loss given default. *International Journal of Forecasting*, 29: 548-562, 2013.

Van Gestel. T., and B. Baesens. *Credit risk management*. Oxford: Oxford University Press, 2009.

Zhang, J., and Lyn C. Thomas. Comparisons of linear regression and survival analysis using single and mixture distributions approaches in modeling LDG. *International Journal of Forecasting*, 28: 204-215, 2012.

CHAPTER FIFTEEN

WHEN SOVEREIGN RISK SUDDENLY MATTERS (AGAIN): EMPIRICAL EVIDENCE FROM THE EUROPEAN DEBT CRISIS[1]

MATTHIAS HAERRI, STEFAN MORKOETTER AND SIMONE WESTERFELD[2]

With the European sovereign debt crisis in 2010-2011, investors began to differentiate in more detail the individual counterparty risk of government debt. As a consequence, the yield spreads between very stable economies and weak economies started to dramatically increase. Against this setting, we investigate the extent to which the counterparty risk of a country—measured by the underlying sovereign CDS spread—affects the refinancing cost of corporates located in the respective country. Based on an empirical analysis of European corporations, we show that sovereign credit default swaps (CDS) are positively correlated with corresponding corporate CDS spreads and are a significant factor for corporate CDS pricing models. In other words, if government yield spreads of a country are increasing, the interest rates of corporates headquartered in this country will follow this pattern. We further demonstrate that this impact increased with the tightening of the European sovereign debt crisis in 2010-2011. Interestingly, we show that the link between higher sovereign

---

[1] This extended abstract is based on the article "Sovereign Risk and the Pricing of Corporate Credit Default Swaps" by M. Haerri, S. Morkoetter and S. Westerfeld (2015, *Journal of Credit Risk*, forthcoming).

[2] Matthias Haerri is with the University of Applied Sciences Northwestern Switzerland. Email: matthias.haerri@fhnw.ch. Stefan Morkoetter is with the University of St. Gallen. Email: stefan.morkoetter@unisg.ch. Simone Westerfeld is with the University of Applied Sciences Northwestern Switzerland.
Email: simone.westerfeld@fhnw.ch.

risk and increasing refinancing costs is stronger for corporations with a high dependency on their domestic market and the local economy respectively.

Institutional Background

For many years, institutional investors around the world appeared to be ignorant about the potential default of countries. The huge losses and asset write-downs of the 1990s, resulting from investments in Argentinean or Russian government debt, seemed to be forgotten. In Europe particularly, sovereign risk was not priced in accordance with individual riskiness. In this setting, less stable Eurozone countries benefited from favorable refinancing conditions. Starting with the financial crisis and the Lehman default in 2008, investors started to become (again) more concerned with counterparty risk. Initially, this led to increasing refinancing costs for banks (also documented by increasing credit default spread levels). Once market participants realized that individual countries were not able to bail out their staggering banking sector anymore, government yield spreads increased dramatically. Such a development made it even more difficult to finance increasing government budget deficits as well as to refinance outstanding debt (see, for example, Greece). Interest rate levels for so-called peripheral countries of the Eurozone (e.g., Italy and Spain) increased steadily, whereas more stable European economies (e.g., Germany) benefited from an opposing trend (see Figure 1).

For our empirical part, we focus on credit default swaps (CDS) and investigate the co-movement between corporate CDS spreads and sovereign CDS spreads. Why should corporate and sovereign capital markets be interlinked? In our paper, we argue that a weak economic environment or even a negative outlook should lead to higher sovereign CDS spreads (e.g., higher refinancing costs). At the same time, an overshadowing economic situation within a country leads by definition to a worse environment for business activities (e.g., lower sales in domestic markets due to a weak economy). However, corporates generating a major share of their revenues in foreign markets should be less exposed as compared to companies, which are highly dependent on their domestic market activities. The less you sell your products in a deteriorating home market, the better you are hedged against a worsening local economy.

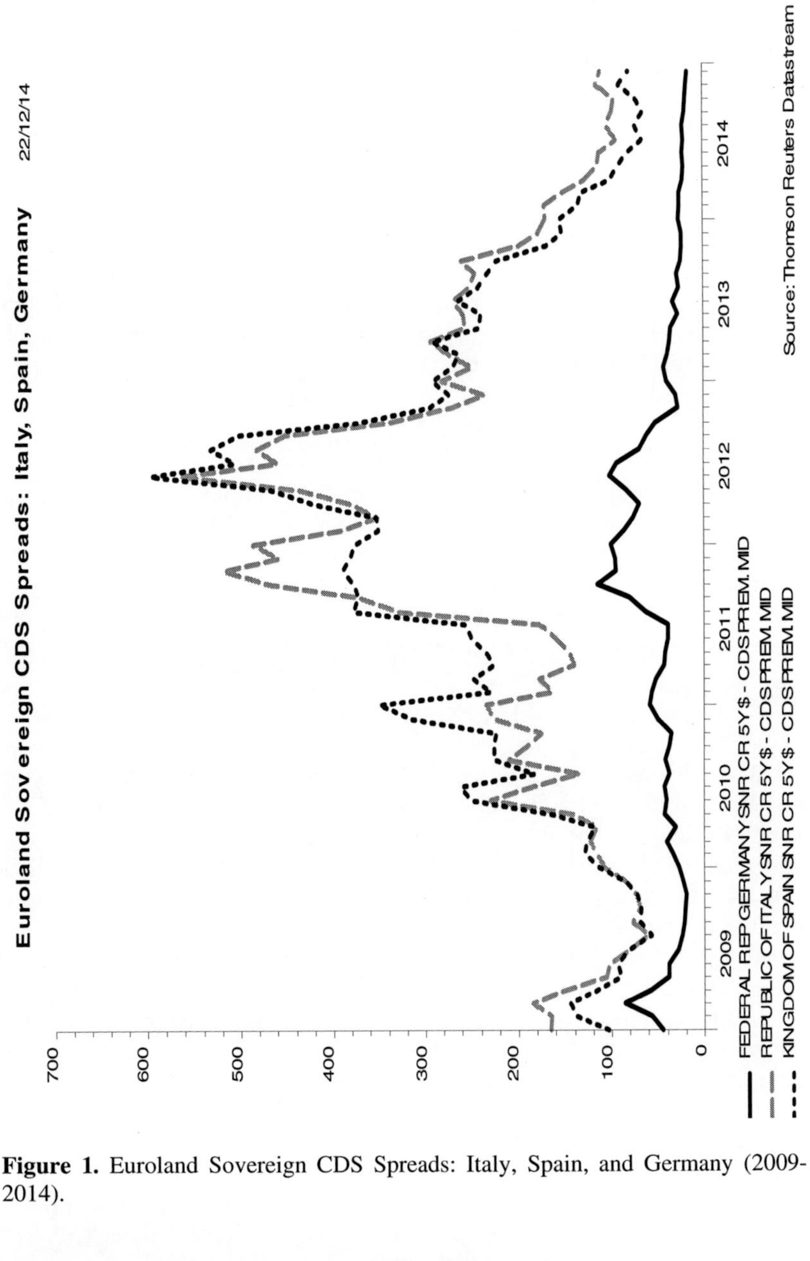

Figure 1. Euroland Sovereign CDS Spreads: Italy, Spain, and Germany (2009-2014).

As already argued, a good time frame and geographical region to study the pricing power of sovereign CDS spreads on corporate risk levels is Europe throughout the recent sovereign debt crisis. In order to empirically demonstrate a positive relationship between corporate and sovereign CDS spreads, we regress the respective sovereign CDS spreads (according to the location of the company's headquarter) on the individual corporate CDS spread. At the same time, we also control for company specific factors to ensure that our results are not driven by entity fixed effects (e.g., size, liquidity, etc.). In a second step, we add the dependence of domestic market sales (ratio domestic market sales over total sales) as an additional independent variable to our model and perform several subsample analyses to observe whether or not a high reliance on domestic markets intensifies the linkage to the home country's sovereign risk.

Data Sample

Our data sample consists of 107 referenced entities from ten different European countries, all members of the Eurozone. All selected reference entities belong to the Markit iTraxx Europe Index and are thus among the most liquidly traded CDS contracts in Europe. We focus on a three-year time period that started in 2009 and lasted for three years, using the last quoted monthly data for the performed panel analysis.

Empirical Results

If our hypothesis can be confirmed, we would expect that sovereign risk has a significant and economically relevant impact on corporate CDS spreads. Indeed, based on our results, we are able to confirm that sovereign CDS spreads are significantly and positively linked (coefficient +0.104***) to underlying corporate CDS spreads. In other words, controlling for several company specific variables, higher sovereign risk levels indeed correlate with higher credit risk levels and thus increasing refinancing costs for local companies.

In addition, a subsample analysis segmenting for the aggravation of the sovereign crisis in 2010 shows that this effect more than doubled when compared to the pre-crisis time sample before 2010 (0.128*** vs. 0.052*). At the same time, we also document that the impact of sovereign risk on corporate risk levels widens in cases of distressed countries (e.g., Greece or Italy) for which investors' sentiment is significantly lower than for other countries of our data sample (e.g. Germany). The documented result does not come as a surprise, but the size of the impact (coefficient of

0.276* for the distressed countries vs. 0.0933*** for the non-distressed countries) is remarkable.

Is a home market bias making it worse?

Based on the above results, we are now searching for a reason behind the pattern. Our assumption is that the dependency of corporate credit-worthiness on sovereign risk might be heavily impacted by the percentage of revenue generated by the corporation in the home market. Therefore, the deteriorating economy in the home country has a more direct link to the riskiness of corporations with revenue concentrated in the home market than to the riskiness of corporations with internationally diversified revenue.

Our results confirm our conjecture: a strong reliance on revenues in the home country contributes positively to the impact of sovereign risk on corporate risk. Once again, the result itself is not surprising; however, the mere size of the effect—almost double the effect for companies with a stronger national exposure in terms of revenues—is quite remarkable (the coefficient for companies with strong home country bias in revenues is 0.139***, whereas it is 0.068*** for the other sample).

Is dependency on local bank financing making it worse?

The business model in continental European banking is built on a strong relationship between local banks and corporations. This means by definition that access to international capital markets is not as distinct as it is for US corporates. However, there are differences with regard to the degree of local bank dependency and the refinancing mix in debt financing of corporations. We hypothesize that a higher dependency on (local) bank debt leads to the higher impact of sovereign counter-party risk on corporate CDS spreads. This assumption is based on the argument that a deteriorating economy directly impacts the creditworthiness of local banks, which spills over to the riskiness of local corporates because access to credit or deteriorating credit conditions might directly impact the refinancing flexibility of corporations. We analyze the refinancing side of companies and the ratio of bank debt over total debt to get an approximation of the dependence on the local/national lending market.

Our results show that the coefficients of the two samples for the impact of sovereign risk are slightly different (0.121*** vs. 0.097***), but due to large standard errors, the resulting difference is not significant. We tested the robustness of our results on a sample without banks because we wanted to ensure that it is not the banking sector only that drives our results and makes interpretation of debt ratios difficult. We, however, observe stable results.

We interpret our results as follows: the reliance of corporate activity on national markets and a lack of international revenue diversification have a strong influence on the exposure of corporates to sovereign risk. This effect is, however, not necessarily confirmed for the refinancing side of the company's balance sheet. We therefore observe an effect that seems to be driven by asset rather than by liability side reasons.

Conclusion

We focused on the impact of the latest sovereign debt crisis in Europe and analyzed how the riskiness of sovereigns spills over to the riskiness of corporations. We find that the linkage between the sovereign and the corporate CDS markets increased tremendously during the crisis and conclude that this effect not only holds for banks but also for corporates from other industries. The impact of sovereign CDS is more pronounced for peripheral Eurozone countries, with a significant increase in the years 2010/11. To explain the results, we studied an asset driven effect and confirmed that a strong reliance on local revenue generation increases the exposure of corporates towards volatility of sovereign risk. Reliance on local bank financing, however, could not be identified as a contributor to the general effect. Going forward, it will be interesting to analyze how correlations develop with lower levels of sovereign risk in terms of CDS spreads and how current discussion about countries potentially leaving the Eurozone, i.e. Grexit (e.g. that Greece might leave the Eurozone), might impact sovereign risk as a pricing component of corporate CDS.